STUDENT'S BOOK WITH KEY

WITH APP & DIGITAL STUDENT'S BOOK

App

READY FOR

C2 PROFICIENCY

FIONA AISH
ETHAN MANSUR
JO TOMLINSON
with ROY NORRIS

macmillan education

CONTENTS

INTRODUCTION

Welcome to *Ready for C2 Proficiency*, a course designed to help you prepare for *Cambridge English Qualifications: C2 Proficiency.*

This book contains a wide range of activities aimed at further improving your English and developing the language and skills you need to pass the examination.

In addition to the Language focus and Vocabulary sections, there is an Idioms page at the end of every unit to deepen your knowledge of non-literal expressions and improve your ability to infer nuances in meaning.

Fiona Aish, Jo Tomlinson, Ethan Mansur and Roy Norris

Overview of the Examination

Reading and Use of English 1 hour 30 minutes

Part	Task Type	Number of Questions	Task Format
1	Multiple-choice cloze	8	A text with 8 gaps; there is a choice of 4 options for each gap.
2	Open cloze	8	A text with 8 gaps, each of which must be completed with one word.
3	Word formation	8	A text with 8 gaps, each of which must be completed with the correct form of a given word.
4	Key word transformation	6	Gapped sentences that must be completed using a given word.
5	Multiple choice	6	A text followed by multiple-choice questions with four options.
6	Gapped text	7	A text from which paragraphs have been removed. Candidates decide which paragraph best fits each gap.
7	Multiple matching	10	A text preceded by multiple-matching questions, which require candidates to find specific information.

Writing 1 hour 30 minutes

Part	Task Type	Number of Tasks	Task Format
1	Essay	1 (compulsory)	Candidates write an essay which is based on key points from two input texts. They summarise and evaluate the ideas in these texts, as well as give their own opinions.
2		5 (candidates choose one)	A task with a clear context, purpose for writing and target reader. Possible tasks are an article, informal letter, formal letter, report or review.

Listening about 40 minutes

Part	Task Type	Number of Questions	Task Format
1	Multiple choice	6	Three short unrelated extracts from either monologues or exchanges between interacting speakers. For each extract there are two multiple-choice questions, each with three options.
2	Sentence completion	9	A monologue lasting around 4 minutes. Candidates write a word or short phrase to complete sentences.
3	Multiple choice	5	A conversation between two or more speakers, lasting approximately 4 minutes. Multiple-choice questions have four options.
4	Multiple matching	10	Five short monologues on the same theme, each lasting approximately 35 seconds. There are two tasks. For each task candidates select the correct option from a choice of eight.

Speaking 16 minutes

Part	Task Type	Time	Task Format
1	Interview	2 minutes	Candidates give personal information in response to questions from the interviewer.
2	Collaborative task	4 minutes	Candidates are given instructions and photos, which they use for discussion, and then a decision-making task.
3	Long turn	10 minutes	Each candidate is given instructions and a written question with prompts, which they discuss. Then the interviewer leads a discussion which is related to the topics discussed by the candidates.

1 THIS IS US

KEY LANGUAGE

The present
Feelings and emotions
Adjectives and nouns with *self*

IDIOMS

Personality

EXAM PRACTICE

Reading and Use of English Parts 1, 2 & 6
Writing Part 2
Listening Part 1
Speaking Parts 1 & 3

Speaking Part 1 Interview

Work with a partner. Discuss the questions.

1 What character traits do you think are the most important in a boss / a neighbour / a good friend?
2 Are your personal interests influenced in any way by global trends or local traditions?
3 How much do you think other people can tell about you from the way you dress?
4 Do you find it easy to get to know new people?
5 Who does society value more: people who are resilient or people who are sensitive?

How to go about it

Respond as naturally as you can, but also try to use a variety of language to impress the examiner.

1 THIS IS US

Vocabulary Feelings and emotions

1 **Complete sentence B with a word from the box so it has a similar meaning to sentence A. There is an example at the beginning (0).**

ballistic besotted despondent elated
engrossed flabbergasted grossed petrified

0A I didn't find the monster too convincing, but the film still **scared me out of my wits**.

0B The monster wasn't given the benefit of depth, but the film still left me **absolutely** *petrified*.

1A Loads of people start to feel **a bit down in the dumps** over the winter season, what with so little sunlight and so many colds around to keep us all miserable.

1B Due to reduced sunlight and the prevalence of the common cold, it's not unusual for people to feel **somewhat** __________ during the winter season.

2A Strangely, there are certain customers who **go apoplectic with rage** when notified of the store's no-return policy, while most others are left unperturbed.

2B It's so strange – there are some customers who **go** __________ at the mere mention of our no-return policy, while most others take it in their stride.

3A 'We're **chuffed to bits**,' said the team captain, holding the award. 'It's something that we feel we deserve, and we've worked hard to get it.'

3B At the ceremony, the team captain was **visibly** __________ as she collected the award, saying that she felt it was hard won and well deserved.

4A Liam is clearly **head over heels in love** with Nora because he immediately goes along with anything she thinks is cool.

4B It's obvious that Liam is **absolutely** __________ **with** Nora, as he is happy to indulge in her every whim at a moment's notice.

5A Her 'food idiosyncrasy', as she calls it, is to feel **completely repulsed by** the mere sight of certain white foods, such as milk or mayonnaise.

5B The poor girl can't even look at white food – things like milk and mayonnaise – without getting **totally** __________ **out**. Who ever heard of such a thing?

6A I was **completely dumbfounded** – my chances of winning the scholarship had seemed all but guaranteed, but I did not even make the shortlist.

6B When I applied for the scholarship, I thought I was a shoo-in, so I was **utterly** __________ to find that I wasn't even short-listed.

7A I couldn't believe it. Instead of watching the children up on stage, one of the fathers spent the entire end-of-year recital **literally glued to** his mobile phone.

7B While the children performed, one father spent the entire end-of-year recital **wholly** __________ **in** his mobile phone. I was in disbelief.

2 **Think of a time when you or someone you know experienced one of the feelings or emotions from Exercise 1. Make notes on when, where and why it happened.**

3 **SPEAK** **Work in small groups. Take turns telling your classmates about your experiences. Ask follow-up questions.**

Speaking Part 3 Long turn

1 SPEAK **Work in pairs. You are going to take turns talking on your own for about two minutes. Before you do the speaking task, read the information in the boxes below.**

Student A: Talk for about two minutes about the question below.

Student B: When Student A has finished, say whether schools or parents should be responsible for teaching values to young people.

What has the most influence on people's values?
- age
- education
- community

2 **Now change roles.**

Student B: Talk for about two minutes about the question below.

Student A: When Student B has finished, say to what extent you think it's important for people to be informed about local political issues.

What are the qualities of a good citizen?
- being respectful
- being responsible
- being helpful

How to go about it

- The examiner gives you a topic card with the question on it, which you need to talk about for two minutes. There are three prompts to help you think of possible discussion areas, but you don't have to address these. You won't lose points for focusing on other ideas, as long as they are relevant.
- Allow yourself time to think before you begin. After the examiner gives you the topic card, you have up to ten seconds of 'thinking time'.
- Organise your ideas using a variety of signposting phrases. As well as demonstrating a higher level of English, this can help the examiner and your partner more easily understand your train of thought.

Useful language

Signposting phrases

Put the phrases in the correct category. Add more phrases to each category.

A case in point is … *Moving on …*
First and foremost … *Now, turning to …*
For instance … *To start off with …*
In summary, … *To recap, …*

Introducing your first main point	Transitioning to another main point	Introducing an example	Summarising

Listening Part 1 Multiple choice

1 1.1 **You will hear three different extracts. For questions 1–6, choose the answer (A, B or C) which fits best according to what you hear. There are two questions for each extract.**

What to expect in the exam

- There are three extracts with two multiple-choice questions for each extract. The extracts are either monologues or interactions between two speakers, such as interviews or conversations. You will hear a variety of accents.
- One by one, you will hear each extract twice.
- The questions can focus on a variety of different aspects of the extracts, including attitude, purpose, opinion, detail and general idea. You may also have to listen for what the two speakers agree or disagree on.

How to go about it

- Carefully read the introductory sentences for each extract. These give you context for what you will hear. Then read the questions and underline key words and phrases.
- Listen carefully to the whole extract before choosing an answer.
- Check your answers the second time you listen.

Extract 1

You hear part of an interview with a psychologist called Sandy talking about clothing.

1 According to Sandy, how has our relationship with clothing changed?
- **A** It is characterised by increased complexity.
- **B** Its connection to tradition has weakened.
- **C** It has become heavily influenced by trends.

2 Sandy says people choose specific clothing brands to
- **A** help them stand out from the crowd.
- **B** ally themselves with social causes.
- **C** reflect their accomplishments.

Extract 2

You hear two friends, a newspaper editor and a dentist, discussing their jobs.

3 What aspect of professional life do they agree on?
- **A** Their work does not satisfy basic psychological needs.
- **B** A healthy work-life balance is not easy to achieve.
- **C** People's attitudes are influenced by their work.

4 What is the woman doing when she talks about her patients?
- **A** questioning their integrity
- **B** condoning their irresponsibility
- **C** criticising their motives

Extract 3

You hear part of a lecture by an academic who is talking about oral history.

5 Why does the professor tell the story of the circus performer?
- **A** to cite a primary source
- **B** to support a prior claim
- **C** to illustrate an important point

6 What is the professor's attitude towards the way history is usually taught?
- **A** He laments its failure to engage students.
- **B** He thinks it leads to mistaken assumptions.
- **C** He is concerned about its lack of objectivity.

2 SPEAK **Which events in history have had the biggest effect on your country's or region's cultural identity, do you think?**

Pronunciation Consonant clusters with /s/

1 Complete the gaps in these sentences from the listening on page 4.

1 Not to **str**__________ too much into jargon, but this is why we behaviour theorists refer to clothing as an 'artefact of extended self'.

2 We **spl**__________ on certain clothing brands because of their association with subcultures or leisure activities.

3 History __________**sts** of stories, and what stories get told and who gets to tell them is important.

2 The words in the box all contain a combination of /s/ and two other consonant sounds. Complete each sentence with one of the words in the box.

boasts risks scrapped springboard streak stroll

1 The school's volleyball team can't seem to lose – they're currently on a 10-game **winning** __________.

2 The visit to my childhood home was a __________ **down memory lane**.

3 Do the potential benefits of space exploration outweigh its **inherent** __________?

4 When its funding was pulled, **plans** for the youth centre were __________ entirely.

5 Abdul is exceptionally proud of his children and often __________ of their academic **achievements**.

6 The scholarship aims to provide a __________ **to success** for talented young kids.

3 1.2 Listen and check your answers to Exercise 2.

Vocabulary Adjectives and nouns with *self*

1 SPEAK In Extract 1 of the listening, the psychologist refers to the 'extended self', the idea that valued possessions form part of our identity. What objects in your life would you consider part of your 'extended self'?

2 Complete the *self-* adjectives in sentences 1–6 with a word from the box.

deprecating indulgent made possessed respecting sacrificing satisfied

1 'I knew I was right,' he gloated, and gave that irritatingly **self-**__________ **smile** he reserves for even his most insignificant successes.

2 Her one-hour stand-up act consisted of her usual **self-**__________ **humour**, an endless string of jokes revolving around her own perceived failings.

3 She received the award for her tireless efforts and **self-**__________ **devotion** to those less fortunate than herself in the community.

4 No **self-**__________ **cook** should ever consider serving instant mashed potatoes!

5 He confronts each problem with the same calm, **self-**__________ **confidence**, never raising his voice, never losing his temper.

6 This modest, **self-**__________ **billionaire** – she built up her clothing empire from absolutely nothing – had no time for a **self-**__________ **lifestyle** and was happier sitting at her desk than lounging by the pool.

3 Underline the correct option.

1 Her dismissal would have been an easy excuse for Hana to **wallow in** ***self-preservation / self-pity / self-delusion***, but she didn't fall into this trap.

2 The book chronicles a young man's struggles with not quite fitting in, living with regrets and **questioning** his own ***self-esteem / self-worth / self-interest***.

3 His attempt to rationalise his bad behaviour is a profound **act of *self-deception / self-aggrandisement / self-assurance*** – but he's fooling no one else.

4 Turn to the Additional materials on page 200 for further practice.

About English

The word 'selfie' was declared the Oxford Word of the Year in 2012, when its use by English speakers spiked by 17,000 per cent.

Do you know the meaning of these other words of the year? Why do you think they were chosen?

goblin mode (2022), *vax* (2021), *climate emergency* (2019), *toxic* (2018), *post-truth* (2016)

Reading and Use of English Part 6 Gapped text

1 You are going to read an article about people who are exceptionally good at remembering faces. Seven paragraphs have been removed from the article. Choose from the paragraphs **A–H** the one which fits each gap (**1–7**). There is one extra paragraph which you do not need to use.

SUPER-RECOGNISERS

Police employ them and scientists study them, but what is life like for the rare few who can never forget a face?

As a child, Yenny Seo often surprised her mother by pointing out a stranger in the grocery store, remarking it was the same person they passed on the street a few weeks earlier. Likewise, when they watched a movie together, Seo would often recognise 'extras' who'd appeared fleetingly in other films. Her mother never thought this was 'anything special', Seo says, and simply assumed she had a particularly observant daughter.

1 ______

It was only as she started using social media that Seo became self-conscious of her skill. 'I would start a new class in uni or I would meet people through social gatherings and I would remember visually what kind of photos I'd seen them in. I'd already be so familiar with them and I'd know in my head: "Oh, you are that person's sibling, or you used to date so-and-so,"' she says. 'But I also knew it'd be really creepy if I said that out loud, so I'd keep it on the down low and just say: "Oh, nice to meet you."'

2 ______

Until the early 2000s, little scientific attention was paid to whether all humans possess the same ability to recognise faces. According to Dr David White, now a lead investigator at the Face Research Lab at the University of New South Wales (UNSW), 'I think intuitively people believe that the way they see the world is the same as others. And I think that scientists had that intuition as well.'

3 ______

It may be, he says, that our brains are organised to perform different tasks, 'like an app on your smartphone.' Along with other researchers, White started examining people without impairments, discovering there is 'tremendous variation' in facial recognition ability. From their research, experts have concluded that facial recognition ability lies along a bell curve, like IQ and other human capacities.

4 ______

The underlying cause is still not entirely clear – it's a new field, with only around 20 scientific papers studying super-recognisers. However, it is suspected that genetics plays a role because identical twins show similar performance, and it has been shown that cortical thickness – the number of neurons – in the part of the brain that supports face recognition is a predictor of superior ability. So it appears that certain people like Seo are born with a superpower, as if they were a character in a comic book. But how exactly does this superpower work?

5 ______

Because this is such a rare phenomenon, in 2017 White and his colleagues at UNSW designed a publicly available online screening tool to try to unearth the world's best super-recognisers. When Seo – then in her mid-20s, gave it a go – her score was so high that White invited her to come to Sydney for more testing. With more than 100,000 people now tested, Seo still ranks in the top 50.

6 ______

For her part, Seo is perfectly happy with her job as a technician at a pathology lab. However, the diagnosis from White did help her see her abilities in a new light. 'It made me realise: oh yeah, it's not crazy – I must have been right the whole time. It's not that I'm creepy, but my brain is just wired that way.'

7 ______

If so, Dr White and his colleagues at the Face Research Lab at UNSW would be delighted to hear from you.

Adapted from *The Guardian*

What to expect in the exam

There is a long text from which paragraphs have been removed, followed by the extracted paragraphs in a random order. You have to decide which paragraph goes in each gap.

How to go about it

- First, quickly read the gapped text and identify the main themes. Take note of where the writer shifts focus. For example, this article starts with a personal story and then moves into a discussion of scientific research.
- Choose a gap and carefully read the sentences before and after. Look for any links to the missing paragraph, e.g. demonstrative pronouns (*this*, *these*), subject pronouns (*he*, *we*), linking words and phrases (*then*, *though*).
- Then, check each extracted paragraph to see if it fits in the gap. Repeat the process for each gap.

A Once though, while working at a part-time job at a clothing store, Seo had good cause to deploy her special ability. Staff were shown grainy, hard-to-decipher CCTV footage of a habitual shoplifter; the next time this person entered the shop, Seo instantly recognised them and alerted the security guard.

B A recent experiment, which used eye-tracking technology, may shed some light on the matter. White observed that super-recognisers spread their 'gaze more around the face, which suggests they might be painting a more elaborate picture of the face in their mind's eye.'

C In fact, most of us are quite adept at recognising the faces of people we know well, no matter how pixelated or grainy a picture may be. Matching unfamiliar faces, though, can be surprisingly challenging even under optimal conditions, and this is problematic because many important tasks depend on this very skill – matching a traveller to their passport or a CCTV image to a police mugshot.

D Seo was unaware that others didn't share her love of the private game she played, where she'd spot a person on a bus or the street and then flick through the vast catalogue of faces she kept in her head, trying to place where she'd seen them before. 'Especially as a child, I remember just really enjoying looking at different faces.'

E So, what about you? Have you also questioned your sanity after recognising a stranger whom you passed on the street years before? Perhaps you easily rattle off a list of movies where you've seen a particular extra, only to be met by blank stares.

F He began to question this while studying a rare condition called prosopagnosia – when a brain injury leaves someone unable to recognise faces. He was intrigued that while people with this condition couldn't recognise the face of a loved one, they could still recognise other objects.

G Perhaps unsurprisingly, the existence of super-recognisers has not gone unnoticed by law enforcement agencies, which have started to actively recruit people with superior facial recognition capabilities. London's metropolitan police, for example, has a special team who examine CCTV footage from crime scenes, and several years ago Queensland police started identifying super-recognisers in its ranks.

H Most people fall somewhere in the middle, but a few possess either an exceptionally good or weak ability to identify faces. The 1–2% of the population at the very top are 'super-recognisers' – people who only need the briefest glimpse to memorise a face, and who can then store that information for months, years, or even the rest of their lives.

2 SPEAK Work in pairs. Do you think being a super-recogniser would be a blessing or a curse?

About English

In journalism and fiction, as well as other neutral / informal contexts, writers often use the dash (–) to:

- indicate an abrupt change in the flow of sentence:

  It made me realise: oh yeah, it's not crazy – I must have been right the whole time.
- set off one or more appositives or modifiers:

  ... and this is problematic because many tasks depend on this very skill – matching a traveller to their passport or a CCTV image to a police mugshot.

  ... and it has been shown that cordial thickness – the number of neurons – in the part of the brain that supports facial recognition...

Language focus The present

1 **Read sentences 1–4, in which both the present simple and present continuous are possible and answer the questions.**

1 Alisa is already quite proficient in Portuguese, but she *always looks* / *is always looking* for ways to improve it.
Which form shows that something happens so often it is characteristic of that person?

2 I *hope* / *'m hoping* you'll be available to help set up for the children's concert.
Which form makes the request sound more direct and less polite?

3 For social media companies, monitoring content *only gets* / *is only getting* harder.
Which form emphasises that a situation is in a state of change?

4 To improve her German, Federica *spends* / *is spending* July in Hamburg.
Which form indicates that the action is only temporary instead of habitual?

2 **SPEAK** **Work in pairs. Some verbs have different meanings depending on whether they describe a state or a dynamic action. Read sentences 1–4 and discuss the differences in meaning.**

1 A For some professionals, like dentists, referrals and word of mouth **appear** to work just fine.
B I hear several of these actors **are appearing** on stage for the very first time.

2 A What first **attracts** me is her sparkling wit.
B Marked by radiant splendour, the refurbished palace **is attracting** visitors from the world over.

3 A The authors of the report **conclude** that contagious yawning is closely related to empathy.
B After days of wrangling, the negotiators **are** finally **concluding** the trade agreement as we speak and details will be made public shortly.

4 A The court may make such enquiries as they **consider** necessary, and may hold a hearing for the purposes of so doing.
B We'**re considering** holiday options for our dog – probably either a sitter or a kennel.

3 **Go to the** **Ready for Grammar section on page 204** **for further rules, explanations and practice.**

4 **Read the anecdote. Underline the correct option in *italics*.**

My dog, Bella – she **(1)** *absolutely adores* / *is absolutely adoring* water. This one day, we **(2)** *hang* / *'re hanging* about at the pool and Bella **(3)** *just wants* / *is just wanting* to swim the whole time. At one point we **(4)** *put* / *'re putting* her in the garage, but less than a minute later she leaps up through an open window. She **(5)** *hits* / *'s hitting* the ground running and she **(6)** *jumps* / *'s jumping* right back in the pool.

5 **1.3** **Listen and check your answers.**

6 **Read the social media post with advice for telling anecdotes. Did the speaker in Exercise 5 follow all the tips?**

7 **Prepare to tell an anecdote about something that happened to you or someone you know. Make sure you follow the tips in Exercise 6.**

8 **SPEAK** **Work in small groups. Take turns telling your anecdotes. Tell each other which details from the story you found most interesting or amusing.**

TOP FIVE TIPS FOR TELLING ANECDOTES

1 Identify the purpose of your anecdote: tell a joke, make a point, teach a lesson, etc.
2 Skip long introductions. Jump right into the action.
3 Bring the story to life with relevant details. But avoid overwhelming your story with unnecessary information.
4 Use present tenses. They make it feel like the action is happening right now.
5 Finish with a bang. Make your ending count.

Reading and Use of English Part 2 Open cloze

What to expect in the exam

- In Part 2, you are given a short text with eight missing words. You must think of one word that fits in each gap. The answer will never be a contraction (*can't*, *I'm*).
- The open cloze tests your knowledge of both grammar (e.g. dependent prepositions and auxiliary verbs) and vocabulary (e.g. phrasal verbs and fixed phrases). To guess the right word, you need to understand the meaning of the whole sentence or even the whole paragraph.

1 **Read the following text about job titles. Do you agree with the writer's views and opinions? Why or why not?**

2 **Read the text again and think of one word which best fits each space (1–8). Use only one word in each space. There is an example at the beginning (0).**

DO JOB TITLES REALLY MATTER?

In a (0) *WORD*, yes. Within an organisation, a person's job title can clarify an employee's role and status. Outside of work, it is often brandished as a marker of one's self-identity, a prism through which we present ourselves to the world. (1) As ____________, these titles should be chosen with care.

Sadly, this is not always the (2) ____________. Many companies today are succumbing (3) ____________ the temptation of job title inflation. This is the practice of levelling (4) ____________ an employee's job title without increasing their responsibilities (or salary) – for instance, adding 'Senior' in front of a 'Software Engineer' position with junior requirements.

On the (5) ____________ of it, job title inflation might seem like a tempting way to soften the (6) ____________ when you can't give an employee their desired pay rise or promotion, but it is ultimately detrimental. (7) ____________ loftier titles be bestowed upon employees at random, it can breed resentment among others doing similar work. Even worse, inflated titles create undue confusion, defeating the (8) ____________ of having a job title in the first place: to tell people who you are and what you do.

3 **SPEAK** **Work in pairs. For a company, what might be the advantages and disadvantages of using inflated job titles when it comes to recruiting new talent?**

4 **Prepositions are often tested in Part 2 Open cloze. In the column on the right-hand side, write the missing prepositions in sentences 1–8. Do NOT write the prepositions in the spaces in the sentences.**

1. It made my day! So many friends came to my birthday! I was so happy my heart felt like it was overflowing ______ joy. ____________
2. The law prohibits any business from discriminating ______ qualified individuals with disabilities in employment. ____________
3. A last-minute injury forced Emma to withdraw ______ the competition, leaving her bitterly disappointed. ____________
4. As a New Year's resolution, the couple committed themselves ______ eating a healthier diet. ____________
5. The fraternisation ______ managers with factory workers was reprimanded, which only reinforced existing class barriers. ____________
6. As a political cartoonist, my job is to make social commentary and poke fun ______ politicians. ____________
7. We had some strong feelings on the matter, but we refrained ______ further comment so as not to upset our guests. ____________
8. It was only when my first daughter was born that I was confronted ______ the reality of being a parent. ____________

5 **SPEAK** **Work in pairs. Cover the column on the right and practise saying the missing prepositions from memory.**

Writing Part 2 Article

What to expect in the exam

- In Writing Part 2, you may have the opportunity to write an article. Usually, the target audience is the readership of an English-language newspaper or magazine (print or digital). The instructions specify the topic and type of publication. This information will inform what style you should adopt.
- In an article, you not only need to convey information, but also to engage the reader's interest in the topic. This can be achieved by using language that is vivid, descriptive, and succinct. You can also include a personal narrative or anecdote, if appropriate.

1 SPEAK Work in pairs. Read the quotations. Have any global trends recently become popular where you live?

'I've started doing yoga. It's originally from India, where people have been doing it for thousands of years, but it's become very trendy in my country in the last 10–20 years.'

'Where I live, hip hop is always on the radio now and I even see teenagers sitting with their friends in the park practising their own verses.'

2 Read the Writing Part 2 task below. What key points do you have to address in your answer?

An English-language magazine is running a series of articles on the ways our personal identities are shaped by global trends. You decide to send in an article. You should briefly describe one or two ways in which your personal opinions or interests have been shaped by global trends. You should also evaluate the extent to which the influence of global trends on our lives is positive or negative.

Write your **article** in **280–320** words.

MANGA AND ME

Most people don't know that the mythic Japanese comic *Akira*, written and illustrated by Katsuhiro Otomo, wasn't originally published as a book. It ran as a serial for eight whole years in the pages of weekly *Young Magazine* from 1982 to 1990. Why do I know this? Because I'm obsessed with manga.

You might be wondering how someone from a small town in southern Italy got sucked into the Japanese subculture of manga, but this sort of thing is common nowadays. For me it's manga; for you, it might be sport or fashion or video games. With the internet, we have all found new ways of organising information around ourselves, new ways to develop and define our personal identities. These days our personal identities have become intertwined with our online activities to such a degree that they are no longer separable from our 'real'-life selves.

Some see global trends as a negative force. Some see globalisation as a juggernaut, squashing local traditions, fomenting social isolation. But, at least for me, that couldn't be further from the truth. I thoroughly enjoy the rhythms of traditional life in my small town. My interest in manga has not dulled my enthusiasm for our local festivities. Our regional delicacies still taste just as good. Although I prefer reading stories that take place in faraway Tokyo, I have no plans to move there. My identity is rooted in the very soil of my hometown and the strong network of family and friends that I belong to here.

And so, if you happen to see me sipping a cappuccino at the local café, sporting my favourite *Akira* T-shirt, looking slightly out of place among my compatriots, set your worries aside. That's just me being me.

3 **Read the model answer and respond to the questions.**

1 Does the writer cover the key points in the instructions?

2 What is the purpose of each paragraph?

3 Does the writer hold your attention, expressing their ideas in a way that's easy to follow?

4 What examples can you find of language that is vivid and/or descriptive?

4 **The use of effective writing techniques is an essential feature of C2 Proficiency writing tasks. Read techniques 1–5 below, then find an example of each technique in the model answer.**

1 Semicolons are a subtle way to show that two separate sentences are working together to make a point.

2 Metaphors or similes can be used to express your idea in a vivid, memorable way.

3 The use of parallel structures, such as starting two sentences in a row the same way, creates a dramatic effect.

4 Another way to create a dramatic effect is to follow a long, complicated sentence with a short, snappy one.

5 To achieve a satisfying feeling of coherence, finish a piece of writing by referring back to something mentioned at the very beginning.

Useful language

Parallelism is when similar words, phrases, clauses, sentences structures or related elements are in harmony within a sentence. It can help make writing more clear and concise, as well as improve its readibility.

Look at the following sentence from the model answer.

With the internet, we have all found new ways of organising information around ourselves, new ways to develop and define our personal identities.

In the sentence above, *new ways <u>of developing</u> and <u>defining</u>* would sound better because it would be grammatically parallel to *new ways of organising.*

Look at the following sentence. Find and correct the mistake in its parallel construction.

The not-for-profit gave up on hosting the second fundraiser because the results of the first one were unsatisfactory and a general lack of enthusiasm among donors.

5 **Now write your own answer to the Part 2 task in Exercise 1. Before you start writing, read the advice in the *How to go about it* box.**

How to go about it

- Read the instructions and identify the key points to include in your answer.
- Brainstorm ideas and think about how to support them with relevant examples, reasons, personal stories or reflections.
- Make a plan. Decide on the main focus of each paragraph before you start writing.
- Grab the reader's attention in the first paragraph by asking them a question, referring to personal experience or sharing an interesting and/or surprising fact.
- You can end with a summary, but many good articles finish with a direct quotation, a funny comment, a final anecdote – anything that brings the piece to a satisfying end.
- To finish, give your article a catchy title.

For more information on writing articles, see page 192.

1 REVIEW

Reading and Use of English Part 1 Multiple-choice cloze

What to expect in the exam

- You read a short text with eight gaps. You must choose the correct option among four (A–D) that best fits the gap. There is always one example.
- This task tests different types of vocabulary, e.g. collocations, set expressions, phrasal verbs, idioms, linkers. It also tests your knowledge of the subtle differences in meaning between similar words, as well as complementation, i.e. words that are followed by specific prepositions or verb forms (gerund/infinitive).

How to go about it

- Read the text once quickly for gist. It can be helpful to guess which words are missing before looking at the options A–D.
- To get the answer right, you must decide which of the options best fits the phrase or sentence containing the gap. It's important to carefully check the words on either side of the gap. However, sometimes you have to take into consideration the meaning of the whole sentence or even the whole paragraph. This is especially true with linking words and phrases.

1 **Read the text quickly. Ignore the gaps. What is the writer's main argument about rental fashion?**

2 **For questions 1–8, read the text and decide which answer (A, B, C or D) best fits each gap. There is an example at the beginning (0).**

Fashion for rent

Fashion allows us to express our mood, personal interests, political leanings and so much more. The rise of fast fashion has made this (0) ___C___ for self-expression more widely accessible, but it has also been an (1) ________ disaster for the environment. We now buy twice as much clothing and keep it for half as long. Are there any viable alternatives?

Enter fashion rental websites, where you can borrow clothes for a fixed period of time. Might this innovation (2) ________ a way forward for those of us who are (3) ________ with fashion but also care about the planet? In theory, rental fashion could reduce the demand for manufacturing new clothing, which in (4) ________ could reduce textile waste.

In practice, however, it (5) ________ to be seen whether rental fashion is really as green as it's (6) ________ up to be. Consider all the energy needed to deliver and clean the items. But, provided a greener infrastructure *were* possible, rental fashion might (7) ________ be a good reason to (8) ________ hope for a more sustainable future of fashion.

	A	B	C	D
0	motive	aptitude	vehicle	alley
1	unassailable	insufferable	unmitigated	inculpatory
2	survey	chart	log	cast
3	bequeathed	besotted	bewildered	besmirched
4	turn	part	excess	short
5	waits	happens	stands	remains
6	banged	kicked	cracked	whacked
7	furthermore	nonetheless	hence	conversely
8	come into	back up	put aside	hold out

Vocabulary Feelings and emotions

Complete the gaps in the bold expressions with a word from the box. The words can be used more than once.

by in out over to with

1 At first you might be **completely repulsed** __________ the idea of eating insects, but they are actually quite nutritious.

2 In the film, Jane falls **head** __________ **heels in love** with a cute department store clerk.

3 I was so **wholly engrossed** __________ my new book that the flight attendant had to remind me to put down my tray for the meal.

4 When another driver suddenly cut him off, forcing him to slam on the brakes, Uncle Jack nearly **went apoplectic** __________ **rage**.

5 It's become a cliché, teenagers **literally glued** __________ their smartphones, but in fact young people use devices more mindfully than we think.

6 As Gael cycled on the narrow road, cars whipped by at over 100 kilometres per hour. Needless to say, he was **scared** __________ **of his wits**.

7 If you're feeling **a bit down** __________ **the dumps** and need a pick-me-up, then listen to some music with an upbeat tempo – it's sure to boost your mood!

8 The restaurant now has a Michelin star, so I was **chuffed** __________ **bits** when my daughter gave me a voucher for it as a birthday present.

9 The pupils crowded around the laboratory table, feeling **totally grossed** __________ yet totally intrigued by the mould experiment.

Language focus The present

Choose the correct alternatives in the following sentences. Either one or both alternatives may be possible.

1 If you *feel / are feeling* ill, why don't you go lie down and rest?

2 Thinking back on it now, I still can't believe I won – I *guess / am guessing* luck was on my side.

3 I *mind / am minding* my own business, in the middle of a relaxing jog, and a dog runs up and starts nipping at my heels.

4 I'm trying to make sense of this information. It *concerns / is concerning* safety protocols and will be applicable to all of us.

5 The parade starts at 10 am and the weather forecast *looks / is looking* good.

6 We *wish / are wishing* to present a brief overview to demonstrate what benefits this technology could provide for your organisation.

7 To avoid potential inconvenience, we *recommend / are recommending* that drivers renew their licences well in advance of the expiration date.

8 He now *holds / is holding* a bachelor's degree in computer science from Tsinghua University in Beijing.

Writing Part 2 Letter

An online magazine is inviting readers to contribute letters on the topic of childhood friends. You decide to write a letter about one of your childhood friends. You should explain what made this friendship special and assess the importance of friends in the lives of children.

Write your letter in 280–320 words.

For more information on writing letters, see page 193.

Idioms Personality

1 **Sentence A has a similar meaning to Sentence B. What advantage to using idioms does this illustrate?**

A He's not someone who likes doing new or different things. He'd much prefer to follow a routine, doing the same things in the same way.

B He's a **creature of habit**.

2 **Match sentences (1–9) to idioms (a–i) which have a similar meaning.**

1 Mena used to be very shy, but these days she is friendlier and more talkative. She seems more confident when speaking to new people.

2 Mark has an inflated sense of his own importance. He thinks of himself as being very special and clever, and he can't help showing it.

3 Sarina has become very enthusiastic about chess. She dedicates nearly all of her time and energy to the game.

4 Jimmy is the kind of person who lies to people and he is likely to cause trouble. He's unpleasant and unkind.

5 Tommaso is always ruining other people's fun. He either refuses to join activities other people want to do – or, if he does join, he stops other people from enjoying the activity.

6 At one point in the past, Alice feels like she was treated unfairly. She has been resentful about this for a long time. When the subject comes up, she takes offence quickly and easily.

7 Georgia is very energetic and determined to succeed. Plus, she seems to be able to handle any difficult situation with ease.

8 Very gregarious and outgoing, Melonie has always had great communication skills. She seems to take real joy in meeting and talking to people.

9 Nnamdi is a stickler for rules. When given instructions on how to do something, he follows them rigorously.

a He's a **nasty piece of work**.

b He does things strictly **by the book**.

c She's **come out of her shell.**

d She **lives and breathes it**.

e He's **full of himself**.

f She's **got a chip on her shoulder.**

g She's a **people person**.

h He's a **wet blanket**.

i She's a real **go-getter**.

Discussing idioms

Discuss the differences in meaning between these idioms:

- a wet blanket / a party pooper
- a people person / a people pleaser
- a go-getter / a high flyer

3 SPEAK **Work in pairs. Decide which of the idioms from Exercises 1 and 2 would typically have a positive connotation and which would have a negative connotation. Are there any that could be either positive or negative depending on the context?**

4 **Think of two characters from books, films or TV series that could be described using the idioms from Exercise 2.**

5 SPEAK **Take turns describing the characters but without using the idioms. Your classmate has to guess which idioms describe your characters.**

2 WANDERLUST

KEY LANGUAGE

Past forms
Adverbs and adverbial phrases
Travel
Adverbs

IDIOMS

Making stories interesting

EXAM PRACTICE

Reading and Use of English Parts 3, 4 & 5
Writing Parts 1 & 2
Listening Part 2
Speaking Parts 1 & 2

Speaking Part 1 Interview

Work with a partner. Discuss the questions.

1 How important is travel to you?
2 How much interest do you take in travel websites, magazines or TV programmes?
3 In the future, do you see yourself travelling more or less?
4 Does the environmental impact of travel outweigh personal or commercial benefits?

About English

wanderlust (n) /ˈwɒndə(r)ˌlʌst/
A strong wish to travel

This word originally comes from German and describes the pleasure or delight taken from hiking. It is used more broadly in English to talk about travel in general.

What other words or phrases do you know in English that originally come from another language?

2 WANDERLUST

Speaking Part 2 Collaborative task

1 **SPEAK** Work in pairs. Look at pictures 1 and 2 below. They show people on different types of holiday. Talk together about what holiday types are suggested by these pictures.

2 Before you do the speaking task, read the information in the boxes below.

3 In pairs, talk together about which picture (1 or 2) interests you more.

4 Now look at pictures 1–4. Imagine an online streaming service is going to create a new series exploring how tourism affects local environments around the world. Talk together about the different effects of tourism on local environments suggested by the pictures. Then decide which issue should be highlighted in the first episode.

How to go about it

- When you discuss the pictures in the first part of the task, be sure to make speculations and not simply describe them.
- Be a good listener. Throughout the task, respond to and build on what your partner says, for example, by using counterarguments. Don't just talk about your own ideas and opinions.
- In the decision phase, don't worry if you and your partner never actually reach a decision, as long as it is clear that you are trying to work towards one.

Don't forget!

Counterarguments are a good way to build on your partner's responses.

› That would be great, except ...
› That's probably true, but ...
› Possibly, but ...
› Even so, ...

Useful language

Responding to and building on your partner's comments

For 1–4 below, complete the sentences with one word in each gap.

1 I like what you said ________ how people should be more mindful of the impact their actions are having on the natural world.
2 What exactly did you mean ________ 'acceptable limits of change'?
3 I largely agree with what you said, except for the part ________ golf courses wasting precious freshwater resources.
4 So ________ you're saying is that saving local environments is a fool's errand?

Online series – effects of tourism

1

2

Vocabulary Travel

1 Underline the adjective in each group that doesn't normally collocate with the noun in capital letters.

1	arduous	occupied	perilous	uneventful	**JOURNEY**
2	alternative	circuitous	scenic	beaten	**ROUTE**
3	faraway	bumpy	smooth	long-haul	**FLIGHT**
4	go-to	world-class	far-flung	over-run	**DESTINATION**
5	fleeting	flying	torrential	impromptu	**VISIT**
6	unrestricted	unacceptable	unavoidable	unforeseen	**DELAY**

2 Write five sentences about a real or imagined trip you went on using collocations from Exercise 1.

3 Complete the sentences with an adjective from box A and a noun from box B. There is an example at the beginning.

A backwater bustling culture discerning iconic leisurely overseas shoddy

B crowds landmark service shock stroll travel traveller villages

0 What might a *discerning traveller* expect from a luxury hotel?

1 What would be the pros and cons of a job that involved frequent ______________?

2 Which would be more relaxing to do on a beach holiday – lying in the sand or taking a ______________ along the coast?

3 For you, what ______________ in your country is a must-see for foreign visitors?

4 When in a major city, do you gravitate toward the ______________ of the city centre or do you try to avoid them?

5 If you experienced ______________ while on holiday, would you make a complaint?

6 Have you ever experienced ______________? Where were you? How long, if ever, did it take you to adjust?

7 Do you think it's more interesting to visit cosmopolitan cities or quiet ______________?

4 SPEAK Work in pairs. Discuss the questions from Exercise 3 with your partner.

Reading and Use of English Part 5 Multiple choice

1 **SPEAK** **Work in pairs. Look at the photos opposite and discuss your ideas on the following:**

1 Do you recognise either of the places? Where do you think they are?

2 What reasons might a tourist have to visit these places?

How to go about it

- Read the title and text quickly for general understanding.
- Look at the first question and underline the key words. Before you read the options (A, B, C and D), find the place in the text where the answer is located and underline the relevant part. Try to answer the question yourself without looking at the options. Then check and choose the option closest to your own answer.
- Don't be put off by difficult vocabulary. Even if you don't understand every word – or even every sentence – in the text, you can still get the answers right.

2 **You are going to read a magazine article about film tourism. For questions 1–6, choose the answer (A, B, C or D) which you think fits best according to the text.**

1 What point is being made about film tourism in the first paragraph?

A It is the reason more producers are choosing to film in real-life settings.

B It has coincided with the rapid growth of international travel.

C It is revolutionising the film and television production industry.

D It has created new opportunities for collaboration between certain industries.

2 Why does the writer refer to *Game of Thrones*?

A It partnered with travel websites to increase tourism at its filming locations.

B It used tourist sites and historical monuments to create a feeling of authenticity.

C It demonstrated the potential effect a TV series can have on tourism.

D It had the ability to transform any film location into a tourist attraction.

3 In the third paragraph, what point about academic research does the writer emphasise?

A her admiration for the careful research done by an academic

B her surprise at the widespread lack of objectivity in academia

C her distrust regarding the motives of some experienced researchers

D her uncertainty about the type of methodology used in recent studies

4 What point is exemplified by the story of Maya Bay?

A Tourists may unwittingly participate in irresponsible holiday activities.

B A natural area may be devastated by tourism unless protective measures are put in place.

C Environmental regulations have a limited ability to restore areas devastated by tourism.

D A balance should be found between creating jobs and protecting the environment.

5 In the fifth paragraph, what do we learn about production incentives?

A They encourage production companies to employ local actors and film crews.

B They allow for independent films to be made with limited resources.

C They aim to create a connection between stakeholders that is mutually beneficial.

D They influence which countries film production companies choose to work in.

6 In this article, the writer is

A examining the trend of film tourism.

B outlining distinct visions of film tourism.

C arguing for more investment in film tourism.

D analysing the sustainability of film tourism.

3 **SPEAK** **Is there a place you've always wanted to visit because of a film or TV series? What are the pros and cons of this kind of tourism for local people?**

As Seen on Screen

Rising to prominence in the 1990s, the trend of 'film tourism' really began to gather steam in the early 2000s thanks to the success of The *Lord of the Rings* film trilogy. In its wake, New Zealand, where the films were shot, is reported to have experienced an astonishing 50% surge in tourism. Over the years, a growing synergy has emerged between the tourism and the entertainment sectors, as countries try to actively promote themselves as settings for films or TV series in hope of reaping the rewards of increased tourism.

Take the ground-breaking, global phenomenon, *Game of Thrones*. The TV series, which originally ran on the streaming network HBO from 2011–2019, was shot on location in various European countries. Particularly around the release of the last season, those locations saw a significant jump in tourism, with bookings to Iceland swelling by 166% and those to Croatia, by 68%. Here the coastal city of Dubrovnik, where the city of King's Landing was set in the series, proved particularly popular. Another prime example would be Zafra Castle in Guadalajara, Spain, which had a 488% increase in searches on TripAdvisor in one year after its appearance in the series, according to the travel platform. These figures coincide with research on the '*Game of Thrones* effect,' which has found a correlation between the frequency and tendency of tourists to post photos of a film spot on social media with both the amount of screen time that spot is given in the show and where characters have the most intense scenes.

But what motivates so many tourists to visit these film locations? In her book, *Fan Sites: Film Tourism and Contemporary Fandom*, postdoctoral researcher Abby Waysdorf identifies a few key factors: the desire to have a novel experience by visiting film locations; prestige aspects, such as the inherent status symbol of posting a selfie of yourself at the setting of a famous film; and a sense of personal involvement with film – fans paying a kind of tribute to something important in their lives. However, Waysdorf approaches her subject with caution (unlike so many amateur researchers who, due to a growing need for positive results, tend to overinflate the significance of their findings) and stresses that film tourism is a more complex phenomenon than it might at first appear.

Tourists may indeed become aware of a new destination because of a film or TV series, but they may decide to visit based on a combination of other factors, such as being lured by attractive travel offers, a desire to learn about the place's history, or simply to enjoy idyllic scenery.

Film tourism has been a boon for many tourist destinations, but an unexpected surge in visitors can have obvious downsides. After watching blockbuster film *The Beach*, hordes of tourists began descending on Maya Bay, a pocket of paradise on the coastline of Ko Phi Phi Leh in Thailand. At one point, up to 6,000 people were arriving daily. This unregulated, out-of-control tourism quickly precipitated coastline erosion and the destruction of coral reefs due to boats docking and shoreline swimming. In October 2018, Thailand's Department of National Parks, Wildlife and Plant Conservation announced that the area would be closed to give the ecosystem time to recover. Maya Bay was eventually reopened, but swimming is now banned and there is a strict cap on tourist numbers.

Despite the possible downsides for local environments and communities, film tourism appears to be here to stay. National governments are even getting involved, proffering generous production incentives, in effect paying production companies to shoot within their borders. In many European countries, for example, even the smallest of independent film studios can bank on a cash rebate of between 20–30% of their production spending. Singapore subsidises a whopping 50% of qualifying expenses. These production incentives vary in scope and structure from place to place, but the objective is universal: a symbiotic financial relationship between countries and film production companies. There are, of course, caveats to consider. Production companies often have to meet a minimum amount of qualifying local expenditure, which can be high. And some countries even require a film or TV series to pass a 'cultural eligibility test.'

Film and TV series are set in some of the most alluring locations on earth. Thus it's unsurprising that viewers would be motivated to travel to these places. The key is to manage it responsibly. If local communities are sufficiently prepared for the deluge of tourists heading their way, through awareness campaigns and other measures, and if local environments do not deteriorate, it seems that cross pollination between the film and tourism industries can be, on the whole, a positive phenomenon for cities and towns keen to boost their local economies.

Language focus Past forms

1 Match sentences 1–10 with the types of past actions (a–e).

1 Did the cabin crew come round with snacks after the seatbelt sign went off?
2 He had a staycation because he hadn't found the time to renew his passport.
3 Her uncle would send her postcards from all the cities he visited.
4 I went off social media because friends were always posting their amazing travel photos.
5 They were on the verge of booking the flights when the website crashed.
6 My teenagers now want to have really exotic holidays! As kids, they used to be happy anywhere with a swimming pool.
7 He was constantly travelling for work those days when his boss couldn't get away.
8 What a shame the museum was closed! Which paintings had you been hoping to see?
9 She had more time to wander around the city after she had seen all the major sights.
10 When they said it was their anniversary, the hotel staff sent complimentary gifts to the room.

a Unfulfilled past intentions. ________ and ________
b Unexpected or annoying past actions. ________ and ________
c Sequential past actions. ________ and ________
d Non-sequential past actions. ________ and ________
e Repeated past actions or states. ________ and ________

2 Complete sentences 1–7 with the appropriate past form of the verbs in brackets. There may be more than one possible answer.

1 My love of Thai food started with a trip to the odd restaurant. But once I ________ (*be*) to all of them and ploughed through all the recipe books, there was only one thing to do and that was go to Thailand itself!
2 I almost went the year before. After one particularly stressful week, I ________ (*about/request*) temporary leave from work, but I let a friend talk me out of it right at the very last moment.
3 Back then, you see, I had a close friend who ________ (*always/question*) whether my plans were realistic or practical. But I eventually overcame this self-defeating pessimism and booked my flight to Bangkok.
4 When I started walking the streets of Bangkok, I ________ (*expect*) to see streets full of cooking schools but I didn't come across a single one!
5 After a while, I was tired and sweaty from walking so I went to a local café. I sat down and ________ (*order*) a drink. It was then that I finally spotted a flyer for what I had been searching for: 'Thai Cooking School.'
6 After we had had a few lessons learning the basics, the other students and I ________ (*begin*) to get to grips with this new world of spice and flavour.
7 I vividly remember how we used to dedicate hour upon hour to cooking and then, come mealtime, the pupils and teachers ________ (*sit*) down together around this big table to taste everyone's creations.

3 Go to Ready for Grammar on page 206 for rules, explanations and further practice.

4 SPEAK Work in pairs. Where there are two or more possible forms in Exercise 2, is there a change in meaning?

5 SPEAK Work in pairs. Prepare to tell your partner about a time when you learned something new or had a new experience while travelling. Make notes on the sequence of events. Think about your intentions when you started travelling and how they might have changed. Take turns describing your experiences.

Listening Part 2 Sentence completion

1 SPEAK Work in pairs. Look at the photo and discuss the following questions.

1 Where in the world do you think it is?
2 What might draw someone to visit somewhere like this?
3 Are there any areas like this in your country?

What to expect in the exam

- In Part 2, you will listen to an informative monologue.
- There are nine gapped or incomplete sentences to answer. You need to complete the gaps with either single words or short phrases. The questions follow the order of the information in the text.
- For some questions you will hear distractors: words or phrases that fit the sentence grammatically, and might seem relevant, but are incorrect.

How to go about it

- You will hear the recording twice. Before you listen, read through all the questions and predict the type of information required.
- Underline the key words in each sentence. This can help guide you through the speaker's monologue. As these tracks are quite long – around four minutes – it's possible to get lost. Knowing what type of information is coming up can help you identify if you have missed a question and need to move on.
- The second time you listen to the recording, check your answers. Make sure that your spelling is correct and that your answer fits the sentence grammatically.

2 ▶ **2.1** You will hear a travel expert and writer reporting on travelling in deserts. For questions 1–9, complete the sentences with a word or short phrase.

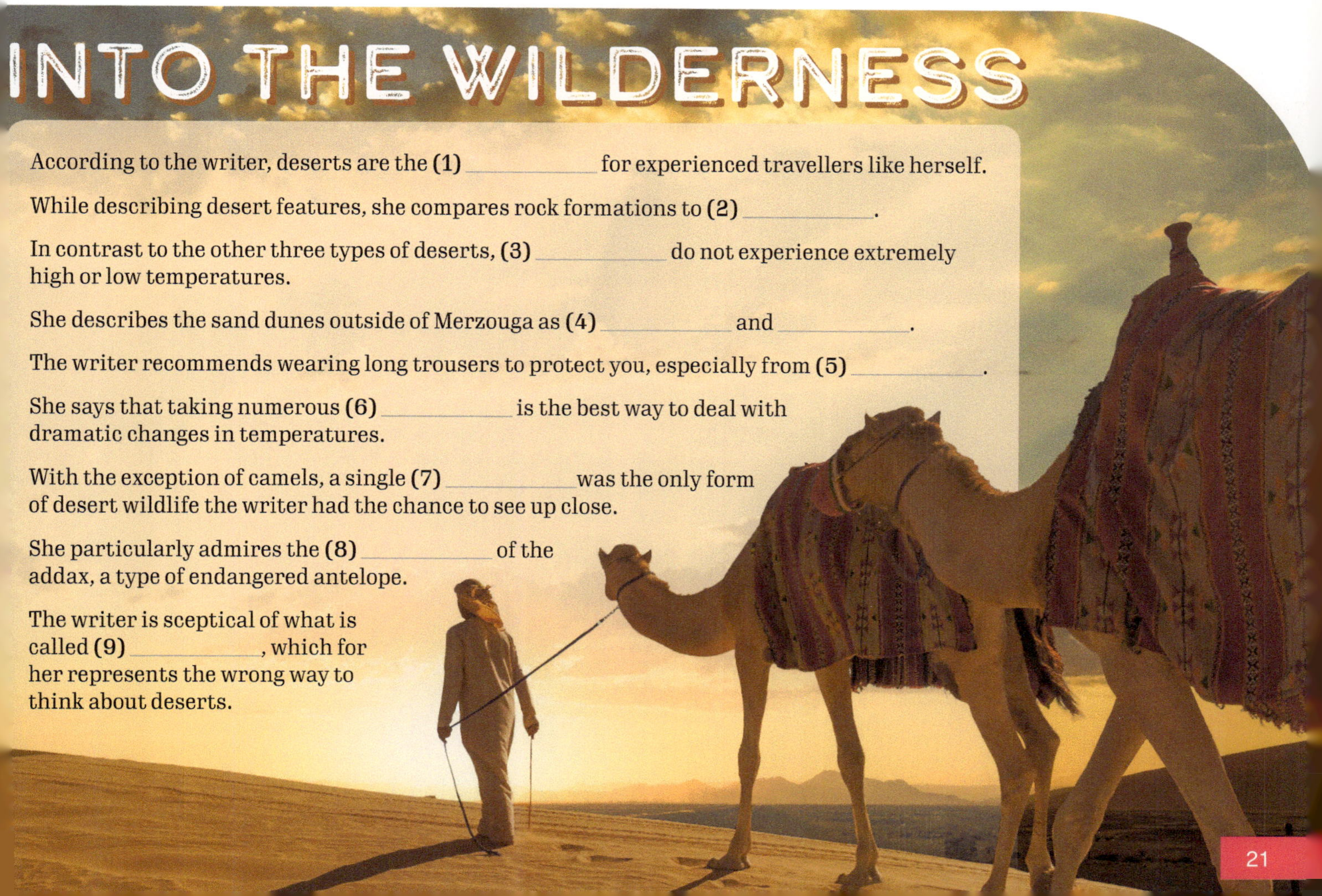

INTO THE WILDERNESS

According to the writer, deserts are the (1) ____________ for experienced travellers like herself.

While describing desert features, she compares rock formations to (2) ____________.

In contrast to the other three types of deserts, (3) ____________ do not experience extremely high or low temperatures.

She describes the sand dunes outside of Merzouga as (4) ____________ and ____________.

The writer recommends wearing long trousers to protect you, especially from (5) ____________.

She says that taking numerous (6) ____________ is the best way to deal with dramatic changes in temperatures.

With the exception of camels, a single (7) ____________ was the only form of desert wildlife the writer had the chance to see up close.

She particularly admires the (8) ____________ of the addax, a type of endangered antelope.

The writer is sceptical of what is called (9) ____________, which for her represents the wrong way to think about deserts.

Language focus Adverbs and adverbial phrases

1 Match each adverb or adverbial phrase (1–3) in **bold** from the listening on page 21 with its type and function (a–c).

1 In the desert, **even** the sound of your own footsteps is different.

2 It is estimated that the current population living **in the wild** could be in the low hundreds ...

3 ... great swathes of land are irrigated intensely with the goal of growing crops, **supposedly** in the name of saving mankind from the climate crisis.

a Adverbial of place: informs us where something happened.

b Comment adverb: comments on, and sometimes distances the speaker from, what they are saying.

c Focusing adverb: highlights one part of the sentence.

2 SPEAK Work in pairs. Read the sentences and look at the adverbs and adverbial phrases in bold. How does the emphasis change when they move to a different place?

1 A The committee **even** got support for the measure from its longest standing members.

B The committee got support for the measure **even** from its longest standing members.

2 A **At one point or another**, boredom hits the most avid of backpackers.

B Boredom hits the most avid of backpackers **at one point or another**.

3 A **Reportedly**, the spy was travelling with a fake passport.

B The spy was **reportedly** travelling with a fake passport.

4 A You **really** should read the instruction manual before trying to assemble the furniture.

B You should **really** read the instruction manual before trying to assemble the furniture.

5 A A bright star appeared **way up in the night sky**.

B **Way up in the night sky** a bright star appeared.

3 Go to Ready for Grammar on page 208 for rules, explanations and further practice.

4 SPEAK Work in pairs. Talk about a memorable journey you have had. Use adverbs and adverbial phrases to give details about your actions before, during and after this experience.

Word formation Adverbs

1 Underline the correct adverbs in the following sentences.

1 The Minister disputed claims she had *knowledgeably / knowingly* misled the public, assuring journalists that she 'would never *purposely / purposefully* deceive anyone'. **KNOW** **PURPOSE**

2 Our kitchen staff coped *admirably / admiringly* with the high demand of the holiday weekend, coupled with the *considerably / considerately* increased workload caused by flu-related absences. **ADMIRE** **CONSIDER**

3 Footballers who are *spatially / spaciously* aware can accurately assess the position of other players on the pitch, and pass the ball *confidentially / confidently* with pinpoint accuracy. **SPACE** **CONFIDE**

4 They reached an agreement *whereby / wherever* each employee would receive a one-off bonus of three thousand pounds. Shortly *thereby / thereafter* the company went bust. **WHERE** **THERE**

2 Choose three of the adverbs from Exercise 1 that were not used and write gapped sentences for each of them. Then, work in pairs. Give your sentences to your partner to complete.

3 Complete the sentences with an appropriate adverb form of the word in capitals. Use each suffix in the box once only and make any further spelling changes necessary.

-ally -less -ly -ward -wise

Crazy, I know, but I once travelled **(1)** ____________ around France, using only local buses – north to east, then south, west, and north again. I prepared it all **(2)** ____________, poring over routes and timetables for hours on end. Nothing would be last-minute or **(3)** ____________ arranged; everything was planned well in advance. I never once deviated from my schedule; even when I felt ill, I carried on **(4)** ____________. I set off at the start of July from Dieppe, and by the end of August, I was back in Normandy and **(5)** ____________ bound. **CLOCK** **METHOD** **HURRY** **REGARD** **HOME**

4 Using the same suffixes as in Exercise 3, write adverb forms for the following words. The same suffix is needed for all three words. Some words may require further spelling changes.

1	length	____________	other	____________	like	____________
2	admit	____________	suppose	____________	repute	____________
3	doubt	____________	never	____________	none	____________
4	strategy	____________	analysis	____________	theme	____________
5	on	____________	back	____________	sea	____________

5 Complete the sentences with the appropriate form of the word in capitals. You may need to add suffixes, prefixes or make other changes to the word.

1 Both players have been **suspended** ____________. It is not known when – or indeed, if – they will return to the side. **DEFINITE**

2 He stammered, **paused** ____________, as though to gather his thoughts, and then relaunched into his speech. **MOMENT**

3 Her research ____________ **focuses** on the issue of adult literacy. **DOMINATE**

4 The webpage is ____________ **updated** with the latest travel restrictions. **PERIOD**

5 The mayor said he ____________ **agreed** with my concerns and would look into my proposal. **HEART**

6 After the story broke, the actor was **pursued** ____________ by the press. **RELENT**

7 The company is suing a former employee for ____________ **stealing** proprietary documents. **ALLEGE**

6 SPEAK Work in pairs. Choose five of the adverbs in Exercise 5. Think of two other contexts for each of them.

*Software is **periodically updated** to fix bugs and make other small improvements.*

*Dictionaries are **periodically updated** to keep pace with the times.*

Writing Part 1 Essay

What to expect in the exam

In Part 1 of the Writing paper, you have to write an essay in which you summarise and evaluate key points from two source texts. There are usually four key points in total – two in each text. The views expressed in the texts are either contrasting or complementary. In addition to evaluating the arguments from the texts, you must also include your own ideas. You should write between 240–280 words.

1 **SPEAK** **Work in pairs. Read the Writing Part 1 texts below. Do you agree or disagree with the views expressed in the texts? Justify your answers.**

Write an essay summarising and evaluating the key points from both texts. Use your own words throughout as far as possible, and include your own ideas in your answer. Write your answer in 240–280 words.

TRAVELLING SOLO

Much has been said about what fun it can be to travel alone, but on a more profound level <u>it's an exercise in self-confidence. You see yourself as a stronger, more independent person</u> after travelling alone, whether it be to a far-flung location or merely a neighbouring town. You will feel more comfortable with being in your own skin, more comfortable in your own company. What's more, solo travel has practical benefits. It enables you to indulge in idiosyncratic whims, such as visiting a quirky museum or even trawling a local antiques shop, because <u>your choices are not contingent on fellow travellers</u>.

MISSING OUT

The inescapable truth is that, despite what many a self-help blogger may claim, <u>life is a great deal more enjoyable in the company of other people</u>. Take travelling alone. Although the quiet contemplation of an unexpectedly beautiful scene does hold a certain appeal, it's ultimately disheartening to have no one with whom to share this sort of experience. There is also the small matter of <u>it being inherently inconvenient to travel on your own</u>. When travelling solo, there is no one to hold you accountable for missteps, no one to bounce ideas off before it's too late and you make a bad decision.

2 **There are four key points underlined in the texts. Read the texts again and answer the questions.**

1 Does the language in the key points tend to be more general, or more specific?
2 Key ideas are never supporting examples. In *Travelling solo*, the writer introduces an example with the phrase *such as*. What other phrases do writers use to introduce examples?
3 Linking words or phrases are sometimes used in the middle of the source texts to move from one key point to another. What examples of this can you find in these texts?

3 **Read the model answer. Decide:**

- whether the writer includes a summary of the key points.
- whether the writer includes their own ideas.

FREEDOM OR FOMO?

Travel is delightful and generally considered to be good for the soul. **But is it a good idea to travel alone**? This largely depends on the purpose of your trip.

Without question, travelling on your own has upsides. It can help you become more independent and self-confident. It can help you grow as a person. In addition, travelling alone means you don't have to negotiate your plans with other people, which is ideal for travellers who like to selfishly indulge in their passions, for example, an architecture nut who enjoys nothing more than visiting every notable building in the city.

However, there are also clear downsides. Not only is it more fun to travel with other people, it is also more convenient. There are certain aspects of travel that can be quite daunting to face on your own, such as exchanging currency or reserving accommodation in a foreign country.

To take a wider view, the purpose of travel is often to spend time with other people – or to get away from them. If you want to disconnect from a demanding job, a solo trip could be just what the doctor ordered. That said, it's a great deal more common to go on holiday with family or friends, who we often don't get to spend enough quality time with. The point of these trips is to be together. Where you go and what you do is of little consequence.

To sum up, when deciding whether or not to travel alone, a good place to start is by asking yourself why exactly you have chosen to leave home in the first place.

4 **Underline the words and phrases the writer uses to paraphrase the four key points from the original texts.**

5 **Look at the phrase in bold. What purpose does it have for the model answer as a whole?**

6 **Rhetorical questions can also be used to introduce the main theme of a paragraph. Rewrite the underlined sentence at the beginning of the third paragraph to make it a rhetorical question.**

7 **Either write your own answer to the task in Exercise 1 or do the task in the Additional materials on page 196. Before you start writing, read the advice in the *How to go about it* box.**

How to go about it

- Start by reading the two source texts and underline the key points.
- Decide to what extent you agree with the views expressed. Make notes about how you will summarise and evaluate them.
- List some relevant ideas of your own to include. Think about how to support these ideas with reasons, examples, evidence, etc.
- Set your essay out into clear paragraphs. Check that the plan includes a summary of key points as well as your own ideas. Remember to include an introduction and conclusion.
- Write your essay using a neutral or semi-formal style.

For more information on writing essays, see page 190.

About English

FOMO (n) /ˈfəʊˌməʊ/

An abbreviation for fear of missing out; used to describe a social anxiety someone may feel when they see what others are doing, especially via social media sites.

What do the following abbreviations stand for?

WFH
BRB
JSYK
IRL
AKA

2 REVIEW

Vocabulary Travel

1 For sentences 1–6, underline the correct alternative.

1 The years of stress at work had taken their toll. He was excited for his adventure, having never been on a long-haul *stroll* / *delay* / *travel* / *flight* before.

2 It was an incredibly long and *alternative* / *arduous* / *iconic* / *far-flung* journey through the mountains on horseback.

3 She was a seasoned traveller and had been to many *shoddy* / *discerning* / *far-flung* / *torrential* destinations.

4 After dinner, you should take a leisurely *service* / *stroll* / *travel* / *visit* from the main square down to the riverside promenade.

5 The hotel apologised for the *shoddy* / *circuitous* / *world-class* / *perilous* service and went so far as to give the family a full refund.

6 Profits at the company took a turn for the worse over the period, with the CEO citing a sharp decline in overseas *landmarks* / *shock* / *strolls* / *travel* as the primary cause.

Reading and Use of English Part 3 Word formation

For questions 1–8, read the text below. Use the word given in capitals at the end of some of the lines to form a word that fits in the space in the same line. There is an example at the beginning (0).

Home away from home

For some, home swapping may not be worth serious **(0)** *CONSIDERATION*, but there are many travellers who enjoy this type of budget holiday option every year. Indeed, this trend is currently seeing **(1)** ______ growth. Ideal for flexible travellers, home swapping **(2)** ______ the need to book hotels, and avid home-swappers rave about the range of **(3)** ______ places they've stayed in. As you might expect, people with **(4)** ______ beachside villas or swanky flats in the city centre **(5)** ______ get first pick of the available options, but don't worry: many swappers are just looking for a decent place that's available when they are.

To get started, **(6)** ______ a list of enticing details about your home to include on the house exchange site. Remember to provide personal references and, of course, lots of photos. After you have uploaded everything, check the site

(7) ______ for any new listings. Once you find a potential swap, be clear about your expectations. Agree on how to handle worst-case **(8)** ______ and pin down all the details before you leave. Then, all that is left is to hope for the best!

CONSIDER
PRECEDENT
VENT
FAR
PICTURE
VARIABLE
PILE
PERIOD
SCENE

Reading and Use of English

Part 4 Key word transformations

For questions **1–6**, complete the second sentence so that it has a similar meaning to the first sentence, using the word given. **Do not change the word given.** You must use between **three** and **eight** words, including the word given.

What to expect in the exam

- Part 4 tests your ability to paraphrase and your knowledge of both vocabulary and grammar, e.g. your ability to change verbs to nouns, move from active to passive, etc.
- Your answer cannot be less than three words nor more than eight words long, and must include the key word. Bear in mind, contractions are counted as two words.

How to go about it

- Carefully read the first and second sentences and think about what information is missing from the second one. It can be helpful to cross off the words in the first sentence that are repeated or paraphrased in the second. This helps you focus on the words and structures you will need to manipulate.
- Once you decide on your answer, double check that you have used the key word. Make sure you have kept the second sentence as similar as possible to the first, in terms of meaning, tense and aspect.

1 As soon as they arrived at the main square, they fell in love with the city.
SET
They fell in love with the city the ______________________ the main square.

2 In the interview, the famous travel writer didn't mention how her mother had influenced her.
REFERENCE
In the interview, the famous travel writer ______________________ of her mother.

3 Did the stock market perform any better yesterday?
IN
Was there any ______________________ yesterday?

4 The way the hotel manager dealt with workplace issues was not always very diplomatic.
LACK
At times, there ______________________ the way the hotel manager dealt with workplace issues.

5 No one had foreseen the mechanical problems that delayed the flight.
HELD
The flight ______________________ mechanical problems.

6 The local residents used to object to how rude the tourists were.
EXCEPTION
The local residents used to ______________________ the tourists.

Writing Part 2 Report

You work for a company that makes travel goods. The company is planning to advertise a new product or accessory on social media. Your manager has asked you to write a report on which social media platform the company should choose for its marketing campaign. You should briefly describe one social media platform and explain why you would recommend it. You should also evaluate the extent to which social media can influence people's purchasing decisions.

Write your **report.**

For more information on writing reports, see page 194.

Idioms Making stories interesting

1 **Guess the missing words in idioms 1–10 used for making stories interesting. The first two are from the listening on page 21.**

1 I did see a scorpion. I almost stepped on it – and it **scared the** ____________ **out of me**!

2 It is estimated that the current population living in the wild could be in the low hundreds ... **Time will** ____________ whether or not they can be saved.

3 I like my little car – **don't get me** ____________ – but it's getting a bit old.

4 And can you believe Megan met her favourite footballer in Lisbon airport. What **a stroke of good** ____________!

5 A wave of dizziness came over me and, **for a split** ____________, I thought I might need to sit down, but then it passed.

6 It can't be easy for Mark and Ruth to share such a small space on such a long journey. They're both quite demanding people, **to put it** ____________.

7 I got the camera repaired and never told Juliet what happened. That's strictly **between you and** ____________, though.

8 I travelled around the world in just 38 days. It was ____________ **down** the best thing I've ever done.

9 I've started taking my holidays in September. **There's a lot to be** ____________ **for it**. Prices are so much lower.

10 He claims he can't go because he has to catch up on work – **a likely** ____________! Tomás is always cancelling plans.

2 **2.2 Listen and check your answers to Exercise 1.**

3 **SPEAK Work in pairs. Discuss the meaning of the idioms in Exercise 1.**

4 **Listen to sentences 1 and 2 again. Underline the words that carry the most prominent stress. The forward slashes (//) indicate the places where the speaker makes a slight pause.**

1 // I did see a scorpion // I almost stepped on it // and it scared the life out of me //

2 // Time will tell // whether or not // they can be saved //

Pronunciation: Speech units

When we speak, we divide our words into groups called speech units. Fixed phrases and idioms are usually pronounced as one speech unit. Within speech units, it's usually one of the content words (nouns, main verbs, adjectives, adverbs) that carries the most prominent stress. For longer words, one of the syllables within the content word carries the prominence, e.g. // it came as a sur<u>prise</u> //.

5 **SPEAK Work in pairs. Practise saying the sentences in Exercise 1. Say each idiom as a speech unit, putting the most prominent stress on the gapped words.**

6 **SPEAK Work in small groups. Play the board game.**

Discussing idioms

Discuss the differences in meaning between these idioms:

- a split second / a New York minute
- don't get me wrong / don't take this the wrong way
- a stroke of luck / a lucky break

Rules

1 Toss a coin. Move two spaces for heads and one space for tails.

2 Use the idiom or fixed phrase from Exercise 1 containing the word in the box to tell a short anecdote, real or imagined.

START	life	Go back one space
hands		mildly
Miss a turn	said	Go forward one space
second		wrong
Go back one space	story	FINISH

READY FOR READING AND USE OF ENGLISH PARTS 1–4

Introduction

In the **Reading and Use of English** paper, you have 90 minutes to complete 7 different tasks. In this section, we will look at the first four tasks, Parts 1, 2, 3 and 4. We will look at Parts 5, 6 and 7 on pages 61–66.

Reading and Use of English Part 1 Multiple-choice cloze

1 SPEAK **Work in pairs and discuss the questions.**

Have you ever heard of a Comic-Con? If not, from its name, what do you think it might be?

What do you think the experience of a Comic-Con might be like?

Now, read the text, ignoring the gaps. Do your ideas match those of the writer?

2 **For questions 1–8, read the text below and decide which answer (A, B, C or D) best fits each gap. There is an example at the beginning (0).**

ANOTHER WORLD

The world of Comic-Cons (comic book conventions) encompasses far more than just comic books, and frequently **(0)** ___*D*___ host to the casts of popular films and TV shows in the realms of fantasy, sci-fi and beyond. Anyone who's anyone in the superhero world turns up to San Diego Comic-Con, but with tickets like gold **(1)** ________, many people miss out on the unique experience. However, it's certainly worth your while going, so if you find yourself with a ticket, you should **(2)** ________ at the chance of attending. One of the largest conventions in the world, what you'll see in San Diego will be beyond your **(3)** ________ imagination. Upon entering the convention you'll find yourself amongst a sea of people, many wearing costumes and every one of them agape at the scenes around them. It would be easy to become overwhelmed by the **(4)** ________ scale of the event, and often the best laid plans go straight out the **(5)** ________ once inside. With so much on offer, time in queues will most definitely **(6)** ________ into any overambitious schedule plan. For both **(7)** ________ Comic-Con fans and newcomers alike, the takeaway is that you can only just **(8)** ________ the surface of an event of this magnitude, so be selective in your choices.

	A	B	C	D
0	gives	sets	takes	plays
1	powder	dust	crumbs	flecks
2	jump	beam	plunge	fly
3	rashest	balmiest	fiercest	wildest
4	utter	sheer	outright	wholesale
5	door	window	picture	scene
6	creep	factor	cut	carve
7	old-school	run-down	laid-back	die-hard
8	scratch	pick	touch	stroke

3 **Look at the answers for Exercise 2 and match them to the descriptions (a–d) below.**

a a phrasal verb

b a noun + noun collocation

c an idiomatic expression

d an adjective + noun collocation

Reading and Use of English Part 2 Open cloze

1 **Read the following text, ignoring the gaps for the moment. What change did Robin Moore manage to procure through his photograph?**

LESSONS FROM BEHIND THE LENS

Although wildlife photographer Robin Moore's 2017 photograph of some of the world's rarest iguanas (0) ___FELL___ short of winning him the Wildlife Photographer of the Year, its influence was extremely wide reaching. When Robin set off to photograph the iguanas, (1) __________ did he know the power the image would come to have. Threatened by government plans to allow construction in (2) __________ forest habitat on Great Goat Island off Jamaica's southern coast, the iguanas' future looked bleak, until it was announced that the plans (3) __________ to be abandoned.

This remarkable change of heart came (4) __________ thanks to the exposure the photograph received online. A short film highlighting the plight (5) __________ the endangered reptiles contributed to the campaign, too, and this was used as a fund-raising tool by charities to (6) __________ the islands designated as a nature reserve.

(7) __________ surprisingly, there was great relief at the news across all sections of the community, and conservationists are optimistic that these creatures will thrive again (8) __________ that they are left alone in their new home.

2 **For questions 1–8, read the text again and think of the word which best fits each space. Use only one word in each space. There is an example at the beginning (0). Write your answers IN CAPITAL LETTERS.**

3 **Look at the example answer (0). The correct answer is *fell* because:**

A it is part of the phrase *to fall short of something*.

B *fall short* is a collocation.

C the meaning of *fall* in this context is 'to fail'.

4 **SPEAK Work in pairs. Look at answers 1–8. Explain why those are the correct answers, thinking about the types of words that were missing.**

Don't forget!

Write your answers in CAPITAL LETTERS on the answer sheet in the exam. Make sure your writing is clear and easy to read.

How to go about it

- Read the title and the whole text so you understand the gist of it before attempting any answers.
- Always read the complete sentences around the gaps and think about the possible answers such as references, conditionals, dependent prepositions, fixed phrases, verb forms, etc.
- Write down the type of word which could go in each space.
- The answer is always ONE word only and it will not be a contraction.

Reading and Use of English Part 3 Word formation

What to expect in the exam

The answers for Part 3 involve transforming the word in CAPITALS. This could mean using a prefix or a suffix (*re-*, *dis-*, *-ly*, *-ation*), making internal changes to the root word (*deep – depth*, *explain – explanation*), or compounding (*fall – downfall*). You may need to make two changes to the word given, for example adding a suffix to a noun to form an adjective and then adding a prefix to make it negative.

Don't forget!

Your spelling must be accurate, or you will not get the mark.

1 **SPEAK** Have you ever watched someone making sushi or tried to make it yourself? What do you think are the most important things to consider when making sushi?

2 For questions 1–8, read the text below. Use the word given in capitals at the end of some of the lines to form a word that fits in the space in the same line. There is an example at the beginning (0). Write your answers **IN CAPITAL LETTERS**.

THE ART OF SUSHI

Sushi is one of the most (0) *ICONIC* foods of modern cuisine, revered in all corners	ICON
of the globe, but becoming a sushi chef is no mean feat. Expectations are high insofar	
as they must produce (1) ____________ high quality dishes and, as such, being a	CONSIST
(2) ____________ is somewhat of a prerequisite.	PERFECT
These delicate morsels of rice and fish (3) ____________ the meticulous attention to detail	EXAMPLE
required of sushi chefs and this is reflected in their training. It may take trainees up	
to two years to learn how to prepare flawless rice. Any (4) ____________ in the balance	CALCULATE
of rice and vinegar could render it unpalatable. Once this has been mastered, chefs	
focus on the (5) ____________ of the other ingredients to ensure the ideal balance of	COMPOSE
flavour and texture. It is this combination which makes sushi so (6) ____________.	RESIST
Rising to the status of master sushi chef is akin to becoming an artist. Their skills	
must be (7) ____________ but additionally, they should bring a creative flair to their	EXCEPT
work to be categorised as master (8) ____________ of their art.	PRACTICE

3 **SPEAK** Work in pairs. In the example answer in Exercise 2, the root word was a noun, which was changed to its adjective form to fit the gap. Describe what changes were needed for answers 1–8 using the words in the box below.

adjective adverb negative noun plural prefix spelling verb

Reading and Use of English

Part 4 Key word transformations

Don't forget!

- The key word must not be changed.
- Any contractions you use count as two words.
- Remember you should only write the words that are needed to complete the gap on the answer sheet. Do not write out the full sentence.
- Bear in mind that in the exam you will not have the two prompt questions.

For questions 1–6, complete the second sentence so that it has a similar meaning to the first sentence, using the word given. Do not change the word given. You must use between **three** and **eight** words, including the word given.

0 This house needs a lot more work before it is finished.

DEAL

There is ___*A GREAT DEAL OF WORK TO BE DONE*___ on this house.

1 Journalists wouldn't go easy on him during the press conference and the minister knew that.

HARD

The minister knew that he ________________________ during the press conference.

What does the 'he' before the gap tell us about the structure required?

What phrase, collocating with 'hard', means to make something difficult for someone?

2 It was a mystery to everybody as to why James kept moving from job to job.

DOWN

Nobody understood why James ________________________ job.

What phrasal verb, with 'down', collocates strongly with job?

What tense should the verb be in to match 'kept moving'? Should it be positive or negative?

3 It's almost certain that Nico's next opponent will win the tennis match.

STAND

Nico ________________________ beating his next opponent.

What preposition often precedes an -ing verb form?

What phrase, meaning likely to be successful contains the word 'stand'?

4 Julia's manager said she shouldn't go into the office until she had recovered from her cold.

WEATHER

Because Julia ________________________, her manager advised her not to come to work.

What tense should the answer be in?

What idiom, with the word 'weather', means to feel ill?

5 Upon arrival, we were disappointed to notice that the hotel looked nothing like the pictures in the brochure.

BORE

Disappointingly, when we arrived at the hotel, we noticed that ________________________ that we had seen in the brochure.

Did the hotel look slightly like the pictures or not at all like the pictures?

What collocation goes with 'bear' to mean look like?

6 The staff were about to walk out when the management finally submitted to their demands.

VERGE

The staff ________________________ when their demands were accepted by the management.

What tense do you need to use in the answer to match the first sentence?

What grammatically precedes and follows the noun 'verge'?

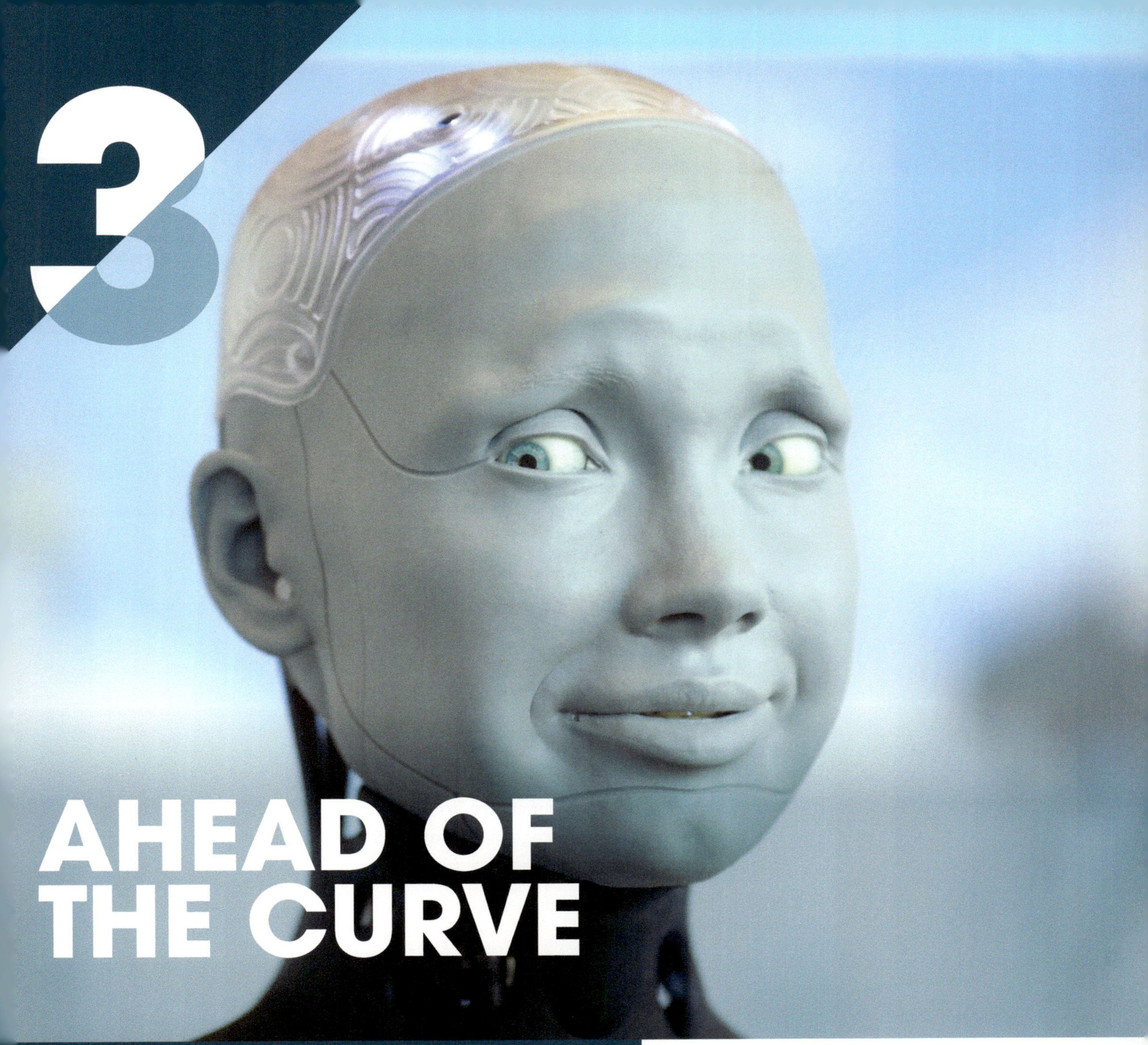

3

AHEAD OF THE CURVE

KEY LANGUAGE

Talking about the future
will, *shall* and *would*
Phrasal verbs and noun collocations
Prepositional phrases with *at*, *in*, *on* and *under*

IDIOMS

Innovation

EXAM PRACTICE

Reading and Use of English Parts 2, 3, 4 & 7
Writing Part 2
Listening Parts 1 & 4
Speaking Parts 1 & 3

Speaking Part 1 Interview

Work with a partner. Discuss the questions.

1 What modern invention would be the hardest for you to live without?
2 How good are you at fixing technological issues?
3 In recent years, has the way you work or study been impacted by technology?
4 Are you an early adopter when it comes to new trends in technology?
5 For you, what has been the worst invention in the last 100 years?
6 What are the possible implications for building machines that are more intelligent than humans?

3 AHEAD OF THE CURVE

Reading and Use of English Part 7 Multiple matching

What to expect in the exam

- In Part 7, you have to match questions to different sections of a text. The text itself could be an article or an extract from a book that has been broken up into sections, or it could be a group of independent texts, for example, different people giving their opinion on a particular topic. There are between four and six sections.
- The questions paraphrase specific information, opinions or attitudes from the text. Note that the same section is often the right answer for more than one question. For instance, Section C could be the right answer for questions 2, 5, and 10.

1 You are going to read an article about innovation. For questions **1–10**, choose from the sections **(A–F)**. The sections may be chosen more than once.

In which section are the following mentioned?

an unwillingness on the part of certain researchers to commit to an opinion	1
the beneficial effects of improved administration at companies	2
the desire to reduce the number of workers needed to do certain jobs	3
a falling benefit–cost ratio	4
the growing need for experts to work together	5
a narrow perspective leading to an incorrect assumption	6
the potential downsides of strong economic performance	7
economic gains resulting from humans altering their environment	8
the failure to take full advantage of innovations that already exist	9
a lack of enthusiasm for innovation at some companies	10

2 **SPEAK** In your opinion, which area of contemporary life is most in need of innovative ideas? Why?

Robotic arm harvesting lettuce

A 3D-printed book cabin

ARE WE REACHING THE LIMITS OF INNOVATION?

A Were there far fewer undiscovered ideas out there than in our more primitive past, how would people know? This is not an idle question; decoding the mysteries of nature, from atmospheric pressure to electricity to DNA, allowed people to bend the natural world to their will, and to grow richer in the process. A dwindling stock of discoverable insights in the pipeline would mean correspondingly less scope for progress in the future – a dismal prospect. And some signs suggest that the well of our imagination is about to run dry. Though ever more researchers are digging for insights, according to new research, the flow of new ideas is flagging.

B But is it? A recent paper by Nicholas Bloom, Charles Jones and Michael Webb of Stanford University, and John Van Reenen of the Massachusetts Institute of Technology provides relevant evidence. Though striking an agnostic position as to whether humanity has used up all its eureka moments, they nonetheless conclude that new ideas are getting more expensive to find. The authors consider four different case studies, within which they compare research 'inputs' (such as the money spent on researchers and lab equipment) and outputs. For instance, the number of transistors that can be squeezed onto a microchip has doubled with reassuring regularity for half a century, every two years or so – a phenomenon known as Moore's Law (after Gordon Moore, a founder of Intel). But companies have run up against a vexing problem: to continue achieving this success, they have to pour more and more resources into the effort over time. The research productivity of each scientist participating in the battle to cram in transistors has correspondingly tumbled.

C Analysing the supply side of the innovation equation in isolation can also be misleading. The demand for new ideas, and, correspondingly, the incentive to tackle difficult questions, also matters. In his analysis of the Industrial Revolution, Robert Allen, then an economic historian at Oxford, sought to explain why it started in Britain rather than anywhere else. Supply-side factors, such as improved literacy and stronger property rights, certainly played a part. But it was the demand for labour-saving innovation, prompted by Britain's relatively high wages at the time, which gave tinkerers a strong incentive to develop and hone the steam engine and its applications.

D Researchers are often like the man searching for his keys under the streetlight, because that is where the light is. Until some pressure is applied to encourage him to look elsewhere, the search will often prove fruitless. It is easy to see why firms might take a lackadaisical approach to some research questions. Disappointing wage growth across advanced economies is a deterrent to the invention and use of labour-saving innovations. Persistently high rates of profit give big firms plenty of money to plough into fancy research labs, but also suggest that the competitive pressures which might prompt them to exploit the resulting discoveries are weak.

E Despair is premature, however. The effort to find new, growth-boosting ideas is not necessarily hopeless, just complicated. Whether herding more researchers into the laboratory raises growth might depend on how intensively the resulting brainstorms are used. Across the global economy, many countries have yet fully to exploit ideas already in use by firms at the cutting edge of scientific knowledge. The problem, in other words, is not that oranges are in short supply or are already squeezed dry, but rather that of the ten workers at the juice bar, only one has learned to do the squeezing. Investments in education and training, to expand the share of workers that can use new ideas, or in the quality of management, to improve how effectively ideas are applied within firms, would do wonders for growth, even if the world's scientists are idly scratching their heads.

F In some ways, the accumulation of knowledge can hold back progress. The more that is known, the more researchers must absorb before they can add to the stock of human knowledge – or the more they must collaborate with other researchers to combine their areas of expertise. But the incomplete exploitation of currently available knowledge is in some way reassuring. It suggests that people are underperforming relative to their potential: both in how they use available ideas and in how they uncover new ones.

Language focus Talking about the future

1 Read the example sentence from the reading and answer the question.

*Some signs suggest that the well of our imagination **is about to** run dry.*

How would the meaning of the sentence change if the word *about* was replaced by *likely*, *bound* or *due*?

2 Match the underlined future forms in sentences 1–5 with their functions (a–e).

1 But of course Berta will have already seen the film. She's obsessed with that director.
2 Will you be visiting your grandchildren this weekend?
3 We'll have been driving for six hours non-stop by the time we reach Hamburg.
4 I'll be passing by the bakery anyway after work, so I can pick up the pastries.
5 By the end of the month, the company will have released its newest software update.

a to make an assumption about the past
b to make a polite enquiry about future plans
c to imagine looking back at an event from a specific point in the future
d to talk about something in the future we perceive as inevitable
e to emphasize the duration of an action from a certain point in the future

3 SPEAK Work in pairs. Create a context for each of the sentences in Exercise 2.

'So, will you be visiting your grandchildren this weekend?' 'Yes, just for the day on Sunday. They're going to a birthday party on Saturday.'

4 Cross out the option that is NOT possible.

1 When the taxi *comes / is coming / will come*, I'll let you know.
2 In June, I *will live / will have lived / will have been living* in my flat for two years.
3 Within a year, the company *aims / is aiming / has been aiming* to release its low-cost battery technology.
4 Future buildings in the area *were to be / were seen to be / were going to be* incorporated into a coherently designed landscape.

**5 Go to the Ready for Grammar section on page 210 for rules, explanations further practice.
and**

6 SPEAK Work in small groups. Follow these steps:

1 Think of a technology that people use in their daily lives, for example, cars or smartphones.
2 Identify a problem – big or small – that people have with that technology.
3 Brainstorm different ways to solve that problem, and then choose one innovative solution.
4 Make a plan for how to put your innovation into practice, e.g. funding, development, testing, marketing, etc.

7 SPEAK Take turns explaining your innovation. Use future forms to talk about how your innovation will improve the user experience and how you intend to make your innovation a reality.

This new type of battery is bound to provide a huge improvement in battery life.

The solar panel will allow the phone to charge itself during daytime hours.

Once we have finished testing our new battery, we'll be ready to start thinking about ...

Vocabulary Phrasal verbs and noun collocations

1 Choose the correct verb to complete these sentences from the reading.

1 But companies have *run / ended / stood / kicked* **up against a** vexing **problem**: to continue achieving this success, they have to pour more and more resources into the effort over time.

2 Persistently high rates of profit give big firms plenty of **money to** *knock / plough / slam / blast* **into** fancy research labs, ...

3 In some ways, the accumulation of knowledge can *stand / revert / hold / scale* **back progress**.

2 Read the following story about Ignaz Semmelweis's life-saving medical discovery. Match a sentence beginning 1–10 with an appropriate ending a–j. The nouns in italics are common collocates of the phrasal verbs.

1 Recently, I was **flicking**
2 As I did so, I **stumbled**
3 Ignaz Semmelweis **came**
4 Handwashing **brought**
5 He wrote a book **drawing**
6 But he was unable to **put**
7 As a result, his theory **met**
8 His fellow doctors **threw**
9 And Semmelweis **held**
10 People would later **come**

a **up with** a *solution* to postpartum infections in his clinic.
b **forward** a scientific *explanation* for his discovery.
c **through** the *pages* of a book on scientific discoveries.
d **with** fierce *resistance* from the medical community.
e **out** little *hope* that his idea would ever receive acceptance.
f **across** the *story* of a 19th-century Hungarian obstetrician.
g **round** to his *way of thinking*, but not until after his death.
h **down** the *number* of cases of puerperal fever, he noted.
i **out** the *suggestion* that they should disinfect their hands.
j **on** his *observations* and outlining his conclusions.

3 SPEAK Work in pairs. Study the sentences in Exercise 2. Cover up endings a–j. Take turns to read out the beginnings 1–10 and complete the sentences from memory.

4 Write the infinitive form of the phrasal verbs from Exercise 2 next to their meaning.

1 reduce something ___*bring down*___
2 reject something ______
3 change your opinion and agree with someone ______
4 receive a certain reaction, often negative ______
5 think of something such as an idea or plan ______
6 find something by accident ______
7 use experiences you have acquired in the past ______
8 suggest something or offer an idea or reason ______
9 think that something may or may not happen ______
10 quickly look through written material ______

5 Complete each gap in 1–5 with the infinitive form of an appropriate phrasal verb from Exercise 2. The nouns in bold are common collocates of the phrasal verb.

1 When writing the television series, Adams was able to ______ his **experience** as a teacher, as well as **interviews** carried out with former colleagues.

2 The government's main aim this year is to ______ the cripplingly high **rate of inflation** and **cost of living** that are plaguing the economy.

3 The proposed development is likely to ______ **criticism** from the local media, and **opposition** from residents and environmental groups.

4 The defence lawyer was confident the judge would ______ the main **charges** against her client, in particular the **claims** of professional misconduct and legal malpractice.

5 Before we can ______ our **ideas** and **proposals** to the board of directors, we need to ______ an effective **strategy** for implementing them and a **solution** to the issue of cost.

6 SPEAK Describe a theory, an innovation or an invention which was originally rejected but later accepted.

Writing Part 2 Review

What to expect in the exam

- In Writing Part 2, you might have the opportunity to write a review. This might be of a book, film, TV series, play, or exhibition but could also be of an event, product or service. It should be between 280–320 words in length.
- Pay close attention to what type of publication you are writing for, as this will tell you who the target reader is and what register and language you should use. It can also tell you what type of information to include.
- An effective review goes beyond general description or narration. You are expected to evaluate your subject, for example, by discussing its strengths and weaknesses.

1 SPEAK Work in pairs. Read these Writing Part 2 instructions. Which app would you choose to review? Why?

A website called *Tech for Today* is preparing a newsletter about apps. You decide to submit a review of an app you have recently downloaded to either your smartphone or tablet. In your review, you should briefly describe what the app is for and how useful it is. You should also evaluate the importance of apps in contemporary society.

2 Read the model review. Does the writer evaluate, rather than just describe, the app?

TECHDAILY News Reviews Buy More ›

Frustrated with my current email app, I went looking for a new one and found Flow, which tries to distinguish itself to more traditional apps by presenting emails as chats. The idea intrigued me, so I thought I'd give it a try.

At first, I was smitten. Flow hides most of the extraneous information that accompanies emails and presents them in bubbles, similar from messaging apps. It also allows you to organise your email according to subject or people. This is **(1) pa**__________ *handy* for tracking long email threads. Just tap in a single email and you can easily scroll through six months of correspondence with one client. What's more, the app **(2) au**__________ *categorises* emails into 'priority' and 'other'. The app's AI is **(3) ex**__________ *good* at this.

Despite my initial enthusiasm, Flow soon got at my nerves because it had so many usability problems. The forward button is **(4) fi**__________ *difficult* to find, and the interface makes it far too easy to **(5) in**__________ *delete* email threads – or indeed, all emails from a single sender. But the big problem is that Flow does a poor job to handling multiple accounts. Its slick organisation quickly breaks down when the same person writes to more than one of your accounts. Setting up multiple calendars with Flow is also problematic.

When I finally got fed up and deleted Flow, a strange thing happened. I started only checking my email by my computer and I loved it. The root of my frustrations with mobile email apps, it turns out, is that a phone is an atrocious place to deal with email. Flow is trying to solve a problem of its own invention, which I think is true from many apps these days. Were it less aggravating to check email on a phone, you wouldn't need a fancy app for it. So, before you download the latest app, consider on a moment the old-fashioned way of doing something. It might be much better.

3 It's important to use a wide range of language in your answer. Complete the adverbs, shown in **bold** in the model text, which go with the words in *italics*.

4 The writer of a review is expected to pass judgment on their subject. Underline words and phrases in the model text that make clear the writer's views and opinions.

5 Accuracy is very important in C2 Proficiency writing tasks. Find eight mistakes with prepositions in the model text and correct them.

6 Read the information in the *How to go about it* box. Then plan and write your own answer to the task in Exercise 1 in **280–320** words.

How to go about it

- A review should be both balanced and thoughtful, but don't be afraid to criticise.
- Set out your review in clear paragraphs. Begin by stating important information the reader will need to know, e.g. title, genre, location, etc. Then provide a vivid, interesting description of your subject, while ensuring there is also enough room for in-depth evaluation.
- To make your arguments convincing, back them up with reasons or examples that are both relevant and specific. At the end of the review, make it clear to the reader whether or not you recommend the product, event, etc.
- Leave time to carefully proofread your review. Look for small inaccuracies that might bring down your mark.

For more information on writing reviews, see page 195.

Reading and Use of English Part 3 Word formation

1 For questions **1–8**, read the text below. Use the word given in capitals at the end of some of the lines to form a word that fits in the space in the same line. There is an example at the beginning **(0)**.

NICARAGUAN SIGN LANGUAGE

Humans possess an **(0)** *IRREPRESSIBLE* urge to communicate. **REPRESS**
What, then, would happen if we were to grow up in a community bereft of any established language system – would we develop a new one? For linguists, the idea of ever being able to conduct any research into this question was **(1)** ________ – until it suddenly wasn't. **CONCEIVE**

In the mid-1980s, the field of linguistics received an unexpected **(2)** ________ when the government of Nicaragua **FALL**
(3) ________ hundreds of deaf children into two newly **ROLL**
built schools. Most started with no understanding of grammar or syntax — they only had rudimentary signs for basic needs, like 'eat' and 'drink.' However, once placed together, the children began to respond to and build on each other's signs, **(4)** ________ creating a new **EFFECT**
language out of thin air.

The invention of Nicaraguan Sign Language is recognised as a **(5)** ________ feat within the field of linguistics. Over the **MOMENT**
years, scholars have patiently **(6)** ________ the **CODE**
language, finding it to be filled with **(7)** ________ and **CURIOUS**
yet strikingly similar to many of the world's languages. Many see this as **(8)** ________ evidence of children's ability not only **DEFINE**
to passively learn languages, but to actively develop them.

2 **SPEAK** In your country, what measures have been taken to support the full integration of people with disabilities into their communities? What more could be done?

Listening Part 4 Multiple matching

What to expect in the exam

- You will hear five monologues on a similar theme, and you will hear each speaker twice.
- There are two matching tasks to do at the same time. For each task, you have to choose the correct answer from eight options (A–H). Three of the options in each column are not used. Each task has a different focus; for example, one might be about identifying main ideas and the other about interpreting the speakers' attitudes.
- The answers do not appear in a fixed order – you may hear the answer to Task Two before the answer to Task One, so you need to watch out for this as you listen.

How to go about it

Before reading the options, pay careful attention to the instructions, especially the ones above each column. Knowing the focus of each task helps you predict what you will hear.

There's more than one effective way to approach this task:

- answer the questions in both tasks at the same time
- listen for the answers to Task One the first time and Task Two the second time
- focus on the most challenging questions the first time and the easier ones the second time

Experiment in class and decide which approach works best for you.

1 **3.1 You will hear five short extracts in which people are talking about their experiences with technology at work. While you listen you must complete both tasks.**

TASK ONE

For questions **1–5**, choose from the list (**A–H**) what reason each speaker gives for the adoption of new technology.

TASK TWO

For questions **6–10**, choose from the list (**A–H**) how each speaker feels now about the technology.

While you listen you must complete both tasks.

A to become more sustainable
B to increase motivation
C to reduce expenses
D to facilitate collaboration
E to improve communication
F to compensate for human limitations
G to stay ahead of the competition
H to speed up an existing process

Speaker 1 [ ] **1**
Speaker 2 [ ] **2**
Speaker 3 [ ] **3**
Speaker 4 [ ] **4**
Speaker 5 [ ] **5**

A resigned to using it
B discouraged by its shortcomings
C surprised by how well it works in practice
D sceptical of its supposed benefits
E concerned about a growing overreliance on it
F optimistic about its future potential
G impressed by its widespread acceptance
H worried about its inevitable misuse

Speaker 1 [ ] **6**
Speaker 2 [ ] **7**
Speaker 3 [ ] **8**
Speaker 4 [ ] **9**
Speaker 5 [ ] **10**

2 **Prepare a short monologue about how a specific technology has changed the way you study or work. Why was it adopted? How do you feel about it now?**

3 **SPEAK Work in small groups. Take turns delivering your monologues. Ask follow-up questions.**

Vocabulary Prepositional phrases with *at*, *in*, *on* and *under*

1 SPEAK Work in pairs. What do these underlined phrases from the listening mean?

1 That's why baseball coaches like me were such early adopters of video analysis ... they came to depend on it in a big way.

2 Our very sanity is under attack, and every day the deluge continues with no solution in sight.

3 People today talk about 'techno-stress'. I'd say, in all likelihood, email is one of the main culprits.

4 ... making adjustments to my irrigation systems on the spot from a phone or computer instead of driving to each field.

5 ... yet another decision aimed at improving the hospital's bottom line that would come at the expense of patient care.

2 Complete each gap with a preposition from the box that can be used before all five of the words and phrases.

at in on under

1	______	siege	wraps	threat	oath	scrutiny
2	______	edge	a par with	the market	display	the lookout for
3	______	awe of	jeopardy	poor taste	retrospect	force
4	______	stake	the forefront of	odds with	a loss	best

3 Complete the gaps with a word or phrase from Exercise 2.

1 Are there any technological issues currently **at** ______________ public debate in your country? What are they?

2 What technological innovations will be needed to save geographical areas currently **under** ______________ from climate change?

3 What professional jobs could be **in** ______________ as artificial intelligence becomes more and more powerful?

4 What aspects of our lifestyle today do you think are fundamentally **at** ______________ achieving a sustainable future?

5 Do you think access to the internet has become a fundamental human right, **on** ______________ the right to privacy or education?

4 SPEAK Work in pairs. Discuss the questions in Exercise 3.

Pronunciation Vowel length before voiced and unvoiced consonants

1 3.2 Listen to sentences 1 and 2. The words in *italics* contain the same vowel sound. In which word is the vowel sound longer?

1 Do you see that *man*? 2 Do you see that *map*?

> Voiced consonant sounds (/d/, /z/, etc.) make your vocal cords vibrate, while unvoiced consonant sounds (/s/, /f/, etc.) don't. The length of a stressed vowel sound is greater when it comes before a voiced consonant sound and shorter before an unvoiced consonant sound.

2 The words below are from the listening on page 40. Underline the words which have a longer vowel sound.

app back big check bet cough come good have leave much reel spot such tool what track

3 SPEAK Work in pairs. Write sentences using the words from the box. Practise saying them aloud.

Listening Part 1 Multiple choice

1 3.3 **You will hear three different extracts. For questions 1–6, choose the answer (A, B or C) which fits best according to what you hear. There are two questions for each extract.**

Extract One

You hear part of an interview with a university professor talking about blended learning – courses that combine online and face-to-face learning.

1 What observation does Professor Yavuz make about her students?

- **A** They responded well to her innovative approach.
- **B** They had a surprisingly self-directed learning style.
- **C** They felt the format of the course was out of date.

2 Professor Yavuz says that one of the advantages of blended learning is

- **A** creating more in-class learning opportunities.
- **B** letting students progress at their own pace.
- **C** giving students greater choice in how they learn.

Extract Two

You hear a woman on a business podcast talking about spreadsheets.

3 What does she say about the invention of the electronic spreadsheet?

- **A** It allowed people to categorise data in a logical format.
- **B** It laid the foundation for a revolution in office work.
- **C** It shifted workers from one economic sector to another.

4 What is her attitude now towards spreadsheets?

- **A** Their merits have been overemphasised.
- **B** They magnify human error to a dramatic scale.
- **C** They are stretched beyond their limits.

Extract Three

You hear a tour guide at a planetarium talking about how an animal inspired the design of a telescope.

5 Why does he mention the lobster's habitat?

- **A** to point out a key vulnerability
- **B** to highlight a creative adaptation
- **C** to illustrate its ability to face adversity

6 When the speaker talks about the telescope, he reveals

- **A** his admiration for human ingenuity.
- **B** his delight in newly made observations.
- **C** his confidence in the technology's potential.

2 SPEAK **Have you or someone you know had any experience with blended learning? Was it positive or negative? Why?**

Language focus *will, shall* and *would*

1 SPEAK Read each pair of sentences and discuss the question in *italics*.

1 **A** Once I'm back at work, I will get to the bottom of this matter.
B Once I'm back at work, I shall get to the bottom of this matter.
Which one expresses more determination?

2 **A** Would you believe the website is down again?
B Do you believe the website is down again?
Which one conveys more surprise and annoyance?

3 **A** That'll be five pounds fifty.
B That's five pounds fifty.
Which one sounds more direct and less polite?

4 **A** Sit down and I will tell you the tale of a bunch of bold, seafaring ruffians.
B Will they make it through unscathed by this strange adventure?
In which one could 'will' be replaced by 'shall' with no change in meaning?

5 **A** That's the kids coming home from school.
B That will be the kids coming home from school.
Which one merely states a fact about a present situation?

6 **A** He is recording his first-ever podcast.
B He will be recording his first-ever podcast.
Which one expresses more certainty about an ongoing event in the present?

7 **A** Employees shall not take home any company property without permission.
B Employees must not take home any company property without permission.
Which one would only be found in a legal document?

2 Go to Ready for Grammar on page 213 for further rules, explanations and further practice.

3 SPEAK Work in pairs. Imagine possible situations where people would say the following sentences. Who do you think they are talking to?

And, would you believe, he didn't even apologise!

But it says right here, "The employee shall be reimbursed for all work-related expenses."

The project manager would reschedule the meeting at the last minute.

Will you pass me the catalogue?

Shall I start or would you like to?

Well, you know what they say, "seek and you shall find".

Speaking Part 3 Discussion

What to expect in the exam

- At the end of Part 3, the examiner will ask you questions that further explore the topics of the long turns. This discussion lasts around four minutes.

Work in pairs. Discuss the following questions.

1 Some people say creativity can be taught. How much truth is there in this?
2 In what ways are you creative in your daily life?
3 What makes some people seek creative professions?
4 Do you think creativity will be more important or less important in the jobs of tomorrow? Why or why not?
5 Is it better to be creative or practical? Why do you think that?
6 It has been said that creativity is the most valuable human resource. What's your opinion?

3 REVIEW

Reading and Use of English Part 2 Open cloze

How to go about it

- Sometimes the item you require is part of a longer word combination, such as an idiom, phrasal verb, fixed expression or linking phrase. Pay close attention to the words before and after each gap.

1 **Read the text, ignoring the gaps for the moment. Why does the title refer to GPS as the 'invisible utility'?**

2 **For questions 1–8, read the text again and think of the word that best fits each space. Use only one word in each space. There is an example at the beginning (0).**

GPS: The invisible utility

Many of us are unaware of the (0) __EXTENT__ to which our daily lives depend on the Global Positioning System (GPS), but the majority of people actually carry this technology everywhere they go because GPS is built into mobile phones. (1) ____________ and every time we make a call, a GPS receiver determines our location by measuring the arrival time of signals from up to four space satellites which are (2) ____________ orbit around the Earth.

What's (3) ____________, GPS is a highly dependable time service. GPS satellites carry clocks synchronised (4) ____________ within 1–3 milliseconds, and mobile networks make effective (5) ____________ of these clocks to timestamp data, scramble it and then unscramble it at the other end. A glitch of just 100 thousandth of a second would (6) ____________ rise to a myriad of problems. And it's not just phones. Stock markets, power grids, cloud computing – all of these rely on different locations agreeing on the time. They rely on GPS.

Suffice to (7) ____________, if GPS ever went down, even just temporarily, we'd all be lost in more (8) ____________ than one.

Language focus Talking about the future | *will*, *shall*, *would*

Cross out the option which cannot be used to complete each sentence.

1. We *won't buy* / *won't be buying* / *won't have bought* our own place until we've put aside enough money for a down payment.
2. It's the age-old problem – too much to do and not enough time. However, I assure you we *will complete* / *will be completing* / *will have completed* the video tutorial before the end of the workday.
3. The university is *to open* / *due to open* / *bound to open* a new state-of-the-art research facility next week.
4. *Would we have* / *Shall we have* / *Are we having* the same old thing or something new this time?
5. The production of the electric SUV *would* / *was going to* / *was supposed to* resume in September, but supply chain issues delayed the start for another six months.

Reading and Use of English

Part 4 Key word transformations

For questions **1–6**, complete the second sentence so that it has a similar meaning to the first sentence, using the word given. **Do not change the word given.** You must use between **three** and **eight** words, including the word given.

1 I love espresso, but the pour-over method undoubtedly creates a smoother, more nuanced taste.

NO

Much ______________________ that the pour-over method creates smoother, more nuanced taste.

2 Ali feels he was criticised unjustly following the loss of the key client.

FOR

Ali feels that he came ______________________ after the loss of the key client.

3 You must not leave this laptop in an unlocked car under any circumstances.

IS

Under ______________________ left in an unlocked car.

4 The policy will not be fully implemented for another two years.

OF

The ______________________ will take another two years.

5 The father told the child clearly and strongly that her tantrums were unacceptable.

UNCERTAIN

The child ______________________ that her tantrums were unacceptable.

6 The substitute teacher seemed to find the outrageous way the children behaved more a source of entertainment than irritation.

BEING

Far ______________________ outrageous behaviour, the substitute teacher seemed to be entertained by it.

Writing Part 2 Article

An online arts magazine is running a series of articles on the relationship between technology and culture. The magazine has asked readers to contribute articles about a recent technological innovation, other than the internet, which has led to an important change in art, music or fashion. You should briefly describe the innovation and assess its impact.

Write your **article** in **280–320** words.

For more information on writing articles, see page 192.

Idioms Innovation

Discussing idioms

Discuss the differences in meaning between these idioms:

- a stumbling block / a chip off the old block
- go round in circles / go round the bend
- a long shot / a shot in the dark

1 SPEAK Read the example sentence and answer the questions.

*When the engineers discovered a fatal flaw in the design, they decided to throw it out and start again **from scratch**.*

1 What is the figurative meaning of *from scratch* in this context?
2 *From scratch* used to have a literal meaning related to running races. What do you think it referred to?

2 Match questions (1–9) to answers (a–i).

1 Does your construction company have any major projects **in the pipeline**?
2 Did you experience any **teething problems** when you first developed this product?
3 Has the recent controversy proved to be a **stumbling block** to obtaining investment?
4 Are we still **on the right track** for continued growth in the wearable technology market?
5 Have the trade negotiations really come to a **dead end**?
6 Jordan's candidacy for mayor is starting to look like a **long shot**, don't you think?
7 Is the company still **at the leading edge** of cyber security?
8 Is it the kind of place that lets you **think outside the box**?
9 Parliamentary debate on educational reform is **going round in circles**, isn't it?

a Yes, it continues to actively recruit top talent and invest in state-of-the-art facilities.
b Yes, the quick adoption we're seeing of smart watches should ensure long-term profits.
c Yes, we have plans drawn up for several new office buildings in various city centres.
d I agree. If she keeps scoring so low in opinion polls, she's got little chance of winning.
e Yes, our reputation has suffered as a result, and we are finding it hard to attract finance.
f Unfortunately yes. We have lost hope of making any progress as both sides refuse to compromise on tariffs.
g Absolutely. Management really encourages us to be creative and challenge conventional wisdom.
h We did have some issues in the early stages, but we managed to solve these quickly.
i Yes, MPs have been discussing the issue for weeks with little to show for it.

3 SPEAK Work in pairs. Discuss the figurative meaning of the idioms in bold in 1–9 in Exercise 2.

***In the pipeline** means that something like a project is in the process of being planned or developed.*

4 With your partner, do the quiz.

Quiz: Which idiom from Exercise 2 originally referred to …

1 a path made by a horse's hoofprints, and then later railway lines?
2 a road, street or path that has no way out?
3 the part of an aeroplane wing that first meets the oncoming air?
4 a puzzle that was popular in the 1970s that involved connecting dots within a square?
5 tubes used to carry oil or water over long distances?
6 the period when the top and bottom incisors first come through a baby's gums?
7 people lost in the wilderness?
8 a cannonball launched from such a distance that it was unlikely to hit its target?
9 something on the ground people tripped over?

5 SPEAK Read the sentences. What do you notice about the way the speakers use the idioms from Exercise 2?

The company really thought **outside the box** with this new eco-friendly packaging.

So, is your brother-in-law's new dental practice having **teething problems**?

6 SPEAK Work in pairs. Choose three of the idioms from Exercises 1 and 2. For each one, write a sentence that plays on the literal and figurative meanings of the idiom.

7 SPEAK Exchange your sentences with another pair. Which is your favourite?

4

MEETING IN THE MIDDLE

KEY LANGUAGE

Modal verbs 1
Noun phrases and nominal clauses
Partitive expressions with uncountable nouns
Closed compounds

IDIOMS

Negotiation

EXAM PRACTICE

Reading and Use of English Parts 1 & 6
Writing Parts 1 & 2
Listening Parts 2 & 3
Speaking Parts 1 & 2

Speaking Part 1 Interview

Work with a partner. Discuss the questions.

1 On average, how much time do you spend with your family a week?
2 Are you usually more productive when working individually or as part of a team?
3 When you're worried or anxious, do you prefer to share your feelings with family and friends or just keep them to yourself?
4 Talk about a time when you had a disagreement with someone you work or study with. How did you resolve it?
5 Does social media contribute to a polarised society? Can anything be done to bring people together?

4 MEETING IN THE MIDDLE

Speaking Part 2 Collaborative task

1 **SPEAK** Work in pairs. Look at pictures 1 and 2 and discuss how the people might be feeling.

2 **SPEAK** Imagine that a business magazine is planning an article on team building activities. The magazine is considering pictures 1–4 to illustrate the article. Talk together about how effective the activities shown in these pictures can be for improving workers' productivity and motivation. Then suggest one other type of team building activity that could be included in the article.

Magazine article – team building activities

1

2

3

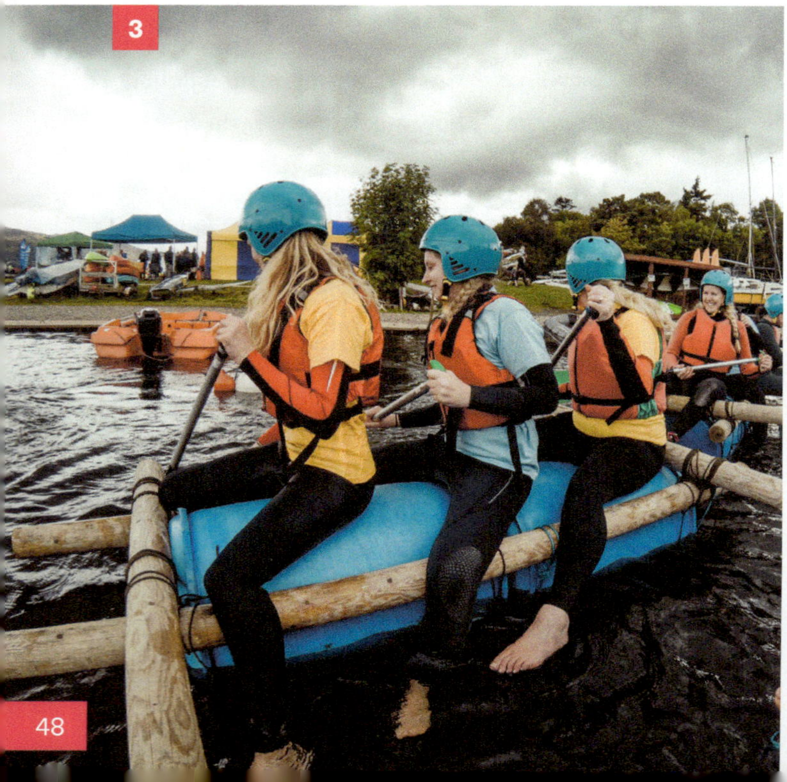

4

Listening Part 3 Multiple choice

What to expect in the exam

Listening Part 3 tests your ability to listen for general ideas, specific details and opinions. You may also have to listen for what two of the speakers agree or disagree on. Ideas are often stated indirectly, so this task often requires inference, i.e. listening 'between the lines', to get the right answers.

How to go about it

One effective strategy for this task is to listen for the answer to the question, rather than listening for the options. Listen carefully to what the speakers say, and once you have understood, look at the options and choose the one closest to what you heard. This strategy has a couple of advantages: 1) it's easier to listen for one thing than four, and 2) you are much less likely to get tricked by the distractors that have been carefully inserted into the incorrect options.

1 SPEAK Do you find it easier or more difficult to make friends now than when you were younger? Why?

2 4.1 You will hear part of an interview with two sociologists, Hanya Richardson and Jeffery Walsh, in which they discuss adult friendships. For questions 1–5, choose the answer (A, B, C or D) which fits best according to what you hear.

1 When discussing the aging process, Hanya and Jeffery agree that
- **A** it causes bonds with childhood friends to weaken.
- **B** social lives fall victim to life circumstances.
- **C** people get stuck in established friend groups.
- **D** adults dedicate too much time to work and too little to leisure.

2 When describing how adults meet potential friends, Jeffery reveals
- **A** his belief that younger people are more open to new friendships.
- **B** his conviction that genuine friendships start organically.
- **C** his impression that people have unrealistic expectations.
- **D** his fear that people are unwilling to put in sufficient effort.

3 What does Hanya say about the use of avoidance strategies?
- **A** It stops us from making an emotional investment in people.
- **B** It allows us to better grapple with awkward social situations.
- **C** It limits opportunities for achieving personal growth.
- **D** It refocuses our minds away from distressing thoughts.

4 What advice is given about how to strengthen a new friendship?
- **A** Embrace taking the initiative.
- **B** Identify activities you could do together.
- **C** Avoid neglecting established social protocols.
- **D** Fulfil your commitments to the other person.

5 In Hanya's view, friends who behave badly
- **A** may overstep boundaries but do so unintentionally.
- **B** can stretch our patience past its breaking point.
- **C** should be given the benefit of the doubt.
- **D** will come to regret their actions at a later date.

Language focus Modal verbs 1

1 Choose the correct modal verb to complete the sentences from the listening.

1 ... try as we *can* / *might* to keep up with people, our friendship circles shrink as we move into adulthood.

2 And so the question is, how *can* / *must* we fill that friendship gap?

3 ... it's not entirely unreasonable that we *can* / *should* make this assumption, ...

4 We *ought not to* / *may not* let ourselves fall into this common trap.

2 Check your answers to Exercise 1 in the Audioscript on page 235.

3 Rewrite the sentences using the modal verb in brackets. There is one example.

0 I hope the bride and groom live a long and happy life together. (may)
May the bride and groom live a long and happy life together.

1 Is it necessary for me to remind you that homework makes up 20 per cent of your overall mark? (need)
______

2 The presence of the prime minister is probably sufficient to bring about the necessary arrangement. (should)
______

3 There was no need for you to pick me up at the airport. (needn't)
______

4 I wish you had told me sooner that you were planning to drop the course! (might)
______

5 It's not a good idea for you to respond to an irritating email before you've had time to calm down. (oughtn't to)
______

6 What a wonderfully thoughtful gift! I feel so grateful. (shouldn't)
______

4 Go to the Ready for Grammar section on page 212 for further rules, explanations and practice.

5 SPEAK Work in pairs. Read the rhetorical questions and create a context for each of them.

1 Must you stay out so late?

2 How can you hope to get better if you don't practise?

3 Need I remind you that we have a contract?

4 Ought we not to allocate more money to improving our schools?

6 Work with your partner. Choose one of the contexts you created in Exercise 5 and write a dialogue which includes at least four modal verbs.

7 SPEAK Join with another pair and roleplay your dialogue from Exercise 6.

Pronunciation Stressed modal auxiliaries

1 4.2 Listen to two versions of this sentence. How does the meaning of the sentence change when the speaker stresses the modal auxiliary *could* in sentence 2?

1 I could have passed my driver's test.

2 I could have passed my driver's test.

2 4.3 You will hear sentences 1–5 twice, once with meaning A and once with meaning B. Decide which one you hear first and which one you hear second.

1 'I will go to the demonstration.'
  A I agree to go.
  B I'm going and you can't stop me.

2 'She might have bought me a birthday present.'
  A I don't know if she bought me one, but I hope so.
  B She didn't, but she ought to have bought me one.

3 'We are going to do our homework.'
  A It's a fact that we're going to do it.
  B You think we aren't going to do it, but that's not true.

4 'He would forget some of the students' names.'
  A He used to do it a lot.
  B It's so typical of him to do that.

5 'I could have played football all afternoon.'
  A I was having so much fun I didn't want to stop.
  B I wanted to play all afternoon, but they didn't let me.

3 SPEAK Practise reading sentences 1–5 aloud with the two different meanings.

Stressed auxiliaries

Modal auxiliaries (*can, could, may, might, must, shall, should, will, would*), as well as other auxiliaries (*be, do, have*), are not usually stressed (except in negatives, short answers and tag questions). But sometimes, to add emphasis or enhance the meaning of a sentence, they are given extra stress.

Vocabulary Partitive expressions with uncountable nouns

1 Choose the correct option to complete the sentence from the Listening task on page 49.

We simply have to get used to those small ___________ of anxiety that come from engaging with new people.

A lumps B doses C dabs D bouts

2 Match each sentence beginning (1–10) with an appropriate ending (a–j).

1 The audience broke into a huge **round of**
2 Fake news often contains a small **grain of**
3 Meeting my future husband was a **stroke of**
4 He admitted to writing the email in a **fit of**
5 The radio host didn't provide a single **scrap of**
6 The community playground was a **breath of**
7 If you are willing to endure the **pangs of**
8 The new sales figures provide a **glimmer of**
9 The teachers belonged to the **school of**
10 The influencer, without the slightest **hint of**

a **thought** that says that cooperation trumps competition.
b **guilt**, a plagiarism-free essay can be yours for £10 a page.
c **evidence** to support his outlandish claims.
d **irony**, wore a T-shirt that declared 'I love ME.'
e **applause** when the speaker took to the stage.
f **hope** that the company's prospects are not as dismal as feared.
g **luck**; if not for the delayed flight, it never would have happened.
h **anger** and regretted his poor choice of words.
i **fresh air** for parents and a feast for young imaginations.
j **truth**, making it easier to digest for busy or distracted readers.

3 SPEAK Work in pairs. Study the sentences in Exercise 2 for a minute. Then cover the second column. Can you remember how each sentence ends?

4 Think of a brief story, real or imagined, that contains one of these sentences.

'But then I felt a pang of regret.'
'At the sight of it, we broke into fits of laughter.'
'It was undoubtedly a stroke of genius.'
'I could detect a hint of bitterness.'
'Then we saw a faint glimmer of light.'

5 SPEAK With your partner, take turns telling your stories. Stop at the part of the story that contains the sentence from Exercise 4. Your partners have to guess which sentence fits into your story.

Reading and Use of English Part 6 Gapped text

1 **SPEAK** What kinds of jobs require excellent negotiation skills? What personal qualities does a person need to be a successful negotiator?

2 You are going to read an article about a negotiator. Seven paragraphs have been removed from the text. Choose from the paragraphs **A–H** the one which fits each gap (**1–7**). There is one extra paragraph which you do not need to use.

The Negotiators

Our everyday lives are punctuated by different types of negotiations, whether discussing divisions of labour within the home, asking for a raise at work or even complaining about bad service. Therefore, it is surprising how unskilled the average human is at undertaking these kinds of negotiations, with results which can vary from having requests fall on deaf ears to inciting a full-blown row.

1 ______________________

This is illustrated by a story from the Middle East, in which three sons are left camels in their father's will. The eldest son is left half of the camels, the middle son one-third, and the youngest, one-ninth. Yet with 17 camels, they were unable to divide them. After much quarrelling, they went to see an old wise man, who listened carefully and then gave them his own camel. The eldest then took half of the 18 camels – nine – the second then took six camels – his third – and the youngest then took two camels – his ninth. And the wise man? Well, he took his left-over camel back!

2 ______________________

Without question, the most important negotiations of all happen in life-or-death situations, like kidnappings or hostage crises, and the procedures for dealing with these situations have been carefully refined. The Behavioural Change Stairway Model (BCSM) is a negotiation strategy developed by the FBI to communicate with dangerous criminals in these kinds of situations.

3 ______________________

Their approach is underpinned by the belief that, in order to gain influence over somebody, both understanding the emotional thinking of the other person, and creating some form of empathy is essential, winning out over logical reasoning every time in such situations. This doesn't mean agreeing with the other party's feelings, but certainly acknowledging and understanding them.

4 ______________________

In addition to this, simply mirroring the final few words of what they have said, or giving a comment that's either positive or neutral, can show that the other party's perspective is recognised and valued. This could be something as simple as 'You seem quite upset. I can see how you feel.' When these statements are followed by a pause, it also gives the other party time to open up further regarding their internal motivations and limits.

5 ______________________

It would be logical to think that due to the success of these kinds of methods, and statistics show they *do* work, they would be expanded into other arenas, and this is indeed the case. When we look to the business world, we can see how emotional connection plays a key role in all sectors where there is any form of decision-making or negotiation.

6 ______________________

In fact, one study found that the success of a negotiation could be predicted just within the first few minutes of interaction, not by measuring what was said, but by looking at volume, pitch, pace of speech and body language as well as cardiogram readouts to show the physical reaction of participants. Where they were more aligned and balanced, there was a better outcome.

7 ______________________

While it's not always easy to take a step back and just listen and absorb what is happening, all the evidence suggests that it might well lead to the best outcome. Perhaps next time you want something from your partner, or boss at work, the best approach may be to diffuse any tension, acknowledge your and their concerns, and get their angle, before coming in with your own.

How to go about it

- Part 6 tests your understanding of text structure, cohesion, coherence and global meaning.
- Carefully read the main text, focusing on how it develops. Consider the progression of events, ideas or arguments.

A In order to achieve these two objectives, communication and listening skills are required. Non-judgemental open-ended questions and statements that ascertain the state of mind of the other person can be the best friend of this kind of interaction. Statements like 'Tell me how that happened' are far more effective than anything more direct and confrontational which can enflame the ire of the other party.

B This indicates that a positive attitudinal outlook may well be more effective in achieving an expected outcome than treating other participants in a more cold, robotic manner. The emotionally intelligent may even have the upper hand over the intellectually intelligent in terms of these kinds of scenarios, as they have the ability to sit back, identify their and others' emotions, how it affects thinking and how this can be managed.

C Coping with any kind of confrontation in general can be quite a difficult scenario. Be it a criminal in negotiation with the police, or a businessman negotiating a deal, often there can be mixed feelings of vulnerability and fear of being tricked or taken advantage of. Perhaps this is why initial impressions can count for so much, to allay these worries.

D Only after all of these strategies have been deployed effectively can any influence be exerted over the decision-making. This part of negotiation is usually what most people jump to first, ignoring all the effort to get the other party on side, yet initiating solutions and agreements is far easier to do, and more successful, when it's negotiated between two collaborators rather than adversaries.

E This is simply because people are usually far too concerned with putting their own opinion across, and showing they are right, to really negotiate effectively with their counterpart. This not only puts the back up of the other party, but it also fails to identify common ground or a third or middle way, which then can ultimately lead to a better solution for all.

F Naturally, the kinds of individuals who negotiate these sorts of transactions need to have a very particular skill set. Usually former police and military, they must have the ability to remain completely unnerved during highly stressful circumstances, and to understand and identify with what many people might consider the unidentifiable.

G But this wasn't always the case. Until recently, emotion was viewed as something that impedes negotiation, with business experts advising people to leave their feelings at the door and focus on the problem rather than the personalities in the room. Yet there is increasing evidence of the flaws in this thinking as more emotionally based insights are coming to the fore.

H The lesson here may seem obvious; that when confronted with a dilemma that seems unsolvable, rather than go in all guns blazing arguing for your position, it's better to step back and look at it from all perspectives to try and find the way forward. While this might be something the average person on the street may struggle with, in many settings this is the first step to tip the scales of success in negotiations.

3 SPEAK In pairs, discuss the questions below.

1 How do you feel when you go into a situation that requires negotiation? Do you use any of the skills in the article?

2 What advice would you give somebody who had to negotiate the following:
- getting money off the price of a product with a slight imperfection
- asking for a deadline extension on an essay at university
- requesting a pay increase at work

Language focus Noun phrases and nominal clauses

1 SPEAK Read sentences A and B. Which sounds less personal and more academic? What changes are made to the underlined words?

A In my department, the person who preceded me in my role was not very organised.

B In my department, my predecessor suffered from a serious lack of organisation.

2 Complete the second sentence so it has a similar meaning to the first. You will need to use the noun form of the verbs and adjectives in bold as well as change the adverbs in *italics* to adjectives.

1 When I *carefully* **analysed** the data, they revealed that the number of couples meeting online had *dramatically* **increased**.

A ________ of the data revealed a ________ in couples meeting online.

2 To make an inference, you *logically* **deduce** or **conclude** something from an established fact.

An inference is a ________ or ________ from an established fact.

3 Last year the government **allocated** health care resources more *efficiently*.

Last year there was a more ________ of health care resources.

4 Research suggests that people are *highly* **tolerant** of small talk when they **encounter** someone *for the first time*.

Research suggests that people have a ________ for small talk during ________.

5 The article **argues** that airlines should **allow** families flying with young children to be able to check more baggage.

The article makes an ________ in favour of more ________ for families flying with young children.

6 If a conversation with a doctor gets too *emotionally* **intense**, a patient might **refuse** treatment.

If the ________ of the conversation between doctor and patient becomes too great, this may result in a ________ of treatment.

3 Choose the correct alternative in the following sentences.

1 One quarter of the participants in the drug trial *was / were* given the placebo.

2 Young trout *is / are* referred to as troutlet, troutling or fry.

3 My sister, together with my parents, *is / are* flying into Buenos Aires today to visit me.

4 Economics *is / are* concerned with finding the most logical and effective use of resources to meet private and social goals.

5 The news out of Canada this week *is / are* both sobering and shocking.

6 The company's CEO, as well as its employees, *has / have* a vested interest in the success of the joint undertaking.

7 Neither the rechargeable batteries nor the baby monitor itself *operates / operate* as intended.

8 A corps of volunteer gardeners *promotes / promote* the selection and planting of appropriate fruit trees.

4 Go to Ready for Grammar on page 214 for further rules, explanations and practice.

5 Work in pairs. Write a paragraph in a formal style answering the following question: *What leads to a successful parent–child relationship?* Use at least five of the nouns from the box.

bond camaraderie delight dependence devotion freedom impatience intimacy isolation offspring parenting persuasion quality reasoning respect sociability surroundings sympathy tenderness tranquillity trust undertaking

6 SPEAK Compare your ideas with another pair of students. Do you agree or disagree with each other's views?

7 Go to the Additional materials on page 201 for practice of word formation with nouns.

Vocabulary Closed compounds

1 Complete the sentences with a word from the box. There are three extra words.

backlash comeback counterpoint forefront
scapegoat stalemate watershed wavelength

1. The board was eager to pin the blame on someone, and so the CEO **became** a convenient ____________ for the company's failures.
2. The teambuilding event went off without a hitch because everyone was **on the same** ____________ and worked well together.
3. The invention of the Gutenberg printing press is recognised as a ____________ **moment** for rates of literacy, first throughout Europe and then the world.
4. An insensitive tweet by the band's lead singer **sparked** an angry ____________ from loyal fans.
5. It had been a considerable undertaking, but after weeks of tough negotiations, the company management and the trade union finally found a workable compromise to **break the** ____________

2 SPEAK Work in pairs. Discuss the meaning of the phrases in bold in Exercise 1.

3 Complete sentences 1–5. Combine one word from box A with one from box B to make closed compounds.

A keep proof short turn will

B comings over power read sakes

1. Our lives are full of clutter. Our houses are crammed with **cherished** ____________ and mementos that it would be better to simply throw away.
2. The best way for companies to avoid high **employee** ____________ is to reward critical staff with more tangible benefits like pay rises or paid time off.
3. There is no personal or professional goal that can't be reached through **sheer** ____________ and self-discipline.
4. It's better to look past the **flaws and** ____________ of our loved ones rather than dwell on them. No one is perfect.
5. **Carefully** ____________ all professional correspondence before it goes out. Typos are a sign of carelessness and they show a lack of respect for the reader.

4 SPEAK Work in pairs. Discuss the statements in Exercise 3, explaining why you agree or disagree with them.

Listening Part 2 Sentence completion

1 4.4 You will hear a woman called Samira Joshi giving a short talk about workplace mediation. For questions **1–9**, complete the sentences with a word or short phrase.

THE MEDIATOR

According to Samira, companies can disregard **(1)** __________ when considering the option of workplace mediation.

She says that **(2)** __________ is the most common reason companies seek out the help of a mediator.

She mentions that some employees contend with stressful work environments through taking **(3)** __________ .

During the first stage of mediation, she advocates for the use of **(4)** __________ while coming up with possible solutions.

Samira states that, to finish the mediation process by the end of the day, **(5)** __________ is an important consideration.

In order to be successful, she thinks it essential that mediators have **(6)** __________ .

She believes that changing each participant's **(7)** __________ is a challenging but achievable goal.

Each participant in the mediation process is accountable for the **(8)** __________ of the final agreement.

Samira uses the phrase **(9)** __________ to describe the approach taken to confidentiality in workplace mediation.

2 **SPEAK** Do you think you would make a good workplace mediator? Why / Why not?

Writing Part 2 Letter

What to expect in the exam

- One of the options in Writing Part 1 may be a letter. You could be asked to write to the director of a company, the principal of a school or college, or the editor of a newspaper or magazine.
- Depending on the task, it may be appropriate to include personal narrative or description in your letter. In other cases, the sole aim is to explain ideas or provide factual information.

1 **SPEAK** Work in pairs. Read the Part 2 task below. What is the purpose of the letter? What points do you have to include?

> An English language magazine has recently published a feature called Have our relationships moved online? The editor has asked readers to write in with their own experiences and views on the topic. You decide to write a letter describing a personal or business relationship that developed online. You should also evaluate the quality of online relationships and consider the extent to which they can replace meeting with people face to face.

Write your letter in 280–320 words.

2 **Read the model answer and complete the notes in the writer's plan.**

Plan

Opening paragraph
– Disagree with arguments made in feature – there are also benefits

First body paragraph

Second body paragraph

Closing paragraph

To the editor,

It was with great interest that I read the recent feature, 'Have our relationships moved online?' The article is a welcome look at an issue that many of us in middle age are still getting to grips with. That said, I'm disappointed by the author's efforts to belittle online relationships, limiting her analysis to a litany of flaws and potential pitfalls. A more fair-minded article would have examined the upsides as well.

'Have our relationships moved online?' triggered memories of one of my own friendships that began online. An avid fan of sustainable interior design, I follow a number of designers on social media. One of my favourites is Maria Suarez, who builds furniture incorporating reclaimed wood and traditional Spanish tiles. Last year, I reached out to Maria and she kindly agreed to custom build a shelving unit for the nook beside my kitchen. Since then, what started as a business transaction has blossomed into a genuine friendship. Maria and I have even met up in person a few times when she's come to Berlin for design-related events.

This example illustrates clear benefits to meeting people through the internet. Firstly, it's undoubtedly easier to break the ice online. Even the shyest of individuals, such as myself, is unafraid of commenting on a social media post. Secondly, the internet facilitates meeting people with mutual interests. Thanks to social media, I've joined a flock of like-minded people, many of whom organise in-person events that I've been lucky enough to attend. Too often to count, the brief, albeit superficial, online communication I had with people prior to meeting with them in person acted as a useful – and, for me, necessary – stepping stone to successful face-to-face interaction.

To conclude, I believe this topic is worthy of further exploration in your magazine and I would encourage you to examine it from a variety of different angles.

Best regards,

Hannah Schulz

3 **Read the sample answer again and assess it with the following scale.**

1 = needs improvement   2 = satisfactory   3 = excellent

Does the writer ...	1	2	3
1 address the points from the task instructions?			
2 begin and end the letter appropriately?			
3 use an appropriately formal style?			
4 organise the letter using a logical structure?			
5 back up arguments with supporting examples and reasons?			
6 use a variety of sophisticated vocabulary and grammar?			

4 **SPEAK** **Work with a partner. Compare your assessments. Justify the marks you chose.**

5 **You are going to write your own answer to the Writing Part 2 task in Exercise 1. Before you start, brainstorm ideas and organise them into a plan similar to the one in Exercise 2.**

6 **SPEAK** **Work in pairs. Discuss your plans. Can you help your partner improve their plan?**

7 **Write your own letter in response to the Writing Part 2 task in Exercise 1. Before handing it in to your teacher, use the chart in Exercise 3 to assess your writing.**

How to go about it

- Read the instructions carefully. Identify and underline the 2–3 points that you need to address. Think about the purpose of your letter – what are you trying to achieve?
- Plan your letter thoroughly before putting pen to paper. Well planned answers are likely to get better marks for both organisation and communicative achievement.
- In your answer, use a wide variety of sophisticated lexis and grammar. You also have to demonstrate you have a good command of the conventions of letter writing.

For more information on writing letters, see page 193.

4 REVIEW

Vocabulary Partitive expressions | Closed compounds

Complete the gaps with words from the unit.

1. When the speaker told a story of finding the **w**__________ to overcome her fear of failure, she received a big **r**__________ **of applause** from the audience.
2. The new advertising campaign was a **s**__________ **of genius** and led the company to an improbable **c**__________ in the South American markets following years of declining sales.
3. In an angry interview, the former CEO claimed he had been made a **s**__________ and insisted there wasn't a **s**__________ **of evidence** to prove the accusations of mismanagement.
4. For the teacher, it was a **b**__________ **of fresh air** to work with a group of students who carefully **p**__________ their essays before submitting them.
5. Paco felt a **p**__________ **of guilt** for giving his grandfather's books, watches and other **k**__________ to charity, but there simply wasn't space for them in his tiny flat.

Reading and Use of English Part 1 Multiple-choice cloze

For questions 1–8, read the text below and decide which answer (A, B, C or D) best fits each gap. There is an example at the beginning (0).

Mentorship

Mentorship programmes have many benefits. Mentors, experienced individuals who **(0)** ___*B*___ knowledge, expertise and wisdom to less experienced individuals (mentees), can facilitate understanding of both practical matters and the more **(1)** __________ aspects of navigating a particular **(2)** __________ of the business world. Mentors know the stresses and fears that come with being the new kid on the **(3)** __________, and by listening carefully and giving advice, they can act as an effective **(4)** __________ board for their mentees. Moreover, when mentors foster a friendly and supportive relationship, displaying patience and empathy, they don't just help **(5)** __________ mentees on the path to success. They also make them feel valued, which has been shown to reduce staff **(6)** __________ and boost morale.

If you have **(7)** __________ in your career, you have most likely had help from another professional along the way – perhaps it was a **(8)** __________ colleague at an entry-level job who showed you the ropes and later set you up for a promotion. Why not extend this opportunity to all new recruits?

	A	B	C	D
0	**A** cultivate	**B** <u>impart</u>	**C** instil	**D** instruct
1	**A** intangible	**B** shadowy	**C** ineffable	**D** rewarding
2	**A** pocket	**B** corner	**C** angle	**D** edge
3	**A** side	**B** block	**C** field	**D** show
4	**A** calling	**B** drawing	**C** proving	**D** sounding
5	**A** set	**B** lay	**C** fix	**D** move
6	**A** uncertainty	**B** turnover	**C** recruitment	**D** incentives
7	**A** delivered	**B** accomplished	**C** culminated	**D** excelled
8	**A** hardened	**B** wary	**C** seasoned	**D** budding

Language focus Noun phrases and nominal clauses

Correct the mistakes in the following sentences.

1 Either Odin's parents or his grandfather are going to pick him up from ballet class.
2 Theoretical physics employ mathematical models to explain and predict natural phenomena.
3 The heiress's inheritance is tied up in different trust.
4 Must you make such a racket? Aerobics don't have to involve such loud stomping!
5 I'm not sure which, but it is either the salmon dish or the salad that contain nuts.
6 It was a risky undertaking. We didn't tell the manager whose decision it had been, but it was Sophie.

Writing Part 1 Essay

Read the two texts below. Write an essay summarising and evaluating the key points from both texts. Use your own words throughout as far as possible and include your own ideas in your answer.

PRIORITIES AND NEGOTIATION

While preparing for a negotiation, the first step should always be to decide on your priorities. If there is more than one, which is most often the case, you'll need to arrange these priorities in order of importance, analysing all the variables in terms of value and cost to each party. When both sides put this strategy into practice, it's easier to make trade-offs. What's more, having clear priorities helps avoid a common problem: as the negotiation draws to a close, it's easy to lose sight of your objectives and make hasty decisions. You may end up giving away too much, leading to an unsuccessful negotiation.

TRUST AND NEGOTIATION

It's a good idea to reveal your priorities at the beginning of any negotiation, whether it be in the context of a business meeting or a discussion among family members. This may sound counterintuitive because the other party could take advantage of this knowledge. However, by disclosing your priorities, you signal cooperation and inspire reciprocity. You also build trust. When trust is at the centre of a negotiation, it's easier to achieve mutual gains, instead of simply trying to get the upper-hand and come out ahead. This is because trust enables negotiating parties to mentally relax and focus on finding innovative solutions that will be advantageous for both sides.

Write your **answer** in **240–280** words

For more information on writing essays, see page 190.

Idioms Negotiation

1 Look at the photo and read the dialogue. Then choose the correct option in the sentence below.

This dialogue illustrates how people sometimes use idioms to *emphasise a particular point* / *imply an idea instead of stating it directly.*

2 4.5 Listen to the sentences and complete the idioms with one or two words.

1 Then, despite their differences, they **found** ____________ when it came to the issue of free speech.

2 That's good to hear, but **the** ____________ **is** that we need to come up with another ten thousand pounds of funding.

3 Farm subsidies have long been **a key** ____________ in these negotiations. I see little or no hope of agreement there.

4 The issue of publicity is still **a bit of a** ____________. It doesn't fit squarely into any one category.

5 I'd like to **clear** ____________ at the start of this meeting and apologise for the recent miscommunication.

6 I know we've already sorted out the basics of the agreement, but do you think two days will give us enough time to **nail down the** ____________?

7 I've tried to convince him to change his mind repeatedly, but to no avail. We finally had to **agree** ____________.

8 Our lead negotiator **got off on the** ____________ with a tactless remark about the office furniture, and we never recovered from that rocky start.

9 It seemed like they wouldn't comply with *any* of our demands. But eventually they did ____________ **halfway** on the most important points.

Discussing idioms

Discuss the differences in meaning between these idioms:

- agree to disagree / see eye to eye
- clear the air / break the ice
- find common ground / stand one's ground

3 Listen again, and then discuss the meaning of the idioms with a classmate.

4 SPEAK Read the information and do the roleplay. Use idioms from the lesson.

STUDENT A

Your company is replacing its office furniture. You are in charge of selling the old furniture. Brand new, it cost 5,000 pounds, but it is now five years old and well-used. The minimum price you would accept is 1,500 pounds. Negotiate with a person who is interested in buying the furniture.

STUDENT B

The non-profit organisation you work for is expanding and you need to buy office furniture for new employees. You find some office furniture on sale. It is second hand but most of it is still in good condition. You think it is worth around 1,000 pounds, but you would obviously be happy to buy it for a lower price. Negotiate with the person selling the furniture.

READY FOR READING AND USE OF ENGLISH PARTS 5–7

Introduction

In this section, we will focus on the techniques and approaches you should adopt in **Reading and Use of English** Parts 5, 6 and 7.

Reading and Use of English Part 5 Multiple choice

1 **SPEAK** Work in pairs. What do you know about citizen science?

2 Quickly read the text about how citizens are contributing to scientific research. Were any of your ideas in Exercise 1 correct? If not, what did you learn about citizen science?

We're all in it TOGETHER

From NASA to Greenpeace to Médecins Sans Frontières via a host of other organisations both governmental and charitable, citizen science has been taking the world by storm. Its benefits as a research tool are nothing short of startling, but what exactly is this phenomenon and why has it become so widespread? In a nutshell, citizen science is a way of harnessing volunteers from all walks of life to help scientists gather data and answer real world questions, and it has made some surprising discoveries along the way.

An often-cited example is NASA, which uses legions of amateur astronomers to scour the night skies for celestial bodies of potential importance. Contrary to popular belief, it turns out that computers aren't really up to the job of spotting patterns in the stars or changes to gas swirls in nebulae. They may well be a whizz at number crunching and processing colossal quantities of information, but it is the human eye that NASA is after to help them spot anomalies in matters of the universe.

Citizen science features heavily in environmental fields too, not least because of the vast network of volunteers always ready, willing and able to assist. Think of the National Bird Survey from the RSPB in the UK to which over half a million people lend their eyes and ears every year. Yet, in some regions citizen science works not because of the hordes of well-meaning volunteers desperate to play a role in conservation, but because of those who have tended the land for generations and therefore possess knowledge indispensable for scientists who may be working from theoretical rather than experiential data. While the former may be involved as a result of a guilty conscience, the latter has an obvious impetus to join the cause.

One such example worth a closer look is China insofar as it demonstrates how locals and scientists can be brought together by NGOs (non-governmental organisations) effectively. Rightly, local residents can be suspicious of outside scientists advocating complex methods, but this is where citizen science can help bridge the gap between traditional and more scientific practices. While scientists conduct their studies, local residents can still apply their traditional expertise. Much of this, from monitoring wildlife populations to tracking desertification, can be carried out via smartphone apps making setting up initiatives and recruiting participants more straightforward without endless ethics forms clogging up the process.

Technology, as one would expect, plays a vital role in citizen science, probably accounting for its recent exponential growth. Smartphone apps are the obvious game changer, but websites, amateur telescopes and digital cameras feature heavily too. Less obvious is the addition of gamification to the tool set. As the name implies, gamification brings elements of games to activities which could otherwise be deemed rather dull. *Worms Watch* is a tool which harnesses the power of gamification to provide data to the medical sector. Citizen scientists play a game where they click on a digital worm whenever it lays an egg, providing insight into the human brain and genetics. These digital approaches remove the need for participants to go to a laboratory, thereby saving the researchers from getting bogged down in a sea of time-consuming documentation.

Although historically Europe and North America have dominated the citizen science landscape, the infiltration of contemporary smartphones has accelerated its use in other regions where the urgency of assessing the quality and quantity of wildlife has escalated. *Green Power* is an organisation in Hong Kong focusing on butterflies and their surveys have been invaluable over the last decade. More recently, in 2023, The Pench Tiger Reserve in central India embarked on a large-scale bird survey, the first of its kind, to investigate biodiversity and species density with 125 volunteers recording sightings on an app. Citizen science has even extended its reach to conservation holidays, which levy a fee to take part in projects such as the tropical butterfly survey in Cameroon run by the African Conservation Foundation.

These latest developments are hallmarks of the ever-evolving nature of citizen science, which shows no signs of slowing down or stagnating. The near future will likely see it mature into a more formalised type of investigation as well as harness emerging technologies and social media. Businesses too will want in on the action; after all, citizen science is not that far removed from market research, and this may well ruffle some feathers amongst the scientific community. Whether they will be able to halt its commercialisation remains to be seen, but citizen science is here to stay.

What to expect in the exam

- In Part 5, you have a text followed by six multiple-choice questions. The task checks your understanding of the main ideas and purpose of the text, as well as smaller details. It also tests your ability to gauge the attitude, opinion or tone of the writer and deduce meaning from context.
- The multiple-choice questions include options that are distractors. Once you have selected all your answers, double-check them against the relevant passage in the text.

2 **You are going to read an article. For questions 1–6, choose the answer (A, B, C or D) which you think fits best according to the text.**

1 The author highlights the fact that technology is
- **A** being challenged by the success of citizen science.
- **B** no match for certain human capabilities.
- **C** less effective at data processing than people think.
- **D** an indispensable tool for observing changes to the universe.

2 What does the author imply about those who take part in citizen science projects?
- **A** Volunteers often do not fully grasp the context.
- **B** Scientists are biased towards certain groups.
- **C** Some have a stronger incentive than others.
- **D** Sections of society are not evenly represented.

3 Charitable organisations are getting involved in citizen science in order to
- **A** foster collaboration between disparate groups.
- **B** channel research to environmental issues.
- **C** ensure it is carried out more rigorously.
- **D** provide educational programmes for local people.

4 What effect has gamification had on data collection?
- **A** It allows more relevant research areas to be addressed.
- **B** It means participants can be drawn from a wider pool.
- **C** It facilitates the use of more innovative methods by scientists.
- **D** It diminishes the requirement for completing paperwork.

5 The author implies that some parts of the world have been slow to adopt citizen science because
- **A** the technology used to be prohibitively expensive.
- **B** richer nations denied them access to resources.
- **C** citizens were largely indifferent until recently.
- **D** it is hard to implement in areas with limited resources.

6 When discussing the future of citizen science in the final paragraph, the author
- **A** predicts its deepening reliance on technology.
- **B** makes a firm assertion that it will become invaluable.
- **C** envisages a development likely to alienate one sector.
- **D** warns of its possible future applications.

3 **For each question, underline the sections of the text that contain the answer and any that include the distractors.**

4 **SPEAK Work in pairs. Compare your answers to Exercise 3 and discuss any similarities and differences in meaning between the questions and distractors.**

5 **Part 5 questions often contain verb + noun collocations related to understanding the author's intention, as in question 1 above: *highlight the fact that*. Go to the Additional materials on Page 203 and do the exercise.**

Reading and Use of English Part 6 Gapped text

1 SPEAK Work in groups. Read the title and subheading of the article. Then, discuss the questions.

1. What international agreements are in place for the world's oceans?
2. In what ways do you think international diplomacy contributes towards their management?

2 Quickly read the text. Were any of your ideas in Exercise 1 mentioned by the authors?

> **Don't forget!**
>
> First, read the whole text to get an idea of the overall meaning, structure and flow. On the next reading, look for links between the extracted paragraphs and the text, including reference words, linguistic devices such as pronoun references and synonym substitutions, as well as any overlaps in ideas or arguments.

MANAGING THE OCEANS

A TALE OF COLLABORATION

It has not all been plain sailing when it comes deciding who owns the oceans and their resources. We take a look at how this tricky area of international diplomacy developed.

Managing the world's oceans has an interesting history that is seldom told in full. While once nations sought to dominate them and assert sovereignty over them for trade purposes, the focus nowadays is on international collaboration to preserve these precious habitats under serious threat after centuries of human exploitation. Satisfying the needs of countries large and small all over the world is no mean feat and one which should be celebrated.

1 ____________________

Humans have traded fish and products derived from sea mammals and plants since they first took to the water in rudimentary sailing vessels several thousand years ago. Sailing technology gradually improved over time resulting in more of the oceans becoming navigable. This in turn led to a global maritime trading network in the 16th century linking regions of the world such as Europe, Asia and the Caribbean.

2 ____________________

This distinction was to give countries jurisdiction over the seas and oceans around their coasts and also started the process of working out how to deal with the high seas. While it was acknowledged that countries should be able to use the oceans bordering their land for their own purposes, deciding what to do with the rest raised questions which were difficult to resolve for obvious reasons until a Dutch legal expert named Hugo Grotius took up the challenge in the 17th century.

3 ____________________

Deciding on the content of a law to ensure 'freedom of the high seas', as the concept became known, was always going to be a daunting task. There were many aspects to take into consideration not least the issue of the distribution of resources in the oceans. While coral reefs and tropical seas are teeming with life, vast stretches of coastlines host far fewer species and as such resources are unevenly spread.

4 ____________________

By this time, it was becoming increasingly clear that any international disagreements would have to be put aside. The oceans were suffering from a raft of issues such as overfishing and pollution, all caused by human activity. There was no doubt that something needed to be done and any action would have to be on a global scale.

5 ____________________

Yet it could not have been accomplished without scientific development. At its heart was the growing understanding that the world's oceans are linked by currents that enable life to thrive and that human impact can have far-reaching consequences. Marine conservationists had started stressing that the only way forward was international cooperation and the United Nations listened.

6 ____________________

As new information was uncovered, more charitable organisations appeared to champion the cause. Spurred on by the success of the UN and bolstered by research data, they too made great leaps in ocean protection, with successful international collaboration projects boosting whale populations, reducing coastal pollution and a host of other improvements.

7 ____________________

In the face of climate change and the devasting effects on marine life, demonstrating effective leadership is necessary. Modern ocean management bears little resemblance to the trade-based treaties of the 17th century and is concerned solely with stewardship rather than ownership. Now that the issues are better understood, modernising old international treaties is of utmost importance.

How to go about it

- Once you have identified the extracted paragraph, check the sentences before and after the gap to make sure it fits with both surrounding paragraphs.
- After you have selected a paragraph for each of the gaps, check that the extra paragraph does not fit anywhere.

3 Seven paragraphs have been removed from the article. Choose from the paragraphs A–H the one which fits each gap (1–7). There is one extra paragraph which you do not need to use.

A Despite the legal work on the *idea* of freedom of the high seas, nothing concrete materialised for centuries. The finer details of an agreement which would satisfy all the nations involved would require serious time and effort; therefore it was not until the mid-20th century that treaties started to be drafted and ratified.

B The birth of the United Nations in the mid-20th century had heralded a sea change in how the world came together to agree on matters of environmental importance. Since then, it has consistently been part of marine conservation and as recently as 2023 created a new agreement. This latest, The High Seas Treaty, will designate 30% of the oceans as protected zones and has been hailed as an historic piece of legislation, an example of working around national interests for a global solution.

C Getting countries to sign up for these types of treaties is a delicate balance of encouragement, incentives and diplomacy. Some can be hesitant until they know what's in it for them, and others can be overly enthusiastic. Emotions can run high in highly polluted regions or areas where fishing is an important livelihood, but negotiations must be entered into in good faith.

D The current international approach to marine conservation has its roots in the development of two key areas during the 17th century, the rule of law and the establishment of trading routes. The initial treaties and agreements, often drawn up between neighbouring countries, focused on getting wider access to the oceans' resources either for feeding ever growing domestic populations or for international commerce.

E This expansion in maritime trade meant that competition for resources grew fierce. Maintaining access to the oceans was vital for many seafaring nations, especially those whose economies depended on fish. As fishermen and traders extended their routes, thoughts turned to protectionism and thus the idea of treating their territorial or coastal waters differently from the high seas was born.

F There were several initial attempts which received a lukewarm reaction in some parts of the world, but in 1982 comprehensive agreement finally prevailed and the United Nations Convention on the Law of the Sea was signed. It was seen as a ground-breaking moment in international law, one which showed how collaboration could be achieved through hard work and determination.

G Back in the 1970s, marine conservation as a discipline was still young, and little was known about the oceans. Scientists had a more thorough knowledge of the moon than the oceans and they had no feasible ways of getting to the depths of the oceans or sea beds in order to carry out research. This changed with the advent of underwater cameras and other enabling technology.

H The initial concept put forward as a potential solution was that of making the high seas free for ships from any country to travel through. As a result of promoting the view that the oceans connect the world and therefore should be a shared resource, this became accepted. This fundamental shift from the idea of territorial acquisition to shared ownership was key to how ocean management would develop over the centuries.

Reading and Use of English Part 7 Multiple matching

What to expect in the exam

- In Part 7, the text is divided into several sections. There are ten questions which should be matched to the correct section.
- There may be more than one statement connected to a section.
- The task focuses on understanding detail, attitude and opinion.

How to go about it

Read the whole question carefully. While elements of the question may be addressed in various sections, only one of the sections will reflect the whole question accurately.

1 SPEAK Work in groups and discuss the questions.

1. Do you own a pair of trainers? Do you wear them on a daily basis or just when you are doing sport?
2. Do you have a favourite brand of trainers? What do you like about them?
3. Why do you think trainers have become such desirable fashion items?

2 Read through *How a love of designer trainers can sneak up on you* on page 66 and decide which of the five people most closely matches your views on trainers.

3 You are going to read an article about trainers. For questions 1–10, choose from the people (A–E). The people may be chosen more than once.

Which person mentions ...

the universally favourable reception given to a pair of designer trainers?		1
the outcome of having had a change of heart about the relevance of trainers?		2
a rational approach to the extravagance of their spending on trainers?		3
an experience which was a determining factor in their employment?		4
the description of an action that was contrary to their usual behaviour?		5
a habit that came about as a result of a one-off unexpected event?		6
the competitive nature underpinning the designer trainer industry?		7
a misunderstanding about trainer fashion which is prevalent amongst the public?		8
a means of making money from trainers that took some time to come to fruition?		9
the way that trainers facilitate their being able to stand out from the crowd?		10

HOW A LOVE OF DESIGNER TRAINERS CAN SNEAK UP ON YOU

A CHARLIE

As an American, they'll always be sneakers to me and I'm afraid to say that social media is responsible for my obsession with, or – as I prefer to call it – *appreciation* of limited edition designs. Despite the widespread belief that the intertwining of basketball with hip-hop and breakdancing is behind this phenomenon, social media had far more impact in terms of collectability. Granted the roots lie in 1970s American street culture but it was actually post 2010 with the rise of online images and internet commerce that things really took off. One day as I was idly scrolling through my feed, my attention was grabbed by these amazing custom designed sneakers. I'd never seen such eye-catching designs and I immediately bought them, ignoring their somewhat eyewatering price tag, and since then I've never looked back.

B RAMONA

Image is fundamental to the world of advertising and as an advertising executive, my employer has high expectations of me to look the part, especially since it's something that affects a client's perception of expertise. Regarding suits, I find understated classics more appropriate than designer gear, but trainers are a whole other story. Quality is first and foremost, something sturdy made from durable materials because I'm on my feet all day long, but that's not to say that design isn't a factor. Scouring the internet for lesser-known brands gives me the opportunity to make a statement with my footwear. While I acknowledge that this attitude is always going to incur substantial financial outlay, I see it as an investment and it's not as though I've built up a huge collection – just a select few pairs.

C JESSIE

It must have been at the beginning of the 2010s when I won my first online auction for a pair of limited-edition trainers. The impulsive nature of my purchase took me somewhat by surprise, but as soon as I spotted them online I knew I had to own them. Their design was unlike anything I'd laid eyes on previously and therefore the compliments and envious glances I received from colleagues, friends and strangers alike came as little surprise. Until then, I'd been oblivious of this 'trainers as collectors' items' trend, one that's often based on celebrity endorsement. Gradually, it dawned on me that selling them could have earned me several times more than I paid, but I wanted to show them off so wore them to death. I kept a close eye on the resale market noticing the incredible markup in some cases and later set up what ultimately turned out to be a reasonably profitable side hustle.

D YOSHIE

Whilst at fashion school, I did an internship with a designer specialising in sports footwear, the leading name at the time, and so a great placement. His designs were extraordinary; radical and flamboyant to the point of being slightly garish at times, but nevertheless they were snapped up by celebrities eager to ditch their swanky designer heels for something comfortable yet stylish. To my utter surprise, at the end of the internship I was given a pair. I couldn't believe my luck and after a matter of days I realised that their comfort was second to none and this was where my career path lay. I managed to land a job as a junior designer in an up-and-coming footwear studio, where I've worked on all sorts of innovative designs and my own style has gone from strength to strength.

E THOMAS

Running a boutique footwear store means I have to keep up to date with my clients' shifting tastes and the boom in designer trainer sales some years ago made me take a more favourable position. Where once heels were the go-to shoe for office wear, sales have declined so much so that it doesn't make any financial sense to maintain a large stock. Replacing them with a selective, but high-quality set of designer trainer brands has done wonders for the business. Clients can also order custom-made designs from a couple of our suppliers which is great as it creates loyalty and repeat business. The sector is pretty cut-throat these days and it pays dividends to stay abreast of all the emerging players on the scene as well as what's trending online among customers.

5 NEWS TRAVELS FAST

KEY LANGUAGE

Cohesion
Demonstratives
Neutral and sensationalist language
Binomials

IDIOMS

Communication

EXAM PRACTICE

Reading and Use of English Parts 1, 2, 4 & 6
Writing Part 2
Listening Part 4
Speaking Parts 1 & 3

Speaking Part 1 Interview

Work with a partner. Discuss the questions.

1 How have our news sources changed in the last 100 years?
2 To what extent do you think word-of-mouth sources can be trusted?
3 How much confidence do you have in online or printed news sources?
4 What issues in the news are most important to you?
5 What issues can work to undermine public trust in journalism?

5 NEWS TRAVELS FAST

Reading and Use of English Part 6 Gapped text

1 SPEAK Work in pairs and discuss the following questions.

1 What do you think draws people in to reading certain news articles?

2 Do you think in general people prioritise trustworthiness over sensationalism? Why / Why not?

2 You are going to read an article on attracting newspaper readership. Seven paragraphs have been removed from the article. Choose from the paragraphs A–H the one which fits each gap (1–7). There is one extra paragraph which you do not need to use.

READ ALL ABOUT IT!

It's good to be *in the know*, so to speak, but how much do we really know of what's going on in the world around us? We tend to assume that news outlets will keep us well-informed on any subject we might care to know about, but we overlook the fact that news isn't just a service, it's a business. In fact, many go so far as to claim that, for some news sources, offering objective information isn't even on their radar.

1 ______

The Great Moon Hoax of 1835, where the *New York Sun* published a series of articles detailing astronomer John Herschel's supposed observations of unicorns and giant man-bats on the moon, is a case in point. Regrettably, Herschel himself, deeply ensconced in study and thousands of miles away in South Africa, was powerless to counteract these absurd claims.

2 ______

Fortunately for us, there are some tell-tale signs of such news articles that are still helpful to the general reader today. Firstly, large graphics and pictures are frequently used to entice the reader, in addition to sensationalist language. After all, hard-hitting words like *scrap* or *oust* can easily draw more attention than boring old *remove* ever will.

3 ______

These techniques have been used by some in the news business since the beginning of the 20th century and still are today. However, where the news once wore its banner of ownership quite clearly, now it's a lot harder to discern its origin. With one click, we can be taken through a tour of any number of news sites without ever knowing who owns them or their veracity.

4 ______

I'm sure I'm not the only one who has clicked on links like 'This is how you earn $1000 an hour' or 'You won't believe what child stars look like NOW!' only to see old, hackneyed information that is no surprise, and certainly no news to anyone. But that's the way sites can make money, and it's everywhere.

5 ______

A study of 200,000 social media users by Beihang University in China, found that posts exploiting those kinds of emotions are three times more likely to be shared or retweeted than any other kind. So, perhaps there is some truth in the old adage that 'bad news travels fast', whether it turns out to be fact or fiction.

6 ______

It is situations like this, and the distribution of far more serious misinformation, that has led to the rise of fact-checking websites in more recent times, which, although perhaps going some way to offering us reliability in our news, are by no means a panacea. There are over 300 fact-checking websites throughout the world, and they are still dwarfed by the sheer volume of misinformation on the internet.

7 ______

What we can say with some certainty is that although the truth may well be out there, it isn't always easy to find. Even the savviest reader can fall prey to a hoax story or two, so how can we expect to know the difference?

A Today's is an endless stream, and dubious or even fake news continues to be an effective way of making money. In fact, many of today's news stories shouldn't genuinely qualify as news. They are simply there to generate clicks by dangling a tasty morsel of a story that inevitably turns out to be disappointing.

B Anything that frequently cites 'anonymous sources' should also be eyed with caution, especially in investigative articles on the rich and famous, as the likelihood is that the source is simply non-existent. Likewise, anything in the article that is overtly fanning the flames of excitement, anger, or controversy should raise suspicion.

C There was uproar on social media when a banned books list was circulated for Florida schools, and on it was the American classic *To Kill a Mockingbird*. The list was shared widely, even though its source was unknown, and in fact, a complete fabrication. Fortunately, in this case, the Florida state government proved that the book was on the schools reading list.

D What makes it impossible to resist a non-news story? Do we truly enjoy these stories, or just read them because they're there? Well, engagement usually starts from an emotional response, so like news headlines, titles of links are there to whip up some form of excitement, and there is some indication that the most effective way to do so is to target anger and indignation.

E However, we shouldn't feel too ashamed of falling for something like this. After all, it happens to the best of us. A number of books, and even the Scottish government had referenced one 'Alan MacMasters' as the inventor of the toaster, unwittingly falling for the fake information put online by a class of students.

F Accusations of 'yellow journalism' were levied against some big-name newspapers virtually at their foundation, proving that this aspersion is not just a 21st century phenomenon. This term described a paper that published salacious and sensationalist stories, the accuracy of which seemed neither here nor there to the newspaper, but in doing so, resulted in increased circulation.

G We, the readers, also have a part to play by thinking and checking before we share news. However, while people who are unsure about an issue tend to look up their sources, unfortunately those with stronger opinions tend not to bother to corroborate any evidence that supports their ideas.

H Needless to say, this supposed scoop of theirs sold in incredible quantities, which was a great bonus for a paper that relied on advertising revenue for its income. After all, why would the advertisers focus on the reliability of stories, when the ones with the biggest reaction sold the most?

3 SPEAK **Work in small groups. Discuss the headlines in the picture.**

1 Why do you think people would click on these links? How do they use language to sell the topic?

2 What do you think the news stories might be about? Are they news?

Language focus Cohesion

1 Find the following sentences in the article on pages 68 and 69 and decide what the words in bold refer to.

1 This term described a paper that published salacious and sensationalist stories, the accuracy of which seemed neither here nor there to the newspaper, but **in doing so**, resulted in increased circulation.

2 Needless to say, **this supposed scoop of theirs** sold in incredible quantities, which was a great bonus for a paper that relied on advertising revenue for its income.

3 After all, why would the advertisers focus on the reliability of stories, when **the ones** with the biggest reaction sold the most?

4 Fortunately for us, there are some tell-tale signs of **such** news articles that are still helpful to the general reader today.

5 These techniques have been used by some in the news business since the beginning of the 20th century **and still are** today.

6 **Today's** is an endless stream, and dubious or even fake news continues to be an effective way of making money.

7 ... titles of links are there to whip up some form of excitement, and there is some indication that the most effective way **to do so** is to target anger and indignation.

8 A study of 200,000 social media users by Beihang University in China, found that posts exploiting those kinds of emotions are three times more likely to be shared or retweeted **than any other kind**.

2 Go to Ready for Grammar on page 216–217 for further rules, explanations and practice.

3 The sentences in Exercise 1 use cohesive ties to avoid repetition and to link ideas together inside and across paragraphs. Decide whether each sentence is an example of reference, substitution, or ellipsis.

4 Complete the text using words from the box. You need to use one of the words twice.

each hers one ones other so such

The Incredible Life of Nellie Bly

When everyone says you can't do something, is your response to accept it or carry on regardless? If so, maybe you should take a leaf out of Nellie Bly's book, an inspiring example of someone who fought against the limitations being imposed on them at the time. (1) ____________ was a life full of ground-breaking adventure and pioneering investigative journalism. She got her start at the *Pittsburgh Dispatch* in 1885, where she was confined to writing about only a limited number of topics, just the (2) ____________ that covered so-called 'women's issues' at the time, like fashion or housekeeping. Wanting more, she decided to try other newspapers, but (3) ____________ of them had the same response as the (4) ____________, a resounding 'No!', until one day, she managed to get a job from the *New York World*. In what was fundamentally investigative journalism, Nellie had to go undercover in a hospital as a patient in order to report on its conditions. In doing (5) ____________, the subsequent article was a great coup for the *New York World*, becoming the first newspaper to publish (6) ____________ a piece – and by a woman, too! But that was not adventure enough for Nellie, and in 1890 she decided to recreate the famous fictional journey of Mr Fogg's in *Around the World in Eighty Days*, the result of which not only saw her best her own goal of 75 days, but by completing it in 72 days she also set a new world record. With determination like (7) ____________, perhaps Nellie's success was never in any doubt. So, remember, even when the odds are against you, like Nellie herself, don't let any opportunity be the (8) ____________ that got away.

5 SPEAK In pairs, discuss the questions below.

1 Which other real-life figures can you think of who have stood up for themselves in the face of adversity and been successful due to their strong sense of determination?

2 What kind of skills do you think good reporters need? Which of these areas do you think you would excel in?

Vocabulary Neutral and sensationalist language

1 **SPEAK** Look at the article on page 68. What two synonyms of *remove* does it mention? What does the article say about these kinds of synonyms?

2 Read the words in the box and match them to the words 1–7 that are closest to their meaning.

axe clash condemn dispute divulge laud leak pledge provoke quash slam spark tout vow

1	stop	*axe*	______
2	criticise	______	______
3	promise	______	______
4	cause	______	______
5	praise	______	______
6	disagree	______	______
7	reveal	______	______

3 Synonyms can sometimes differ slightly in meaning, how they fit grammatically within a sentence, or which words they collocate with. For the headlines (1–7) below, decide if both words in italics can be used with little change in meaning or if only one of the words is possible.

1. Closure of iconic cinema *sparks* / *provokes* protests from local community.
2. Three-time Oscar nominee *touted* / *lauded* to clean up for portrayal of US leader in recent release.
3. Residents *clash* / *dispute* with police after three days of violence in the area.
4. Long running drama *Crossways* to be *quashed* / *axed* after ratings slump.
5. The Prime Minister has now *vowed* / *pledged* his support to organisations struggling during the recession.
6. Business leaders *slam* / *condemn* government for funding cuts.
7. 'I never *divulge* / *leak* my age to anyone but my husband,' claims screen star.

4 Complete the news article with the correct form of a word from the box.

clash dispute divulge laud leak quash vow

The NEWS Watch live

Home UK World Politics Climate Science and Technology Travel Sport

TOP STORIES

As expected, those implicated in the **(1)** ______ documents were quick to deny their involvement and distance themselves from the allegations of financial misconduct. Ministers have moved swiftly **(2)** ______ the claims, labelling the information as fabricated and questioning its authenticity. They vehemently deny any wrongdoing and **(3)** ______ to prove the revelations to be a politically motivated ploy by the opposition to undermine current reforms.

Voices from the opposition however **(4)** ______ the leaks, arguing that the documents released provide irrefutable evidence of abuse of power by those currently in position. They are demanding accountability and transparency from the government, calling for those involved to be removed from position with immediate effect.

While the government and the opposition continue to **(5)** ______, the public look for clarity on who to believe. With the origin and veracity of the information highly **(6)** ______ and with those who published the material refusing to **(7)** ______ their sources, there is no doubt this issue will be fiercely debated for days to come.

Speaking Part 3 Long turn

1 SPEAK Work in pairs. Read the topic cards and questions.

Student A: Talk for about two minutes about the question below.

Student B: When Student A has finished, say to what extent you agree that instantaneous and widespread coverage of local and world events has benefitted society.

How do different types of media have competing functions?
- to inform
- to educate
- to entertain

Student B: Talk for two minutes about the question below.

Student A: When Student B has finished, discuss how far the rise of video calls and virtual meeting platforms has affected our communication skills.

What is the most effective way for governments to communicate information to citizens?
- directly through email or post
- on social media
- via the press

Useful language

You can use the following phrases to hedge your opinion and make it less definite:

I suppose it's conceivable / possible that ...

I'm not sure how feasible / plausible it would be ...

I'm no expert, but maybe ...

I (kind of / sort of) feel that ...

It's not up to me but maybe ...

If I had to hazard an opinion / guess ...

It's pure conjecture, but ...

This is just speculation, but ...

I wouldn't like to say for sure ...

It's certainly not clear cut, but ...

I'm inclined to think / believe ...

2 Take turns to answer one topic card each.

3 SPEAK In the final part of Part 3 of the Speaking test, the examiner will ask you questions which are related to the topics you have just discussed. Discuss the following questions.

1 In what ways do you think technology helps or hinders the quality of news information?

2 Do you think it is the responsibility of governments to keep their citizens informed, or is it up to individual responsibility?

3 They say 'news travels fast, and bad news travels faster'. To what extent do you agree with this?

4 It is said that the media can do more harm than good. To what extent do you agree with this opinion?

5 In what ways, if at all, do you think the press should be regulated?

Reading and Use of English Part 1 Multiple-choice cloze

1 For questions **1–8**, read the text below and decide which answer (**A**, **B**, **C** or **D**) best fits each gap. There is an example at the beginning (**0**).

FURY OVER LEAKED PYLON PLANS

An unnamed energy company has the **(0)** ___B___ for an extensive network of pylons to be constructed across the Welsh countryside, according to documents leaked to *The Weekly Bulletin*, causing **(1)** ________ among local community groups and charities alike.

The proposed plans would see over 60 miles of transmission cables and a series of 100-foot pylons link up electricity users throughout the region, plans which are completely at **(2)** ________ with local preservation efforts.

Campaigners have repeatedly **(3)** ________ to both the company and government ministers to come **(4)** ________ with the public about their agenda for power provision in the country, fearing an initiative such as this. A nature preservation charity spokesman **(5)** ________ the plan as putting 'a permanent scar on the beautiful natural surroundings that Wales has to offer'.

Many environmental groups are up in **(6)** ________ about the plans, citing that for an energy company to put these plans down in writing is a bold move, yet these plans are far from being cut and **(7)** ________. Government approval is outstanding, and many hope they will be **(8)** ________ rejected, but many are asking questions of why the government hasn't released this news, rather than discovering via a leak.

	A	B	C	D
0	schemes	blueprints	layouts	frameworks
1	frenzy	hassle	mayhem	uproar
2	edge	odds	stake	risk
3	appealed	claimed	dictated	challenged
4	clean	out	open	true
5	castigated	maligned	condemned	belittled
6	heads	arms	hands	shoulders
7	clothed	copied	dried	drained
8	broadly	commonly	abundantly	roundly

2 **SPEAK** In pairs, discuss what kind of newspaper this article has come from. What evidence from the text do you have to support this?

Vocabulary Binomials

1 Binomials are two words joined by short linking words (usually *and* or *or*) to form a fixed expression. Look at the binomial *cut and dried* in the text on page 73. Discuss the meaning using the context to help you.

2 Complete the sentences with the correct binomial ending in the box.

cheese	error	foremost	forth	go	large	outs	starts	take	tested	white

1 **First and** ____________, you must enjoy talking to people if you want to work in the media.

2 My father has worked in international business for over 20 years and knows all the **ins and** ____________ of negotiating with overseas clients.

3 We can go **back and** ____________ all day over the edits for this article, but I don't think we'll be any closer to agreeing.

4 **By and** ____________ the book was well received, although a few people questioned its historical accuracy in places.

5 It was **touch and** ____________ at first for both drivers involved in the collision, but they have both pulled through.

6 Learning to speak another language is a case of **trial and** ____________ I find. You're bound to get things wrong at first, but the more you practise, the better you'll get.

7 One **tried and** ____________ cure for writer's block is to get away from the screen and spend some time in nature.

8 The government's attempts to do something effective about crime seems to come in **fits and** ____________. They announce all these big plans, then nothing happens for months.

9 My boss and I are like **chalk and** ____________; she's always stressed and juggling a million things, while I'm more relaxed and take it all in my stride.

10 Relationships are all about **give and** ____________. Things are never one-sided and it's always important to see your partner's point of view, even if you might not necessarily agree.

11 Press freedom isn't a **black and** ____________ issue; while freedom of information and transparency is essential, so is the right to privacy for those in the news.

3 Complete the text about journalism with some of the binomials in Exercise 2.

THE 'DOS AND DON'TS' OF GOOD JOURNALISM

The road to a career in journalism can often be a rocky one, where competition is fierce and opportunities are scarce, but don't let this deter you if it's your dream job, as it certainly is a rewarding career once you get your foot in the door. Before you go down the path of journalism, let's work out if it's the right career for you with our top tips:

1 **(1)** ____________________, remember it's your job to dig up the facts and pass them on, so your communication skills need to be top-drawer. Put people at ease to give you that advantage when it comes to getting the facts.

2 Don't lose your patience! Stories don't always develop as you'd like them to. They tend to go in **(2)** ____________________ – you could be waiting for ages for a development and then suddenly it's all go. So, be patient, but be ready!

3 Try to be objective and find out the facts. A good journalist goes **(3)** ____________________ between different primary sources in order to double-check their facts and make sure they get multiple perspectives.

4 Know your stuff – understanding all the **(4)** ____________________ of a story is paramount, so spend time doing lots of research. At first, this is bound to be a time-consuming and daunting task, but soon enough you'll establish **(5)** ____________ methods for getting all of the information you need.

5 Working your way through difficult investigations can be hard. **(6)** ____________________, they tend not to be **(7)** ____________________. On the contrary, they will often throw up more questions than they answer, which can get frustrating. But don't throw in the towel. It's your job to get down to brass tacks.

6 Remember – as with all jobs, it takes time to be a good journalist! You'll find things out through **(8)** ____________. Don't worry about making these mistakes, they are part and parcel of starting any new career.

4 SPEAK Discuss the questions.

1 Is there anything else you would you add to the list of dos and don'ts?
2 Do you think you have what it takes to work in journalism? Why / Why not?
3 Do you think you are a good communicator in general? In what social situations do you find it easier or more difficult to interact with others?

Pronunciation Binomials

1 5.1 Binomials using *and* often have a common pronunciation pattern. Listen to the example *chop and change* and answer the questions.

1 Which word has the longer vowel sound, *chop* or *change*?
2 Which word is stressed more, *chop* or *change*?
3 Which word is connected to the *and*?

2 SPEAK Look at the list of binomials on page 74. Discuss whether they follow the same pattern as *chop and change*.

3 5.2 Listen and check your answers to Exercise 2.

About English

Did you know that there are trinomials, too? One example of a trinomial is *cool, calm and collected*. Think of some more trinomials that you might know. Use these words to help you:

here, … hook, … beg, … blood, …

4 SPEAK In groups, look at the list of binomials that are connected by the words *or* and *by*. Do they follow the same pattern as those connected by *and*?

all or nothing bit by bit sooner or later step by step

Listening Part 4 Multiple matching

1 5.3 You will hear five short extracts in which people are talking about communication errors.

Don't forget!

Use your time carefully before you listen. Read the instructions and each of the options carefully. Consider any differences and similarities between the options before you listen.

TASK ONE

For questions **1–5**, choose from the list **(A–H)**, what caused each of the communication errors.

TASK TWO

For questions **6–10**, choose from the list **(A–H)**, what the effect of the error was.

While you listen you must complete both tasks.

Task One

A an unplanned comment
B background noise
C mistaken identity
D being distracted
E confusing fact and fiction
F mishearing information
G careless reading
H a speech impediment

Speaker 1 [ ] 1
Speaker 2 [ ] 2
Speaker 3 [ ] 3
Speaker 4 [ ] 4
Speaker 5 [ ] 5

Task Two

A the loss of a job
B a confession of what happened
C the anger of a politician
D an enlarged audience
E the cancellation of an important visitor
F an awkward public appearance
G an unintended good time
H a feeling of embarrassment

Speaker 1 [ ] 6
Speaker 2 [ ] 7
Speaker 3 [ ] 8
Speaker 4 [ ] 9
Speaker 5 [ ] 10

2 SPEAK Discuss the questions in groups.

1 Which of these stories would you consider the funniest or the most embarrassing?
2 In which of these stories did the *news travel fast*? Why?
3 Have you or anyone you know ever experienced any crossed wires like this? What happened?

Language focus Demonstratives

1 Complete the sentences from the listening. Use ONE word in each space.

1 I wanted to visit my uncle in Australia, and there was __________ flight I saw online that was a bargain.

2 I still wonder how many people are telling __________ ridiculous 'fact' of mine.

3 It's so hard to plan for __________ sorts of deviations.

4 Well, __________ error of mine caused the biggest turnout they'd ever had!

2 Go to Ready for Grammar on page 216 for further rules, explanations and practice.

3 Look at the sentences in Exercise 1 again and discuss how they are connected to the rules. Which sentences are positive, negative or neither?

4 Complete the text with *this*, *that* or *those*.

'In my college, they've got **(1)** __________ custom of using spoken assessments. I hadn't read the prospectus properly so had no idea and was absolutely panic-stricken when I found out. I'm not one of **(2)** __________ people who enjoys being in the limelight – at all. My friend said she had **(3)** __________ book about helping nervous people speak. Although, I'm not into **(4)** __________ kinds of self-help theories, I thought I may as well give it a go. One piece of advice was to own up to the audience and admit my nerves. Well, **(5)** __________ tip of his really saved me. Before, I'd thought of public speaking as a confrontational activity, but now I feel it's much more collaborative. I'm positive that **(6)** __________ new skill of mine will help me one day get a job in marketing.'

Writing Part 2 Article

Don't forget!

Articles should be engaging as well as informative, so it's important to grab the reader's attention at the start and then hold the reader's attention throughout the article.

1 Read the Writing Part 2 task below. Underline the points you need to include in your article.

A magazine is running a series of articles on effective communication in international contexts. You decide to submit an article in which you describe someone who demonstrates the ability to communicates effectively in a second language. You should also explain what personal qualities help make people effective communicators in international contexts.

Write your article in 280–320 words.

2 **Read the model answer to the Part 2 task in Exercise 1. Choose which option below (A or B) is the most appropriate introduction for the article.**

A Effective communication is of the utmost importance in international contexts, and nowhere is this more evident than in sports. This article describes one particularly effective communicator, the multilingual tennis star Roger Federer, with the goal of showing what personal qualities can help a person communicate effectively in a second language.

B He thinks carefully before he responds. Throughout the four interviews, each conducted in a different language, his answers are thoughtful yet concise and easy to understand. You might think I'm describing a high-level diplomat, but you would be wrong. The person who I am describing is the tennis star, Roger Federer.

(1) ______________

During his 25-year career, Federer travelled the world, playing thousands of tennis matches but also giving thousands of interviews. No matter who he spoke to, no matter how exhausted or disappointed he was after a match, Federer was always friendly and polite, looking just as comfortable in front of the camera or microphone as he did on the court. And he would regularly give four interviews in a row – in English, French, German and Swiss German.

Federer is from Basel, Switzerland, and grew up multilingual. He was educated in German but at home spoke Swiss German with his father and English with his mother, who is from South Africa. As a teenager, he moved to the French-speaking part of Switzerland to pursue his tennis career. There he quickly mastered French.

But what makes Federer an effective communicator is not his vocabulary or grammar. Indeed, it is when he reaches his limits that he really shines. Let me explain. Federer speaks his second, third and fourth languages well but far from perfectly. He makes plenty of mistakes, but he does not seem the least bit bothered. When he doesn't understand something, he just smiles and says, 'Sorry, I didn't get that.'

In international contexts, people often focus on avoiding misunderstandings. But Federer demonstrates a better approach: If you are modest and polite, people will give you the benefit of the doubt when you say the wrong thing or misunderstand something, allowing the interaction to quickly get back on track. It might be a bit messy, but this is what real effective communication consists of in international contexts.

3 **Read the following tips (1–6) for holding the reader's attention. Which ones did the writer follow in the article about Roger Federer?**

1. Choose a topic their readers will find interesting.
2. Alternate long and short sentences. This creates a nice flow.
3. Create anticipation, for example, by using phrases like 'Not convinced?' or 'Here's why.'
4. Tell a story. The reader will want to know what happens next.
5. Avoid information overload. If you go into too much detail, readers get bored.
6. Make it personal. Don't be afraid to refer to your own experiences.

4 **SPEAK** **Compare your answers to Exercise 3 with a classmate. Give examples.**

5 **Now write your own answer to the task in Exercise 1. For more information about articles, see** **page 192****.**

5 REVIEW

Reading and Use of English Part 2 Open Cloze

For questions **1–8**, read the text below and think of the word that best fits each space. Use only one word in each space. There is an example at the beginning **(0)**.

BUSINESS COMMUNICATION

Communication is important in **(0)** *ALL* walks of life, that's for certain, but no more **(1)** __________ than in business, where it can **(2)** __________ the scales between success and failure. While there aren't any hard and **(3)** __________ rules for good communication, certainly one advantage is to know your audience inside out, and tailor your communication accordingly. This involves discerning the others' wants, needs and goals, as well as recognising your **(4)** __________. For example, if you work in IT support, clarity and patience may serve you well, but in sales an ability to conjure **(5)** __________ an image of how your product can improve a client's life is essential. Additionally, try to think on your feet, adapt to your audience and remember there is only so **(6)** __________ talking you can do: you *must* listen too. Communication is very much a two-way street, and only **(7)** __________ paying close attention to the people around you will you be able to understand their needs. We may **(8)** __________ it as read that communication doesn't exist in a vacuum, but you'd be surprised at how many people forget this most basic fact.

Vocabulary Neutral and sensationalist language | Binominals

Complete the text with the words in the box. Change the word forms if needed.

axe black and white cut and dried leak spark touch and go tout tried and tested

According to reports, one of the largest employers in insurance services, Demnity, is set to **(1)** __________ over 5000 employees from its regional offices in the coming months. The move has **(2)** __________ widespread outrage from employees and unions alike. While a spokesman for the company claimed that the situation was far from **(3)** __________ and no formal decision had been taken, an official document **(4)** __________ to us from an inside source indicates there is no going back on the issue. Demnity's future has been **(5)** __________ for months after its annual report revealed the company had faced losses of over 30 million pounds in the last year. **(6)** __________ as a game changer in the insurance industry only 10 years ago, the downfall of Demnity has been rapid and severe. With their decline now being reported in **(7)** __________, we could well see a return to the more **(8)** __________ insurance model of the past.

Reading and Use of English

Part 4 Key word transformations

For questions 1–6, complete the second sentence so that it has a similar meaning to the first sentence, using the word given. Do not change the word given. You must use between three and eight words, including the word given.

1 I can't persuade her to stand in for me, despite my great efforts.

MIGHT

Try ______________________________ her, she won't stand in for me.

2 I only thought about becoming a writer because of my English teacher's influence.

BEEN

If ______________________________ of my English teacher, I'd never have considered becoming a writer.

3 Jennifer believes she's got the best job in the world, but I don't think it's that great.

END

Jennifer thinks her new job is the ______________________________ all, but I don't agree.

4 Millions of mites around us can only be seen under microscopes.

NAKED

Millions of mites around us are ______________________________ eye.

5 The flavour of the dish won't be as good if you use a shop-bought stock.

EXPENSE

You can use a shop-bought stock, but it will ______________________________ the dish's flavour.

6 The fact that all the governments agreed to the treaty is absolutely miraculous.

SHORT

It's ______________________________ that all the governments agreed to the treaty.

Writing Part 2 Report

You are a volunteer writer for a college newspaper. The editor is considering including a section dedicated to national news in the paper. You have been asked to write a report to the editor assessing two national newspapers or news websites. You should briefly describe the style of the newspapers, as well as the types of news stories and features they cover. You should also consider their reputation, and evaluate how each of these sources will appeal to the college audience.

Write your **report** in **280–320** words.

For more information on writing reports, see page 194.

Idioms Communication

1 5.4 Listen to the two conversations and answer the questions.

1 What do you think the contexts are?

2 Which conversation is more polite? How do you know?

2 5.4 Listen to the conversations again. Write the idioms you hear next to their meanings.

0 divulge some information *spill the beans*

1 avoid talking about the main point or issue ______

2 hear something for the first time ______

3 get confused and failed to understand each other ______

4 to understand (despite missing information) ______

3 Use the words in the box to complete the definitions below.

boo to a goose | out of the loop | something off your chest | the wrong end of the stick | touch base

1 When you **are** ______ you are unaware about information relating to a certain matter.

2 When you ______ **with someone** you make or renew contact with them.

3 If you **get** ______, you have misunderstood something.

4 People who **don't say** ______ are very quiet, shy people who do not like speaking up.

5 To **get** ______ means to tell someone about something that has been bothering or annoying you, making you feel relieved to talk about it.

4 SPEAK Look at the meanings and their corresponding idioms in Exercises 2 and 3. Which idioms soften their original meanings?

5 Decide if the following sentences below could be softened by an idiom and rewrite the ones that could.

1 Why don't we **have a meeting** next week to discuss your idea for the article?

2 Thw storm warning wasn't very clear and many people **were totally confused** and went out anyway!

3 This programme really **avoids talking about the true issues** on the topic of politics.

4 I haven't heard anything from the sales team for so long, **I have no idea what's going on**.

5 Look, I know something's wrong – you've been acting completely out of character. Come on, **tell me!**

6 SPEAK Work in pairs. Discuss the following questions.

1 When was the last time you completely **got the wrong end of the stick** about something? What happened?

2 How often do you **touch base** with old friends?

3 Do you prefer people to **beat around the bush** or get straight to the point when discussing important things with you?

4 Why is it important for people to **get their problems off their chest**? Do you think this is always the right thing to do?

About English

Sometimes idioms can be used to soften language, for example to say *I'm out of the loop* is a softer, more polite way of saying *nobody told me.*

Think about your own language. Do idioms sometimes soften your speech in the same way?

Discussing idioms

Discuss the differences in meaning between these idioms:

- be out of the loop / be in the dark
- touch base / cover all the bases
- get something off your chest / get a monkey off your back

6 HIGHS AND LOWS

KEY LANGUAGE

Conditional clauses
Expressions and phrases with *pay*
Rise and *fall*

IDIOMS

Money and wealth

EXAM PRACTICE

Reading and Use of English Parts 3, 4 & 7
Writing Parts 1 & 2
Listening Parts 1 & 2
Speaking Parts 1 & 2

Speaking Part 1 Interview

Work with a partner. Discuss the questions.

1 What kinds of jobs are you attracted to? Why?

2 Do you view your job as an integral part of your identity?

3 Which would interest you more, any well remunerated position in a company or a prestigious managerial role?

4 It is said that the best things in life are free. How much truth is there in this?

5 How important is it to have diversity, equity and inclusion in the workplace?

6 HIGHS AND LOWS

Listening Part 1 Multiple choice

1 SPEAK Work in pairs. Answer the questions.

1 Which of your family or friends has the most unusual or interesting job? What makes it so unique?

2 If money were no object and your job enabled you to work from anywhere in the world, where would you choose and why?

2 6.1 You will hear three different extracts. For questions 1–6, choose the answer (A, B or C) which fits best according to what you hear. There are two questions for each extract.

Extract One

You hear someone talking about their job on a yacht.

1 The speaker says that her job satisfaction depends on

A the people onboard.

B her professional conduct.

C having convenient hours.

2 What does the speaker say about yacht owners?

A Their numbers have dwindled.

B They have an enviable lifestyle.

C The majority are not affluent.

Extract Two

You hear part of a conversation between two colleagues about work.

3 How does Jacob feel about his work?

A He is likely to remain with his current employer.

B He lacks confidence in his performance.

C He would like a more challenging position.

4 Zandra's dream work location would be somewhere

A far from civilisation.

B close to her relatives.

C without any ties.

Extract Three

You hear part of a podcast about money-saving tips.

5 What is the advisor's main message?

A It's vital to protect against unforeseen financial circumstances.

B When it comes to financial planning, people ignore the future.

C People should save as large a proportion of their income as possible.

6 The advisor says that saving money is

A easier said than done.

B at odds with modern life.

C within everyone's reach.

3 SPEAK Are you good at saving money? Do you think saving for the future is important? Why / Why not?

Pronunciation Assimilation

1 **Read the extracts from the listening and practise saying them aloud. Focus on the pronunciation of the underlined consonants and select the sound you hear.**

1	in more detail	/ŋ/	/m/	/n/
2	the right captain	/k/	/b/	/p/
3	I've been getting	/n/	/ŋ/	/m/
4	they're good people	/d/	/k/	/b/
5	earn plenty of money	/m/	/b/	/ŋ/
6	you'd be surprised	/p/	/b/	/k/

2 **6.2 Now listen and check your answers to Exercise 1.**

3 **Read the the information about assimilation in the box.**

4 **SPEAK Work in pairs. Practise saying the sentences in the box.**

5 **For extra practice go to the Additional materials.**

Student A: Turn to page 196 and follow the instructions.

Student B: Turn to page 199 and follow the instructions.

Assimilation

In connected speech some consonant sounds at the ends of words change depending on the consonants at the beginning of the following words.

A Final consonants /t/ and /d/ sound more like /p/ /b/ /k/ or /g/ before words beginning with those sounds.

You should paint that bench with a different bright colour.

The company suffered great damage but got back on track later.

B Final consonant /n/ sounds more like /m/ before words beginning with /p/ /b/ /m/ or /ŋ/ before words beginning with /g/ or /k/.

When people earn money they want even more fine clothes.

Just ten minutes of rain gave us clean garden paths.

Vocabulary Expressions and phrases with *pay*

1 **Use the words from the box to complete definitions 1–9 of the expressions and phrases with *pay*.**

a compliment dividends it forward lip service the price through the nose tribute to your own way your respects

1 When you pay ________________, you don't allow others to pay for you.
2 The expression 'to pay ________________' is used when you do a kind action because another person was kind to you.
3 You pay ________________ to someone by welcoming them to somewhere new or by honouring them and attending their funeral after they die.
4 If you pay ________________ for something you have done, you experience something negative as a result.
5 Something that pays ________________ will bring a good result in the future.
6 An informal phrase used if you pay too much money for something: you pay ________________ for it.
7 If you pay someone ________________, you say something nice about or to them.
8 People that say they believe in something, but don't do anything to show their support, are said to be paying ________________ to it.
9 The phrase pay ________________ someone is often used on formal occasions to praise someone or something.

2 **SPEAK Work in groups. Discuss the following questions using the expressions from Exercise 1.**

1 The nicest compliment anyone has ever paid you. Who was the person? What did they say? How did it make you feel?
2 Something you bought that you had to pay through the nose for. What was it? Do you regret buying it?
3 A time when you chose to pay your own way instead of accepting money from someone. Why did you make this decision?
4 A mistake you made that you paid the price for later. What was it? What were the consequences?

Language focus Conditional clauses

1 Complete the extracts from the listening on page 82 with a phrase from the box.

even if in case of provided that supposing

1 ______________ you don't want to earn a fortune, the job is great.
2 And of course, the range of crafts is huge, so anyone can own one if they want, ______________ their budget isn't enormous.
3 ______________ your job was remote, like a digital nomad, so all you need is a laptop and your passport and you're good to go.
4 Just by putting aside a small amount per week would mean you'd soon build up a large enough nest egg ______________ a nasty surprise.

2 Cross out the options that cannot be used to complete each sentence.

1 I've been building up a nest egg, so we'd still manage to get by for several months *in the event that* / *on provision that* / *provided that* either of us got made redundant.
2 *But for* / *In case of* / *What if* a fire alarm, all staff should gather at outside the rear entrance to the building and remain there until they are told it is safe to return.
3 The flexible working policy allows all staff to work around their commitments, *so long as* / *in the event that* / *supposing* they do the allocated number of hours over a week.

3 Match the underlined conditional structures in sentences 1–5 to the type of conditional in the box.

zero first second third mixed

1 Imagine you had the opportunity to start your career over, what would you choose to do instead? ______
2 I have no objection to you brightening up the office with some plants so long as you don't go overboard. ______
3 The market can make a fool of first-time investors if they don't know what they're doing. ______
4 If I hadn't taken a gap year from university, I would be a qualified dentist by now. ______
5 What if we hadn't picked up the error in the report for the client? That would have been embarrassing. ______

4 Which of the sentences in Exercise 3 considers an imaginary situation in the past and its result in the present?

5 Match each mixed conditional sentence (1–5) with one of the explanations (a–e).

1 But for the success of their new smart phone, the company might have gone out of business.
2 If we hadn't missed our flight connection, we'd be going to the concert tonight.
3 Had you gone to the dentist like I told you to, you wouldn't be in so much pain now.
4 Were I not leaving the company next week, I would have been a speaker at the conference.
5 If my house wasn't being painted next week, I wouldn't be looking for a hotel.

a a present condition with a past result
b a past condition with a present result
c a past condition with a future result
d a future condition with a past result
e a future condition with a present result

6 Go to Ready for Grammar on page 218 for further rules, explanations and practice.

7 SPEAK Work in groups and answer the questions.

1 Imagine you had to organise a social event for your class. What would you choose and why?
2 If you hadn't learnt English, what other language would you like to have learnt?
3 What if you could start a new business, what would it be and why?

Vocabulary *Rise* and *fall*

1 SPEAK Work in pairs. What verbs can you think of that mean *rise* and *fall*?

2 In sentences 1–6, choose the words that collocate with the nouns in bold. For each sentence, one, two or all of the alternatives may be possible.

1 As oil prices rise, consumers have been hit by *spiralling / waning / soaring* **costs** in supermarkets and other stores. There are fears that landlords will soon *hike up / mount / dwindle* **rents** as they try to cover the recent spike in mortgage repayments.

2 Markets have been rocked by the announcement that the region's largest car producer will close several factories. **Sales** of diesel vehicles have gradually *swelled / waned / dwindled* in recent years and the company's **debt** has been *escalating / plummeting / mounting.*

3 By midday the **crowds** waiting to see the newly elected president had *hiked up / swelled / spiralled* to over fifty thousand.

4 Initially, **enthusiasm** for the strike saw a sharp increase among the workforce, however it began to *wane / hike up / dwindle* after months of negotiations took their toll and no resolution was reached.

5 Following a massive reduction in customer spending, **profits** at the firm *spiralled / mounted / plummeted* dramatically.

6 The government's economic policies proved to be their downfall as *spiralling / soaring / escalating* **unemployment** caused **discontent** to *soar / hike up / mount* among the younger population.

3 Put the verbs from Exercise 2 into the correct column. Which verb can mean both *rise* and *fall*?

rise	*fall*

4 Add the following verbs to the table in Exercise 3.

accelerate diminish plunge recede skyrocket slump surge

5 Decide which word (a, b, c or d) best fits the gap in each pair of sentences. The word you choose must fit both sentences.

1 a **House prices** in the area are ____________ thanks to the new shopping centre.
b ____________ **unemployment** is the most pressing issue facing the government.
a swelling b hiking up c accelerating d skyrocketing

2 a **Shares** in the company ____________ following the news that the CEO had quit.
b The box fell out of the window and ____________ **into the sea**.
a diminished b plummeted c waned d receded

3 a The designer ____________ the **price** of his clothes after he won the reality TV show.
b When they ____________ the **tax rates**, I was forced to close down my business.
a spiralled b soared c hiked up d escalated

4 a It's amazing how the band's **popularity** has never ____________, even after all these years.
b My **interest** in the business ____________ after I watched the documentary.
a slumped b waned c spiralled d plunged

6 SPEAK Work in pairs. Talk about some of the following topics in relation to your country/region using the vocabulary in Exercise 2.

- The state of the economy (unemployment, inflation, currency)
- The popularity of a certain TV series, music group or technological product
- The cost of living (food, travel, household bills, eating out)
- The financial performance of a major industry (retail, hospitality, manufacturing, IT)

Reading and Use of English Part 7 Multiple matching

1 SPEAK Work in groups and discuss the questions.

What are some of the main reasons why businesses fail?

Have there been any products or companies whose bankruptcy or failure has surprised you?

What companies have made products you can't live without?

2 You are going to read an article about famous businesses which failed. For questions 1–10, choose from the sections (A–D). The sections may be chosen more than once.

In which section does the writer do the following?

refer to a number of situations beyond a company's control	1
highlight the role that one retail chain played in its own downfall	2
mention how ignoring customers can be fatal to a business	3
advocate for revision of the ways companies do business	4
highlight the pitfalls of continuing to adhere to a particular sales model	5
weigh up the core factors which contribute to a business's failure	6
mention that success can be a double-edged sword	7
disagree with the standard explanation for one company's failure	8
explain how a company's commitment to quality can inadvertently contribute to its demise	9
show how quickly a company can fall out of favour with consumers	10

Don't forget!

Remember that ALL the information in the questions must match the paragraph you choose. There may be more than one paragraph with similar information but only one will be an exact match.

3 SPEAK How can businesses prepare for unknown events? How much should they focus on continuity plans and preparing for unexpected events?

BOOM AND BUST

A Making money is a fickle business and in order to stand the test of time companies have to withstand such onslaughts as random world events, changes in legislation and shifts in consumer behaviour. Yet none is more liable to bring about their undoing than a failure to innovate and keep pace with their competitors. Probably the most often cited example is the sad tale of how Blockbuster, the once ubiquitous video rental store found in every town in the UK and the USA, and with countless branches worldwide, went from boom to bust in little more than a quarter of a century. Whether or not this was entirely due to the rise of online video rental and subsequently streaming services, as is frequently cited, is not cut and dried. After all, it could have reacted to the rapidly changing preferences of its customers and embraced the new technologies emerging, but instead chose not to evolve in line with its competitors.

B Sometimes circumstances behind a business's success or failure are beyond anyone's control. History is littered with examples of ventures large and small that suffered at the hands of natural disasters or political events, but those that make the headlines tend to be large organisations, often household names, which have either formed part of the economic bedrock of a country for generations or are globally recognised, seemingly unbreakable corporations. And it is precisely this renown and perceived stability which means that their downfall is so shocking to the public. The classic example is Pan Am, America's iconic airline of the 1960s and a hugely lucrative business in its heyday. It prided itself on two of the cornerstones of aviation, renowned customer service and a fleet of modern aircraft. What it could not have predicted, however, was the oil crisis of the early 1970s which caused fuel costs to soar. Had it not been for the high fuel consumption of their aircraft, they may have weathered the storm, but they were forced to hike ticket prices and soon after customers responded with their feet.

C Another area where companies are vulnerable to failure is in how they do what they do. Like the products and services they sell, this should be subject to scrutiny and periodic reassessment in order to be alive to the need for change as and when it arises. Kodak, the photography giant, is a prime example of complacency setting in and the results of turning a blind eye to the limitations of a specific approach. The company followed the 'razor and blades' model of selling one product at low prices with complementary products at vastly inflated prices. In their case, the cameras were the razors, and the processing of the film was the blades. As digital photography came of age, the costs of cameras and printing photos began to change but rather than adjust to the new trend, Kodak wasted a decade attempting to convince people of the superiority of analogue photography, all in vain as it finally lost the fight and filed for bankruptcy in 2012.

D These days if you were to ask any adolescents or twenty somethings if they'd heard of Myspace, you'd likely be met with blank looks all round, but in the mid-2000s, it was the social media start-up on everyone's lips. It soon became a victim of its own success, sending shockwaves across the business world. Bought by a large news media corporation for over $500 million, it was touted as a master stroke of a takeover. However, it was plagued by technology issues and users found the excessive advertising overwhelming and off-putting. This lack of attention to the user experience was instrumental in its downfall, to the extent that it would never be able to regain users' trust. Surprisingly, in this case there was an even more destructive element that sealed Myspace's fate. The new owners had a distinct lack of understanding of the agile mentality needed to run a social media company and attempted to integrate it into their corporate way of doing things. As such, Myspace lost out to its competitors and soon the market was overtaken by the social media giants we know today.

Writing Part 1 Essay

1 SPEAK Work in pairs and discuss the questions.

1. What are the most important factors for companies to consider in order to ensure good working environments?
2. How do you think people can best achieve a work-life balance?
3. What are the benefits of contented employees to wider society?
4. In what ways can employees be involved in improving their workplaces?
5. What role should governments play in improving working conditions?
6. What are the most effective ways to sustain employee motivation?

Don't forget!

You should paraphrase the key points from the text in your essay. One way to do this is to convert positive verbs and structures to negative. Additionally, including noun phrases and nominalisation can help achieve a more formal tone.

2 Read the Writing Part 1 texts below. Make notes on the main ideas in each text.

Write an essay summarising and evaluating the key points from each text.

Use your own words throughout as far as possible and include your own ideas in your answers.

Write your answer in **240–280** words.

MEANINGFUL WORK MAKES MOTIVATED WORKERS

Contrary to popular belief, financial compensation is not the be all and end all when it comes to employee satisfaction. Countless studies have drawn out the complex nature of human beings' relationship with their work. Topping the list in employee surveys with increasing regularity is how work is connected to an individual's perception of their identity, something which is nebulous and personal, not like the clarity of a salary. Employees cite feeling appreciated by senior management for specific character traits and being allocated demanding work as key factors to workplace satisfaction. Unfortunately for employers, individuals are highly unlikely to interpret these key indicators in the same way, meaning there is much more to understanding them than meets the eye.

It's not about the money ... until it is

A 2010 study in the USA showed that earnings in excess of $75,000 make little difference to happiness, but while this might be thought-provoking in some ways, we shouldn't ignore the vast swathes of people who take home nowhere near this figure, suggesting that actually it is all about the money for them. Many of the hardships faced by those working in retail or manual jobs could be avoided by a modest salary hike and not, as much research would have us believe, by unnecessary lifestyle benefits or a pat on the back from management.

3 **SPEAK** Work in pairs and compare the notes you made in Exercise 2. Do you agree? Why / Why not?

Useful language

Using noun phrases in essays

Noun phrases have a more formal and academic tone than verb-based sentences, so they are an appropriate register for essays. In addition, these noun phrases use a wider range of grammatical structures and vocabulary and can help paraphrase the ideas in the texts.

1 **Relative clauses**: The solution which is most likely to be successful is increasing performance bonuses.
2 ***to* clauses**: The question to be considered in more detail is whether hiking prices to meet our mounting costs will pay off in the long run.
3 **Prepositional phrases**: Best practice from a range of sources could be incorporated into our new policies.
4 ***-ing* clauses**: Techniques pertaining to relevant theories are likely to be of more interest to our human resources department.

Rewrite sentences 1–4 using less academic language. For example:

1 *We think that we would be more successful if we increased performance bonuses.*
2 ______
3 ______
4 ______

4 Read the model essay and underline sentences that use the noun phrase structures from the Useful language box.

Employers are keen to more fully understand the psychology of motivation in the workplace, given that the extent to which employees are satisfied by their roles and responsibilities can both positively and negatively contribute to their effectiveness and thus the overall performance of an organisation. However, the factors described by employees can differ immensely and as such may reveal more areas for analysis than immediate solutions for employers to implement.

There is a wealth of options for companies that would like to address issues of motivation in their workforce. Initially, the recourse which should not be overlooked is whether or not a pay rise could positively impact staff productivity and wellbeing. Although there is a threshold above which income makes fairly little difference, this figure is quite high and certain individuals in the organisation might react well to such a measure.

Inevitably, the likelihood of this applying to employees in more senior positions is low, therefore a question to be discussed in more detail by a company´s management is how best to incentivise those employees for whom money is not a decisive factor. While money may make a difference to people whose current life circumstances would benefit from it, such as younger employees or those with a growing family, others may view financial compensation as less enticing. In these instances, rewards expressing gratitude in a more personal way could be worth considering, perhaps extended leave or experience gifts.

However this process is addressed, companies would do well to bear in mind the need for sensitivity when discussing motivation with their employees.

5 Now write your own answer to the task in Exercise 2. Use some structures from the Useful language box and paraphrase the ideas from the texts.

For more information on writing essays, see page 190.

Listening Part 2 Sentence completion

1 SPEAK Work in pairs. Discuss the following questions.

1 Do you think you could turn any of your hobbies into a profitable business? Why / why not?

2 What do you think the challenges are of starting up a small business? And what are the rewards?

2 6.3 You will hear a business advisor talking about the trend of hobby-based businesses. For questions 1–9, complete the sentences with a word or short phrase.

SIDE HUSTLES

1 The modern interpretation of a side hustle is related to ______________ more than work.

2 People with a ______________ usually reap the most rewards from side hustles.

3 The advisor comments that the products from side hustles are often of ______________ quality.

4 Acquiring a ______________ is higher in traditional forms of employment.

5 Asserting control over one's work life gives a greater sense of ______________ for people.

6 The rising interest in the idea of side hustles can be attributed to ______________ from online sources.

7 People could be squandering ______________ on side hustles for no good reason.

8 Most of the ______________ from side hustles lies with highly qualified individuals.

9 The main draw is the potential to build a ______________ start-up.

3 SPEAK Work in small groups and discuss the questions.

1 What are the benefits and drawbacks of working for yourself as opposed to a company?

2 What personality traits do entrepreneurs often have?

Speaking Part 2 Collaborative task

1 **SPEAK** Work in pairs. Look at pictures 2 and 4 below, which show different types of employee incentives. Talk together about how effective the different types of incentives would be.

2 Now look at pictures 1–4. Imagine that a website is writing an article about what companies should invest in to improve employee satisfaction. Talk together about the benefits and drawbacks of investing in the things shown in these pictures. Then decide which would have the most positive impact on employees overall.

Useful language

Use these phrases when trying to make a decision.

I'm torn between ... and ... What do you think?

My instinct is to go for ...

The one that stands out for me is ...

Okay, so we need to make our minds up between ... and ...

Are we on the same page about this?

I think ... is a no brainer.

In my view we should opt for ...

I'm happy to go along with that.

It looks like we've settled on this one.

This would be the best one to go for.

Website article – employee satisfaction

1

2

3

4

6 REVIEW

Reading and Use of English Part 3 Word formation

For questions 1–8, read the text below. Use the word given in capitals at the end of some of the lines to form a word that fits in the gap in the same line. There is an example at the beginning (0).

DON'T BANK ON IT!

The mutilated currency division is an obscure part of the American government where citizens can send their damaged banknotes to **(0)** *UNDERGO* examinations for authenticity. They can also have their value redeemed in cases where they can be verified **(1)** ____________. This kind of work requires serious attention to detail as well as procedures to be highly **(2)** ____________ in order to ensure their accuracy. To make sure that **(3)** ____________ claims are spotted, analysts must apply a range of tests **(4)** ____________. Should the notes pass, their value will be redeemed. However, if more than half the note is **(5)** ____________, no payment is made. It is unsurprising that the division's guides have amusing cases to recount on their tours, and given that they are not subject to the **(6)** ____________ rules that apply to other employees, these stories invariably become public knowledge. Perhaps the most entertaining was that of a farmer who mailed in the stomach of a slaughtered cow, convinced that it had eaten his wallet. It turns out the evidence was **(7)** ____________ and the famer got his payment of several hundred dollars. The moral being that it is **(8)** ____________ sending in your mutilated currency just on the off-chance of a pay-out.

GO
SATISFY
STANDARD
FRAUD
SYSTEM
IDENTIFY
CONFIDE
DISPUTE
WORTH

Vocabulary Phrases with *pay*

Complete the texts with the words in the box. There is one extra word you do not need.

compliment consequences dividends forward lip service nose price respects tribute way

There will be a memorial service for our former mayor and town legend, Jack Henderson. Business leaders and community members have been invited to pay their **(1)** ____________ to him at the town hall on Saturday. The town council is also considering erecting a statue to pay **(2)** ____________ to his achievements.

These one-to-one 15-minute meetings are just paying **(3)** ____________ to the idea of empathetic listening. Proper engagement with the idea would pay **(4)** ____________ in the long run.

I used to believe in paying my own **(5)** ____________ as a matter of principle, but this meant that I would often miss out on whatever was happening because I didn't have the cash. Rather than asking a friend to help, I paid the **(6)** ____________ for being so stubborn.

I wasn't expecting Hannah to pay me that lovely **(7)** ____________ on how I handled the discussion. Afterwards, I noticed a glowing feeling inside and I realised the impact they can have so I want to pay it **(8)** ____________ and do the same for one of my colleagues this week.

Instead of sticking to the budget, Caroline paid through the **(9)** ____________ for that new coffee machine. I imagine she'll live to regret that decision when senior management find out.

Reading and Use of English

Part 4 Key word transformations

For questions 1–6, complete the second sentence so that it has a similar meaning to the first sentence, using the word given. Do not change the word given. You must use between three and eight words, including the word given.

1 Without the appropriate training, puppies can become difficult to manage around other dogs.

HAND

It's necessary to train puppies to prevent their behaviour ______________________ around other dogs.

2 I think that if you don't intervene too much, the students will work much harder in class.

DEVICES

In my view, the students work better when ______________________ in class.

3 Working or studying long hours into the night rarely produces the results people expect.

BURNING

Although it sounds like a good idea, ______________________ can be counterproductive.

4 By limiting pleasantries and focusing on the agenda, Jane is able to keep meetings short.

STRAIGHT

Jane always ______________________ in meetings so as not to waste anyone's time.

5 When they shook hands, it was akin to an agreement.

INTENTS

The handshake was, ______________________, an agreement.

6 Damian's good nature really shines through whenever people come to visit him.

BEST

Having a house full of guests always ______________________ Damian.

Writing Part 2 Letter

Your college principal is keen to find out more about experiences of kindness or generosity that students have had either in a classroom setting or as part of an extracurricular activity organised by the college. Write a letter in which you describe a recent experience of this nature and say how it impacted you.

Write your letter in 280–320 words. You do not need to write any postal addresses.

For more information on writing letters, see page 193.

Idioms Money and wealth

1 Complete the expressions 1–5 with the correct word. Use your dictionary to help you if necessary.

Whenever a recession takes hold, it's not long before companies start **feeling the** (1) *pinch / stretch / touch / stitch*. However, the effects vary considerably depending on the sector. Industry and light manufacturing are often the first to take a financial hit and many companies find it challenging to **keep their heads above** (2) *earth / ground / surface / water*. Consumer spending **is their bread and** (3) *cheese / jam / butter / honey*, so when that slows in a recession, they're forced to make tough decisions. They simply cannot afford to invest in new ventures on top of managing all the hidden costs associated with running a business. In the finance world, however, recessions can be extremely profitable. Far from **being hard** (4) *over / out / up / off*, bankers are often reported to be (5) *swimming / rolling / playing / laughing* **in it** during or after a recession.

2 Which of the expressions in Exercise 1 mean:

a to provide the main source of income ______________

b to not have much money ______________ and ______________

c to manage to keep a business working despite not having much money ______________

d to have a lot of money ______________

3 For sentences 1–5 choose the phrase (a or b) that could replace the idioms in bold.

1 The sales department have **been on a roll** this quarter. Let's hope it continues.
a had a lot of success **b** experienced a drop in their figures

2 Her family must **be made of money** judging by her lavish lifestyle.
a have financial issues **b** be very well-off

3 Even though the accountancy firm we use charges exorbitant fees, Tom wouldn't change them **for love nor money**.
a unless he had to **b** in any situation

4 It's all very well Michaela promising we'll move to new premises, but she really has to **put her money where her mouth is**.
a ask us what we want **b** take some action

5 I'm astounded the client is paying us for this – it's just **money for old rope**.
a payment for hardly any effort **b** will involve a lot of hard work

4 SPEAK Work in groups. Explain how the context of the sentences helped you choose your answers for Exercise 3.

Discussing idioms

Discuss the differences in meaning between these idioms:

- be on a roll / be in the groove
- money for old rope / money for nothing

READY FOR LISTENING

Introduction

The **Listening** paper contains four parts and lasts approximately 40 minutes. At the end of the test, you are given an additional five minutes to transfer your answers onto the separate answer sheet. You will hear each recording twice.

Listening Part 1 Multiple choice

What to expect in the exam

- In Part 1 you will hear three short extracts, each with a different theme. The extracts are a mixture of monologues and dialogues.
- Each question will focus on a different aspect of the extract.

1 0.1 You will hear three different extracts. For questions 1–6, choose the answer (A, B or C) which best fits according to what you hear. There are two questions for each extract.

Extract One

You hear a news report about a road closure.

1 In the report, the newsreader
  A is condemning the response to essential maintenance.
  B is revealing the extent of the area's poor road conditions.
  C is highlighting the council's inadequacy in communicating.

2 The newsreader suggests that the response to complaints
  A showed little remorse on the part of the council.
  B will leave local residents feeling puzzled.
  C was not issued in a timely enough manner.

Extract Two

You hear two people discussing the recent bad weather conditions.

3 What do the two speakers agree about?
  A That strong weather is becoming more frequent.
  B That the effects of the weather were severe.
  C That the country should be better prepared.

4 Why is the wildlife suffering so much from the weather?
  A They aren't accustomed to dealing with such cold weather.
  B They do not receive assistance to ensure their safety.
  C They cannot cope with unexpected weather changes.

Extract Three

You hear an interview with a government minister talking about a new housing scheme.

5 What is the core rationale for the new grant scheme?
  A To ease population strain in cities.
  B To breathe new life into abandoned areas.
  C To create new environmentally friendly housing.

6 What is the interviewer's opinion of the funding scheme?
  A It fails to address the main housing issues.
  B It is a distraction tactic from failing policies.
  C It is a short-term answer to a long-term problem.

2 Check your answers by looking at the Audioscript on page 241. How have the answers been paraphrased? What clues are there in the audio script that might make you think a wrong answer is correct?

Don't forget!

Make sure you listen to each extract in full before you choose an answer. Speakers may discuss one idea and then go on to rule it out later in the script. Do not pick an answer based on them saying a word that matches the extract.

Listening Part 2 Sentence completion

What to expect in the exam

- In Part 2 you will hear an informative monologue.
- There are nine questions testing your understanding of specific information.
- The questions follow the order of information in the recording.
- The answers you need to write will be words or short phrases from the recording.
- The words/phrases must fit the sentence grammatically and your spelling must be correct.

How to go about it

- Read the sentences carefully before the listening starts. Underline key words to help you focus on the meaning.
- Look carefully at what goes before and after each gap and consider what fits into the structure of the sentence.
- For each question, you may hear distractors – words which might at first seem relevant, but do not complete the sentences correctly.
- Always write words that you hear.
- Check your spelling carefully and make sure your writing is clear.

1 0.2 You will hear a talk by an expert about ways in which energy can be generated. For questions **1–9**, complete the sentences with a word or short phrase.

THESE NEW ENERGY SOURCES ARE MAKING WAVES BUT NOT NECESSARILY IN OUR OCEANS

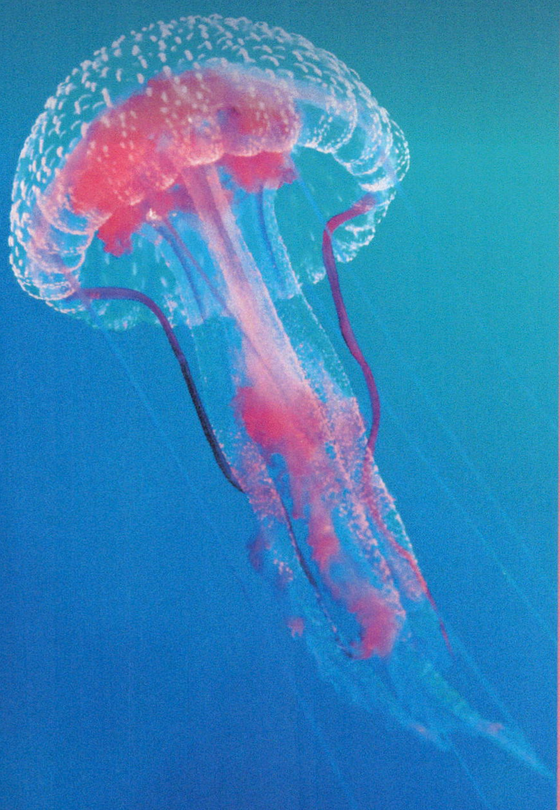

Due to the study of alternative energies advancing by (1) ________________, many new energy sources are emerging onto the scene.

The (2) ________________ of gravity is one of its biggest assets for exploiting it as an energy source.

People in Kenya have managed to almost eliminate the (3) ________________ of lighting by using the GravityLight.

With the continued research into kinetic energy, it's possible that human (4) ________________ will be a source of power.

The speaker uses the term (5) ________________ to describe how solar energy may be adapted and used for inexpensive green energy production.

The problem with solar energy is that the material used as a (6) ________________ is expensive and energy hungry to produce.

Scientists are aiming to use the same protein that is responsible for the (7) ________________ in jellyfish in solar panels.

New solar panels using proteins could be (8) ________________ or put to use floating in the seas.

Researchers are turning away from (9) ________________ resources in order to deal with modern energy challenges.

2 **SPEAK** Compare your answers with a partner's. Are they the same or are there any key differences? Can you see any wrong answers that could have been easily avoided, such as spelling or grammatical errors?

Listening Part 3 Multiple choice

What to expect in the exam

- In Part 3 you hear two people talking about a particular topic, with a third person, the interviewer, prompting them with questions.
- The recording will contain opinions and attitudes, which are expressed both implicitly and explicitly.
- There are five multiple-choice questions with four options each. These focus on understanding the points raised.
- Questions follow the order of the information in the recording.

1 SPEAK Before listening, look at Question 1 in Exercise 3. In groups, try to think of as many ways as possible the speakers might refer to the ideas in the question and the possible answers.

e.g. *If it were up to me, I'd ...*

... let's not put it all on them ...

... already do quite a bit ...

2 Now read the remaining questions and answer options in Exercise 3 and spend a few minutes thinking about possible ways the speakers might express the ideas in the questions and possible answers.

3 0.3 You will hear a councillor, Kevin Eastwell, and a conservationist, Julia Wright, discuss cats in New Zealand. For questions 1–5 choose the answer (A, B, C or D) which fits best according to what you hear.

1 In response to Julia's comment about cats having killed off many bird species, Kevin
  A disputes that cats are the main cause of bird loss.
  B corrects how she has described the cat threat.
  C claims she is too sensitive to the issues at hand.
  D accuses her of pointing the finger at owners.

2 Bird populations are being destroyed so dramatically in New Zealand because
  A they struggle to recognise predators.
  B their numbers are already relatively small.
  C their evolution has been slow.
  D they are ill equipped for danger.

3 Kevin explains that in the early 19th century, the population of the Lyall's wren was
  A flourishing on the main islands.
  B confined to one particular place.
  C entirely eradicated across the country.
  D slowly diminishing on the main islands.

4 When it comes to managing household cats, Julia advocates
  A enforcing a ban on all domestic cats roaming neighbourhoods.
  B instituting a license system for new cat ownership.
  C making owners ensure that their cats can't reproduce.
  D limiting the number of cats each household may have.

5 Julia and Kevin agree that
  A dealing with a range of predators is worthwhile.
  B cats are not the most dangerous predator.
  C wildlife organisations need to reassess their priorities.
  D the issue of feral cats is widely underestimated.

4 Look at the Audioscript on page 242 and use it to work out where and why you chose the right or wrong answers. How was paraphrase used to help or distract you?

Listening Part 4 Multiple matching

What to expect in the exam

- You hear five short monologues on a specific topic or theme and while you are listening, you have to complete two tasks. You may be asked to identify gist, main points, details, or the speaker's attitude, opinions or feelings.
- You will hear each monologue twice. Remember that each one will contain information that may seem like the right answer but is just distraction.

How to go about it

There is no 'correct' approach to doing Part 4. You may choose to answer both tasks simultaneously, answering the easier questions on the first listening and the harder questions on the following listening. Alternatively, you may choose to answer Task 1 on the first listening, and Task 2 on the second listening.

1 SPEAK In groups, look at the task below. Remembering that you will listen twice, discuss strategies you could use to answer these questions.

2 0.4 You will hear five short extracts in which people are talking about doing very long races called ultramarathons.

TASK ONE

For questions **1–5**, choose from the list **(A–H)** how each speaker views ultramarathons.

TASK TWO

For questions **6–10**, choose from the list **(A–H)** what advice each speaker gives ultramarathon runners.

While you listen you must complete both tasks.

Task One

- **A** an activity which requires continual adjustment
- **B** a discipline that builds resilience in everyday life
- **C** a way of gaining pleasure that's unobtainable elsewhere
- **D** an activity to remember but also to regret
- **E** an all-consuming obsession in their lives
- **F** a sport that creates a unique bond between runners
- **G** a fulfilling activity to push the limits of capability
- **H** a way to keep their body internally and externally fit

Speaker 1 [1]
Speaker 2 [2]
Speaker 3 [3]
Speaker 4 [4]
Speaker 5 [5]

Task Two

- **A** ask other runners for advice before and during races
- **B** think of solutions to practical problems beforehand
- **C** it's impossible to anticipate what you might face
- **D** ensure you give your body what it needs while racing
- **E** remember that not finishing a race is OK
- **F** it's essential to have mental toughness
- **G** learn techniques from more experienced runners
- **H** you must be strict with yourself in training and racing

Speaker 1 [6]
Speaker 2 [7]
Speaker 3 [8]
Speaker 4 [9]
Speaker 5 [10]

3 Check your answers using the Audioscript on page 243. Underline the location of each correct answer and circle any words or phrases that could distract you from the correct answer.

7

WORKING IT OUT

KEY LANGUAGE

Modal verbs 2
Adjectives and fixed expressions
Phrasal verbs of deduction and investigation
Verbs of confusion and deceit
Adjectives

IDIOMS

Mystery

EXAM PRACTICE

Reading and Use of English Parts 2, 4 & 6
Writing Part 2
Listening Part 3
Speaking Parts 1 & 2

Speaking Part 1 Interview

Work with a partner. Discuss the questions.

1 Do you enjoy problem-solving activities like escape rooms, strategy board games or crosswords? Why / Why not?
2 Why do you think some people are attracted to mysteries and solving puzzles?
3 What is the biggest real-life mystery you would like explained?
4 How can problem-solving skills drive personal performance in the workplace?
5 What puzzle-solving skills are required when trying to glean meaning from something in English that you don't understand?

7 WORKING IT OUT

Listening Part 3 Multiple choice

1 SPEAK Look at the film posters and book covers. In groups, discuss the questions.

1. What makes these forms of entertainment exciting?
2. What techniques do you think writers and film-makers use to add excitement to their work?

2 7.1 You will hear a discussion between a film-maker and a psychologist on the topic of mystery and suspense. For questions 1–5, choose the answer (A, B, C or D) which fits best according to what you hear.

1 What point does Anthony make about creating suspense in a film?

A The story should unfold gradually.
B The plot should give the audience a sense of uncertainty.
C The audience should feel they are solving a puzzle.
D The plot should portray a credible threat.

2 When discussing audience exposure to suspense, Helena reveals that

A it helps them feel safe in the real-world.
B it helps them develop coping strategies.
C it helps them consider similar scenarios.
D it helps them experience danger safely.

3 Anthony thinks most directors fail to provide enough suspense by

A creating characters the audience don't care about.
B mis-timing their moments of suspense.
C making suspenseful moments too low risk.
D relying on effects over storyline.

4 What does Helena indicate is the particular reason for people's enjoyment of detective novels?

A They make us feel more intelligent.
B They improve our problem-solving skills.
C They play to our natural curiosity.
D They take our minds off daily life worries.

5 Helena states that the increased risk of spoilers for television shows

A has led some people to reduce their social interactions.
B is often perpetrated with malicious intent.
C is purely down to increasing social media activity.
D has created a greater impatience amongst viewers to reach the end.

3 SPEAK Work in small groups.
Choose a film or book that you found suspenseful:

- Outline the plot of the film or book.
- Describe a particularly dramatic scene and what techniques were used to heighten the suspense.

Language focus Modal verbs 2

1 Complete these extracts from the listening on page 100. Write two words in each gap.

1 ... know that the character ______ end up in grave peril and hope they don't.

2 It's ______ be quite tricky to write that kind of story ...

3 ... the speculation of who could or ______ been the culprit, suddenly becomes terrifying.

2 Check your answers in the Audioscript on page 237.

3 Match sentences 1–3 in Exercise 1 with functions a–c.

a Used when speculating about a lack of possibility in the past ___

b Used when drawing a conclusion or expressing probability ___

c Used when expressing possibility in the present and future ___

4 Go to Ready for Grammar on page 220 to check your answers to Exercise 3 and for further rules, explanation and practice.

5 Complete the sentences below with a modal verb from the box and the correct form of the verb in brackets. You can use each modal verb only once. There may be more than one answer.

could	couldn't	got	may	might	must

1 'Thank you to the British Film Board and Midway Productions, without whom this film ______. Nobody else could see our vision for this project, so thank you for believing in us and providing the funding to bring this to life.' (*make*)

2 It ______ really interesting to study suspense and mystery as a psychologist, but I bet it's impossible to watch a film without deconstructing it. (*be*)

3 It ______ incredibly difficult to write a book like that with so many unexpected twists and turns, especially in such a short time. Could you tell us how you went about it? (*be*)

4 With regards to our findings from the study, from the data collected, it ______ that there is a strong correlation between the release of an in-demand series and lack of productivity at home. (*deduce*)

5 Everybody was expecting to be watching the film through their fingers, but it ______ much more terrifying in my view. (*be*)

6 I ______ watching that new series tonight if I get home from work early enough. I've got nothing else on, I think. (*start*)

6 SPEAK Read the puzzle. Use modal verbs of possibility, probability and deduction to try and find the answer to the question.

PUZZLE

Maria and Eliza went out for drinks together. They both ordered lemonade. Maria was really thirsty and finished three in the time it took Eliza to drink just one. Later, it was discovered that both of their drinks had been poisoned, but only Eliza died. How?

Vocabulary Phrasal verbs of deduction and investigation

1 Complete the definitions with the correct phrasal verb in the box.

keep something back   mull something over   stumble across something

1 ______________________ – to find something unexpectedly
2 ______________________ – withhold some information
3 ______________________ – think deeply about something

2 Check your answers in the Audioscript on page 237.

3 Complete gaps 1–8 in the story with the correct sentence endings A–H.

Detective Santos had been trying to **track** (1) __________. He'd been **staking** (2) ______________________, but there had been absolutely no movement. No wonder really. Surely only a fool would go back to their house after robbing a bank?! But he knew this man of old, and he was no mastermind. He'd attempted to **nose** (3) ______________________, asking locals if they knew his whereabouts, but it was hard to size (4) ______________________. Communities like these were often closed off to giving any real information to the police, in fear of repercussions. This made it even harder to **root** (5) ______________________ in the community, like this guy. He decided to go back to the station and **sound** (6) ______________________. Maybe they'd be able to suggest some way forward in the investigation. He knew he'd **hit** (7) ______________________ to discover his whereabouts eventually. If Detective Santos was anything, he was determined. He wouldn't stop until this man's crime had **caught** (8) ______________________, whether it be sooner or later.

A **up with** him
B **out** his house
C **upon** a new idea
D **down** the suspected thief for the past 24 hours.
E **out** the other detectives there.
F **out** any criminal elements
G **up** whether people were really telling the truth
H **around** the area

4 Complete sentences 1–8 with the correct form of a phrasal verb from Exercises 1 and 3. Put the phrasal verb in the correct form.

1 The mayor was primarily elected because of his commitment to ______________________ **corruption** in the city.
2 The detectives had been ______________________ **the house** from across the street for over 48 hours without a sign of movement.
3 Leaving a job can impact almost every area of your life, so it's better to ______________________ **the decision** carefully.
4 Despite talking a good story, the police knew he was ______________________ something ______________________ **from** them.
5 Every mistake he'd made in the past had suddenly ______________________ **him** and there was nothing he could do to stop it.
6 When the officer first ______________________ **the idea** of scouring CCTV footage of the area, everyone doubted it would turn up any leads.
7 It had been months since the crime had taken place, and the police still hadn't ______________________ **the perpetrators**.
8 Those men had been ______________________ **the property**, going through rubbish and looking in windows, but nobody could call the police because they hadn't done anything wrong.

5 SPEAK Work in pairs. Using the words in the box, answer the questions below.

a claim   the competition   a person   a problem   a solution   territory   troublemakers

1 What TWO things can we **root out**?
2 What thing can we **hit upon**?
3 What TWO things can we **size up**?
4 What TWO things can we **stake out**?

Reading and Use of English Part 2 Open cloze

1 **For questions 1–8, read the text below and think of the word which best fits each space. There is an example at the beginning (0).**

THE LIMITS OF OUR KNOWLEDGE

Given the astonishing list of discoveries and achievements **(0)** *MADE* by modern scientists, you might think that we would understand our own bodily processes back to front, but you'd be surprised at the many things still **(1)** ________ uncovered about the human body. One such discovery revolves **(2)** ________ why we dream. While we can say **(3)** ________ some degree of certainty that dreaming is an essential function and vital to our health, scientists are still at a **(4)** ________ as to why memories of dreams are random or why we dream in the first place. And as for why we yawn – the once prevailing theory that we yawn to gain oxygen and thus keep us awake has now been **(5)** ________ into question, and some now hypothesise that we actually yawn to cool down the brain. Finally, don't bank **(6)** ________ laughter as just being a simple reaction to your off the **(7)** ________ humour either. Studies have shown that, in fact, it is a social tool to form bonds rather than a reaction to anything funny. So, the next time someone laughs at your jokes, remember, they could just be trying to get you on **(8)** ________!

Pronunciation Chunking and asides

1 **Speech is often broken up into meaningful chunks by pausing and intonation. Look at the dialogue below and mark where you think the speaker should pause or make a change in intonation. The first one has been completed for you.**

'I had no idea / that we don't know why we dream. I thought / science had more or less wrapped up / all the mysteries of the human brain. I guess I was wrong / and there's quite a lot / of scientific research to do!'

'Of course! The brain is an extremely complex organ. When I did my psychology course, which I had to drop out of, we learnt a great deal about the mysteries of the brain and the limits to our scientific knowledge.'

2 **7.2 Now listen and check your answers.**

3 **7.3 Listen to extracts 1–5 and identify the asides in each sentence.**

1. One thing I've always been curious about is the deep sea. I've actually read that, incredibly, we know less about it than we do our own solar system.
2. I think it's an exciting time for scientific research and I, for one, can't wait to see what the next few years will bring. Immune responses has been one of the areas that has been so hard to fathom, but science is getting there slowly but surely.
3. One thing that truly makes me wonder is my dogs! I'd love to know what's going on in their minds and be able to speak to them. Although maybe what I love so much about them is that they don't answer back, unlike my kids.
4. What has always puzzled me in regard to the human body is why we have a dominant hand. What makes it so hard for me to write with my left hand, it literally looks like a five-year-old's writing, and not my right?
5. Space has to be the ultimate mystery! The vastness of it all is unthinkable, and I'm positive there must be life, of some form, on other planets.

4 **7.4 Now listen to the sentences without the asides and note how the intonation changes.**

5 **SPEAK Work in pairs. Rewrite sentences 1–5 in Exercise 3 by using a different aside in each. Take turns to practise saying each of the phrases. Try and chunk the speech, lower your tone for asides and consider intonation.**

About English

Asides, like *between you and me* are usually said as a separate chunk, and in a lower tone, than the other parts of the speech. They often give a remark or comment on what is happening, and can even be secretive in nature.

Look at the examples below and identify the aside:

1. *I've been working my fingers to the bone to get this project finished. Well, not completely, I had a few days off last week. I'm so pleased with how it's looking.*
2. *Frank, unusually for him, got a great mark in his end of term report. They said he's almost top of the class.*

Speaking Part 2 Collaborative task

1 **SPEAK** Work in pairs. Look at the pictures. They show people working in areas that present some of the biggest mysteries for humankind. Take turns and talk for one minute each about pictures 1 and 3. Discuss which of the mysteries interest you more.

2 Now look at pictures 1–4. Imagine that a college is going to have a debate about what the most fundamentally important mystery facing mankind is. Talk together about the importance of the different mysteries suggested by the pictures. Then choose one other mystery that could be included in the debate.

Useful language

In the Speaking test, try to vary your language to show you can use a wide range of vocabulary. A way to do this is to use synonyms or near synonyms to avoid repetition.

Match the synonyms in the box with these words.

baffled	breakthrough	contemplate	finding	mystified	ponder	revelation	stumped	wonder

- think about (v) ________ ________ ________
- puzzled (adj) ________ ________ ________
- discovery (n) ________ ________ ________

Discuss the slightly different ways these synonyms might be used. Use a dictionary if necessary.

Debate – mysteries

1

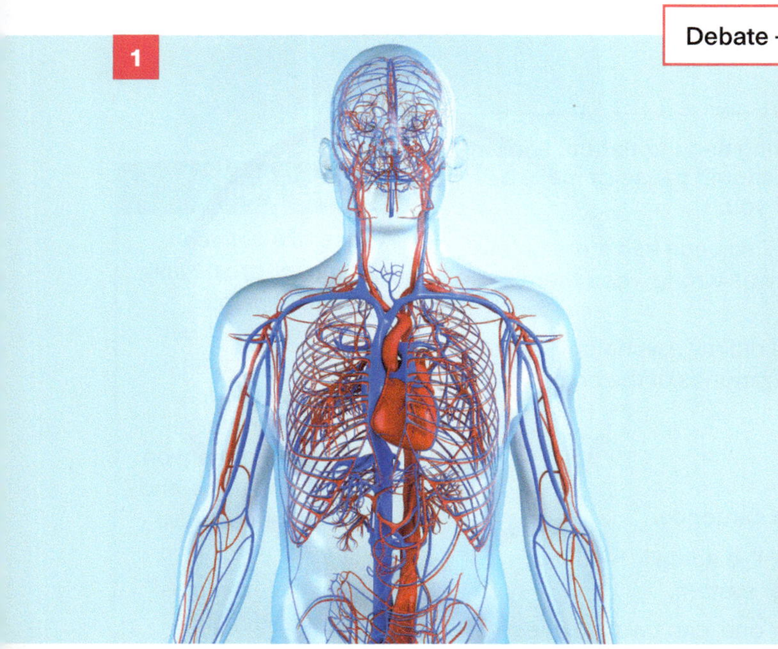

2

3

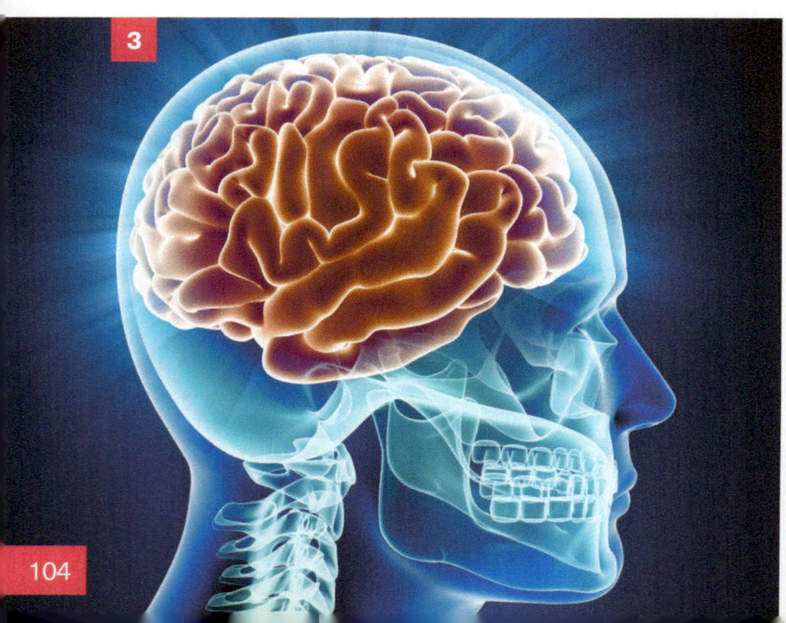

4

Word formation Adjectives

1 In 1–7 below, the words in each line can all form an adjective with the key suffix in bold, except one. Write the adjective forms of each word and identify the odd one out on each line.

1 **-ant**	hesitate *hesitant*	vacate	comply	repent	fraud
2 **-ent**	abhor	reminisce	decipher	appear	prevail
3 **-ous**	mischief	infect	poison	miracle	convince
4 **-able**	repel	tolerate	redeem	regret	laud
5 **-ible**	reverse	perceive	access	mercy	discern
6 **-less**	harm	thought	awe	relent	blame
7 **-some**	trouble	rebel	fear	whole	irk

2 Use the word given in capitals to form a word that fits in the gap. You may need to add prefixes.

1 The sound was so faint that it was ____________ to most of the others on the jungle expedition, but for George it was loud and clear. **PERCEIVE**

2 Although the evidence against him was overwhelming, he remained ____________ when in the dock, staring the victims in the face. **REPENT**

3 At first, the symptoms were ____________ in those who contracted the disease. It was only after three days that it became clear something very strange was happening. **APPEAR**

4 The scrolls discovered in the deep sea are covered in a script that is ____________ at present, although the world's greatest cryptographers are working on it. **DECIPHER**

5 Without immediate intervention, the growing distance and tension between the couple could be ____________. **REDEEM**

6 Once the situation at work became ____________ for Anya, she decided to hand in her resignation and move on. **TOLERATE**

7 What could not have been predicted is that this behaviour will have ____________ effects on the environment. **REVERSE**

3 Write a gapped sentence using a word from Exercise 1. Then give your sentence to your partner to complete.

4 Turn to the Additional materials on page 202 for further practice.

Reading and Use of English Part 6 Gapped text

1 SPEAK Skim read the article about encrypted texts and discuss the questions.

1. What do you think drives people to work so diligently to decipher the messages in such texts?
2. What kind of information do you imagine might be learnt from these kinds of encoded messages?

CRACKING THE CODE

Voynich manuscript

Sit on any commuter train or in any café and you are bound to spot people around you consumed by the challenge of doing a puzzle. It is a hugely popular pastime, whether in the form of a simple crossword or Sudoku puzzle, Wordle, an online strategy game, or even an escape room challenge. And yet, the most formidable of puzzles can't be found in black or white in the daily news, or behind some unassuming shopfront entrance. They are the enigmas of secret ancient texts and the keys needed to unlock them have been lost in the mists of time.

1 ______

Usually, these kinds of communications require a 'cipher', essentially the blueprint to interpret the secret code, which should be known only to the original agents. However, the luxury of a cipher doesn't always exist. When trying to 'crack a code' that doesn't have any cipher, the cryptanalyst needs to gather as much information as possible from the original text, so the bigger it is the better, and then to use all the techniques in his or her arsenal to try and unlock it.

2 ______

This, done by hand, can be a painstakingly slow, difficult, and sometimes, fruitless task. Firstly, this technique has to assume what language the original code was written in, as well as that the original cipher has failed to hide these common patterns. It's therefore a technique which relies on the cipher being simplistic, which, while true of some earlier forms of coded messaging, is rarely the case these days.

3 ______

In retrospect, the flaws in this method of encryption are obvious. However, there are many codes of the past that do indeed require a genius to unlock their mysteries, the most famous of which is the Voynich Manuscript, a 15th century book, written in an unknown script, featuring a never-before-seen alphabet. With over 170,000 beautiful, looping letters, as well as illustrations, this manuscript is the pinnacle of puzzle solving, and remains a complete mystery to professional and amateur cryptologists alike.

4 ______

People can make up their own mind about it, however, as the entire work is publicly available online for anybody to try their hand at solving. It is one of many mysterious texts now accessible to the general public and waiting to be cracked. In fact, there is a plethora of enigmatic communications from throughout history that remain shrouded in mystery, many of which have a fascinating background.

5 ______

But perhaps the Beale Ciphers might be of more interest to a wider audience of puzzle enthusiasts. These three cryptic texts date back to the 1880s and apparently conceal the location of one Thomas J Beale's buried treasure in Virginia. Some parts of these texts have been solved, such as what the treasure contains and that the hiding place is 'roughly lined with stone', making it all the more compelling.

6 ______

Stories such as these often create a frenzy of excitement, but, even if there is no monetary value in it for the solver, cracking any secret code pays dividends when it comes to the sense of achievement you get. After all, they were meant for only certain eyes that do not include our own – who wouldn't be interested in trying to find out their hidden meanings? This is why amateur cryptography can be such a fulfilling pursuit.

7 ______

With the sheer range of coded texts in existence, however, wherever an individual's aptitudes lie, there will always be the very puzzle for them. The visually minded perhaps lean towards the Dorabella Cipher, while the linguistically focused could view the Voynich Manuscript as their Everest. And for those who are more commercially minded, the Beale Ciphers might be just the ticket.

Dorabella cipher

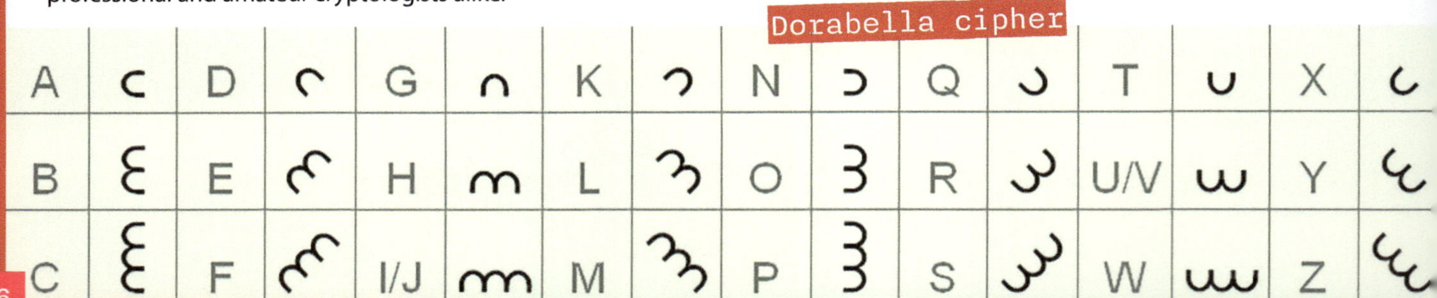

2 Seven paragraphs have been removed from the text. Choose from the paragraphs A–H the one which fits each gap (1–7). There is one extra paragraph that you do not need to use.

A Simple as they may appear now, basic coded messages signalled a huge leap in communication forms of the past. In fact, an elementary form of cryptography was practised by Julius Caesar, who sent his generals coded messages using what is commonly known today as the Caesar cipher – a technique where, put simply, one letter in an original message was replaced by another in a fixed position, usually three letters down the alphabet. So, for example, DON'T MOVE becomes GRQW PRYH.

B What inspires people to design these kinds of cryptic messages, while sometimes stemming from practicality, can in other cases be a complete mystery. One such example of this is the Voynich Manuscript, where the reasons for creating such a vast important tome in a language not readily accessible seems unfathomable.

C The Dorabella Cipher, for example, written by composer Edward Elgar, is a message to a family friend, consisting simply of various squiggles oriented towards different directions. It looks unlike any other kind of text, but to this day, nobody has been able to decipher it, even the recipient herself. Some even believe it to not be a text at all, but rather a coded musical composition.

D When seeking to unlock the simpler codes, frequency analysis is often considered a useful method. This involves looking for letters that appear more frequently than others. So, for example, if the original text is considered to be in English, then identifying frequent occurrences of a letter or groups of letters, such as vowels or consonant clusters, may help decode the text.

E Reasons why messages might be obscured can vary widely – whether to conceal military plans from the enemy, create distractions or quite simply due to audacity, the only commonality being that the message must be hidden from those who are not the intended or worthy recipients. Within the study of Cryptography, the sender is referred to as Alice or A, the intended recipient is Bob or B , and amongst many other monikers, Eve or E is the eavesdropper.

F There is still debate over the purpose of the text, but the illustrations would seemingly point to it being some sort of encyclopaedia of the natural world. Some argue that the work is not encoded at all, but rather written in a language that died out without record. One school of thought even considers the entire thing to be a hoax and that the 'writing' is simply gibberish.

G But before, reader, you go searching through every cold, dark and dangerous cave in the area, as many have before you, be warned that it may all just be an elaborate ruse. After all, the texts were sold in pamphlets for a princely sum at the time, putting the veracity of the whole story in question.

H Getting started couldn't be easier, with a multitude of books on the subject, ranging from titles for the beginner code breaker to more advanced works on specific cyphers, as well as a number of websites devoted to code breaking, many with accompanying brain teasers. Although, with more modern codes, having a good grounding in maths and computer sciences is imperative.

Don't forget!

When answering a gapped text, do not worry about answering the questions in order. It is better to read the text and complete the gaps with the paragraphs you are most certain of first.

3 SPEAK Understanding words from context is another way of deciphering meaning that is unclear. In pairs, find the following words in the text and use the context around the words to help you work out the meaning.

eavesdropper fruitless gibberish princely squiggles unfathomable

Language focus Adjectives and fixed expressions

1 **Choose the correct alternative in the following extracts from the Reading on pages 106–107.**

1 In *perspective* / *retrospect*, the flaws in this method of encryption are obvious.

2 But before, reader, you go searching through every *cold, dark and dangerous* / *dark, dangerous and cold* cave in the area, as many have before you, be warned that it may all just be an elaborate ruse.

3 The beauty of coded texts, however, is that wherever an individual's aptitudes lie, there will always be the *really* / *very* puzzle for them.

2 **Match examples 1–3 in Exercise 1 with the explanations a–c below.**

a Adding detail to a sentence with a string of adjectives.

b Intensifying meaning by using a degree adjective.

c Adding focus by using a fixed expression.

3 **Go to Ready for Grammar on page 220 to check your answers to Exercise 2 and for further rules, explanations and practice.**

4 **Complete the story extract with the phrases in the box.**

all in all	all of a sudden	in actual fact	sure enough	up to this point

This was thirty-two floors all reeking of business. Looking around the place, you could tell he must've had quite the fortune to call this place his company office. With modern, understated décor, the latest technology on all the walls and large windows looking onto killer views – (1) ______________________, it was the kind of place that screamed success. His secretary gestured for me to sit on the couch. I sat there taking it all in. I knew what to expect. In my line of work, you meet these high-flyer types all the time. (2) ______________________, what I found when I finally entered the office, was a man sitting slouched down at his desk, like a schoolboy in detention. He tried to meet my eyes, with some difficulty. 'Mr Baresi? Please sit down.' I took my time, sizing him up with every step, and took a seat opposite him. (3) ______________________, he got up and started pacing back and forth behind his desk. 'So, how can I help?' I asked, stumped at what I was doing here and sick of moving my head metronomically in his direction. 'No police, OK? But I want you to help me. I heard you were my best shot. I've got a problem ... it's my wife, she's missing. I came home two days ago and she was gone. All I've found is this note.' He pushed a piece of paper over to me, his perplexed expression imploring me for answers. It read, QRZ/LV/WKH/WLPH/OHWV/JR. (4) ______________________, the whole scenario had been surreal. But, as I looked at the message, it all started to make sense. I'd seen this code before. I scribbled down some letters in my notebook. (5) ______________________ the answer was staring me in the face and I had news for Mr Allman.

5 **SPEAK Think of eight other adjectives or fixed expressions you could add to the story.**

6 **SPEAK In pairs, answer the questions.**

1 Can you crack the secret message?

2 Do you know what happened to the wife? How?

Vocabulary Verbs of confusion and deceit

1 Choose the correct verb to complete the sentences.

1. The gallery was *duped* / *perplexed* **into** believing that the artwork was an authentic Picasso; it was, in fact, painted by the seller's brother.
2. If you think that one fifteen-minute walk a week will help you lose weight, you're *deluding* / *hoodwinking* **yourself**.
3. She knew almost nothing about the company and its products, but she managed to *bluff* / *hustle* **her way** through the interview, and was given the job.
4. The getaway driver *blackmailed* / *double-crossed* his gang by hiding away some of the money and reporting the other gang members to the police.
5. The defendants were accused of *stumping* / *swindling* a total of nearly three million pounds **out of** hundreds of vulnerable people.
6. It sometimes can be difficult to remain objective when solving crimes, and many new detectives tend to *confuse* / *scam* a lack of cooperation **with** guilt, when there could be many reasons for it.
7. Thieves *baffled* / *conned* the security guard **into** letting them into the building by disguising themselves as cleaning staff.

2 SPEAK Look at the options presented for each sentence in Exercise 1. Discuss the difference in meaning between each of the options. Use a dictionary if necessary.

Writing Part 2 Review

1 SPEAK Work in pairs and answer the questions.

What, for you, makes a film or book particularly good? Do you generally go for thought-provoking, intense storylines, or do you prefer more whimsical, escapist plots?

★★★★★ compelling stuff

★☆☆☆☆ wouldn't put my worst enemy through it

Useful language

Building more complex sentences

We can use premodifiers, postmodifiers or both to build a more complex sentence that is rich in detail. For example:

This film revolutionised the hackneyed detective narrative.

This little-known film set on the moon revolutionised the hackneyed detective narrative.
(adjective + noun + reduced relative clause)

This cult film from South Korea revolutionised the hackneyed detective narrative.
(noun modifier + prepositional/adjectival phrase)

Now try to add some complexity to the starting sentence yourself.

This ________ *film* ________ *revolutionised the hackneyed detective narrative.*

2 Read the writing task below. Then, look at the model answer on page 197. Underline where the writer has added extra information to the nouns in bold.

A mystery website is asking for reviews of mystery films or books, examples of which are brilliant instances of their genre. You decide to send in a review of a mystery book or film to the website. Include why the film or book you have chosen is such an excellent example of the genre and also include examples of how the writer or director has achieved this.

3 Now, write your own answer to the task in Exercise 2. Add extra information to nouns where appropriate. Write between 280–320 words.

4 SPEAK Swap your writing with another students'. Read and discuss where information has been added to the nouns. Would you change anything?

For more information on writing reviews, see page 195.

7 REVIEW

Language focus Modal verbs 2

Choose the correct word to complete the text. Sometimes both are correct.

Who was the Babushka Lady?

Many mysteries surround the assassination of John F Kennedy, one of which is the identification of the Babushka Lady, which confounds experts to this day. The lady, named after her old-fashioned Russian style scarf, **(1)** *must* / *may* have been an unsuspecting bystander like any other, but certain details about her appearance and manner that fateful day lead some to suspect that she was far from being just another member of the public. Firstly, her headscarf concealed her appearance, and secondly, amidst what surely **(2)** *must* / *could* have been a most traumatic event, she was standing calmly, photographing the scene when everyone around her was logically scrambling and taking cover. The reaction from the police and the public after seeing her image was natural: 'Something **(3)** *has got* / *must* to be up with this woman.'

Police at the time appealed for the woman to come forward, but nobody did until decades later. However, many people think this claimant **(4)** *mightn't* / *couldn't* have been the Babushka Lady. Why? Well, she would have been a tall 17-year-old at the time of the assassination and a completely different build to the figure that appears in the photo. Additionally, she also claimed to be have been holding a camera that wasn't even invented at the time. Some of the more outlandish theories that continue to surround this woman and who she **(5)** *could* / *must* have been include that she **(6)** *must* / *might* have been a spy for some government. But after so many decades, it **(7)** *may* / *must* be surmised that now, after so much time, we **(8)** *can* / *could* well never really know her true identity.

Reading and Use of English

Part 4 Key word transformations

For questions **1–6**, complete the second sentence so that it has a similar meaning to the first sentence, using the word given. **Do not change the word given**. You must use between **three** and **eight** words, including the word given.

1 All exams will be held in classrooms for now.
TIME
All exams are taking ________________ being.

2 Joe is determined to be a stunt man, even though it sounds dangerous.
SET
As dangerous as it sounds, Joe is ________________ a stuntman.

3 The rumours of the head teacher hitting the jackpot are untrue.
CONTRARY
Despite stories ________________ hit the jackpot.

4 Regardless of how difficult the exercise, you must keep trying.
ACCOUNT
Despite the difficulty of the exercise, ________________ give up.

5 The weather will stay bad for the next few weeks.
LIKELY
The weather ________________ better any time soon.

6 We can tell from the results of carbon dating that it's impossible Plato wrote that text.
HAVE
The carbon dating results indicate that Plato ________________ text.

Vocabulary

Read the text and choose the correct word (A, B or C) that best fits the space.

THE LOST COLONY

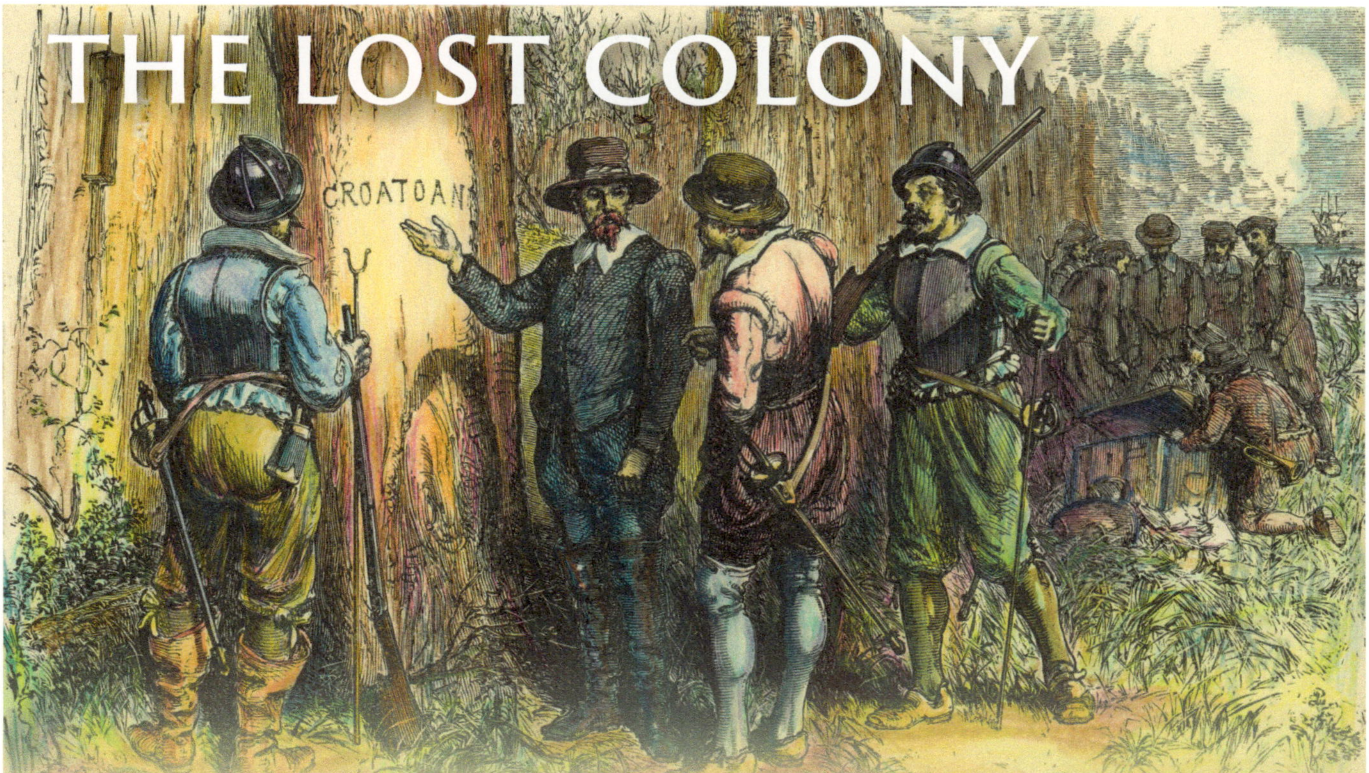

One mystery that still **(1)** ______ people to this day is the disappearance of an entire colony of people in what was then referred to in Britain as the 'New World' – 1500s America. The Roanoke Colony was a group of about 100 men, women and children who were sent from England to the New World in order to **(2)** ______ the new territories by creating settlements. Early into the colony's establishment, the governor, John White, returned to England for more supplies, but on his return to the colony, he was shocked to discover that all the settlers had disappeared. Try as he might to **(3)** ______, there was simply no trace of any of the colonists. The only visual evidence he **(4)** ______ was the word 'Croatoan' cut into a tree – but this only served to **(5)** ______ him further. Today, theories abound over what happened to them, but once these are carefully **(6)** ______, it becomes easy to see the flaws: if they moved on to a new place, where did they go and why didn't they leave a message? If they died of disease or were attacked by local tribes, where were the bodies? If they were **(7)** ______ people into believing they'd disappeared, what was the motive?

	A	B	C
1	**A** hustles	**B** dupes	**C** baffles
2	**A** stake out	**B** stumble across	**C** nose around
3	**A** keep them back	**B** track them down	**C** root them out
4	**A** hit upon	**B** sounded out	**C** sized up
5	**A** hoodwink	**B** delude	**C** perplex
6	**A** caught up with	**B** mulled over	**C** rooted out
7	**A** confounding	**B** hoodwinking	**C** hustling

Writing Part 2 Article

A newspaper has asked readers to submit articles on the subject of mystery for their special weekend supplement. The article should briefly describe a mystery, and touch upon why it is mysterious. The article should then broaden out to discuss why people find mysteries so captivating.

Write your **article**.

For more information on writing articles, see page 192.

Idioms Mystery

Murder Mystery night at THE GRAND CENTRAL HOTEL

If you're a lover of all things mysterious, why don't you join us for a night of mystery and suspense at the Grand Central Hotel, where there's much (1) **more to this** New Year's Eve party **than meets the eye**.

Host and multi-millionaire, Victor Del Fuente has more than a few (2) **skeletons in his cupboard**, and these catch up with him during his star-studded bash. Having got (3) **caught red-handed** in some dodgy dealing, his business associates aren't best pleased with him, and his family (4) **smell a rat** about what he's done with the family investments. And who's that mysterious woman in the shadows who looks familiar, yet nobody can (5) **put their finger on?**

With (6) **red herrings** aplenty, you'll need to keep your wits about you to stay in with a chance of solving the murder.

Discussing idioms

Discuss the differences in meaning between these idioms:

- ring a bell / strike a chord
- keep something under wraps / keep something under your hat
- be barking up the wrong tree / get the wrong end of the stick

About English

Idiomatic language is a common feature of English. In general, idioms which can be applied to a broader range of contexts are more common than those with a specific usage. For example, a *skeleton in the cupboard* can only be used in certain situations, but many things can be *more than meets the eye*.

1 Read the text and match the words in bold (1–6) with their meanings (a–f).

a begin to suspect deception
b to have an unpleasant secret about something you did in the past
c more difficult or involved than it at first seems
d a misleading clue
e spot someone in the act of wrongdoing
f to be able to identify, or say, exactly what something is

2 SPEAK Look at the idioms in Exercise 1. Which idiom do you think is only used in a context of crime?

3 Decide which idiom (a or b) best fits each gap.

1 They're ____________ by investigating that man. He's got a watertight alibi and barely any motive.
a keeping something under wraps b barking up the wrong tree

2 Elisha ____________ and told everyone she was the murderer instead of creating a cover story.
a let the cat out of the bag b rang a bell

3 Everybody at the party was ____________ and we had to try and work out the truth.
a keeping something under wraps b putting their finger on it

4 We thought the man's name ____________ and it turns out he's the long lost brother of the victim.
a smelt a rat b rang a bell

4 SPEAK In pairs, discuss the questions.

1 Can any of these idioms be translated into your own language? How common are the expressions?
2 What other expressions do you have in your language that have a similar meaning?
3 Why might people want to use idiomatic language for these kinds of situations?

8

HUMAN IMPACT

KEY LANGUAGE

Comparatives
Expressing contrast
Environment collocations

IDIOMS

Noticing similarities and differences

EXAM PRACTICE

Reading and Use of English Parts 3, 4 & 5
Writing Parts 1 & 2
Listening Parts 2 & 4
Speaking Parts 1 & 3

Speaking Part 1 Interview

Work with a partner. Discuss the questions.

1 Would you consider yourself environmentally minded? Why / Why not?
2 In what ways does your lifestyle impact the environment?
3 Do you think attitudes towards environmental issues are changing? If so, how? If not, why not?
4 How do you feel about the future of the planet?
5 How will a switch to a less carbon-intensive economy affect society?

8 HUMAN IMPACT

Speaking Part 3 Long turn

1 **SPEAK** Work in pairs. You are going to take turns talking on your own for about two minutes.

Student A: Talk for about two minutes about the question below.

Student B: When your partner has finished talking, discuss what campaigns there are in your country to raise awareness of environmental issues and how effective they are.

What do you think schools should focus on in terms of environmental education?

- energy
- transport
- waste

2 Now change roles.

Student B: Talk for about two minutes about the question below.

Student A: When your partner has finished, say what aspects of your local environment are threatened by climate change and to what extent.

What should the public prioritise in order to make an environmental difference?

- waste production
- travel habits
- power use

Don't forget!

You will need to speak for two minutes so remember to expand your answers. You can do this by giving reasons, making predictions and speculating.

Useful language

Speculating about the future.

Choose the correct words to complete the sentences.

Reducing meat consumption *should* / *may* well be the best solution to reduce the environmental impact of farming.

I think it's *highly* / *deeply* likely that the next generation will change their living habits completely.

Renewable fuels are *bound* / *verge* to be cheaper in the long run than fossil fuels.

Will we *have* / *be having* these same conversations about the environment in 20 years' time? Will we *have learnt* / *be learning* nothing?

3 **Work in pairs. Take it in turns to ask and answer the questions below.**

- How does consumerism affect the environment?
- What more can energy companies do to reduce their environmental impact?
- How realistic is it for national governments to deal with global environmental problems?
- Should green energy or public transport be subsidised for all citizens? Why / Why not?
- Why do you think environmental problems are not taken seriously by some groups in society?

Don't forget!

When you do the task, don't cross off any options. They could be the answer to another speaker.

Listening Part 4 Multiple matching

1 8.1 **You will hear five short extracts in which people are talking about working in conservation.**

TASK ONE

For questions **1–5**, choose from the list (**A–H**) what each speaker does as part of their job.

TASK TWO

For questions **6–10**, choose from the list (**A–H**) which positive impact of their job each speaker mentions.

While you listen you must complete both tasks.

A manages people
B does scientific experiments
C allocates finance
D liaises with other organisations
E reviews documents
F advises local businesses
G speaks about an initiative
H responds to complaints

Speaker 1 [1]
Speaker 2 [2]
Speaker 3 [3]
Speaker 4 [4]
Speaker 5 [5]

A more efficient use of resources
B improved bureaucracy
C new government policies
D investment in national parks
E a change in public opinion
F better public health
G more green spaces
H protection for native species

Speaker 1 [6]
Speaker 2 [7]
Speaker 3 [8]
Speaker 4 [9]
Speaker 5 [10]

2 **SPEAK Discuss the questions in groups.**

1 Which, if any, of the jobs mentioned in the listening could you see yourself doing?
2 What does conservation mean to you? Do you value it?

Language focus Comparatives

1 Complete these sentences with one word from the listening on page 115.

1 Before, after several months people would get requests for more documents and still be ____________ further along in the process.

2 Unfortunately, all they see is a blot on the landscape and trying to explain the environmental benefits to them doesn't make the ____________ difference.

3 The only issue is that climatic conditions are ____________ changeable these days ____________ we have to review everything year on year.

4 The scientific side of things is far beyond me I'm afraid, but my team are ____________ competent a group ____________ you'd find in any university research department.

5 And to be honest, figuring out how to reduce air pollution is tantamount ____________ figuring out the size of the universe!

2 Check your answers in the Audioscript on page 238.

3 Match each sentence in Exercise 1 with the correct meaning a or b.

1 **a** providing extra information sped up the application process
b providing extra information made no difference to the application process

2 **a** explanations only make a very small difference
b explanations make no difference at all

3 **a** reviews happen as a result of climate changes
b reviews happen to counter climate changes

4 **a** they are one of the most competent research departments
b they are more competent than other research departments

5 **a** dealing with air pollution is harder than figuring out the size of the universe
b dealing with air pollution is as difficult as figuring out the size of the universe

4 Go to Ready for Grammar on page 222 for further rules, explanations and practice.

5 Read the email of complaint. Rewrite the underlined sections using the comparison forms in the box.

as if | not that much | so ... as | tantamount to | the slightest

Dear Sir/Madam,

I recently visited your store in Newport and I am writing to let you know that I was absolutely appalled by the quantity of plastic packaging on your products. For a company the size of yours to persist in the continual use of plastic packaging, despite the growth in more environmental alternatives, is **(1)** the same as gross negligence, environmentally speaking. In fact, your supermarket runs **(2)** like environmental issues do not exist!

These plastics end up in our seas and land for thousands of years. If you could be **(3)** forward thinking enough to change your packaging, then this would be far better for the planet. In my view, changing this wouldn't make **(4)** any difference to you. On the contrary, it would only increase your reputation. If you must provide packaging, cardboard packaging **(5)** is only a little more expensive than plastic equivalents, yet significantly better for the environment.

I would be happy to discuss any of the above points further. I really hope you will take my concerns into consideration.

Regards

Yolanda Barrett

6 Make brief notes on one topic below using comparatives.

Nuclear vs renewable energy
Buying locally vs buying organic
Recycling goods vs reducing buying

7 SPEAK Work in pairs. Take turns to talk about your topic. Your partner should ask you questions about your views to find out more.

Vocabulary Environment collocations

1 Read the newspaper article, then complete the collocations with the nouns in the box.

catastrophe disposal erosion habitats tourism waste wind farms

ACT NOW SAYS PUBLIC OPINION

Astonishingly, just 30% of local citizens think the council is doing enough to prevent an **ecological** (1) ____________, according to a recent survey by a prominent campaign group. Following major storms over the past few weeks, **coastal** (2) ____________ is said to be increasing at an unprecedented rate. The impact of this is not just alarming to homeowners on that stretch of land, but also to local wildlife groups, who point to the cliffs as breeding ground for puffins, amongst other species.

A series of newspaper articles exposing the shocking levels of plastic pollution on our beaches has resulted in more being done to promote **sustainable** (3) ____________ in the region, especially ahead of peak seasons, such as summer. With opinion polls already at an all-time low, it is perhaps no surprise that meetings are now said to be hurriedly taking place with the MP for the region. In an apparent bid to appease critics who point to his lack of action on the renewable energy pledge he made two years ago, discussions are reported to be centred on the option of building several **offshore** (4) ____________ on our eastern coastline.

However, development of such a project is sure to concern sea life charities, who are bound to point to the impact such a project would have on already fragile **marine** (5) ____________. Since the national scandal three years ago, which found a number of factories to have been dumping **hazardous** (6) ____________ into the sea, killing fish populations, charities have been granted more oversight of the area. While this has led to more responsible **waste** (7) ____________ in the area, fish populations are still said to be below previous levels.

2 Which four nouns from Exercise 1 do each of the following sets of or words collocate with?

1 climate / environmental / humanitarian ____________
3 gradual / soil / wind ____________
4 household / industrial / organic ____________
5 natural / shrinking / woodland ____________

3 Complete the table with the collocations 1–7 in the article.

Adjective + noun	Noun + noun

4 Choose four of the collocations in Exercises 3 and write sentences about the impact of humans on coastal regions.

5 **SPEAK** Work in pairs. Compare your sentences with your partner. Do you agree with each other's statements?

Reading and Use of English Part 5 Multiple choice

Don't forget!

When answering multiple choice questions, read the question carefully to find out exactly what you need to know.

Some answers may be paraphrased directly in the text, which require you to examine a few sentences.

Other questions may require a more abstract understanding of larger stretches of the text as well as what the author implies.

1 SPEAK Work in pairs. Look at the picture and discuss these questions.

1 What types of food do you tend to eat more frequently?
2 Where do you think it comes from?
3 What foods are produced in your region?

2 Skim read the article on page 119 and answer the question.

How has Almeria changed in the last 100 years?

3 You are going to read an article about greenhouses. For questions 1–6, choose the answer (A, B, C or D) which you think fits best according to the text.

1 What is the author's objective in the first paragraph?
  - A to explain why the greenhouses in Almeria exist
  - B to suggest the importance of the greenhouses in Almeria
  - C to highlight the scale of the greenhouses in Almeria
  - D to describe how the greenhouses in Almeria are overlooked

2 What does the writer admire about farmers in the 1950s?
  - A their resourcefulness in adapting to conditions
  - B their resistance to the climate conditions
  - C their persistence in developing growing conditions
  - D their skilled approaches to poor conditions

3 The writer says that the owners of the greenhouses
  - A employ more people than any other industry in the region.
  - B consist of families that were generally native to the region.
  - C have more wealth than any other social group in the area.
  - D are generally well-dispersed across the entire province.

4 What is the writer's view on plastic waste in the area?
  - A It is a necessary evil that the area must live with.
  - B There's little incentive for farmers to deal with it.
  - C It makes the surrounding area less desirable.
  - D Farmers will probably come up with an ingenious solution.

5 How does the greenhouse industry in Almeria contribute to sustainability?
  - A It largely functions on natural resources.
  - B It keeps seasonal temperatures consistent.
  - C It creates less transport pollution.
  - D It generates energy that is used in the area.

6 What is the writer's overall opinion on intensive farming?
  - A It is a pragmatic food supply option to cater for growing needs.
  - B It is a trend that is unlikely to continue in the future.
  - C It needs some slight adaptations before being adopted internationally.
  - D It has to further consider the environmental effects of production.

4 SPEAK Work in small groups.
Discuss the following questions.

1 What are the environmental impacts of eating meat and how do they compare to having a plant-based diet?
2 How could people limit the impacts of global food export and consumption?
3 How do you think food production might change in the future?

PUTTING THE 'GREEN' IN GREENHOUSE

When we think about views of the Earth from space, normally awe-inspiring ancient constructions spring to mind like the Great Wall of China or incredible natural wonders like the Great Barrier Reef. One vista that few tend to think of lies in south-eastern Spain, in the province of Almeria, where there is an expanse of greenhouses which cultivate vegetables for much of Europe, conspicuously standing out from the desert-like surroundings.

Known as the 'mar de plastico', or 'sea of plastic' in English, the area is somewhat of a modern-day phenomenon that has completely changed the fortunes of the region. In the middle of the 20th century, Almeria was one of the poorest of Spain's provinces, with a barren climate, remote location, and little industry. However, this all changed when farmers started to question how they could exploit their year-round temperate climate and counter the dry conditions that were so detrimental to growth.

The answer came in the form of greenhouses, which retain water and heat while keeping the harsher elements out. With this ingenious development came the emergence of a new-found wealth within the region, and as farming in the region consisted of many family-owned smallholdings, this fanned out throughout the region, giving more horizontal growth and offering plentiful job opportunities unlike anything the area had seen previously.

Almeria plays a crucial role in catering for ever-increasing demands for produce throughout Europe, exporting to nearly every country in the continent throughout the year. In a modern society which expects seasonal produce throughout the year, fulfilling these demands is essential, and Almeria continues to go from strength to strength in doing this. As well as creating a booming agricultural industry, a whole host of research and development companies have set up shop in the area. Nonetheless, intensive farming in the province is not without its fundamental challenges, especially in terms of sustainability and the local environment.

One area which needs careful consideration in the long term is the methods of using water. Water scarcity may become an issue due to widespread use of water from underground sources for use in cultivation. Many environmentalists claim that in an area so arid as Almeria, the underwater sources can't replenish at the rate of their depletion. However, many farms have adopted more sustainable practices to help combat this, such as drip-feeding irrigation and the use of hydroponics, a soil-free method of plant-growing, which can reduce water use by around 80%.

The other, more pressing, sustainability issue surrounding Almeria is the plastic waste generated by these greenhouses. The three-year lifespan of the plastic greenhouses causes a considerable amount of waste in the area, and its disposal leaves a lot to be desired, with much plastic waste polluting the surrounding environment. Addressing this is a rather more complex issue. While there are waste management services for farmers to use, they are not generally cost effective. A more environmentally-friendly answer may be in replacing plastic with glass. Albeit the material of choice for some large farming areas in northern Europe, many farms in the Almerian province, especially the smallholdings, are put off by the massive investment this would require.

However, while these sustainability challenges are important to consider, the delicate interplay of progress and its environmental effects is far from cut and dried, especially when it comes to this kind of farming. In many ways, the greenhouses of Almeria could be considered a pinnacle of natural sustainability. Although this may seem strange, given the vision of plastic it displays, there are many ways in which Almeria is ecologically very sound. Firstly, the greenhouses, thanks to mild temperatures and abundant light, need little heating, which means very little traditional energy consumption is involved considering the large-scale of the food production, even taking into account transportation effects. Additionally, an unintended effect of the greenhouses has been to cool the area in the long-term, as the roofs reflect the sunlight. In a world which is constantly getting hotter, Almeria is one of the exceptions to this, which could be an important discovery for wider consideration.

Finally, what cannot be forgotten is that with increasing demands, increased production is essential. If large-scale intensive farming like that of Almeria isn't used to feed populations, then alternatives are few and far between. Upscaling food production significantly, while reducing the environmental footprint may be the ideal objective, but real-life indicates that there always has to be some form of trade-off, and at the moment, Almeria, with perhaps a few tweaks, seems well-placed to be the food production model of the future.

Listening Part 2 Sentence completion

1 SPEAK Work in pairs. Discuss the following questions.

1 How often do you buy new gadgets?

2 What do you do with them when you no longer want them?

2 8.2 You will hear an expert talking about the problem of electronic waste and some possible solutions. For questions 1–9, complete the sentences with a word or short phrase.

E-WASTE E-MERGENCY

Electronic waste underpins the performance of the (1) ________________ .

Humans are naturally (2) ________________ , as evidenced by their ability to use their environment for practical purposes.

Supplies of precious metals are now far less likely to be found (3) ________________ than they were in the past.

To ensure future sales, some consumer items are designed to (4) ________________ quickly.

Reductions in the cost of consumer electronics meant that people didn't need to (5) ________________ them.

Manipulating product design to increase consumption is a (6) ________________ practice nowadays.

Changes in legislation in one country were brought about by (7) ________________ from a single organisation.

Innovation in materials could remove the need to manage (8) ________________ waste disposal.

Several (9) ________________ may soon be made use of in the manufacture of electronic components.

> **Don't forget!**
>
> Write only words from the audioscript. Do not paraphrase them.

3 SPEAK Work in small groups and discuss the questions.

1 Some people say that compared to our modern throwaway society, products in previous generations were 'built to last'. To what extent do you believe this to be true?

2 What do you think of the phrase 'buy cheap, buy twice'?

Language focus Expressing contrast

1 Look at these extracts from the listening and complete the sentences with one word that best fits the gap.

The cycle of production, use and waste is constant and is repeated across almost all industries. Even ________, I want to stress that humans are not wasteful by nature.

It wasn't until the birth of the modern consumer lifestyle in the mid-20th century that we became passive over-consumers instead of active makers and menders. And ________, here we are a few decades later in a world where most of the world's gold reserves can be found ...

2 Match the beginnings of the sentences (1–5) with the correct endings (a–e).

1 Fixing your malfunctioning vacuum cleaner could be tricky,
2 There has been a substantial improvement in consumer rights,
3 Despite the population as a whole not recycling many gadgets,
4 There are plenty of free courses on how to fix consumer goods,
5 Replacing precious metals in gadgets with man-made ones is the way forward,

a we have, nonetheless, seen a modest rise in the practice amongst teenagers.
b challenging though that may sound at the moment.
c although easier if you found some instructions online.
d and yet very few people take advantage of them by enrolling.
e albeit gradually since the beginning of the century.

3 Go to Ready for Grammar on page 222 for further rules, explanations and practice.

4 Decide which of the underlined sections is wrong in the pairs of sentences and correct it.

1 a Though <u>unusual it seemed</u>, the idea was an excellent example of sustainable living.
  b The issue with the project is that it is likely to be <u>more complex than costly</u>.
2 a Very few consumers actually need to keep buying new gadgets <u>and yet</u> spending shows no signs of slowing down.
  b The researchers found the question posed challenging <u>even so</u> they persisted until they worked it out.
3 a This proposal for reducing traffic in the city centre is the <u>most comprehensive solution by a long way.</u>
  b <u>Although it well designed</u> in principle, the new recycling system did not prove popular with consumers.
4 a Many companies claim they are committed to green policies but financing them <u>has been difficult nonetheless</u> to achieve.
  b Many so-called environmentally-friendly products are <u>nothing like as effective</u> as many people believe.
5 a <u>Albeit the problem is difficult,</u> the government really needs to get its act together and deal with climate change.
  b Recent recorded temperatures in the region have been <u>considerably higher</u> than were predicted by scientists.

5 Complete the following sentences to make a contrast.

1 Important though improving public transport is, ...
2 Although in favour of recycling and repairing as much as possible, ...
3 Becoming vegetarian is an admirable lifestyle change, albeit ...
4 There is less packaging in supermarkets these days. Even so ...

6 SPEAK Work in pairs and compare your sentences from Exercise 5.

Writing Part 1 Essay

1 SPEAK In groups, discuss the following questions.

1 What threats to the environment does overpopulation pose?

2 What approaches can you think of to tackle the issue of overpopulation?

SAVING THE WORLD ONE BUSINESS SOLUTION AT A TIME

With the world population currently at over 8 billion and rising, manufacturing businesses are working towards lessening human impact on the environment. New business models such as the circular economy, where all waste from production is recycled or repurposed, are being implemented with immediate positive effects. High-income countries are expected to shoulder the responsibility of investing in this and other ideas which explore new technologies such as 3D printing and man-made materials instead of mining and other environmentally damaging processes.

GOVERNMENTS MUST TAKE THE LEAD ON CHANGE

It is unrealistic to expect that scientific or economic miracles will mitigate the environmental issues caused by overpopulation. People need to change their lifestyles and behaviours radically and governments should incentivise their citizens to have fewer children in the long term. In terms of environmental legislation, there needs to be far stricter laws against deforestation, as well as international cooperation on protecting water supplies and making food production more sustainable. Governments should show their commitment to change by amending international law as soon as possible. There's no time to lose.

2 Read the texts about overpopulation.

3 SPEAK Work in pairs. Take it in turns to summarise the ideas in each of the texts.

4 What ideas do you agree and disagree with in the texts? Explain your answers.

5 Read the model answer and answer the questions.

1 What sections of the essay paraphrase the texts?

2 Where are the student's own views on tackling overpopulation?

3 What do you like about the essay? Why?

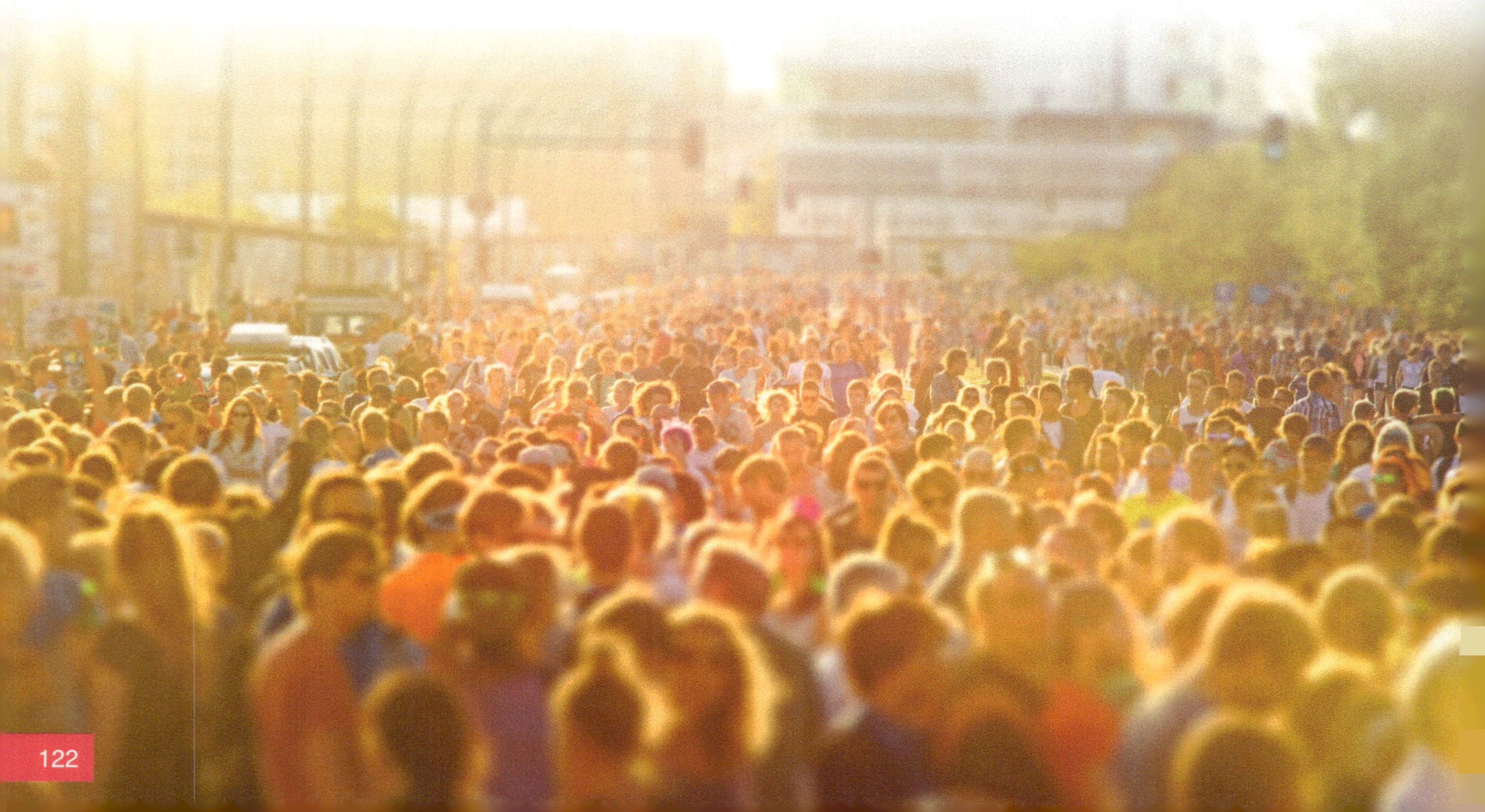

THE WAY FORWARD IS TOGETHER

The negative effects on the environment brought about by overpopulation are extremely concerning and should be addressed immediately through a variety of strategies and innovations. These texts present contrasting solutions, one from a business perspective, and the other based on government intervention.

The first text highlights the potential for business solutions to combat the impact of humans on the environment by describing a more sustainable economic model. The text states that the responsibility lies firmly with companies in high-income countries insofar as they have the financial resources to explore new approaches. To some extent, high-income countries are no more suited to solving complex problems such as overpopulation than lower income countries in my view as innovation has no geographical limits. Notwithstanding this, these countries do have larger funds to invest, which means that they could research techniques and approaches to rectify the current situation more effectively.

The second text argues that governments should be responsible for addressing the issue of overpopulation firstly by encouraging certain behaviour amongst individuals and thereafter through legislation. Although painfully slow to react at times, I believe governments have the advantage of being able to implement new laws which can encourage people to adopt better lifestyle choices. It is true that science is also in a position to contribute innovative solutions to worldwide problems. However, many successful conservation ideas have originated from scientists or university departments collaborating with governments and businesses rather than working in isolation.

In conclusion, collaboration between people and organisations everywhere is highly likely to be the most effective way forward. Creative ideas, legislation and sufficient funding are what is required to address overpopulation and reduce its negative impacts.

6 **Look at the problem-solving verbs in the box. Underline two verbs that means *reduce* and one verb that means *defeat*.**

address alleviate combat compound deal with exacerbate
face minimise overcome rectify remedy tackle

7 **Match the verbs in the box in Exercise 6 to the correct function.**

1 Solve a problem: ______
2 Make a problem worse: ______
3 Make a problem less serious: ______
4 Manage / respond to a problem: ______

8 **Choose the correct verb to complete the sentences.**

1 One idea which could *minimise* / *compound* habitat loss in forests is to plant more fire-resistant trees.
2 Contrary to popular belief, organic farming is not always the best way to *combat* / *face* soil erosion.
3 Each year vast regions of the world *remedy* / *deal with* the consequences caused by drought.
4 Urban expansion is *exacerbating* / *tackling* air pollution in cities across the country.
5 The World Wildlife Fund has the unenviable task of deciding which issues to *alleviate* / *address* with their limited funds.

9 **Now write your essay. Use some expressions to talk about problems, and if possible, some language of comparison.**

Write your answer in **240–280** words.

For more information on writing essays, see **page 190**.

8 REVIEW

Reading and Use of English Part 3 Word formation

For questions 1–8, read the text below. Use the word given in capitals at the end of some of the lines to form a word that fits in the gap in the same line. There is an example at the beginning (0).

MORE THAN A TUNNEL

A Victorian tunnel, built in the 1890s, may be the newest tourist attraction for south
Wales, with plans to **(0)** _REPURPOSE_ it from its original use for trains, to one of **PURPOSE**
Europe's largest cycle and walkways. The two-mile long tunnel is part of an ambitious
aim to promote sustainability and **(1)** ________________ a long-neglected area, with a **VITAL**
focus on attracting visitors to the area.

The tunnel fell into **(2)** ________________ in the 1960s partly due to the cost of **REPAIR**
maintenance, which became **(3)** ________________ after reports found that some **REAL**
parts of the tunnel were hazardous to use. However, many community groups
now see this tunnel as signifying a new start for the area, which, due to the
collapse of much industrial activity, has seen widespread **(4)** ________________ **DEPRIVE**
in recent decades.

The tunnel repairs are estimated at around 18 million pounds, an **(5)** ________________ **SIGNIFY**
small amount of investment compared to the money it could draw to the local area.
At the moment, the potential for tourism in this area remains **(6)** ________________. **TAP**
However, with some **(7)** ________________ breath-taking natural scenery, the area is **ORDINARY**
perfect for lovers of nature who want a different destination. An ecologically sound
way of bringing money into the area could be the perfect antidote to years of being
(8) ________________. **LOOK**

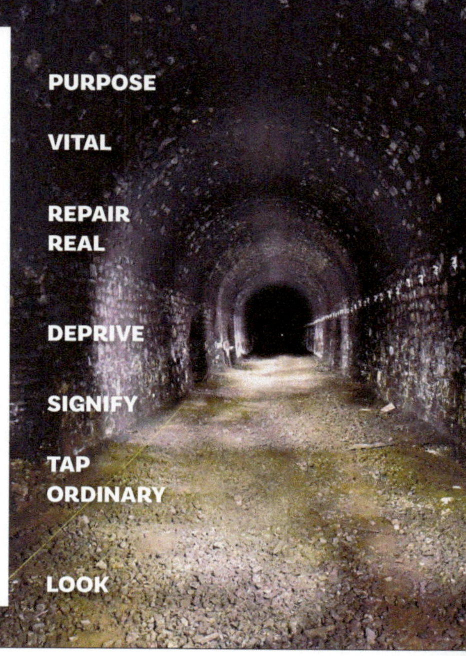

Vocabulary Environment collocations

Complete the sentences with the correct word or phrase in the box.

coastal erosion ecological catastrophe habitat preservation household waste
marine habitat sustainable development waste collection

1 It will take a concerted effort from all citizens to convince the council that the frequency of our ________________ should be increased.
2 The last international meeting of climate experts described ________________, especially forests and jungles, as the most important issue facing humanity today.
3 This ________________ was caused by the river, which burst its banks and flooded after torrential rains.
4 Agriculture should be more focused on ________________, irrespective of the challenges and costs involved. We should be able to meet society's needs today without compromising those of tomorrow.
5 Some countries still send far too much of their ________________ to landfill instead of investing in upgrading recycling facilities.
6 The pollution levels in a ________________ like a coral reef only have to increase slightly before they have devastating effects on the wildlife.
7 Governments of low-lying countries must address the continued ________________ that is affecting communities living by the sea.

Reading and Use of English

Part 4 Key word transformations

For questions 1–6, complete the second sentence so that it has a similar meaning to the first sentence, using the word given. Do not change the word given. You must use between three and eight words, including the word given.

1 People weren't surprised at all when the government added a pollution tax on cars.

IN

When the government introduced the pollution tax nobody ________________ slightest.

2 She thought she'd wait for the applause to stop before starting her closing speech.

DIE

Before starting her closing speech, she decided ________________ down.

3 Jake thought he might like to grow his own vegetables even though he worried it might be too time consuming.

UP

Although Jake was worried it might ________________, he was considering growing his own vegetables.

4 Louise was too busy to attend the climate conference despite the fact that it interested her.

THOUGH

Louise was too busy to attend the climate conference, ________________ seemed.

5 I didn't find the film that exciting, but it did make me think.

THOUGHT-PROVOKING

For me, ________________ exciting.

6 The next service station was 30 kilometres away, and they were nearly out of petrol.

LOW

They were ________________, and there was still 30 kilometres to the next service station.

Writing Part 2 Letter

You recently went on a tour which was advertised as an eco-adventure, but you were shocked at the lack of consideration the tour guide had for the environment. The tour guide ignored your complaints at the time. Write a letter to the director of the tour company outlining the issues you had with the tour and the guide, and how you would like the matter to be resolved.

Write your **letter** in **280–320** words. You do not need to write any postal address.

For more information about writing letters, see page 193.

Idioms Noticing similarities and differences

1 SPEAK Work in pairs. Use the contexts in texts A and B to help you work out the meanings of the idioms in bold. Do the idioms have similar or different meanings?

A

USER096

All these corporate promises to put the environment at the heart of what they do **ring hollow** to me. I mean there's little evidence to prove they're taking action.

Posted 5mins ago

CATFAN3

I recently read a press release from an oil company, and I'm inclined to believe that they're committed to change. The tone of it just **rang true** to me.

Posted 16mins ago

B

... and the trial concluded yesterday. The judge ruled that the factory was not guilty of leaking dangerous levels of toxic chemicals into the water table. A spokesperson for the company said they were delighted to be **in the clear**. This ruling is likely to be met with disapproval from environmental groups campaigning to have the company called to account, and with several other charges pending, the company is not **out of the woods** yet. Campaigners said they intend to ...

About English

The internet is full of stories about the origin of idioms which sound believable but aren't true. Pinning down their origins is notoriously hard since they evolved at a specific point in time and reflect that culture and society. This is also why they often don't translate across languages or even cultures with a shared language.

What idioms from your language don't translate well?

Discussing idioms

Discuss the differences in meaning between these idioms:

- rock the boat / upset the apple cart
- be in a tight spot / be a tight squeeze
- make your blood boil / get your back up

2 SPEAK Work in pairs. Discuss the meanings of the following pairs of idioms. Do they have similar or different meanings? What clues in the sentences helped you decide?

1 A When I realised what was about to happen in the horror film, my **blood ran cold.**

B It **makes my blood boil** just knowing that the council could easily improve air quality by reducing vehicle access to the town centre, yet they choose not to take the opportunity.

2 A It's imperative that no one says anything to **rock the boat** at this delicate stage in the negotiations. We want this deal wrapped up as soon as possible.

B Laura's been **making waves** with her comments about the lack of resources and budget on this project, but I don't know whether her views carry any serious weight.

3 A Either we have to make a few of the team redundant or ask everyone to take a salary cut. We're **stuck between a rock and a hard place** on this.

B Louis helped me when I **was in a tight spot** financially a while back, so if ever he gets into any trouble himself I'll be here to bail him out.

4 A Throwing litter on hiking trails **is out of line** when plenty of bins and recycling points are provided and clearly signposted at various stages.

B What started out as a civil discussion about graffiti in the community soon **got out of hand** as emotions rose and accusations of blame were thrown around.

3 Work in pairs. Write definitions for the idioms in Exercise 2. Check your answers in the Additional materials on page 197.

9 BY DESIGN

KEY LANGUAGE

Expressing concession, contrast, purpose and reason
Passive and causative structures
Prepositional phrases with *by*, *in* and *out of*
Describing art and architecture

IDIOMS

Art and creativity

EXAM PRACTICE

Reading and Use of English Parts 1, 2 & 7
Writing Parts 1 & 2
Listening Parts 2 & 3
Speaking Parts 1 & 2

Speaking Part 1 Interview

Work with a partner. Discuss the questions.

1 If you could be a famous artist or designer from any time in history, who would you be and why?
2 Do you prefer to design and create art yourself or admire the work of others?
3 To what extent can art and design have a positive impact on people's wellbeing?
4 Should museums remove artworks that offend visitors?
5 Should art museums commit to showing equal numbers of female and male artists?

9 BY DESIGN

Landscape with Wheat Sheaves and Rising Moon Vincent Van Gogh, 1889

The Scream, Edvard Munch, 1893

Group X, No. 1, Altarpiece, Hilma af Klint, 1915

Composition 8, Wassily Kandinsky, 1923

Autumn, Giuseppe Arcimboldo, 1573.

Lady with an Ermine, Leonardo Da Vinci, c. 1490

Reading and Use of English Part 7 Multiple matching

1 SPEAK Work in pairs. Look at the paintings and discuss the questions.

1 Do you like any of the paintings? Why? / Why not?
2 Do you consider AI-generated art to be 'real' art? Why? / Why not?
3 To what extent should artists and designers be concerned by AI and other technological innovations, such as 3D printing?

2 You are going to read an article about art and AI (artificial intelligence). For questions 1–10, choose from the sections (A–E). The sections may be chosen more than once.

Which person mentions the following?

the dividends that maintaining a positive mindset pays when things look bleak	1
the feeling of unease that AI induces throughout the wider artistic community	2
the naïvety of artists in their expectations for change	3
the lack of resemblance of artists' contemporary working lives to past practices	4
the consequences of collaboration between humans and computers	5
the progress being made in the art world despite resistance to innovation	6
the need for AI to be prevented from overriding the rights of artists	7
the qualities brought to art by humans that cannot be replicated by computers	8
the implausibility of one particular situation	9
the virtual undetectability of artworks generated by AI	10

3 Rewrite the sentences from the article putting the information in a different order using a word or phrase from the box.

as a result of even though therefore

1 Now that I've had this experience, I'm even more convinced that there's no threat.
2 I know more than most about losing out to AI as our whole industry was turned upside down by new technology in the 80s.
3 They might be surprised by what it's like working with AI, however counterintuitive it may seem.

Don't forget!

In reading and listening parts of the exam, texts and questions may be paraphrased by changing the order of the information. In sentences 1 and 2, the meaning is the same, but the information is in a different order and the connecting words are different.

1 *Artists and AI actually complement each other* ***since*** *one cannot generate output without the other's input.*
2 *Artists have to teach AI how to generate images* ***so*** *the two actually complement each other.*

The robots are taking over

A Jack

AI art doesn't concern me in the slightest; <u>however</u> you can understand why it causes so many artists so much discomfort. I suspect it's related to the unpredictability of where it will all end up. For my part, having been involved in a collaborative project with a gaming company recently, I can see how they go hand in hand. Over 50 artists were employed on the project, and I found it fascinating to observe firsthand the interplay of both these creative forms and how this produced an altogether better product. Artists and AI actually complement each other <u>since</u> one cannot generate output without the other's input. <u>Now that</u> I've had this experience, I'm even more convinced that there's no threat. With all that I can bring to the table, I won't be sidelined in the foreseeable future. I just wish I could get others to believe this too.

B Valentina

As a graphic designer I know more than most about losing out to AI <u>as</u> our whole industry was turned upside down by new technology in the 80s with many people being made redundant. And this has been replicated more recently in the impact of digital on the music industry as well as print media. People are often reluctant to change, and this is no different, it's just part of the evolution of art. A recent example is graffiti artists who are always being denounced for ruining art when, in actual fact they're a long overdue breath of fresh air in a dusty old artworld. AI is on a collision course with artists for better or worse and that won't be derailed by anything human artists say or do, and nor should it be as far as I'm concerned. So the sooner artists from all walks of like stop deluding themselves that things are going to go just how they'd like them to go the better, because there's little likelihood of that.

C Phoebe

You have to hand it to the programmers writing the algorithms and training the AI – the creations are simply incredible by any standard. Would judges in any art competition be able to single out AI generated paintings without exception? To be honest, I wonder whether anyone can reliably answer that as plenty of experts have been fooled by AI generated pieces. For me, it's tantamount to theft, though, when AI reproduces paintings or uses photos without permission. Intellectual property is fundamental to artists to ensure they don't get ripped off and can earn a decent living. Something should be done about this while the genre is still in its infancy, otherwise I imagine we can expect further issues down the line.

D Richard

Many artists seem to fear AI, <u>whereas</u> I'm all for it! In my humble opinion, this is all about artists not wanting to move with the times. I think they are blinkered, <u>in that</u> they don't see the benefits of the technology. Gone are the days when artists could hole themselves up in a remote studio alone, painting in their same old style, and still expect to remain relevant. That kind of lifestyle is out of the question these days and artists can't risk being out of touch with what clients and society want from them, as we're expected to be diverse in what we produce. After all, artists are selling something and those who embrace technology rather than bemoaning the loss of our traditional careers will come across opportunities. They might be surprised by what it's like working with AI, however counterintuitive it may seem.

E Kiki

Nowadays technology steamrolls over everything while genuinely skilled practitioners are left bringing up the rear. If it were up to me, I'd have these AI people spend time with some of our professionals <u>so as</u> to emphasise the hard graft and unique skill that is part and parcel of creativity. You've got to know your Da Vinci from your Kandinsky in terms of objectives, theories and movements as well as have a grasp of differing artistic techniques. It's about representations of the world from different perspectives, not how lifelike the computer image is because it's made from a million pixels.

4 SPEAK Work in groups. What do you think about the opinions expressed in the reading? Which do you agree / disagree with? Why?

Vocabulary Prepositional phrases with *by*, *in* and *out of*

1 Complete the extracts from the reading text on page 129 with the words in the box.

by in out of

1 You have to hand it to the programmers writing the algorithms and training the AI – the creations are simply incredible ____________ **any standard**.

2 Something should be done about this while the genre is still ____________ **its infancy**, otherwise I imagine we can expect further issues down the line.

3 That kind of lifestyle is ____________ **the question** these days and artists can't risk being ____________ **touch** with what clients and society want from artists as we're expected to be diverse in what we produce.

2 Match the sentences 1–8 with the definitions (A–H) of the prepositional phrases in bold.

1 **By all means** make a suggestion as to how my plan could be improved. I need all the help I can get!

2 Did you have a clear vision of the artwork **in your mind's eye** before you started or were you inspired during the creative process?

3 It was a fairly uneventful day at work; nothing **out of the ordinary** happened.

4 **In essence** the painting reflects the artistic style of its era more than anything else.

5 I'm afraid I can't take you to the opening night of fashion week. It's **by invitation only** and there's no plus one.

6 I don't care how we do it, but we're going to need to meet the deadline **by any means necessary**.

7 Only jokes that are **in good taste** should be incorporated into your speech – I don't want anything controversial.

8 That horrible 1960s style office looks **out of place** compared to all the stylish modern ones surrounding it.

A something strange or unusual

B only specific people can attend

C not suitable, uncomfortable in a situation

D of course/ certainly

E doing whatever it takes

F the most important aspect of something

G in someone's memory or imagination

H appropriate for a situation

3 Complete the questions with a prepositional phrase from Exercise 2.

1 Have you ever been to an exclusive event which was ____________?

2 When you think back to your childhood, what images do you see ____________?

3 Has anything ____________ happened recently which surprised you?

4 Name a situation recently where you felt uncomfortable and ____________?

5 Has anything ever been so important to you that you had to do it ____________?

4 SPEAK Work in pairs. Ask and answer the questions in Exercise 3.

Language focus

Expressing concession, contrast, purpose and reason

1 **Find the words in the box underlined in the reading on page 129. Complete the table according to the function of the words in context.**

as however in that now that since so as to whereas

concession	contrast	purpose	reason

2 **Rewrite the sentences, replacing the words in bold with a word or phrase from Exercise 1.**

1 I'm extremely fortunate **because** I had the financial means to support myself through university.
2 My children have flown the nest, **so** I'll be able to recycle some of their old clothes.
3 Lia loves Van Gogh **but** Tom prefers modern art.
4 This painting was drawn by a computer, **even though** that sounds far-fetched.
5 We went out of our way to see the piece **because** it's moving to a private collection.

3 **Go to Ready for Grammar on page 224 for further rules, explanations and practice.**

4 **SPEAK Work in pairs. Complete the sentences so they are true for you and then compare your ideas.**

When it comes to artistic and creative things, I'm not very good at ... **whereas** ... .
For me art is about ... **in that** ... .
Doing creative activities is important/ not important to me **since** ... .

Reading and Use of English Part 1 Multiple-choice cloze

1 **For questions 1–8, read the text below and decide which answer (A, B, C or D) best fits each gap. There is an example at the beginning (0).**

Scientists and engineers have long been (0) ___C___ by the Leaning Tower of Pisa's remarkable ability to remain standing over several centuries despite its almost four-degree tilt and having been at the (1) ________ of numerous earthquakes since its construction was completed in 1372. To the naked eye, it appears extremely precarious and likely to collapse at any moment, and yet it has (2) ________ the test of time. New research suggests that the tower's (3) ________ can be attributed to the soil it is built on and a pause early on in the construction works that had the unintended effect of strengthening the foundations.

Over the course of the 12th century, the city of Pisa engaged in several battles with other nearby towns and cities which caused construction to cease. Experts now suggest that in all (4) ________ this was responsible for the tower being so (5) ________ since it allowed it to gradually sink further into the soft soil. (6) ________, the soft soil which caused it to lean in the first place has (7) ________ to be its saviour too. Restoration work carried out in the early 20th century to reinforce the foundations has (8) ________ confidence amongst scientists and engineers, and they believe that the tower is unlikely to collapse any time soon. In fact, not for at least another two hundred years.

0 **A** deluded **B** conned **C** baffled **D** fazed
1 **A** mercy **B** forefront **C** expense **D** spot
2 **A** held **B** lasted **C** stood **D** remained
3 **A** resilience **B** fortitude **C** tenacity **D** resistance
4 **A** eventuality **B** appearances **C** odds **D** likelihood
5 **A** concrete **B** stable **C** anchored **D** substantial
6 **A** Flippantly **B** Ironically **C** Incongruously **D** Ambiguously
7 **A** revealed **B** arisen **C** materialised **D** transpired
8 **A** transfused **B** instilled **C** lodged **D** permeated

Vocabulary Describing art and architecture

1 SPEAK Work in pairs and discuss which of the words in groups 1–3 have a different meaning from the other two.

1 ostentatious / flamboyant / renowned
2 understated / vulgar / minimalistic
3 swanky / unassuming / utilitarian

2 For 1–12, choose the correct alternative to complete the text.

INTERIOR DESIGN: different strokes for different folks

Interior design for the average person has come on leaps and bounds since the advent of home makeover TV shows back in the 1970s, and one thing that these shows have made crystal clear is the distinctive nature of taste. After all, as the saying goes, beauty is in the eye of the beholder and this is definitely the case when it comes to how we decorate our homes.

Some people believe interior design should have a (1) *garish / utilitarian / whimsical* look and feel, considering embellishments, such as cushions to be unnecessary as they detract from purpose and function. These people tend to splash out on a few timeless pieces of furniture from (2) *renowned / vulgar / unassuming* designers or shops, rather than have lots of bits and pieces at a lower price point. They would choose (3) *imposing / understated / vulgar* elegance over anything that could be considered (4) *minimalistic / ostentatious / utilitarian* or showy.

This (5) *flamboyant / minimalistic / renowned* approach is synonymous with contemporary design. Replete with sleek fixtures and fittings, many (6) *garish / imposing / swanky* modern offices have adopted this look in order to denote a level of success, sophistication and quality.

Not everyone is into this however, and for the more (7) *flamboyant / imposing / utilitarian* amongst us, when it comes to curtains, cushions, rugs and ornaments, the more (8) *unassuming / utilitarian / whimsical* the approach, the better. These people enjoy being surrounded by items that will stand out and take centre stage. They are likely to choose (9) *imposing / minimalistic / unassuming*, eye-catching colours for the walls to create a bold contrast with those of the furnishings.

Then, there are those who love an eclectic, vintage look. These people are often to be found at flea markets looking for items to collect that reflect the motifs and styles of bygone eras, from wallpaper and colour schemes to furniture and accessories. Take the 1980s, for instance, when bright, (10) *garish / minimalistic / swanky* colours were all the rage. While this style may still be loved by fans of vintage, others consider it to be (11) *renowned / vulgar / understated* and a sign of poor taste.

At the end of the day, whatever your style preference, be it the wild and the wacky or something altogether more muted and (12) *garish / renowned / unassuming*, the best advice is probably to embrace it and enjoy it.

3 Complete the definitions with adjectives from Exercises 1 and 2. Some have more than one possibility.

1 An eyesore is something you think is ______
2 Something playful or fun is ______
3 If you are in awe of something, it is ______
4 Something that doesn't stand out is ______
5 If something is famous, it is ______
6 Two adjectives to describe artistic or architectural styles are ______
7 If something is designed to attract a lot of attention, it is ______

4 SPEAK Work in pairs. Describe the objects and buildings in the photos below using the words from Exercise 2.

Listening Part 2 Sentence completion

1 SPEAK Work in pairs. Discuss the following questions.

1 Why do you think some companies spend a fortune on their offices?
2 What image do modern skyscrapers project? Is this important or not?
3 What impact does the interior design of offices have on the way people work? Why?

2 9.1 You will hear a lecture on unusual office buildings. For questions 1–9, complete the sentences with a word or short phrase.

MAKING A MARK

Many architects are driven to create a **(1)** ____________ that will stand the test of time.

The **(2)** ____________ of the majority of the world's most renowned cultural buildings is comparable, irrespective of location or the era in which it was built.

The public reception to the more innovatively designed office buildings has tended to be **(3)** ____________.

In order to create its vast, minimalist interior, Lloyds of London had some of the **(4)** ____________ commonly associated with a building reimagined and repositioned.

As far as 20th century architecture is concerned, the Lloyds of London building is widely regarded as one of the most **(5)** ____________ examples there is.

Initially, the twisted F & F building was intended as a **(6)** ____________ case study.

According to the lecturer, what makes the F & F building **(7)** ____________ is that it was relatively cheap to build for a building of its magnitude.

Showcasing their architects' **(8)** ____________ is one of the reasons behind the quirky designs of the Lloyds of London and the F&F buildings.

The Fisheries Board office is a contradiction to other **(9)** ____________ buildings.

3 SPEAK Work in small groups and discuss the questions. Which of the buildings described in the listening would you prefer to work in? Why? If you were an architect, what issues would you prioritise in office design?

Pronunciation Juncture

1 9.2 Listen to the phrases from the listening and tick what you hear.

1	an aim	☐	a name	☐
2	my turn	☐	might earn	☐

2 Check your answers in the Audioscript on page 239.

3 9.3 Listen to the following phrases. Which phrase do you hear first and second? Write 1 or 2 next to A and B.

1	A the sky	___	B this guy	___
2	A send to all	___	B centre wall	___
3	A keep sticking	___	B keeps ticking	___
4	A an ice	___	B a nice	___
5	A its wings	___	B it swings	___
6	A a tax on	___	B attacks on	___
7	A a monk swimming	___	B amongst women	___
8	A the cross-eyed bear	___	B the cross I'd bear	___

About English

When people mishear song lyrics or poems the resulting changes are called 'mondegreens'. The term was coined by American writer Syliva Wright in 1954 when she heard her mother say the line 'layd him on the green' from a poem as 'Lady Mondegreen'. The word mondegreen entered the dictionary in 2000. You can find lots of examples of mondegreens from famous songs online.

Have you ever misheard any song lyrics in English or your language?

Language focus Passive and causative structures

1 Correct the passive forms in the sentences from the listening on page 133.

1. But these buildings share a function in that they're cultural, designed for pleasure and entertainment and, as a genre, had been reimagined and had been reworked over and over.
2. However, the plans have been drawn up with plenty of attention to function rather than form, it is understandable that the initial reception could be described as lukewarm at best.
3. It's intriguing to note that the spiral design actually started out as a theoretical project by the architect company, but despite not has been intended as an actual building, it caught the eye of one the company's clients and a decision was made to go ahead with the project.

2 Match the passive structures in bold in the quiz to the uses A–E.

ARE YOU AN ART AND DESIGN CONNOISSEUR?

Put your knowledge to the test with our quiz.

1 **Having been born** in Malaga, which famous Spanish artist moved to Barcelona and then Paris, where he spent the rest of his life?

2 Which spectacular white building did an Indian emperor **have his chief architect design** to house the tomb of his wife?

3 Which iron tower that was initially disliked and **criticised** by artists and intellectuals for its design went on to become one of the world's most recognisable and iconic landmarks?

4 In spite of **having been taught** only reading, writing and basic mathematics, which artist from Florence became one of the world's greatest inventors?

5 Which Dutch artist, whose paintings are some of the most valuable in the world, **had their work ignored** during their lifetime?

A to avoid repeating the same passive auxiliary form in a sentence ___
B to give background information to help explain or clarify something in the past ___
C as a complement when following a preposition ___
D to describe making someone do something ___
E to focus on the victim of a negative or unwanted action or event ___

3 SPEAK Work in pairs. Do the quiz in Exercise 2.

4 Go to Ready for Grammar on page 224 for further rules, explanations and practice.

Speaking Part 2 Collaborative task

1 Work in pairs. Look at pictures 1 and 4. They show people doing different types of jobs. Talk together about what might attract people to these jobs.

2 Now look at pictures 1–4. Imagine that a newspaper is writing an article on the provision of arts and culture employment opportunities for young people. Discuss what could be done to increase these opportunities. Then suggest other jobs in art and design that could be included in the article.

3 SPEAK Which of the jobs in the photos do you think would be the most challenging? Why?

Article – arts and culture

1

2

Listening Part 3 Multiple choice

1 SPEAK Work in pairs. What are the people in the pictures doing? What skills do you think these people have to possess to do this?

2 9.4 You will hear part of a discussion in which Olga Jenkins, an art restorer and Edward Blackwell, an artist who specialises in reproduction, discuss their work.

For questions 1–5, choose the answer (A, B, C or D) which fits best according to what you hear.

1 What is Edward's assessment of his customers?
   - **A** They lack an appreciation of quality.
   - **B** Their tastes are varied and eclectic.
   - **C** Their requests are often predictable.
   - **D** They're impressed by his work ethic.

2 What do Edward and Olga agree on with regard to their jobs?
   - **A** There is a lack of appreciation for what is involved.
   - **B** Both of them use specialist equipment.
   - **C** Some of the necessary skills cross over.
   - **D** They invested a lot of time in their training.

3 What does Olga say about the time needed for restoration work?
   - **A** Big projects are notorious for having lengthy delays.
   - **B** The nature of the work makes planning impractical.
   - **C** Experts are consulted about an appropriate timescale.
   - **D** Time taken at the start of the project can upset the schedule.

4 Edward questions whether his paintings might be improved if he
   - **A** made some adjustments to his environment.
   - **B** focused on improving his concentration.
   - **C** worked in short intervals instead of one long stint.
   - **D** was able to receive feedback as he worked.

5 Olga and Edward both mention achieving certain outcomes by
   - **A** the process of trial and error.
   - **B** a tried and tested solution.
   - **C** tending to minute details.
   - **D** the use of certain tricks.

3 SPEAK Work in groups. Discuss the following questions.

1 Who is your favourite artist? Why?

2 Look at the list of art galleries and museums below. Where are they? What can you see in them? Which would you like to visit? Why?

The Louvre	The Guggenheim	The Rijksmuseum
MOMA	The Victoria and Albert Museum	The Deutches Museum
The Tate Modern	The Acropolis Museum	The Uffizi Gallery

Don't forget!

Think about how the wording in the sentences could be paraphrased in the listening as you read the questions. The paraphrases may involve using synonyms, different grammatical structures or changing the order of information.

3

4

Writing Part 2 Review

1 SPEAK Work in pairs and answer the questions.

1. Would you like to go to any of the exhibitions in the photos? Why? / Why not?
2. Why might an exhibition curator choose these formats?
3. What are the intended effects of these types of exhibitions?
4. Have you ever been to an exhibition that had a profound effect on you? What would you say to convince someone else that it was worth seeing?
5. Have you ever been to an exhibition that you didn't enjoy? What was unpleasant or disappointing about it?

2 Read the Writing Part 2 task and the model answer on page 137. What is the purpose of each paragraph? Which parts of the answer cover the points in the task?

> A local magazine is posting a series of reviews of art exhibitions that readers have visited recently. You decide to send in a review in which you describe an exhibition and evaluate the layout, installations, and overall experience.

3 Underline the different tenses used in each paragraph. Why are these tenses used?

4 Look at the underlined phrases in paragraph 1. Are they usually followed by information or opinions that are more neutral in tone or more extreme?

Useful language

Persuasive vocabulary

Reviews use extreme vocabulary to persuade the reader to engage with or avoid something.

1. Look at the bold words in the model answer which are neutral and replace them with the persuasive words below.

dazzling	enthusiasts	exploded	exquisitely	meticulously	mighty
poignant	powerful	radiating	renowned	triumph	turbulent

2. Work in pairs. Which one word in Exercise 1 is negative? Can you think of opposites for the words above?

INFINITELY GOOD

A long-awaited new exhibition at The Tate Modern opened last week, billed as a **(1) great** display of works from Yayoi Kusuma, one of the world's most celebrated artists and as expected it was nothing short of a **(2) big success**. Titled *Infinity Mirror Rooms*, the exhibition explores themes of infinite space and endless replication through two immersive mirror room installations, reflecting her long career in conceptual and minimalist artwork since she **(3) arrived** onto the New York art scene in the late 1950s.

The installations are accompanied by photographic works **(4) carefully** documenting the artist's early sculptural work as well as images of her working in her New York studio, giving the viewer context so as to interpret the artist's work more deeply and see her as the **(5) strong** artistic force that she is. Some images explore the **(6) emotional** experience of moving to New York, where feelings of alienation hint at this having been a **(7) difficult** period in her life.

The curation of the exhibition has been **(8) nicely** done, with attention to detail in the layout and flow throughout the gallery. The main draw is without doubt the installations themselves in which tiny, suspended lights give the impression of **(9) shining out** in all directions. It gives a sense that the light has filled the **(10) large** Tate modern building beyond the confines of the installation rooms.

This exhibition would be well worth a visit for **(11) fans** of the artist herself, but additionally it could easily capture the hearts of any installation art lovers as a fascinating way to experience a talented and **(12) famous** artist.

5 SPEAK Work in pairs. How do the persuasive words affect the reader's reaction to the review?

6 Decide whether the adjectives below are positive or negative. Write + (positive) or – (negative).

appalling	___	dubious	___
disillusioned	___	flawless	___
formidable	___	mediocre	___
profound	___	crude	___

7 Complete the text with some of the words from Exercise 6.

Not the one for me

Attending the opening night of the latest exhibition of local artists at The ONE Gallery, I was immediately struck by how underwhelming the display was. Overall, I would rate the works as **(1)** ______________, at best. There were few pieces containing anything original, while the technical prowess on display was somewhat **(2)** ______________, with glaring errors in perspective and clumsy brushwork. In addition, the pieces were organised by artist, meaning it was nigh on impossible to discern any overriding thematic connection, which made the curation feel rather **(3)** ______________.

The promotional materials had suggested that the work on display would give insight into the people and culture of the region and visitors would leave with a more **(4)** ______________ understanding of their contribution to our national heritage. I left, **(5)** ______________ at the state of art in the region and suggest that art lovers head elsewhere, perhaps Galerias Inc., whose latest exhibition is almost **(6)** ______________ in terms of professionalism.

8 Choose the sentences or parts of sentences in Exercise 7 that you could use to:

1. describe the exhibition's layout
2. give background information on the exhibition
3. say if you would recommend the exhibition
4. explain the subject/topic of the exhibition.
5. give a response to the content of an exhibition

9 Now write your answer to the task in Exercise 2. Use some words from the *Useful language* box.

Write your **review** in **280–320** words.

For more information on writing reviews, see page 195.

Don't forget!

Organise your review clearly so that the reader can understand where you are giving a description and where you are evaluating or making recommendations. Write your review in paragraphs, give it a title and remember to give a recommendation as well as an evaluation.

9 REVIEW

Language focus Concession, contrast, purpose and reason | Passive and causative structures

1 Read the email and underline the correct alternative.

From: Sam

Hi Casey

I just wanted to put your mind at rest regarding the designs for the new 3D printing machine.

However disruptive it **(1)** *may / may be / is being* to have the engineering department constantly going back and forth on the designs at this stage, it shouldn't delay the project too much, **(2)** *since / however / whereas* we've already managed to get the marketing and distribution strategies underway. This should save us time further down the line.

In spite of **(3)** *having been hindered / having hindered / having to be hindered* by recent discussions, we just need a couple more meetings so as to finalise the design and then we're good to go. Since we started having meetups on a Friday, things are progressing at a steadier pace. I'm also going to have the head of engineering **(4)** *check / checking / to check* in with me personally.

The team is functioning **(5)** *so as to / whereas / in that* they are communicating clearly and focusing on outcomes. As **(6)** *for myself / to me / with mine*, leading the project continues to work well. **(7)** *Having to be / Have being / Having been* involved from the beginning**,** I have a thorough understanding of the complexities and the team dynamics.

Anyway, that's all for now.

Best wishes,

Sam

Vocabulary Prepositional phrases with *by*, *in* and *out of*

Match the sentence halves.

1 If you have any ideas, **by all**
2 All modern art is, **in**
3 Politicians are so **out of**
4 Borrowing my car is **out of the**
5 I can see my old house **in my**
6 Your comments on art weren't **in**
7 Jess is determined to succeed **by any**
8 The new treatment is still **in its**
9 The product launch event **is by**
10 The painting isn't high quality **by any**
11 That vintage vase looks **out of**
12 It's a relief that nothing **out of the**

A **mind's eye** quite clearly.
B **ordinary** happened on my commute today.
C **invitation only**, I'm afraid.
D **good taste** during the gallery tour.
E **place** in this minimalistic space.
F **means** share them in the group chat.
G **standard**, so don't buy it.
H **touch** with the mood of the nation.
I **means necessary**, which is a great attitude.
J **essence**, a product of rebelling against tradition.
K **question** this weekend.
L **infancy**, but it sounds promising.

Reading and Use of English Part 2 Open cloze

For questions **1–8**, read the text below and think of the word that best fits each space. Use only one word in each space. There is an example at the beginning **(0)**.

SOUNDS ABOUT RIGHT

Getting the right tone in restaurant design is **(0)** ___*NO*___ mean feat since it is such a sensory experience. While restaurant design primarily tries to emulate or reflect the taste of the cuisine, as the food is what is centre **(1)** ____________, this is shortly followed by sight to get that all important wow factor, especially in high-end establishments. Invariably the most frequently overlooked sense is that of sound. **(2)** ____________ been subjected to all sorts of soundscapes in restaurants, many of them unpleasant, a growing number of diners now regard the volume and type of background noise as a fundamental consideration when deciding **(3)** ____________ or not to make a reservation.

(4) ____________ to popular belief, music is deemed less intrusive by diners than ambient noise. Silence in a restaurant can make people feel ill at **(5)** ____________, so restaurants often splash out **(6)** ____________ sound equipment to create the right ambiance. However, it is the noise from the diners that impacts the soundscape the most, therefore when assessing the acoustic properties of a restaurant space, it is essential to **(7)** ____________ this in mind. In addition, materials can play a vital role in that installing acoustic wall panelling, carpets and velvet upholstery count **(8)** ____________ reducing the noise footprint of a restaurant since they all possess sound absorbency properties.

Writing Part 1 Essay

Read the two texts below.

Write an essay summarising and evaluating the key points from each text. Use your own words throughout as far as possible and include your own ideas in your answer.

WHEN CULTURE BECOMES EXCLUSIVE

Unfortunately, people are increasingly being priced out of various forms of culture and it's not just those mediums that have always been considered exclusive and the reserve of the financially elite, such as the opera or A-list celebrity concerts. Even entrance tickets to museums and attractions have skyrocketed, leaving many families and lower-income earners bereft of affordable cultural experiences. Part of the issue is due to cuts in funding as well as rising production costs. This is being felt across all types of business with increased costs passed on to end users. In this way, the arts and entertainment industries are no different.

Funding culture pays dividends

It's notoriously difficult to pin down an entirely satisfactory definition of culture, but irrespective of what it encompasses, the benefits it brings to society are enormous. Whether musical theatre, movies, concerts or museums and galleries, life is enriched in a myriad of ways through engagement with the arts. Essentially, it's about engaging in creativity, new ideas and alternative ways of interpreting the world around us. These experiences have greatly contributed to the development of every aspect of society for generations.

For more information on writing essays, see page 190.

About English

Idiomatic phrases are often coined by people working in different professions. For example, the artist Peter Arno first used *back to the drawing board* in a comic strip in *The New Yorker* in 1941. It shows a man holding some engineering plans walking away from a damaged plane. The caption says *"Well, back to the drawing board."*

Idioms Art and creativity

1 Match the idioms (A–C) to the situations that explain them.

1 Nothing much happens in the first half hour or so of the film, but it picks up later on.
2 This is not the image we want to portray in our advertising campaign. You'll need to rethink it.
3 I'm really glad I kept this 1990s video game console – I could get quite a lot money for it if I sold it online.

A It's back to the drawing board. **B** It's a slow burner. **C** It's a collector's item.

2 SPEAK Work in pairs. How did the situations help you choose the idioms?

3 Complete the sentences with the art words from the box.

art canvas eye mark mould

1 Like other celebrated artists of the 20th century, Dali **left his** ________ **on the world** through both his art and his personality.
2 There's no fixed job specification so you can take it in the direction you see fit. It's **a blank** ________.
3 As I turned the corner, the building **caught my** ________ due to its garish colours.
4 After experimenting for ages, she's managed to get her photoshop skills **down to a fine** ________.
5 Jennifer **broke the** ________ in her family by becoming an artist rather than a doctor like everyone else.

4 Match the idioms 1–4 to their definitions a–d.

1 to be a breath of fresh air
2 to bear no resemblance to something
3 to go down a storm
4 to reinvent the wheel

a to be very popular
b to waste time and effort doing something that someone has already done well
c to be new and make everything feel more interesting and exciting
d to have a completely different appearance

5 Complete the sentences with the correct idiom from Exercise 4.

1 The family-orientated scheme for the new community centre is going to ________ with the local parent groups.
2 Portraits are not my strong point; this last one of my mother ________ her.
3 Let's just use the same plan as before. We don't need to ________ here.
4 James's creativity and enthusiasm ________ in this old stuffy organisation.

6 When learning idiomatic language, it is helpful to record its structure. Match the phrases in Exercises 1, 3 and 4 to the structures below.

1 Noun phrases
A adjective + noun: ________, ________
B noun + noun: ________
C noun + prepositional phrase: ________

2 Verb + noun
A verb + noun with definite article: ________
B verb + noun with indefinite article: ________

3 Longer phrases
A verb + noun + preposition ________
B verb + pronoun + prepositional phrase ________
C verb + pronoun + noun ________
D verb + prepositional phrase ________

7 SPEAK Work in pairs. Take turns to make sentences using the idioms in Exercise 1, 3 and 4. Listen to each other and correct any mistakes you hear with the structures.

Discussing idioms

Discuss the differences in meaning between these idioms:

a blank canvas / a clean slate

go down a storm / go down like a lead balloon

catch your eye / catch your breath

READY FOR SPEAKING

Introduction

The **Speaking** paper consists of three parts and lasts 16 minutes. You usually take the test with one other candidate (a group of three is possible) and there are two examiners: the interlocutor, who conducts the test, asks the questions, and sets up your tasks, and the other is the assessor, who listens and assesses your performance. The interlocutor also assesses how you perform in the test overall and contributes to your final mark.

Complete the following information about the test with the words in the box.

appropriate attention contributions decision-making
demonstrate initiate interact interruption opinions
organise reaction speculating willing written yourself

TASKS

Part 1 is a social exchange. The examiner asks you questions and you need to respond with general information about **(1)** ________.

Part 2 is done with your partner and has two stages. The first focuses on your **(2)** ________ to a visual input, usually a maximum of two pictures. The second stage is a **(3)** ________ task involving four pictures.

In Part 3 you are given a **(4)** ________ question on a topic card, which you respond to individually. This will then lead to further questions and discussion about the topic.

COMMUNICATION

Part 1 does not require you to **(5)** ________ with the other candidate(s) when answering questions.

However, in Part 2, it is important to collaborate with your partner(s) and show your ability to engage in and successfully manage a discussion.

You have the opportunity to speak without **(6)** ________ in Part 3. When your partner is speaking, you must pay **(7)** ________, so you are ready to answer a follow up question.

LANGUAGE

(8) ________ a range of language functions such as giving opinions, **(9)** ________ and evaluating among others.

You need to **(10)** ________ discussion, make positive **(11)** ________ and be **(12)** ________ to take turns.

Remember to **(13)** ________ your thoughts logically and express your **(14)** ________ clearly using **(15)** ________ language.

Speaking Part 1 Interview — Total time: 2 minutes

1 **Work in pairs. Look at the topics that might come up in Part 1 of the test. Write one question for each of the topics.**

What for you is the most interesting characteristic of your hometown?

- hometown / local area / neighbourhood
- free time / leisure / hobbies
- languages / language learning
- work / studies / skills
- travel / festivals / celebrations

2 **Work in groups. Ask and answer the questions you wrote in Exercise 1.**

3 **0.5 Watch or listen to Sofia and Mario do Part 1 of the Speaking test and answer the questions.**

1 How relevant are each of the student's responses?

2 How well does each student develop their responses?

How to go about it

Listen to the questions and keep your delivery natural. Don't memorise answers as this will sound stilted.

Develop your answers and give examples, when relevant.

Speaking Part 2 Collaborative task Total time: 4 minutes

What to expect in the exam

- Part 2 has two stages. First, you will be shown several pictures, and will be asked to give your reaction to a maximum of two of them. You have one minute to speak and you should talk together with your partner.
- In the second stage, you will be given instructions for a decision-making task that focuses on all of the pictures. You are expected to interact with your partner to try and reach a decision collaboratively. You have about three minutes for this part of the test.

How to go about it

- Use language of speculation and comparison to discuss the pictures.
- Give opinions but also take the initiative to seek opinions and ideas from your partner.

1 **Work in pairs. Look at these pictures. They show people in different situations. Look at pictures 1 and 2 and discuss how these people might feel.**

2 **0.6 Watch or listen to Sofia and Mario discussing the pictures. Answer the questions.**

1 How well do Sofia and Mario interact with each other?
2 How well do they use language to achieve this part of the task?

Magazine article – personal achievement

1

2

3

4

How to go about it

- Listen carefully to what your partner says so that you can give a genuine and logical reaction. Try to respond to what they have said and develop the discussion further.
- It is OK if your opinion differs from your partner. Explain why you hold a different view and give examples. If you agree with your partner, make sure you provide extra reasons and develop your response.
- Remember that there is no 'correct' answer to this task but that it's important to show you are negotiating and working towards a decision with your partner.
- Use language of comparison, evaluation and opinion. Make suggestions to your partner to keep the discussion moving.

3 Work in pairs. Look at all the pictures 1–4. Imagine a lifestyle magazine is planning an article on the theme of personal achievement. They need a picture to accompany the article. Talk together about the ways in which these activities contribute to personal achievement and then decide which image you think would be best to use.

4 0.7 Watch or listen to Sofia and Mario discussing the task. Answer the questions.

1. How well do the students respond to the task?
2. Do they interact effectively?
3. How relevant and coherent are the students' contributions?

Speaking Part 3 Long turn — Total time: 4 minutes

What to expect in the exam

- In this part of your test, each candidate is given two minutes to speak on a topic without interruption.
- The examiner will give you a card with a question on it for you to answer. The card will also have some prompts on it, which you can include in your answer, if you would like to. Alternatively, you may discuss other ideas, as long as they are relevant to the question.
- You can take around ten seconds to think about what you want to say and to organise your thoughts. Your partner will listen to you carefully and will not interrupt you.
- When you finish your long turn, the interlocutor will ask the other candidate a follow-up question related to the topic.

1 Work in pairs and do the task.

Student A: Talk for two minutes about the question below.

How does the sense of competing against others affect people?

- in sport
- at work
- amongst friends

2 Now take it in turns to answer the follow-up questions.

Follow-up questions

Student B: Are you a competitive person?

Student A: How about you?

Speaking

3 Now change roles.

Student B: Talk for two minutes about the question below.

What benefits and drawbacks do large sporting events bring?
- host nations
- sports players and athletes
- fans

4 Now take it in turns to answer the follow-up questions.

Follow-up questions
Student A: Do you think competitions in sports in general is a positive thing?
Student B: What do you think?

5 ▶ 0.8 Watch or listen to Sofia and Mario discussing the task. Answer the questions.

1. How well-organised and cohesive are the students' contributions?
2. Do they show a wide range of vocabulary and grammatical structures to discuss the topics effectively?

Speaking Part 3 Discussion — Total time: 6 minutes

1 Work in pairs. Read the questions and discuss them with your partner.

Do you think more competitive people tend to be more successful than people who aren't very competitive?
Do we learn to be competitive or are we born competitive?
Do you think it's ever a good thing to compare yourself against other people?

2 ▶ 0.9 Watch or listen to Sofia and Mario answering the questions. Consider the following:

1. How well do Sofia and Mario develop their answers?
2. How appropriate and detailed are their responses?
3. How well do they express their own opinions and respond to those of their partner?

10

ADAPTATION

KEY LANGUAGE

Inversion
Creating emphasis and cleft sentences
Describing books and films
Similes

IDIOMS

From literature

EXAM PRACTICE

Reading and Use of English Parts 1, 3, 4 & 5
Writing Parts 1 & 2
Listening Part 4
Speaking Parts 1 & 3

Speaking Part 1 Interview

Work with a partner. Discuss the questions.

1 In what ways can reading literature facilitate the process of learning a language?
2 What do you imagine are the fundamental things playwrights and scriptwriters have to consider when adapting a book for stage or screen?
3 When watching films in another language, do you prefer them to be dubbed or subtitled? Why?
4 What challenges do you imagine translators are faced with when trying to remain faithful to the original meaning of a text?
5 Should we ever judge literature based on the personal lifestyle or views of the writer?

10 ADAPTATION

Listening Part 4 Multiple matching

1 SPEAK Work in pairs. Discuss the questions.

1. Why do you think the design of covers for the same book can differ across cultures?
2. What are the challenges when dubbing films or writing subtitles for the screen?
3. What are some of the most typical ways to promote new books, films or theatre productions?

2 10.1 You will hear five short extracts in which people are talking about problems they experienced while working on adaptations of fiction for different purposes.

TASK ONE

For questions **1–5**, choose from the list **(A–H)** the reason for the issue they describe.

TASK TWO

For questions **6–10**, choose from the list **(A–H)** what they learnt from their challenges.

While you listen you must complete both tasks.

A ignoring expert advice
B choosing an easy option
C a quarrel between those involved
D poor leadership
E targeting the wrong market
F failing to include significant details
G financial difficulties
H a lack of resources

Speaker 1 [1]
Speaker 2 [2]
Speaker 3 [3]
Speaker 4 [4]
Speaker 5 [5]

A the advantage of keeping a process simple
B the benefit of investing in equipment
C the importance of giving clear instructions
D the benefit of having structure
E the need for professionals
F the importance of managing stress
G the value of resisting pressure to change
H the merits of saying no

Speaker 1 [6]
Speaker 2 [7]
Speaker 3 [8]
Speaker 4 [9]
Speaker 5 [10]

Don't forget!

The answers for Task One and Task Two are generally in order on the recording, but in one or two cases, the answer to Task Two may come before the answer to Task One.

3 SPEAK Work in pairs and discuss the questions.

Have you had a challenge recently that you can learn something from? What happened?

Pronunciation Accents

1 10.2 Listen to speakers 1–5 from Exercise 1 saying the sentence below. Match each speaker (1–5) with the country or region you think they come from (A–E), judging by their accent.

The data shows our fiction sales are up about 30% this year, which is really interesting.

A Australia [ ] **B** Ireland [ ] **C** Northern England [ ]
D Scotland [ ] **E** The USA [ ]

2 SPEAK Work in pairs. Look again at the sentence in Exercise 1. The pronunciation of which sounds varies the most between the different speakers?

3 SPEAK Work in pairs. Take it in turns with your partner to say the sentence in Exercise 1 copying the different speakers' accents.

4 SPEAK Work with your partner. Discuss the following questions.

1. Which accents in English do you find easiest to identify and understand?
2. Are there many different accents in your language? Discuss some of the most typical variations.

Language focus Inversion

1 **10.3 Listen to these four extracts from the Listening task and write the missing words in each gap.**

1 ________________ I discover that they'd gone way over budget on the CGI …

2 ________________ how it would end up, I would have definitely approached things differently.

3 ________________ been involved in such a disastrous film adaptation of a book.

4 ________________ they started coordinating the discussions than the production schedule got back on track …

2 **Check your answers in the Audioscript on page 240. Why do the speakers use inversion? What is the effect on the listener?**

3 **Rewrite the underlined sections of the text so that they begin with the words in brackets. Remember to make any further grammatical changes necessary.**

THE TALENTED LIN-MANUEL MIRANDA

(1) The musical *Hamilton* opened in 2015 and it became a roaring success (No sooner), first at the Public Theatre in Lower Manhattan and then on Broadway, launching its creator Lin-Manuel Miranda to immediate stardom. **(2)** Miranda could never have predicted Hamilton's incredible worldwide appeal (Under no circumstances), but the number of accolades it's received speaks for itself. **(3)** It won 11 Tony awards, 8 Drama Desk Awards, a Grammy, an Emmy and a Pulitzer Prize (Not only). **(4)** His remarkable talent for writing songs that can communicate huge amounts of emotion and depth in relatively few words became apparent then (Only then).

Disney were quick to spot this gift. His collaboration on the 2016 film *Moana* and the 2021 film *Encanto*, saw him picking up two grammys and receiving two Academy Award nominations, both for Best Original Song. In fact, **(5)** shortly after the latter film was released on Disney+, the song *We don't talk about Bruno*, became an international hit (Scarcely), reaching number one on US Spotify and becoming the top trending music video on YouTube.

Despite his extraordinary triumphs as a songwriter, actor, singer, filmmaker and playwright, Miranda himself suggests that his success might not have happened at all **(6)** if it were not for two influential people in his life (were it), his long-time university friend and director Thomas Kail and his wife, Vanessa Nadal.

Whatever he turns his attention to next, whether it be more musical theatre or directing for the big screen, you can be sure that Lin-Manuel Miranda is here to stay.

4 **Go to Ready for Grammar on page 226 for further rules, explanations and practice.**

5 **SPEAK Work in pairs. Tell your partner about someone extremely talented that you know about. Use some inversion structures.**

Vocabulary Describing books and films

1 Complete the book and film reviews with the words in the box.

box office hit critically acclaimed cult classic far-fetched hard-hitting heart-wrenching long-awaited page-turner spellbinding spine-tingling star-studded tearjerker

ONLINEREVIEWS LATEST BOOKS FILMS TV STREAMING SEARCH

1 Set in 1930s Liverpool, this emotional story of a young orphan is a real **(1)** ______________ that will have you reaching for the tissues on more than one occasion. It's a sorrowful, **(2)** ______________ tale of a child's quest to belong but the author's writing style, just as much as the story, is what makes it such a **(3)** ______________; you just can't put down.

2 It's an odd and fairly **(4)** ______________ story that challenges the viewer's credibility; a black comedy that focuses on the friendship of 20-year-old Harold and Maude, who is 79. It is, however, without a doubt a **(5)** ______________, its passionate aficionados defending it to the hilt at any and every criticism. Interestingly, it wasn't that well received initially, but on its second release it became a **(6)** ______________.

3 *Where are the Children Now* is the **(7)** ______________ follow-up novel to *Where are the Children* by Mary Higgins Clark, published in 1975. In keeping with her usual material, the story is a **(8)** ______________ thriller with twists and turns in the narrative, which are bound to keep you on the edge of your seat. The book explores motherhood, what it means to lose a child and be wrongfully convicted of a crime and is a **(9)** ______________ exploration of the failures of the justice system. While, not for the faint hearted, it is highly recommended.

4 Featuring a remarkable **(10)** ______________ cast of some of Hollywood's finest, the new film from director Christopher Nolan is nothing short of a masterpiece, with **(11)** ______________ performances from its main protagonists, some of whom are hotly tipped to be amongst this year's Oscar nominees. In particular, Cillian Murphy's portrayal of a physicist grappling with the devastating effects of science on the world is so utterly **(12)** ______________ that you'll be mesmerised throughout.

2 Write the words from Exercise 1 next to their meanings.

1. a film that is very successful and earns a lot of money ______________
2. something that captures your attention completely ______________
3. a story that is intended to make people cry ______________
4. something exciting or frightening in a way that people enjoy ______________
5. something hoped for or expected for some time ______________
6. something that makes you feel very emotional or sad ______________
7. a film or play that has a lot of famous actors ______________
8. something difficult to believe because it's unlikely ______________
9. a very exciting or interesting book ______________
10. something that critiques something in a very strong, honest and direct way ______________
11. a film with a select group of dedicated and passionate fans ______________
12. something that has received excellent reviews from critics ______________

3 **SPEAK** Work in pairs. Tell your partner about

- a critically-acclaimed film or book that you found to be overrated or simply didn't enjoy
- a cult classic film or novel from your country
- a page turner that you have read recently
- a book, play or film with a spine-tingling plot or scene
- a long-awaited book, film or TV series you enjoyed
- a film or theatre performance that you found spellbinding
- the premise to a book, film or TV series that sounds far-fetched

Speaking Part 3 Long turn

1 SPEAK Work in pairs. Discuss the questions below.

1 Who do you consider to be the greatest author ever to have lived that wrote in your language?

2 Who do you think is responsible for ensuring that children have good standards of literacy?

2 10.4 Work in pairs. Listen to the conversation and complete the sentences with one word. Then check your answers in the Audioscript on page 240.

STEFAN: **(1)** As I ____________ it, reading is the most valuable skill we can give our children. It's fundamental to getting on in life and I'm a firm **(2)** ____________ in parents taking every opportunity they can to read with their kids.

CARLA: Well, I'm not sure that forcing children to read more than they want to is particularly beneficial.

STEFAN: Um, sorry. What I **(3)** ____________ to say was parents should read with their children often, but in a way that generates a love for it.

CARLA: Ah, okay I see what you mean. You know it doesn't always follow that children who read a lot continue to do so as adults. Reading can become more or less attractive at different times in our lives.

STEFAN: Hmm. Now you **(4)** ____________ it, maybe it depends on the child and their circumstances. As you say, we all change our interests, even as young children and adolescents.

Useful language

Expressing and clarifying your opinion

When discussing with your partner, you may need to rephrase or clarify what you have said, or even to change your opinion on something as the discussion progresses.

1 Complete the phrases with the words in the box.

come mind perspective put reflection thoughts way words

A On second ____________

B In other ____________

C From my ____________

D On ____________

E Let me put that another ____________

F To my ____________

G ____________ to think of it

H To ____________ it differently

2 Put the phrases in the table below.

Expressing your opinion	Rephrasing your opinion	Changing your mind

3 Add the four phrases from Exercise 2 to the table.

4 Which two phrases for changing your mind are more informal than the others?

3 SPEAK Work in pairs. Discuss the questions.

1 Why do some works of literature stand the test of time and others date quickly?

2 What are the pros and cons of literary and film awards?

3 In a world where films and TV series are readily available to stream, it is argued that more traditional arts, such as theatre and literature have taken a back seat. To what extent do you agree with this?

4 Go to the Additional materials on page 198 for further practice with discussion questions.

Reading and Use of English Part 5 Multiple choice

1 SPEAK Work in pairs and answer the questions.

1 Do you read crime novels? Why? / Why not?
2 Why do you think crime novels are always on bestsellers lists?
3 What skills do writers of crime fiction need?

2 Read the text quickly and answer the questions.

Where is the story set?
Who are the principal characters?
Is there any dialogue?

3 You are going to read an extract from the short story *No Place to Park* by Alexander McCall Smith. For questions 1–6, choose the answer (A, B, C or D) which you think fits best according to the text.

1 What does the writer suggest about the average reader of crime fiction?
A Their perceptive nature is evident in how they conduct themselves.
B They tend to have an overblown opinion of their own intellectuality.
C Their lives are a far cry from those portrayed in such novels.
D They prefer to socialise with like-minded people at literary events.

2 How is the communication between the critic and the writers depicted?
A The exchange has an element of confrontation.
B It is essentially a lesson in effective debate.
C The conversation is full of thoughtful speculation.
D It is basically one of mutual disrespect.

3 What point is the critic trying to make about crime novels?
A The market is completely saturated with them.
B Readers tend to prefer one particular setting over others.
C They have lost all sense of perspective.
D Many of the characters lack credibility.

4 Why might George be reluctant to actually write his new book?
A It may fail to provide much scope for his fertile imagination.
B The subject matter is too close to home.
C He is unclear as to who the target audience would be..
D He thinks the storyline might be too far-fetched.

5 What makes George take the critic's suggestion seriously?
A He enjoys the thrills associated with rising to a challenge.
B The extent of his literary output has declined in recent years.
C His lifestyle would remove the need for extensive research.
D It resonates with something that has been on his mind.

6 The author begins the story with the panel discussion to
A provide a realistic context for the story to unfold.
B outline why the crime fiction genre needs rethinking.
C reveal tricks of the literary trade to the reader.
D evoke sympathy for authors of crime novels.

4 SPEAK Work in pairs and discuss the questions.

1 What do you think happened after this extract?
2 What do you like or dislike about it? Consider the plot, characters, setting, writing style.
3 Would you like to read any of the author's other books? Why? / Why not?

No Place to Park

by Alexander McCall Smith

It started as a challenge, the unforeseen outcome of an absurd conversation at a writers' festival in Western Australia. There was the usual panel on stage, and an audience made up of the sort of people who frequent crime panels – predominantly women, with a sprinkling of men, highly educated, highly literate, and highly imaginative. They were a group bound together by a fascination with the gory details of behaviours in which they themselves would never engage. These people would never commit murder, not in their wildest dreams. Nor would they mix with people who did such things, no matter how fascinating they might find their company on the page. But they loved to read about murder, about the sudden, violent termination of human life, and of how it was done.

The panel was discussing realism in crime fiction. Two practitioners of the art, writers of well-received *policièrs*, had been pitted against the literary critic of a local paper. The critic, who read very little of such fiction expressed the view that there was a surfeit of realistic gore in the contemporary mystery.

'Look at the average crime novel these days,' he pointed out, stabbing at the air with an accusing finger. 'Look at the body count. Look at the compulsory autopsy scenes. Some actually start with the autopsy, would you believe it! The autopsy room, so familiar, so comforting! Organs are extracted and weighed, wounds examined for angle-of-entry, and it's all so ... well, it's all so graphic.' He paused. From the audience came a brief outbreak of laughter. It could not be graphic enough for them.

The critic warmed to his theme. 'But there are crimes other than murder, aren't there? There's fraud and theft and extortion. There's tax evasion, for heaven's sake! And yet all we read about in books of this genre is murder. Murder, murder, murder.' He paused, then looked accusingly at the two authors beside him. 'Why not write about more mundane offences? Why not write about things that actually happen? Murder's very rare, you know. Not that one would think so to read your books.'

One of the authors grinned at the audience. 'Weak stomach,' he said, gesturing to the critic. 'Can't take it.' The audience laughed. They had no difficulty taking it.

'Seriously, though,' said the critic. 'How about it? How about a realistic crime novel dealing with something day-to-day, some commonplace low-level offence.'

'Such as?' asked one of the authors.

The critic waved a hand in the air. 'Oh, anything,' he said lightly. 'Parking violations, perhaps. Those happen all the time.'

Everybody joined in the laughter, even the critic. 'Go on,' he said to the authors. 'Why don't one of you people do something like that? Give up murder. Get real. Start a new genre.'

One of the authors, George Harris, a successful crime writer from Perth, stared at him. He had been laughing, but now he looked thoughtful.

Whenever he went surfing nowadays, thoughts of what might be in the water beneath him were always on his mind, nagging fears, repressed but still there, somewhere below the surface. Eight months earlier somebody whom he knew, although only vaguely, had been taken by a great white within a stone's throw of the edge of the beach. The incident had brought home to him the fact that surfing in Australia had its perils and it had also given him an idea for his next book. The plot would involve rivalry amongst surfers which would lead to one surfer planning to dispose of another. And what better way to do so than to fake a shark attack? The killing strike would be administered from below the waves by a large knife which the murderer had specially made in his garage. The knife would have a number of serrations along the edge, each carefully honed to the shape of a shark's tooth, in order to leave just the right wounds for the coroner to come to the inevitable conclusion – death by shark attack. It was a good plot, even if it would not make comfortable reading for surfers, or comfortable writing, for that matter, for a crime novelist who also happened to be a surfer.

He had barely started this new novel, this surfing story, and was tempted to give it up. He had once before persisted with a book his heart was not in, and he had wasted eight months in the gestation of something that did not work and that had to be abandoned. Determined not to make the same mistake again, he had been open to new ideas when the critic at the panel had made his comments. The suggestion that a crime novel should concern itself with something as minor as illegal parking had been made in jest, of course, but when one thought about it, why not?

Language focus Creating emphasis and cleft sentences

1 Read the sentences and answer the questions.

1 It was at a writers' festival that George got the idea for his next book.
2 Not a single crime novel deals with commonplace low-level events.
3 What might be in the water beneath him came into his thoughts more nowadays.
4 The unfortunate truth is that crime fiction is often formulaic and predictable.

Which underlined structure (1–4) emphasises:

a some factual information?
b what someone is thinking about?
c a problem or issue?
d the lack of something?

2 Complete the sentences so they have the same meaning as the sentences in Exercise 1.

1 George ______
2 There aren't ______
3 Nowadays he ______
4 Unfortunately, ______

3 Go to Ready for Grammar on page 226 for further rules, explanations and practice.

4 SPEAK Work in pairs. Complete the sentences with your own ideas.

What I find most *interesting* / *disappointing* about adaptations of books is ...
The best adaptation of a *book* / *play* I've ever seen is ...
An adaptation of a *book* / *play* I'd like to see is ...
The *author* / *director* / *playwright* I'd most like to meet is ...

Vocabulary Similes

1 Complete the sentences with the correct forms of the verbs from the box.

fight get on sleep stick out watch

1 Joanne and I ______ **like a house on fire** at the party. We just have so much in common and virtually identical tastes in music, food and movies.
2 I didn't want the kids to have an accident, so I ______ **them like a hawk** while they rode their bikes down the street.
3 The building didn't blend in with its surroundings. In fact, it ______ **like a sore thumb**.
4 All families tell tales of sibling rivalry, where sisters and brothers are so different that they constantly ______ **like cat and dog**.
5 After such an exhausting day, I suspect that I'll ______ **like a log**.

2 Complete the sentences with an adjective from the box.

clear dull mad sly tough

1 There's a fine line between being called eccentric or **as** ______ **as a box of frogs**!
2 The book was **as** ______ **as ditch water**; I've never read anything so tedious.
3 Luis won't be upset at this setback – he's **as** ______ **as old boots**.
4 No one can fix the printer – the instruction manual is **as** ______ **as mud**.
5 She's **as** ______ **as a fox** in business negotiations largely due to her ability to read people's weaknesses.

3 SPEAK Work in groups and discuss the questions.

1 Were you able to guess the meaning from the context of the sentences in Exercise 1 and 2? Why? / Why not?
2 Which of the similes have more literal meanings and which are more abstract?

Reading and Use of English

Part 4 Key word transformations

For questions 1–6, complete the second sentence so that it has a similar meaning to the first sentence, using the word given. Do not change the word given. You must use between **three** and **eight** words, including the word given.

1 James was afraid of holding the vase in case he should drop it.

FOR

James didn't want to hold the vase ________________________ it.

2 Please refrain from touching this machine while it is being operated.

IN

Do not touch this machine while ________________________, please.

3 We haven't quite decided which place to go for our next holiday, but it'll be one of two destinations in Europe.

NARROW

We've managed ________________________ to a couple of places in Europe.

4 After some initial clashes of opinion at the climate change conference, the countries reached an agreement.

COMMON

Countries finally overcame their differences and ________________________ at the climate change conference.

5 I didn't think that it was appropriate for Zeina to speak like that to her colleagues.

OUT

From my perspective, Zeina's comments ________________________ in the workplace.

6 I had never skied before, but after only a day of practising, I had learned how to do it.

HANG

It only took me a day ________________________ having done it before.

What to expect

In Part 4, the transformations are separated into two parts, so it's possible to earn 0, 1 or 2 marks depending on how close your response is to the official answer key.

Writing Part 1 Essay

1 SPEAK Work in small groups and discuss the questions.

1. Do you read blogs or self-published books? Why? / Why not?
2. Should writers be allowed to write about any subject they want? Why? / Why not?
3. Are there ever any circumstances where censorship is justified or advisable? Why? / Why not?

WHAT IS ~~CENSORSHIP~~ ANYWAY?

Censorship usually conjures up ideas of banning of books in medieval times, whereas in contemporary society it manifests itself in more subtle ways. These days writers and journalists can have their work sidelined inconspicuously; a series of damaging reviews, or a change of leadership at a publishing company can relegate certain author voices to a less prominent position and move the public perception in a different direction, effectively acting as a form of censorship. Publishing tends to reflect the public interest and as such whichever genre or subject has captured people's attention will be more heavily commissioned.

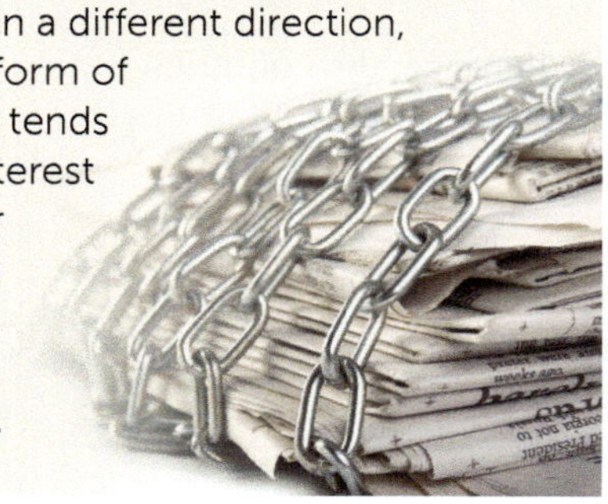

FILTERING OUT THE HATE

Unfortunately, the modern world is more complex and nuanced than many care to admit, and censorship is no longer as clear cut an issue as it once was. Self-publishing and blogging have given authors platforms to write about anything without the oversight which would previously have come from an editor, giving us access to a variety of new and surprising perspectives. The downside is that we can also be exposed to writing which may be unnecessarily upsetting, damaging or misleading. What constitutes censorship for some is merely a way of protecting the vulnerable for others, and in some ways, this is a laudable aim.

2 Read the Writing Part 1 texts and underline the main ideas.

Useful language: evaluating ideas

You can evaluate specific points raised in input texts or focus more broadly on general ideas about the topic. The phrases below will help you to organise your ideas.

Referring to the texts

There are some fundamental flaws in that ...

Weighing up all the points raised, ...

It is potentially more contentious because ...

They make a compelling argument for / to ...

______

______

______

Referring to ideas in general

A salient / pertinent / striking aspect of this matter is ...

Central to this idea is ...

On further inspection, ...

Something often overlooked is that ...

______

______

______

3 Read the model answer on the next page. Add the underlined phrases to the correct category in the Useful language box.

4 **Now read the model answer again and make notes on which parts of the Writing Part 1 texts the writer refers to.**

The topic addressed is whether the works of authors and journalists should be censored in today's world. The texts put forward the idea that perhaps it is time for society to reassess how this term is understood and rightly question whether censorship is being applied correctly or being wielded as a tool for questionable purposes.

While the first text asserts that contemporary writers are being censored indirectly, and that this is a potential road to disaster, the second takes the view that some censorship may be desirable. They come from very distinct standpoints, however both make valuable points which should be explored further.

There is no doubt that freedom of speech for writers should be upheld whatever the circumstances, yet that ignores the fact that fewer contemporary writers are subjected to the editing process, whereby another person or persons assesses the acceptability of a piece of writing prior to publication. Professional writers and journalists must abide by the writing styles and approaches of the organisations they work for, such as newspapers, magazines and publishing companies. In other organisations who are less concerned with the sensibilities of their readership, or more keen to take a controversial stance, the rules are murkier and the standards of writing looser.

Never before has society been in this situation, with so many disparate voices wanting to have their say and so many platforms available for them to do so. What is undeniable is that the way in which we police the writers and journalists of our time needs a thorough review to ensure the system remains fit for purpose.

5 **Clear organisation and appropriate paragraphing are essential features of all C2 Proficiency writing task types.**

Which of the two plans below (A or B) does the model answer follow?

	A	**B**
First paragraph	A summary of the ideas in the first text + the writer's own ideas	A summary of the ideas shared across both texts
Central paragraphs	A summary of the ideas in the second text + the writer's own ideas	A reference to distinct ideas in each text
Final paragraph	A summary of the ideas shared across both texts + the writer's own ideas	A presentation of the writer's own ideas

6 **Which plan do you prefer? Why?**

7 **Which ideas from the texts would you like to focus on in your essay? Why?**

8 **Now write your own answer to the question in Exercise 1. Remember to refer to the texts and use some expressions from the Useful language box and/or the model essay.**

For more information on writing essays, see page 190.

About English

The definite article *the* is the most common word in English and accounts for 5% of all words used. This is mainly due to its various grammatical functions. It is used more in written than spoken English and is especially important in academic essays, where precise meanings are necessary.

Do you know which word is most common in your language?

10 REVIEW

Language focus Inversion

Choose the correct alternatives in the following sentences. Either one, two or all three alternatives may be possible.

1 *Never must / Under no circumstances should / Never again will* you contact him again as I sincerely doubt we can trust him.
2 *Around the corner was sitting / There he sat / There sat* a dapper elderly gentleman waiting patiently for something.
3 *Only then / Only when / Not until* the last prisoner had been released did John feel that justice was done.
4 *So / As / Only* late was it when they arrived that there was nowhere open to grab a bite to eat.
5 *But / Were if not / Had it not been* for Veronika's suggestion, we wouldn't have found a way out.
6 *Barely / Rarely / Scarcely* had I fought off one illness than I came down with another.
7 *Had / Should / Were* Esther realised in time, she would have kept her mouth shut, but it was too late.
8 *Hardly ever / Rarely / Not since* do the managers venture down to this part of the building, so something must be up.

Reading and Use of English Part 1 Multiple-choice cloze

For questions 1–8, read the text below and decide which answer (A, B, C or D) best fits each gap. There is an example at the beginning (0).

I was recently offered free tickets to the opening night of the theatrical adaptation of Alfred Hitchcock's *Rear Window* at the Sun Royal Theatre. Naturally, given the press hype **(0)** ____*A*____ the production, not to mention the exorbitant ticket prices, I jumped at the **(1)** ____________. Having seen the movie countless times and with vast sections of the script **(2)** ____________ to memory, I was intrigued to experience the stage adaptation of the story.

On the night in **(3)** ____________, I eagerly took my seat in the stalls and waited for the curtain to open. That night there was a full **(4)** ____________ and you could palpably feel the anticipation hanging in the air. The curtains drew back and revealed a set which had been **(5)** ____________ modelled on the New York apartment in the movie, so much so that there was an audible **(6)** ____________ from the audience in recognition of the attention to detail. The female **(7)** ____________ was played to perfection by a little-known actor, who managed to really capture the essence of her onscreen **(8)** ____________. Overall, a magnificent production.

	A	B	C	D
0	surrounding	encompassing	binding	corresponding
1	occasion	moment	outcome	chance
2	entrusted	committed	assigned	accomplished
3	principle	question	effect	hand
4	crew	audience	house	group
5	faithfully	decisively	obediently	steadfastly
6	pant	gasp	groan	rumble
7	main	head	chief	lead
8	comrade	fellow	counterpart	peer

Reading and Use of English Part 3 Word formation

For questions 1–8, read the text below. Use the word given in capitals at the end of some of the lines to form a word that fits in the gap in the same line. There is an example at the beginning (0).

Budding writers should consider self-publishing

They say that writing a novel is an **(0)** *attainable* goal for anyone and the — **ATTAIN**
advent of self-publishing has at least improved everyone's chances, if not entirely proved the point. While a contract with a publishing company is still the most sought after option, self-publishing is frequently touted as the next best thing.

Although the writing process is relatively straightforward, be sure to pay a
professional editor to review your work, as **(1)** ____________ of how good a writer you — **RESPECT**
are, there will invariably be errors that an editor will pick up on. Additionally, having
a passable **(2)** ____________ awareness is advantageous when it comes to choosing — **TECHNOLOGY**
a platform to launch your work.

Sales and marketing are a tricky area without a publisher and newly self-published
authors can become **(3)** ____________ by poor sales initially, but it is important to try to — **COURAGE**
remain as emotionally **(4)** ____________ from your work as possible. Bear in mind — **ATTACH**
that it is now a product which must be sold. There is an **(5)** ____________ that just by — **ASSUME**
releasing a novel into the world, it will be read. **(6)** ____________ this is not — **REGRET**
the case, and some promotion will be required to build up **(7)** ____________. — **READ**
Once your **(8)** ____________ as a writer has been established, sales are sure to follow. — **CREDIBLE**

Writing Part 2 Review

An online book club is going to feature a review of books that are inspiring for different reasons and it is asking its members to make recommendations. You decide to send in a review in which you explain what it was that was inspirational from your perspective. You should also suggest reasons why other people might find it inspirational.

Write your **review** in **280–320** words.

For more information on writing reviews, see page 195.

Idioms From literature

About English

A large number of the idioms currently in use by English speakers are thought to have been coined by Shakespeare. Although it is unclear whether he was the original creative force behind the idioms found in his literary works, he is likely to have been the first person to write them down, which is why so many are attributed to him.

Discussing idioms

Discuss the differences in meaning between these idioms:

- a wild goose chase / a lost cause
- an Achilles heel / a chink in the armour
- give you the creeps / give you the chills

1 Match the authors to their books. Some authors wrote more than one of the books.

Lewis Carroll   Miguel de Cervantes   Geoffrey Chaucer
Charles Dickens   Thomas Hardy   Joseph Heller   Homer
Walter Scott   William Shakespeare   Jonathan Swift

Romeo and Juliet   *A Pair of Blue Eyes*   *David Copperfield*

Catch-22   *The Canterbury Tales*   *Don Quixote*

Ivanhoe   *The Merry Wives of Windsor*   *Iliad*

Alice in Wonderland   *A Christmas Carol*

A Complete Collection of Genteel and Ingenious Conversation

2 SPEAK Have you ever read any of the books from Exercise 1? Do you know what they are about?

3 Read the sentences and discuss the meaning of the phrases in bold.

1. Antonio calling me lazy when he doesn't even have a job is **the pot calling the kettle black**.
2. The company wants to hire new people to expand and make profit, but it can't afford the additional wages – it's a **Catch-22** situation.
3. Mastering the art of building realistic characters is the **Achilles' heel** of many budding authors and the primary reason for getting rejected by publishers.
4. Shifting attitudes to work mean people want more flexibility and control in their working lives instead of full-time employment, resulting in **freelance** work becoming more common.
5. The cabin, now just a couple of hours' walk away, would be **a sight for sore eyes** for the exhausted climbers.
6. I only meant to have a quick glance through a couple of holidays websites, but before I knew it I'd **gone down the rabbit hole** and had more than twenty tabs open.
7. By planting false evidence, Harrison had managed to lead the detectives on **a wild goose chase** involving the fruitless search of a warehouse, which gave him time to escape.
8. The dilapidated house at the end of the lane, covered in ivy and rumoured to be haunted, was seldom visited by the villagers as it **gave them the creeps.**
9. As someone who's still young with few commitments and no dependents you could do anything or go anywhere – **the world is your oyster**.
10. My phone was **as dead as a doornail** after I accidentally dropped it in a puddle.
11. His friends knew that Isabel was not a great match for Sam but **love is blind** so he didn't heed their warnings.
12. Season 1 ends on such a **cliffhanger**, with the central figures left fighting for their lives in the jungle, that audiences are clamouring for Season 2 to be released earlier than scheduled so they can find out what happened.

4 Match the phrases in bold in Exercise 3 with the books they come from in Exercise 1.

5 SPEAK Work in pairs. Which idioms and phrases come from literature in your language?

11

TALK OF THE TOWN

KEY LANGUAGE

Reporting structures 1
Reporting structures 2
City dwelling
Phrasal verbs for problems and solutions

IDIOMS

Talk and *tell*

EXAM PRACTICE

Reading and Use of English Parts 2, 4 & 7
Writing Parts 1 & 2
Listening Part 1
Speaking Parts 1 & 3

Speaking Part 1 Interview

Work with a partner. Discuss the questions.

1 In what ways has your town remained unchanged over the past 50 years?
2 What do you enjoy about the place where you live and what would you change if you could?
3 How do you think someone's living environment can affect their quality of life? Does living in an urban or a rural area affect this? In what ways?
4 How would you describe the local community where you live?
5 In cities, what tensions are there between culture and heritage on the one hand, and commercial land use on the other?

11 TALK OF THE TOWN

Vocabulary City dwelling

1 Skim the two articles. Which one is closer to your perspective of cities? Why do you think that?

2 Choose the correct words to complete the collocations in each text.

affluent affordable commuter derelict tight-knit tree-lined

BRIGHT LIGHTS, BIG CITY

What's not to love about the city? It's so exciting. It's here that you can find something happening 24/7 as well as meet people from all walks of life. Diversity is on every street corner – in one direction there may be some abandoned or (1) ____________ **buildings** but then just a stone's throw away there's some highly (2) ____________ **neighbourhood** with shady, (3) ____________ **streets**. Some people claim that the city is a soulless place where you're just another number, but there are plenty of really (4) ____________ **communities** where I live – a city is just a lot of little neighbourhoods, in my opinion. Some people prefer to live in the (5) ____________ **belt** and just travel in for work, but for me, nothing beats being right in the thick of; it is just so exciting. And now that more (6) ____________ **housing** is being built, it means more young people and families can get on the property ladder right here in the swing of things.

antisocial concrete congestion low-emissions rustic welfare

RAT RACE FOR RATS ONLY!

Who would choose to live in a city? Not me, that's for sure. I much prefer the (7) ____________ **charm** of an old cottage in a quiet village to that of living in a hot, polluted, overpopulated, (8) ____________ **jungle**. I know they have introduced (9) ____________ **charging** for vehicles in many cities to try to reduce carbon emissions, as well as (10) ____________ **zones**, but I am not convinced these have made such a big difference or reduced the health risks for city dwellers. And it's not just health related issues, either! I feel really safe in my lovely rural community, where we don't have to worry about tackling (11) ____________ **behaviour** or any other crimes. I think that the reason there is such a strain on the (12) ____________ **system** is thanks to many of the issues derived from city living. I'll take a field and a bit of peace and quiet any day of the week over life in the 'Big Smoke'.

3 Write four sentences about the place where you live using any of the vocabulary in Exercise 2.

4 **SPEAK** Compare your sentences with a partner.

Speaking Part 3 Long turn

1 **SPEAK** Look at the photos. What issues do you think they represent? Do you recognise these issues in any of the cities near where you live?

2 **SPEAK** Look at the two questions below. In pairs, discuss how you might answer the questions and what the bullet points might be.

Student A: How has shopping changed in urban areas?
- ________
- ________
- ________

Student B: What is the most important factor in making a city liveable for all its residents?
- ________
- ________
- ________

3 Read the *Don't forget!* and *Useful language* boxes.

Don't forget!

› The bullet points are provided to help you. You do not have to use them in your answer and can use your own ideas instead.

› Remember to talk for about two minutes each.

Useful language

Highlighting cause and effect

When answering a question like this, connect your ideas using language to highlight cause and effect:

Decide which word does not collocate.

1 This is *largely* / *profoundly* / *primarily* / *effectively* due to ...
2 ... the many *knock-on* / *refined* / *secondary* / *adverse* effects
3 It's *primarily* / *closely* / *simply* / *probably* down to ...
4 This could *trigger* / *bring about* / *give rise to* / *account for* greater availability of affordable accommodation.
5 The *circumstances* / *implications* / *ramifications* / *consequences* of this include fewer consumers shopping via conventional methods.

4 Check your answers to Exercise 2 in the Additional materials on page 198. Take turns to answer the questions.

5 **SPEAK** In pairs, discuss the questions.

1 In what ways is city living more stressful than living in smaller towns, villages or the countryside?
2 To what extent do you believe the development of new shopping centres or out-of-town hypermarkets is a positive step?
3 Do you think people should think more carefully about the impact of online shopping on local businesses?
4 What are some of the biggest challenges facing the place where you live and what is being done to deal with them?
5 What do you think are the biggest issues facing cities globally and what can be done to deal with these?
6 In what ways do you imagine global population increases will affect our current lifestyles?

Reading and Use of English Part 7 Multiple matching

1 SPEAK In pairs, discuss the questions.

1 How many litres of water do you think you use a day? What do you use it for?
2 Where does the place where you live get its water from? How clean do you think it is?
3 What issues do you think there are surrounding cleaning and reusing water?

2 You are going to read an article about water problems in cities. For questions 1–10, choose from sections (A–E). The sections may be chosen more than once.

Don't forget!

You may find some overlap between specific details in the paragraphs (e.g. several paragraphs may mention groundwater problems) but in order to match the sentence to the correct paragraph you need to dissect the information in each of the sentences 1–10. By doing this, you'll ensure that you don't just match part of an idea – you'll match the complete idea.

In which section are the following mentioned?

recognition of a need for more variation in water supply sources		1
insufficient investment resulting in some obstacles to be overcome		2
residents who tolerate their water problems		3
the need for the authorities to keep abreast of developments		4
purposeful cuts in the water supply		5
an escalation in water source contamination		6
a risk stemming from geographical circumstances rather than climate change		7
a water supply that has failed to keep pace with progress		8
plans to exploit further natural resources to bolster the water supply		9
a city affected by unpredictable, severe weather changes		10

3 SPEAK Work in small group. Discuss the following questions.

1 What ideas did the article give that could help places suffering from water emergencies?
2 Are there ever any restrictions on water use in your country? How is it restricted?
3 What can be done to ensure the sustainable management of water supplies for the future?

Jakarta

Bengaluru

Mexico City

In deep waters

A With a population of over 22 million inhabitants, according to UN figures, **Mexico City**'s water supply is in great demand, yet this metropolis has seen what can only be described as a water famine, with water access limited to a few hours a week for some homes during times of drought. The cause of the city's massive water shortage stems from a range of factors, such as disrepair in the pipe network which gives rise to heavy water losses. This damage is largely compacted by the fact that the city is sinking at an alarming rate. In addition to this, with an estimated 40% of its water being imported from outside the city, a lack of large-scale water recycling systems and increasing numbers of droughts brought about by climate change, access to sufficient water is becoming critically scarce. This issue continues to hang in the balance as initiatives to mitigate the problem continue to run up against issues such as shortfalls in funding.

B A water crisis also plagues residents of **Bengaluru**, in Southern India. Despite, or in fact because of, its rapid rise to become India's technological hub and its ensuing population boom, the city has stretched existing water stocks far beyond the capacity for which they were designed. This growth has also meant that, disastrously, a large number of the houses in the city do not have access to tap water, impelling some people to resort to taking what they need from the city's lake, a source which is heavily contaminated. Although consecutive governments have vowed to find a solution, some residents criticise initiatives as failing to address over reliance on groundwater, which thanks to reduced rainfall during monsoon season – largely due to climate change – is even more scarce than it was.

C The Egyptian capital, **Cairo**, has not escaped its share of water issues, despite being located on the banks of the River Nile, and these ripple out across the entire country. While the world-famous river is the source of 97% of Egypt's water, it is becoming increasingly polluted by untreated residential and agricultural waste, leaving it unusable for many. For Cairo, unlike other cities, relying on rainwater is ruled out as an option due to its arid climate, further narrowing down its options to existing river, lake or sea sources, using groundwater supplies and water storage. Unfortunately, climate change has meant that many of these supplies are dwindling. Efforts to solve the issues are taking shape, with a National Water Resources plan to invest $50 billion into the system in many different ways, including increasing desalination to tap into marine water.

D For **Jakarta**, the issue surrounding water is even more complex. Home to around 10 million people, Jakarta stands on a slowly sinking swampy delta with 40% of the city already sitting below sea level. North Jakarta has already sunk by 2.5 metres in the last 10 years and every year the situation deteriorates, with the prospect of 95% of this district being submerged by 2050, regardless of any further climate change issues. Some buildings have been long abandoned as ground floors are filled with stagnant water, while in others, residents try to block out the creeping submergence with makeshift solutions. And despite all this, property continues to be developed to meet demand, and many residents, with a host of critical infrastructure problems to contend with, refrain from focusing too much on the dire water situation. The problems are exacerbated by rising sea levels and excessive ground use which deflates the land over time. A solution may lie in the Great Garuda, a 32km sea wall, however many experts have warned against relying on a one-dimensional approach, stating that this really should be done in conjunction with confronting overextraction of groundwater.

E **New Orleans** is no stranger to harsh weather events, especially flash flooding, occurring when high tides correspond with heavy rain, which has caused catastrophic destruction of whole areas of the city in recent years. Like most flood-prone cities, it suffers from low elevation, and has fundamental flaws in its drainage infrastructure. As sea levels continue to rise, New Orleans is in an increasingly precarious position, with some experts forewarning that almost all of the city's residents may be displaced by 2050. An extensive flood protection project costing around $15 billion is now in place, setting many residents at ease. However, many believe that systems that have been implemented are not keeping pace with the escalating risk of rising sea levels and stronger, more frequent storm surges. Moreover, vanishing wetlands, which once acted as natural flood barriers, mean that governments need to urgently keep up with changing predictions and conditions rather than rest on their laurels.

Vocabulary Phrasal verbs for problems and solutions

1 Complete the phrasal verbs from the article on page 163. The letters in brackets refer to the sections of the text in which the phrasal verbs appear.

1 ... initiatives to mitigate the issue continue to ______ **up against** issues, such as shortfalls in funding. (A)

2 ... impelling some people to ______ **to** taking what they need from the city's lake, ... (B)

3 ... relying on rainwater is ______ **out** as an option, due to its arid climate. (C)

4 ... further ______ **down** its options to existing river, lake or sea sources. (C)

2 Check your answers to Exercise 1 in the text. Use the context to work out the meaning.

3 Complete the phrasal verbs in the text below with the correct form of one of the verbs in the box.

call flood resign revert run saddle talk

The wheels of administration don't always run smoothly, and sometimes even the most experienced of officials have had to **(1)** ______ **themselves to** *the fact that* they're responsible for an almighty blunder. Take for example some employees at Swansea Council, who were **(2)** ______ **with** *complaints* about their bilingual signage. Instead of writing the correct Welsh translation on a road sign, they had inadvertently put the translator's automatic out of office reply on the signs instead, assuming it was the equivalent text. Welsh speakers **(3)** ______ **for** immediate *action*, demanding that the sign be removed immediately and replaced with a correct one.

While this is undoubtedly an embarrassing error, it isn't as costly as the mistake made by Spanish officials, who **(4)** ______ **up against** *a major issue* with their transport plans. They had ordered commuter trains that couldn't fit in the tunnel network, resulting in a two-year delay to the delivery of the project. As the most senior people on the project, they were **(5)** ______ **with** *the blame*, and were forced to resign from their posts. While they were able to **(6)** ______ **back to** the smaller, original designs they had put forward initially, these would be delayed significantly, nonetheless. We may wonder how no one spotted the error sooner so that they might have **(7)** ______ the decision-makers **out of** *their plans* before it was too late!

4 Record the phrasal verbs from Exercise 3 in your vocabulary notebook, together with the collocates shown in *italics*. Paraphrase each collocation to show the meaning.

Example:

1 *resign themselves to the fact that – accept that*

5 Record each of the following groups of nouns with the infinitive form of the phrasal verb from Exercises 1 and 2 that they frequently collocate with.

0 *a decision / retiring / making a mistake* — *talk someone out of*
1 *the possibilities / your options / the list* ______
2 *the blame / the debt / the burden* ______
3 *change / action / unity* ______
4 *the fact / the possibility / the situation* ______
5 *emails / phone calls / complaints* ______
6 *a (previous) state / an (original) plan / the norm* ______
7 *the prospect / the chance / the use of* ______
8 *problems / challenges / constraints* ______
9 *drastic measures / violence / legal action* ______

6 SPEAK Work in pairs. Prepare two questions for your partner using the collocations in Exercise 5. Take turns to ask and answer the questions.

*Can you think of a time when you had to **talk someone out of** making a mistake?*

Language focus Reporting structures 1

1 Choose the correct reporting verbs to complete the summary of the reading text on page 163.

Water is a key issue for many cities in the world, with some research **(1)** *suggesting / threatening* that huge numbers of citizens in some of the worst affected areas could be displaced in the coming decades. Experts have **(2)** *pleaded / warned* against taking these challenges too lightly, and many governments are being **(3)** *urged / insisted* to do more to counter the effects of the water crises, with some citizens even **(4)** *accusing / blaming* policymakers of not taking adequate steps to safeguard against the environmental changes. Until governments **(5)** *reckon / persuade* certain industries to take more drastic action, little can be done to **(6)** *reassure / convince* these city residents of their futures.

2 Match each sentence beginning (1–5) with an appropriate ending (A–E). The reporting verb and any dependent prepositions are in bold. Do you agree with the sentiments in the sentences? Why? / Why not?

1 It is of great use to **hypothesise**
2 Many governments across the globe have been **accused**
3 City residents ought to **demand**
4 Most governments **concede**
5 People living in cities should be **reassured**

A action to make more fundamental improvements to their environment.
B that their lives are unlikely to be significantly impacted by environmental changes in the short term.
C **about** what the long-term effects of climate change in cities might be.
D **of** putting off making unpopular decisions that might aid the environment.
E that due to population growth in cities, resources are already under increasing strain.

3 Go to Ready for Grammar on page 228 to check your answers to Exercise 2 and for further rules, explanations and practice.

4 11.1 Complete the news report with the correct form of a verb from the box. Then, listen and check your answers.

argue blame encourage remark speak urge vow warn

DIMMING THE LIGHTS

'Many environmentalists are taking to the streets today (1) ______ governments to reduce light pollution in cities, which has been exacerbated by the introduction of LED technology, which was previously considered an environmentally-friendly option of light supply. They (2) ______ against the reliance on these kinds of lights in cities, which not only have a negative effect on human sleep patterns, but can also have a catastrophic effect on some wildlife. Such white light is now thought to be (3) ______ for changes to certain animal behaviours, for instance, altered migration patterns in some birds, changes to feeding patterns, loss of habitat and even declining populations of wildlife species.

Recently, several prominent astronauts (4) ______ of the dramatic extent to which white light has spread throughout cities in recent decades, emerging like bigger and bigger luminous spider webs covering our planet. As the only people who can visibly see the Earth and its development, they (5) ______ on how the change is increasingly obvious. Many cities (6) ______ to take decisive action on this matter, with some having already introduced periods of dark sky, when lights are turned off. However, environmentalists want to go further and (7) ______ citizens to think carefully about their energy use and the impact of it on wildlife habitats around them, (8) ______ that we must all remember to switch off our lights.'

5 SPEAK In pairs, choose THREE of the following topics and discuss them. Ensure you use some reporting verbs and verb patterns.

- a time when you had a warning
- something you volunteered to do
- something that you regret
- a good suggestion someone gave you
- something you apologised for
- something you were told off for

Listening Part 1 Multiple choice

1 11.2 You will hear three different extracts. For questions **1–6**, choose the answer **(A, B or C)** which best fits according to what you hear. There are two questions for each extract.

Extract One

You hear a councillor explaining a new initiative during a city council meeting.

1 The councillor feels that at present the city …

A is hardly leading the way in green initiatives.

B is failing to give residents any quality of life.

C is suffering from the lack of investment it deserves.

2 Why does the council want citizens to give their views?

A to ascertain whether people have any concerns

B to understand what they consider most important

C to gauge their enthusiasm for introducing smart tech

Extract Two

You hear part of a conversation between a community centre manager and a local resident.

3 The local resident's main complaint about the centre is to do with

A the anti-social behaviour around the centre.

B how poorly the whole place appears to be managed.

C the length of time it has taken to improve hygiene standards.

4 The local resident implies that she

A reflects the views of residents.

B will get other people involved.

C has been asked to speak on behalf of others.

Extract Three

You hear part of an interview with transport planner, Matt Reid.

5 When considering adding a new route, Matt has to

A ensure not just road users are consulted.

B foresee anything that could go wrong.

C assess whether it is convenient.

6 Matt finds one of the challenges of his job lies in

A dealing with existing infrastructure issues.

B convincing people that change is necessary.

C managing the competing priorities of others.

Language focus Reporting structures 2

1 Which of the speakers from the listening said these sentences?

1 One of them even went off at an old man last week, I saw it for myself.
2 People aren't very sympathetic towards a new route when it's more inconvenient.
3 As such, we're inviting all residents to consult on our plans.

2 Underline the key words in the sentences in Exercise 1 that report speech.

3 SPEAK Work in pairs. Which of the key words in Exercise 1 do you consider the most informal?

4 SPEAK With your partner, read the sentences with reporting verbs. Discuss the similiarities and differences between the verbs.

1 The man **droned on** in a monotonous voice for hours **about** computer programming.
2 The salesperson on the phone has been **blathering on about** their latest deals for ages. I wish they'd just give up!
3 My neighbour's always **banging on about** next door's dog and how we should complain, but I don't want to. It's his constant complaining that's more of a bother.
4 My boss picks holes in almost everything I do. I wish he wouldn't **keep on at** me.
5 I can't believe how my husband **went off at** that cyclist yesterday. I know the cyclist cut him up, but he really lost it!

5 Go to Ready for Grammar on page 230 to check your answers to Exercise 2 and for further rules, explanations and practice.

6 Complete the texts below using the words in the box. Some words may need to be changed to an appropriate form to fit the gap.

adamant admit be keep insist refuse sound unsure

1

Did you hear that the construction company that are building that new apartment complex has **(1)** ____________ to using some dodgy materials? Apparently, they're not up to the safety requirements, and the company has pocketed the savings!

No way. I bet the people who have put a deposit down already have **(2)** ____________ off to them about it.

Well, the company are **(3)** ____________ that the apartments will be perfectly liveable in.

2

I was **(4)** ____________ about whether or not to move to this area. It's got a bit of a bad rep, but now that I'm here, I'm so glad I did. I really like it! It's edgy but not too much. My mum **(5)** ____________ on at me about leaving though – she doesn't like it at all.

3

My landlord tried to put my rent up. He **(6)** ____________ like "it's because costs have gone up". But I **(7)** ____________ to agree to it because I'm still under contract. He kept on **(8)** ____________ it was fair, but if he carries on, I'll just take it up with a lawyer. There's no way I'm paying more than I should.

7 SPEAK Work in pairs. Choose two of the following situations that are relevant for you. Tell your partner about your experience. Use reporting structures to explain what happened.

- A time you made a complaint
- A time you celebrated something
- A misunderstanding you had
- A time you and a friend made up after an argument
- A time you didn't tell the truth

About English

The type of colloquialisms you hear on the streets of English-speaking countries vary widely from place to place. However, across the UK, in informal conversations, it is commonplace for people to use *go*, *be* and *like*.

The traffic warden was pretty rude and without even looking up she ***went*** *'you can't park here' and gave me a ticket, and I* ***was like*** *'I can park here, can't you see my resident's permit?'*

Pronunciation Stress timing

1 11.3 **English is a stress-timed language. This means that we usually stress the important words and speed up the words in between. Listen to the extract from the listening and note down the stressed words.**

Planners like me have to anticipate any potential hazards ... these could be blind spots, bottle necks et cetera.

2 SPEAK **Work in pairs. Take it in turns to practise saying each of the following sentences. As they get longer, try to keep the stress at around the same time.**

	PLANNERS		ANTICIPATE		HAZARDS
	PLANNERS	have to	ANTICIPATE	any	HAZARDS
All	PLANNERS	like me have to	ANTICIPATE	any potential	HAZARDS

3 **Go to the** Additional materials **on** page 203 **for further practice.**

Reading and Use of English Part 2 Open cloze

1 **For questions 1–8, read the text below and think of the word that best fits each space. Use only one word in each space. There is an example at the beginning (0).**

THE INCREDIBLE Baron Haussmann

The wide boulevards, and grand Baroque architecture of Paris (0) ___MAKE___ it a breath-taking place to (1) ____________ up some European culture. But (2) ____________ it not been for Baron Haussmann and Napoleon III, the city would have a very different aesthetic. As little as 200 years ago, Paris was an overcrowded, filthy place, plagued by diseases, primarily caused by the lack of sewage systems. Its narrow lanes were crowded and chaotic, making it difficult to navigate your (3) ____________ through. This was simply because Paris had not been subject to any strategic planning.

Originally a village, the city (4) ____________ shape haphazardly. In order for Paris to keep its status both nationally and internationally, Napoleon III tasked Baron Haussmann (5) ____________ transforming the city. He (6) ____________ most of the centre of Paris to rubble, and constructed 34,000 new buildings, all with a similar but striking design. In addition, he (7) ____________ in place the requisite infrastructure for a modern and safe city, like wide roads, sewage systems and major train stations. Haussmann's effect on the city of Paris is (8) ____________ dispute, perhaps more so than any other of his countrymen.

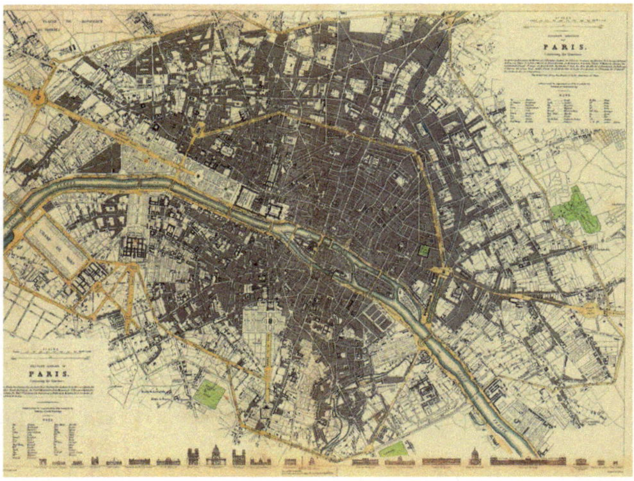

2 SPEAK **In pairs, discuss the questions.**

1. What other cities do you know that have been through a major reconstruction?
2. What are the benefits and drawbacks of carrying out major regeneration projects in cities? Do you think the advantages outweigh the disadvantages?

Writing Part 2 Report

1 **SPEAK** **Work in groups. Talk about your city or a city you know and discuss what you think the major transport issues are. You can choose from the following as well as include your own ideas.**

- reliability
- frequency
- accessibility
- variety
- environmental effects
- capacity

2 **Note down some of the problems you discussed and make a list of solutions for each problem.**

Problems	Solutions
There are always traffic jams during the peak hours of the day.	*Encourage residents to take other routes, or encourage firms to offer flexible working.*

3 **Read the Part 2 task below and then answer the questions.**

There was a town-hall meeting where suggestions were made on how to improve transport problems within the area. You have been asked to write a report for a councillor, identifying two or three of the main issues that were discussed. Outline the problems, explaining why they need to be addressed, and offer any solutions to alleviate this problem.

Write your **report** in **280–320** words.

1 Who is the target reader of the report?
2 What problem and solutions will you include?
3 How will you structure your report?
4 What headings will you use?
5 What vocabulary and language structures will you use to demonstrate your level?

How to go about it

There are some key differences between writing a report and other types of writing.

- The structure of the report is very important. Before you write, carefully consider the question and what information you need to include. This will help you organise the text. You should also consider what advanced vocabulary and language structures to include.
- The report should be organised into clear sections, which should have sub-headings that identify what points those sections cover. Remember that there will also be a subheading for the introduction and conclusion. The conclusion should cover your overall assessment of the task and make any recommendations.
- Remember that reports are factual and objective. As such, an impersonal tone should be taken. This includes using passive structures and more factual rather than opinionated language.

4 **SPEAK** **Go to the Additional materials on page 200.**

5 **Write your own answer for the task in Exercise 3.**

For more information on writing reports, see page 194.

Useful language

Using impersonal structures in reports

Introducing the report

This report outlines / suggests / proposes / identifies …

The aim / purpose of this report is to …

Highlighting issues and evaluating solutions

Buses are (widely) accepted / found / considered / to be …

Traffic jams were recognised / identified as being …

It is anticipated / estimated / expected to …

It could be suggested that …

These problems may have been exacerbated by …

Many / Some residents see this as …

There are many proposed solutions …

This could / may be regarded as …

One solution could be …

11 REVIEW

Language focus Reporting structures 1 and 2

Complete the blog with the correct form of the words in the box.

adamant admit bang rumour suggest urge

Alberobello – the most beautiful place you've (probably) never heard of!

Last night, I finally made it to Alberobello. My Italian cousins had been (1) __________ on at me about visiting there for such a long time. I must (2) __________ to not having given their advice much thought, but when I was invited to a friend's wedding in a nearby region, I was (3) __________ that we had to go. And I am so glad we did! It's a gloriously beautiful place and its quirky architecture is guaranteed to blow you away.

As it's a relatively small place, with only a few museums, I'd (4) __________ just staying overnight, or maybe even just making it a day trip. Be sure to head to the Rione Monti district, where you can find the picture-perfect Trulli buildings. These wonderfully unusual limestone dwellings are (5) __________ to have been designed this way, with makeshift roofs, so as to avoid taxes. However, I'm not sure anybody really knows the true history of these buildings. If you want to splash out, you can actually stay in one of these houses overnight. Whatever your budget, if you're in southern Italy, I (6) __________ you to consider taking some time out and heading over the Alberobello – it's worth the extra miles!

Vocabulary City dwelling | Phrasal verbs

Choose the correct alternatives to complete the text.

THE REGENERATION OF King's Cross

King's Cross is one of the most well-known districts in central London, and these days a fashionable hub of activity, but it didn't always use to be this way. A relatively (1) *affluent / tight-knit* neighbourhood of industrial activity in the 1800s, by the end of the 20th century the area had fallen into decline. With issues such as (2) *derelict / welfare* houses and (3) *rustic / antisocial* behaviour, much of it was considered a no-go zone for the average Londoner. When, in the late 1990s, plans came about for the relocation of the terminus of the Paris to London high-speed train to the area, reinvigorated efforts to regenerate the area were urgently (4) *called / run* for. The aim was to (5) *resign / revert* the area back to its former glory, or even surpass it, but the regeneration plans (6) *ran / stuck* up against challenge after challenge. The developers were saddled (7) *with / for* a number of problems ranging from reluctance for change within the local community to a range of environmental restrictions and problems. However, after extensive consultation and planning, they finally managed to (8) *reduce / narrow* down the key issues and transform the area, creating (9) *rustic / affordable* housing and (10) *tree-lined / commuter* streets. Today, you will find a bustling commercial district, brimming with vibrant plazas, trendy restaurants, fashionable shops and galleries.

Reading and Use of English

Part 4 Key word transformations

For questions 1–6, complete the second sentence so that it has a similar meaning to the first sentence, using the word given. Do not change the word given. You must use between three and eight words, including the word given.

1 If the person who defaced the wall doesn't come forward, everyone will stay behind after class.

OWNS

Everyone will stay behind after class until ______________________________ the wall.

2 As far as they know, the match is still going ahead despite the weather alert.

BEST

The match is still going ahead ______________________________, regardless of the weather alert.

3 Patty realised her keys had been in her pocket the whole time after spending ages searching for them.

ONLY

Patty had spent ages searching for her keys ______________________________ right under her nose, in her pocket.

4 The president received a lot of criticism, yet his party continued to vigorously support him throughout it all.

THROUGH

Despite the criticism the president received, his party stuck ______________________________ thin.

5 Even though they were separated at birth, Andres never gave up hope of seeing his brother again.

CLUNG

Andres ______________________________ see his brother again, despite being separated at birth.

6 I knew Alan had talked about leaving his job, but I didn't think he'd actually do it!

THROUGH

I never thought Alan ______________________________ his job, even though he'd talked it.

Writing Part 1 Essay

Read the two texts below.

Write an essay summarising and evaluating the key points from both texts. Use your own words throughout as far as possible and include your own ideas in your answers. Write your answer in 240–280 words.

UNFIT FOR PURPOSE

It seems to be all the rage to regenerate an area, but from my perspective, officials should prioritise the practicalities, as more often than not, restoration doesn't go far enough. Residents often have to live with outdated insulation in their housing and below par facilities, all in the name of respecting the cosmetic heritage of the neighbourhood. Shouldn't we primarily be considering the quality of life of citizens? If the buildings and facilities in an area aren't really up to scratch, why not start again with a blank slate?

CHERISHING THE HISTORY AROUND US

At the root of almost all of our urban areas is history. In fact, it's what makes a city so great. Only a handful of people would go to the ends of the earth to see a modern building but look at the enormous queues you see for the great historical structures like the Colosseum or the Tower of London. While nobody would dream of knocking down these monuments, with every single traditional building that is wilfully destroyed, a piece of history is lost.

For more information on writing essays, see page 190.

Idioms *Talk* and *tell*

1 Complete the sentences with the correct form of either *talk* or *tell*.

1 'Sorry to ____________ **shop** outside of the office, but we really must get the Vital Industries contract signed next week.'
2 'This project is pretty difficult.' 'Yeah, ____________ **me something I don't know** – I've been working on it for weeks and I don't seem to be getting anywhere.'
3 'The IT giant's share prices have plummeted after it announced heavy losses last week, but **as far as anyone can** ____________, there is no danger of the company folding.'
4 'That dress looks terrible on you!'
'____________ **to the hand**! You've got no idea about fashion – this is designer.'
5 'I'd had enough of his constant criticising of my cooking, so I ____________ **him where to get off**.'
6 'Half the time I've no idea what the interviewers are talking about when I go for a job, but I ____________ **the** ____________ and usually get an offer!'
7 'My son doesn't listen to a word I say when he's playing on his Xbox. **It's like** ____________ **to a brick wall**.'
8 'Taking the metro into town this early is a real pain.'
'____________ **me about it**. I get the metro at 6 am every day and it's always packed.'

2 Match each highlighted expression (1–8) in Exercise 1 with one of the following paraphrases (a–h).

a made it very clear I disagreed
b speak in a confident way to make it sound as if I am an expert
c he completely ignores me
d I'm not going to take any notice of you
e to discuss work
f I completely agree
g from what we know
h I completely agree (in a sarcastic / humourous context)

3 SPEAK Work in pairs. Look at the following way of recording new phrases or idioms. Discuss the positive and negative aspects of this method.

(to make) **small talk** (uncountable noun) – to talk about unimportant things (often with someone you don't know well)
Common use: Very common
Example sentence: *"I hate going to conferences because I'm not good at making small talk with other people."*
Paraphrase: The ability to make conversation on trivial matters is a skill that not everybody has.

About English

Sarcasm is a common feature of English, but it's not always easy to detect. When someone is being sarcastic, usually they say the opposite of what the context indicates, and their tone of voice might change or their speech might seem exaggerated. You can also look out for visual clues like raised eyebrows or eye rolls, or in emails people may use an upside-down smiley face.

4 Choose ONE of the phrases below. Look up its meaning and make a record of it, including the different elements above.

- talk your ear off
- tell it like it is
- tell someone a thing or two

5 SPEAK Share what you have written with others with the group. How could you improve your way of recording these phrases?

6 SPEAK In groups, discuss the questions.

1 How can you group idioms that you learn? (e.g. by key word, by subject etc)
2 How do you try and incorporate phrases like these into your speech? Do you think it is more useful to know them receptively rather than use them?
3 What advice would you give someone who wanted to improve their idiom use?

Discussing idioms

Discuss the differences in meaning between these idioms:

- small talk / idle talk
- talk the talk / put your money where your mouth is
- tell me about it / tell it like it is

12

ON THE RIGHT TRACK

KEY LANGUAGE

Participle clauses
Verb patterns
Health and fitness
Multi-word verbs

IDIOMS

Sports

EXAM PRACTICE

Reading and Use of English Parts 1, 3, 4 & 5
Writing Part 2
Listening Part 3
Speaking Parts 1 & 3

Speaking Part 1 Interview

Work with a partner. Discuss the questions.

1 To what extent and in what ways do you prioritise your emotional and physical wellbeing?
2 What do you do to help yourself relax?
3 What do you find to be the most effective thing when you're under the weather?
4 In your opinion, do alternative therapies provide a real alternative to medicine? Have you ever tried any? If so, which?
5 Do you think people in general prioritise physical health over mental and emotional health?
6 To what extent do social media and the wellness industry influence your lifestyle?

12 ON THE RIGHT TRACK

Reading and Use of English Part 5 Multiple choice

1 SPEAK Work in pairs. Look at the photo and answer the questions.

1 Have you or anyone you know ever read a self-help book? Was it effective? Why? / Why not?
2 Do you think these kinds of books work? Why? / Why not?
3 Why do so many of these titles become bestsellers?

2 Scan the reading text on page 175 and decide which of the following best describes the type of text it is:

- an informative article
- an opinion piece
- a critical review

3 You are going to read a text about self-help books. For questions 1–6, choose the answer (A, B, C or D) which you think fits best according to the text.

1 What is the author's assessment of self-help books?
A She believes the caliber of advice varies.
B She is sceptical in general of their merits.
C She finds them life-affirming.
D She is appalled by the contents.

2 The author implies that the self-help genre
A promotes some addictive behaviours.
B is aware that it exploits the naïve.
C prioritises financial gain over health.
D steals its ideas from classical writings.

3 In the third paragraph, the writer uses the phrase 'in thrall' to
A convey the fascination that self-help advice holds for people.
B clarify which group of people in particular are drawn to self-help books.
C justify people's significant interest in self-help advice.
D explain how the self-help genre is responsible for people's increased interest in reading.

4 What does the writer conclude about the content of current self-help books?
A It should be better researched.
B It has become less relevant.
C It needs more diverse writers.
D It would benefit from fresh subject matter.

5 What do academics have to say about self-help books?
A Their is an element of irony to the basic premise when you consider the habits of their readership.
B There is a tendency to grossly undermine the work of professionals.
C Reading them can make for a distressing experience for a proportion of readers.
D When you consider the population at large, their commercial success is entirely predictable.

6 According to psychologists, self-help books ...
A sustain people's resolve to change.
B skirt around the issue of individuality.
C align with human thought patterns.
D neglect the impact of good fortune.

4 SPEAK Work in groups and discuss the questions.

1 What's the best advice you've ever received?
2 Where do you usually turn for advice? Why?

Don't forget!

If you're unsure of an answer, leave it and come back to it at the end. If, after looking again, you don't know the answer, just guess. You won't lose marks for a wrong answer.

THE ROAD TO BETTERMENT

Often labelled as disingenuous at best, and mere psychobabble nonsense at worst, self-help books have long captivated the masses with their promise to help you on your path to self-knowledge, betterment and eternal happiness, and I appear to be no different. Despite not having learnt Chinese, mastered the art of meditation or acquired the inner peace that would stop the trivial family arguments, I could conceivably achieve any one of those things at any moment, thanks to the bookshelf in my study currently groaning under the weight of my collection of self-help books.

Tantalisingly just out of reach at all times, my perfect self may lie within the pages of one of those life manuals. Perhaps it is just a question of me not having found the right one for me. And yet, having consumed vast quantities of this content and still not found enlightenment, I fear that I'm none the wiser and would have been better off reading literally anything else. Lurking in the back of my mind are the nagging thoughts ever querying whether my time would in fact be better spent reading the classics like Plato or Marcus Aurelius. But then another self-help tome appears, one which promises to help you reach nirvana and I'm sucked in again. And this, essentially, is what the self-help book industry knows and preys upon.

At its most basic level the self-help or self-betterment genre encourages people to read, which is a thing to be encouraged. In fact, reading for betterment has existed since the ancient world of the aforementioned Greeks and Romans. However, today's version is nothing short of a goldmine, its admirable original aims long since consigned to history as we go searching for a quick fix to our problems in a world where competition for everything is fierce. Some blame globalisation for our obsession with improving ourselves; others see the rat race of employment as the culprit. Whatever the root, people are now in thrall to these self-styled gurus, churning out dubious advice, things which many people would say is common sense and wouldn't dream of paying a penny for.

Publishers will have us believe that self-help is the bestselling non-fiction genre, and a recent trip to my local bookshop bore out these claims. Shelves upon shelves of enticing aspirational titles sat vying to be the one to take me to the promised land of health, happiness and riches. Browsing the shelves, I was struck by the similarity of their content as advertised by the slogans and straplines on the covers, but perhaps this is not surprising. With so many writers having jumped on the bandwagon over the years, the market is now saturated, and one suspects there is little of any value left to say, especially given that the advice has always been more anecdotal than rigorously researched in the first place. This is in stark contrast to its academic counterpart, the field of psychology.

Unfortunately for many of the writers in this field, academia is catching up with them and what it has to say makes for uncomfortable reading. Psychologists have long viewed self-help books with a dose of skepticism and rightly so. Few studies carried out on their efficacy have anything positive to report. Recently, I read some online articles vigorously refuting all sorts of claims made by self-help authors about human behaviour and the inner workings of the human brain. But for me, the observations that struck a chord were more about the commercial elements. Several researchers have pointed out that the people most likely to purchase a self-help book were those who had bought one in the previous year.

And as some have drily commented, surely the whole idea of a self-help book is that only one should be necessary.

Talking to psychologists can shed some light on this as they have identified some cognitive biases, or errors in thinking, which drive us to this genre over and over. The narrative fallacy, which I for one am definitely guilty of, states that when assessing our successes, humans tend to remember positive points not negative ones, and self-help books are full of what worked rather than what didn't. Another bias is the fundamental attribution error, which is my personal favourite. When other people make mistakes, we think it's due to their character, but for ourselves, it's down to our life circumstances. But this ignores something that many successful people mention, and that, of course, is luck. So next time you find yourself about to part with some hard-earned cash for another self-help book, you might want instead to move on to the Classics aisle.

Language focus Participle clauses

1 Match the underlined participle clauses in the following extracts from the reading with rules a–e.

1 ... having consumed vast qualities of this content and still not found enlightenment, I fear that I'm none the wiser and would have been better off reading literally anything else.

2 Whatever the root, people are now in thrall to these self-styled gurus, churning out dubious advice, things which many people would say is common sense and wouldn't dream of paying a penny for.

3 Browsing the shelves, I was struck by the similarity of their content as advertised by the slogans and straplines on the covers, but perhaps this is not surprising.

4 With so many writers having jumped on the bandwagon over the years, the market is now saturated.

5 Recently I read some online articles vigorously refuting all sorts of claims made by self-help authors about human behaviour and the inner workings of the human brain.

a Participle clause used with *with* + in a formal context to introduce a new subject.

b Participle clauses to replace a non-defining relative clause.

c Participle clause replaces *after ... ing* to highlight that the action happens before the other.

d Participle clause to replace defining relative clause.

e Participle clause replaces *while* / *as* to highlight two actions happen simultaneously.

2 Combine the information in the following sentences using participle clauses.

1 They had enough money. They decided to book premium economy tickets.

2 There were so many films to choose from. They knew they'd spend ages flicking through all the channels.

3 Everybody looked at the man. He was causing a massive scene in the restaurant. He found a hair in his food.

4 She finished the book. She decided to write a review about it.

5 He was tired after a long day. He headed straight to bed.

6 The apartments were a nightmare to sell. They were built on a toxic waste site.

3 Go to Ready for Grammar on page 230 for further rules, explanations and practice.

4 SPEAK Work in pairs and discuss other ways of saying the following sentences, both with and without participle clauses. Use the example to help you.

Carrie had read up on natural remedies and decided to take melatonin for her insomnia.

- *Having read up on natural remedies, Carrie decided to take melatonin for her insomnia.*
- *Before taking melatonin for her insomnia, Carrie had read up on natural remedies.*
- *After reading up on natural remedies, Carrie decided to take melatonin for her insomnia.*

1 Josh worked such long hours that he needed a cleaner to keep his flat tidy.

2 Fiona trained hard every day at the pool as she hoped to take part in the next Olympics.

3 The simple breathing exercise has been tried and tested many times and can produce favourable results.

Vocabulary Health and fitness

1 Read the articles below and for 1–12 choose the word that does NOT collocate with the noun in bold.

STRUGGLING WITH INJURY? TRY GOLD PHYSIO.

Are you struggling with a **(1)** *severe / damaging / persistent* **injury**? Do you suffer from **(2)** *constant / cognitive / chronic* **pain** that nags away despite **(3)** *medical / surgical / burning* **intervention**. Gold Physio could be for you! We'll look at a range of holistic options including **(4)** *alternative / complementary / genetic* **therapies** to bring you back to your pain-free self. Don't delay, make your appointment today.

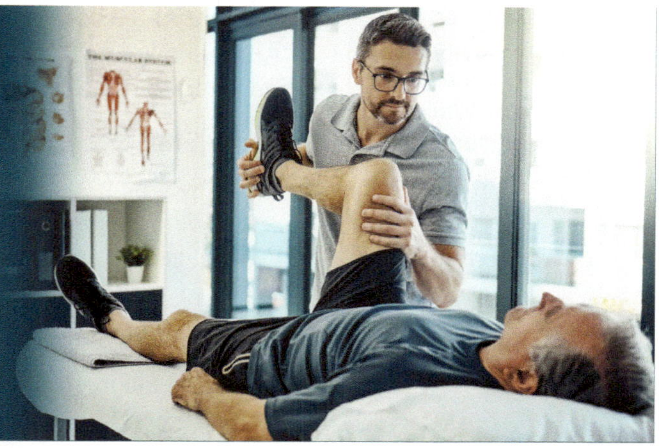

DON'T SUFFER IN SILENCE

Dieting is not just for weight loss. **(5)** *Restricted / Special / Fad* **diets** can actually benefit a whole host of ailments, from **(6)** *poor / bad / limiting* **circulation** to problems with your **(7)** *health / digestive / immune* **system**. Come along to our Wednesday evening group to find out more about this. We'll offer advice as well as help with the **(8)** *intelligent / emotional / mental* **resilience** needed to stick to such diets. With a **(9)** *fresh / conservative / balanced* **perspective** and the right diet, you could see incredible results.

Muscles you can count on!

Do you see little improvement in your (10) *core / physical / superior* **strength**, no matter how many times you go to the gym? Remember, it's not always easy to change your build – it's often part of your (11) *genetic / demographic / physical* **makeup**. But don't get disheartened as help is at hand. Using (12) *effective / established / proficient* **practices** from the east, we'll show you the secret of building muscle that will last! Call us now on 080039393.

2 The groups of adjectives below can combine with one of the nouns from Exercise 1. Add the noun for each group.

1 healthcare / legal / nervous ______
2 brute / considerable / inner ______
3 balanced / varied / staple ______
4 alternative / personal / historical ______
5 increased / blood / air ______
6 unfair / employment / recommended ______
7 chest / acute / sharp ______
8 government / humanitarian / divine ______

3 **SPEAK** Work in pairs. Prepare four questions for your partner using the collocations Exercises 1 and 2 above. Take turns to ask and answer the questions.

Have you ever tried any complementary therapies?

Speaking Part 3 Long turn

Don't forget!

You are examined on your language ability, rather than your opinion. While you must ensure you answer the question, including a variety of advanced structures and vocabulary in your response is the priority.

1 SPEAK Work in pairs. You are going to take turns talking on your own for about two minutes.

Student A: Talk for about two minutes about the question below.

Student B: When Student A has finished, say what governments or employers could do to reduce these factors.

What are the biggest contributing factors to poor health in your country?
- poor eating habits
- sedentary lifestyles
- stress

Student B: Talk for about two minutes about the question below.

Student A: When Student B has finished, say whether you think emotional wellbeing should be taught in schools.

What is the best way for someone to improve their emotional wellbeing?
- getting a pet
- walking more
- cultivating relationships

Useful language

Advanced Structures

1 Match the sentence beginnings 1–8 to the endings A–G. One ending can be used twice.

1	If people were to	5	Supposing everyone
2	Rarely	6	It could be argued that
3	It has been suggested that	7	Having
4	Not only should	8	An approach which

A people be more physically active, but also they could improve their diets.
B been a dog owner for many years, I feel like I'm well placed to comment on this.
C could be beneficial is to encourage investment in sporting facilities.
D have governments shown the right commitment to public health.
E ate less meat, it could reduce the level of chronic diseases.
F devote more time to exercise, the situation might improve.
G food production processes need to be radically overhauled.

2 Match the sentences in Exercise 1 to their structures A–E below.

A	Passive	C	Inversion	E	Participle clause
B	Relative clause	D	Conditional		

2 Go to the Additional materials on page 198 and discuss the follow-up questions to Part 3.

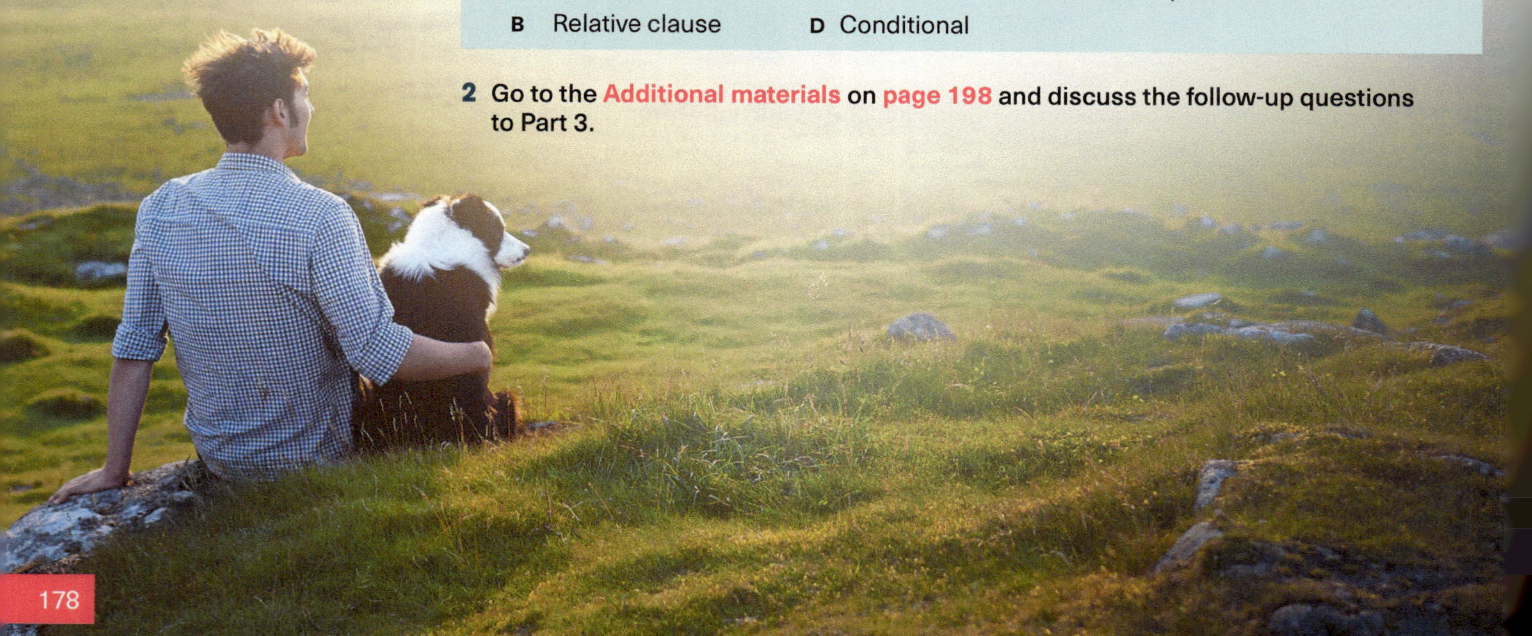

Language focus Verb patterns

THE ADVENTURES OF JUDE

I'd always watched them doing capoeira in the street, and I'd fancied doing it myself, but I felt I **daren't go** and ask them if I could try. I mean, as a 50-year-old woman, I'm not built like your average *capoeirista*! But, one day I plucked up the courage and asked them if **they'd mind my joining them**. Well, they couldn't have been more welcoming, and some of the basic movements are quite accessible. They even mentioned a club I can join! So, next time you're thinking about trying something, but feel out of your depth – just go for it! After all, **wouldn't you hate to miss out** on something that is incredible?

1 Read the text and complete each of the rules (1–3) with the words from the box.

gerund | infinitive with to | bare infinitive (without to)

1 The ____________ is used with modal verbs and certain other verbs (e.g. *let, dare, had better*)
2 The ____________ is used after a possessive pronoun when the subject of the main verb is different.
3 The ____________ is used when certain verbs of liking are combined with *would*.

2 Complete the short dialogues. Put the verb in brackets into the correct form using verb patterns. Decide if any other words or additional structures are needed.

'Would you object to **(1)** ____________ (try) your dish? I'm not sure mine tastes like it should.'
'No of course not. Be my guest. The teacher left me **(2)** ____________ (prepare) this, but to be honest, I've no idea what I'm doing.'
'It's your first time though, and you're on this course **(3)** ____________ (learn) so don't worry.'
'Still. I'd hate for it **(4)** ____________ (taste) bad!'

'I'm sorry, but now the change of the class time clashes with my uni course. I'd hate **(5)** ____________ (be able) to come, so I'm going to look into seeing whether I can change my study schedule.'
'Oh what a pain! I really hope you manage to change it. I couldn't imagine you **(6)** ____________ (attend) the class! You've been coming to this class since the very beginning, haven't you!'
'I have – honestly, it's completely changed my fitness. I'm very reluctant **(7)** ____________ (have to) leave.'
'Yes, for you **(8)** ____________ (come) to all the classes for all this time only **(9)** ____________ (stop) now would be very sad. You've really got the capacity **(10)** ____________ (be) a great swing dancer, but I understand you must **(11)** ____________ (put) your studies before your hobbies!'

3 Go to **Ready for Grammar** on **page 232** for further rules, explanations and practice.

4 SPEAK In pairs, choose one of the classes from Exercise 2 and role play a dialogue. Try to include some of the following phrases in your dialogue.

Would you mind my showing you ... ?
I don't know why he / she / you / they left ...
I'd hate to ...
Let's try to quietly / quickly / slowly ...
It's no use ...
I can't imagine ...
For you / him / her / them / me to be able to ...
It's not worth ...

Writing Part 2 Letter

1 SPEAK Work in pairs. Read the Part 2 task below and discuss how you might answer it.

> A popular lifestyle magazine has invited readers to write in, sharing stories about changes they have made to their lifestyle in order to become healthier. You decide to send in a letter in which you briefly outline the changes you made, the reasons why you decided to make them, and what advice you'd give others wanting to change their lifestyles.

2 Read the model answer in the Additional materials on page 199. Was the response similar to your ideas in Exercise 1?

3 Plan your answer to the task in Exercise 1. Note down in the table what information you need to include in the letter and make a note of your ideas.

Points to be included	Ideas
Outline the changes I made	*Went to dancing classes, etc ...*

Useful language

Avoid repetition in your answer by varying your language. This will indicate that you can use a wide range of appropriate vocabulary.

Complete the synonymous phrases by using a word from the box.

altering fierce incremental losing realistic staying

1 changing (one's) lifestyle / adjusting routines / ____________ habits
2 having achievable aims / attainable targets / setting ____________ goals
3 making small changes / little adjustments / taking ____________ steps
4 having strong motivation / great incentive / ____________ determination
5 keeping at it / maintaining focus / ____________ committed
6 becoming despondent / giving up hope / ____________ heart

4 Write your answer to the task in Exercise 1. Write your letter in 280–320 words.

For more information on writing letters, see page 193.

Listening Part 3 Multiple choice

1 **12.1** **You will hear part of a discussion in which Alex Rogers from a community action group and Nadiya Thompson from the National Parks Service are discussing disabled access to national parks and other outdoor spaces. For questions 1–5, choose the answer (A, B, C or D) which fits best according to what you hear.**

1 What is Alex's opinion about the National Parks Service?
- **A** It fails to understand the needs of disabled walkers.
- **B** It has only provided the bare minimum of disabled access.
- **C** It prioritises disabled access less than other organisations.
- **D** It imagines disabled people have little interest in hiking.

2 According to Nadiya, the new disabled access plan came about
- **A** because of pressure from organisations with vested interests.
- **B** after negotiations between disparate groups of people.
- **C** by approaching the problem with a different mindset.
- **D** due to revisions in the process for enacting new policies.

3 When discussing the National Parks Service, both Alex and Nadiya agree that
- **A** it should take the lead on securing more funding.
- **B** it has failed to grasp the extent of the issue.
- **C** it needs guidance from a wider range of experts.
- **D** it has been slow to enact the necessary changes.

4 When discussing her work, Alex reveals her hope to help disabled people
- **A** have a higher degree of self-belief.
- **B** be more inspirational.
- **C** take more risks.
- **D** be more observant of the natural beauty.

5 Why do some schemes not get implemented in national parks?
- **A** Their complexity makes them impractical in many parks.
- **B** It is difficult to get agreement on the finer details.
- **C** They are neglected in favour of more urgent matters.
- **D** The National Parks Service does not have sufficient resources.

2 **SPEAK Work in groups and discuss the questions.**

1 How accessible are building, services and facilities in your town?

2 What measures are being taken to improve its accessibility and do you think these go far enough?

Pronunciation Reading between the lines

About English

In English, sometimes people say one thing but mean something different. Listening carefully to a person's intonation can help us work out the implied meaning, i.e. the meaning hidden behind their words. This is called 'reading between the lines'.

1 12.2 Listen to the extracts from the listening on page 181. What is implied by the speakers ...

1 when Alex says *'It's good to finally get this plan agreed.'*?
  A I understand that your job is difficult.
  B I think the process is much too slow.

2 when Nadiya says '*I appreciate your frustration Alex,*'?
  A I too think the situation could be improved.
  B It's good that you are being direct with me.

3 when Alex says *'We have been trying to get involved for some years now.'*?
  A It took much too long for us to be consulted.
  B We were happy to wait to be consulted.

4 when Nadiya says *'In <u>my</u> view, yes it is.'*?
  A Other people's opinions are not as relevant.
  B Not everyone she works with shares her view.

2 Work in pairs. Create a short conversation between two people with one or two phrases like those in the discussion. Give your conversation to another pair of students and ask them to read between the lines and work out the hidden meanings.

Vocabulary Multi-word verbs

1 Match the multi-word verbs in bold (1–4) from the listening with their meanings (a–d).

1 In recent years complaints have been **mounting up** from groups such as yours.
2 Community action groups like mine have to ... **keep at it** in order for change ...
3 We want to **urge them on** to be more adventurous and challenge themselves ...
4 ... we have to actually **go through with it** and not just pay them lip service.

a continue trying to do something
b encourage someone
c increase gradually
d complete something agreed (usually difficult)

2 Write the multi-word verbs from Exercise 1 next to their type and structure (a–d).

a Intransitive phrasal verb: verb + preposition ____
b Transitive phrasal verb: verb + (object) + preposition + (object) ____
c Prepositional verb: verb + preposition + object ____
d Phrasal prepositional verb: verb + particle + preposition + object ____

3 Complete the sentences with the correct form of the multi-word verbs from the box. You may need to include a relevant object.

bottle up catch on catch up with cling on to count in get through get to go without

0 People should be encouraged to process their **emotions** as there is plenty of evidence that *bottling them up* can lead to mental and physical health issues.
1 All his days of sitting in front of the TV, mindlessly eating fast or processed food finally ____________ when his doctor told him how much damage he'd done to his body.
2 Just ____________ **the hope** that your forefather's longevity will be passed on to you.
3 Perfectionism, which may seem like a positive quality, can actually be incredibly damaging as **the stress** of trying to attain such levels can really ____________ you.
4 It ____________ **saying** that enjoying nature does wonders for our general wellbeing.
5 In many countries, travelling by scooter or bike has really ____________ and is now a popular and convenient way to get around in the city centre.
6 As long as I can ____________ **my speech** without any mistakes, my parents' anniversary dinner should be a thoroughly enjoyable occasion.
7 Joaquin said to ____________ for the camping trip next weekend.

4 SPEAK Work in pairs. Look at the multi-word verbs in Exercise 3. Discuss which type of multi-word verb each one is and when you might use them.

5 In 1–4, decide which of the nouns do not collocate with the verb.

1	bottle up	anger / stress / pain / madness
2	cling on to	hope / fear / power / life
3	mount up	pressure / time / debts / costs
4	get through	your job / the day / an ordeal / an exam

6 SPEAK Talk to your partner about:

- a time when you **bottled up** your disappointment about something
- an idea or belief that you **clung on to**
- a time when you had problems or difficulties **mounting up**
- a situation which was difficult to **get through**

Reading and Use of English Part 1 Multiple-choice cloze

1 For questions 1–8, read the text below and decide which answer (**A**, **B**, **C** or **D**) best fits each gap. There is an example at the beginning (**0**).

FOOD SUPPLEMENTS – *friend or foe?*

A fast growing and immensely profitable industry in many countries, there are (0) ____*D*____ of dietary supplements on the market, with individuals taking them whether they are feeling out of (1) ____________ or simply aiming to stay on form. However, whether they have any true efficacy is another matter entirely.

For many current researchers, the jury doesn't seem to be just out, it has come back with quite a (2) ____________ verdict that there are almost no tangible benefits to (3) ____________ on such supplements. Firstly, they cite that nutritional (4) ____________ *don't* necessarily need to be addressed by supplements, since such a wide variety of food products, especially in countries like the US, are (5) ____________ with vitamins and minerals to ensure a balanced diet. Additionally, these supplements aren't (6) ____________ to the same manufacturing standards as medicines, meaning that some of the more unscrupulous supplement providers can oversell the health benefits without providing a (7) ____________ of evidence. So, perhaps the lesson for us all here is that when it comes to health you just can't (8) ____________ a balanced, varied diet.

0	**A** haul	**B** mounds	**C** glut	**D** <u>heaps</u>
1	**A** mend	**B** sorts	**C** touch	**D** elements
2	**A** malicious	**B** elusive	**C** fatal	**D** damning
3	**A** forking out	**B** pressing on	**C** chipping in	**D** bouncing back
4	**A** infractions	**B** deficiencies	**C** inadequacies	**D** shortages
5	**A** embodied	**B** doctored	**C** fortified	**D** garnished
6	**A** held	**B** shown	**C** pinned	**D** drawn
7	**A** strip	**B** snatch	**C** shred	**D** shave
8	**A** whip	**B** strike	**C** crush	**D** beat

12 REVIEW

Vocabulary Health and fitness | Multi-word verbs

For questions 1–8, read the text and think of a word from the unit that best fits each gap. Use one word in each gap.

The common cold is an annoyance that almost everyone has to suffer at one time or another in their life, but some people, due to their genetic **(1)** ____________ suffer more frequently and more severely than others from such colds. For them, it's impossible to get **(2)** ____________ their cold without a couple of days in bed and, in extreme cases, it could lead to something more serious requiring medical **(3)** ____________, and even a stint in hospital.

It is important to recognise when things have taken a turn for the worse, and seek medical advice. Unfortunately, some people **(4)** ____________ on to the belief that they'll be fine, yet ask any doctor and they'll soon tell you how this attitude can be quick to **(5)** ____________ up with those who are unaware that they have compromised **(6)** ____________ systems. In these cases, symptoms can quickly **(7)** ____________ up and drain people's physical **(8)** ____________, which in turn makes the body susceptible to more serious illnesses.

Reading and Use of English Part 4 Key word transformations

For questions 1–6, complete the second sentence so that it has a similar meaning to the first sentence, using the word given. Do not change the word given. You must use between three and eight words, including the word given.

1 Julian knew he'd end up with the project as he always got the worst jobs in the company.
SADDLED
Julian always got the jobs that nobody wanted, so he was bound ____________________ the project.

2 I've never heard any of the local residents say anything good about the parking rules.
SAY
The local residents have never ____________________ the parking rules.

3 We decided to be cautious and stick to the original plan.
ERR
Deciding to ____________________, we stuck to the original plan.

4 Everyone was sure that Daily would win the race as he was in the best form of his life.
WHATSOEVER
Being on the best form of his life, nobody ____________________ that Daily would win the race.

5 The practical joke was ingenious, fooling his son completely.
IN
His son ____________________ the ingenuity of the practical joke.

6 They were only in this dire situation because of Julio's terrible map reading skills.
FAINTEST
If ____________________ read a map, they wouldn't be in this dire situation.

Reading and Use of English Part 3 Word formation

For questions 1–8, read the text below. Use the word given in capitals at the end of some of the lines to form a word that fits in the space in the same line. There is an example at the beginning (0).

THE RISE OF PICKLEBALL AND PADEL

Only a decade ago, were you to have asked someone to name their favourite
leisure (0) *PURSUIT*, tennis was almost guaranteed to have been a common answer. **PURSUE**
Its popularity is (1) ____________ due to it being very social as well as a good workout. **DOMINATE**
However, padel and pickleball are fast becoming challengers. Many people attribute
this to their relative (2) ____________ compared to tennis, which is often seen as a **SIMPLE**
more complex and (3) ____________ sport, requiring expensive resources and high **COMPROMISE**
levels of physical fitness. Padel and pickleball, in contrast, are somewhat less
(4) ____________ demanding. **TECH**

Another thing in their favour is their accessible nature. While many tennis
clubs maintain an air of (5) ____________, which can seem intimidating, padel **EXCLUDE**
and pickleball clubs are not seen as quite so (6) ____________ to less affluent **ATTAIN**
members of the community. It's unlikely that tennis will pale into (7) ____________ **SIGNIFY**
in the coming decades, but one thing that we can say with some certainty is that
both padel and pickleball are changing the (8) ____________ of racket **LAND**
sports, and look set to continue.

Writing Part 2 Report

The town council wants to improve sports initiatives in your local area. You have been asked to submit a report about a neighbouring area. You should briefly describe what sports facilities are provided and the programmes which are on offer, evaluate whether they would be suitable for adoption in your area, and make recommendations about any other ideas that could encourage more participation.

Write your report in 280–320 words.

For more information on writing reports, see **page 194**.

Idioms Sports

1 SPEAK Read the speech bubbles below and then complete the table with your own ideas.

Some idioms have a metaphorical or symbolic meaning based on their literal origins. For example, *step up to the plate,* which means to take action in response to something, has a more literal meaning in baseball, where it refers to standing in a position ready to bat. These two meanings are very similar.

Once you've **learned the ropes** and settled in, you'll feel far less anxious about your new job.

Make sure you train gently at first – don't **jump the gun** and sign up for a marathon!

Sara **threw in the towel** halfway through the marathon because she pulled a muscle.

My boss is always **moving the goalposts,** so I never end up looking good no matter what I do.

Johan's resolve and determination are what **give him the upper hand** when negotiating deals.

Making sure your children's diet is full of nutritional value means they'll **have a head start** in life.

Idiom	Sport	Literal meaning	Metaphorical meaning
Learn the ropes	Sailing	To learn about tying knots in ropes on a boat	1
Jump the gun	Athletics	To start running before the sound of the starting gun	2
Throw in the towel	Boxing	To throw the towel on the floor to quit a fight	3
Move the goalposts	Football	To change the position of the posts and make the game easier or harder	4
Have/give the upper hand	Cards	To have good cards and therefore a better chance of winning	5
To have a head start	Horse racing	A horse that has its head slightly in front of the others at the start of a race	6

About English

Because idioms have metaphorical meanings they often exist in many languages. There may be some that have shared ideas, but the actual words may be very different as they often depend on cultural and historical factors. Does your language have idioms or phrases to express the ones in this unit?

Discussing idioms

Discuss the differences in meaning between these idioms:

- jump the gun / jump on the bandwagon
- throw in the towel / throw your hat in the ring

2 Complete the idioms with a word from the box.

ballpark   barred   bowled   chin   target

1 The first company quoted us a fee of $400,000 to redesign the complex. I can't remember the exact figure given by the second company, but it was **in the same** ____________.

2 James has put a great deal of practice into his chess game, and if he continues like this, he'll be **on** ____________ to win the national championship.

3 Her autobiography was quite shocking really. There were **no holds** ____________ when it came to what she thought about her teammates.

4 The generosity of his co-workers ____________ **him over** as he's only been there for a year and his leaving present was incredible.

5 He knew he was to blame for his team losing the match, and when the coach ranted and raved at him, he **took it on the** ____________ and didn't complain.

3 SPEAK Understanding the literal meaning of an idiom can sometimes help us understand the metaphorical meaning. Read the sentences in Exercise 2 and discuss from which sports you think the idioms originated.

COLLOCATION REVISION UNITS 1–12

1 **Write one word which can be used in all three expressions. The question numbers also refer to the relevant unit of the book where the collocations appeared. If necessary, use the box with the words in to help you.**

Adjective + noun

1 self-indulgent / self-satisfied / self-possessed ______

2 far-flung / go-to / tourist ______

3 vexing / age-old / usability ______

4 considerable / joint / risky ______

5 anonymous / inside / primary ______

6 spiralling / hidden / mounting ______

7 forensic / overwhelming / visual ______

8 household / hazardous / industrial ______

9 flamboyant / garish / whimsical ______

10 critically-acclaimed / star-studded / heart-wrenching ______

11 knock-on / adverse / secondary ______

12 brute / core / inner ______

Verb + noun

1 ______ somebody's day / something public / sense of something

2 ______ a leisurely stroll / a turn for the worse / its toll

3 ______ round to something / up with a solution / to a dead end

4 ______ the stalemate / the ice / with tradition

5 ______ the ins and outs / the difference / your stuff

6 ______ the price / a compliment / dividends

7 ______ upon an idea / the jackpot / out at (someone / something)

8 ______ a threat / a question / as somebody else

9 ______ down a storm / hand in hand / out of your way

10 ______ for your life / like cats and dogs / off an illness / infection

11 ______ change / action / unity

12 ______ anger / pain / stress

bottle up break call for come costs design destination effects evidence fight film go hit know make pay personality pose problem source strength take undertaking waste

2 **Use other collocations from the book to help you create your own exercise. Write three words or expressions which can all be used with the same adjective, verb or noun, in the same way as in Exercise 1. Write four examples like this for another student to complete.**

READY FOR WRITING

Introduction

In the **Writing** paper you have 1 hour and 30 minutes to complete two different writing tasks. The first is the compulsory Part 1 Essay task, where you should write 240–280 words. In Part 2, you select from a choice of three and should write 280–320 words.

Writing Part 1

In Part 1, you are given two source texts which contain contrasting or complementary views. You write a discursive essay in which you summarise and evaluate the key points from both texts, using your own words as much as possible. You must also include your own ideas.

Writing Part 2

In Part 2, you choose one task from a choice of three. Possible tasks include: an article, a letter, a report and a review.

Marking

Your writing is marked based on assessment criteria that consists of four subscales. Match the General advice A–D to the Assessment criteria 1–4 in the table below.

ASSESSMENT CRITERIA

1	2	3	4
Content	Communicative achievement	Organisation	Language

GENERAL ADVICE

A	B	C	D
Use the appropriate conventions for the task type, including **structure** and **register**. Communicate **complex ideas**. **Hold the reader's attention**. ___	Make sure your information is **logically ordered** and **flows clearly,** both from sentence to sentence and throughout piece of writing. Effectively use **cohesive devices** and **organisational patterns**. ___	Use a wide **range** of grammatical structures and lexis and ensure these are **accurate**. Where appropriate, use some **less common vocabulary**. ___	**Understand all points** of the task and **do everything required** by the task instructions. Make sure everything is **relevant**. ___

SPEAK **Read the General advice again. Identify which of the areas in bold you think you are strong at, and which you need to work on. In pairs, discuss what you can do to improve on your weak points.**

Planning and checking

Match steps 1–8 to the general advice A–D in the Marking section to which it corresponds.

1 While reading the task instructions, underline the points you have to address. ___
2 Identify the communicative purpose(s) of the piece of writing, e.g. persuading, evaluating, explaining, etc. ___
3 Consider the target reader. This will help you know what register to use – formal, neutral or informal – and help you decide what information to include. ___
4 Brainstorm ideas. Once you have decided what general ideas to focus on, think of specific supporting reasons or examples that the reader will find convincing. ___
5 Plan your paragraphs. Think about how you will transition from one section to the next and develop your argument through the piece of writing. ___
6 While writing, don't only rely on cohesive devices like *however* or *as a result* to connect your ideas. Also use organisational patterns: parallelism, topic sentences, rhetorical questions, ordinal adverbs (*first, second, last*), coordinating conjunctions (*not only … but also*, *whether … or …*), and so on. ___
7 Aim for a degree of sophistication in your writing. Show the reader that you can express your ideas effectively and precisely using just the right words. ___
8 Accuracy is key in C2 Proficiency, so leave time to proofread. Look for small errors that will bring down your mark. ___

Task conventions

Match task conventions 1–8 with the types of writing in the box. Sometimes more than one answer is possible.

article essay letter report review

1 You may choose to use headings to guide the reader through the piece of writing. ___
2 You need to evaluate abstract arguments made by another writer. ___
3 It's important to think of a 'catchy' title, so the reader will choose to read the piece of writing. ___
4 The target audience for your piece of writing is your teacher or tutor. ___
5 You may choose to include a personal anecdote. ___
6 At the beginning, you need to provide basic information about what you will be criticising, such as the title and author of a creative work. ___
7 You may be writing to the editor of a newspaper or magazine. ___
8 Instead of summarising main ideas, it is often appropriate to finish by giving recommendations. ___

Writing Part 1 Essay

Read the two texts below.

Write an essay summarising and evaluating the key points from both texts. Use your own words throughout as far as possible, and include your own ideas in your answer.

Write your Essay.

BUY CLEVER, NOT OFTEN

We need to all take a long hard look at our mindset and alter our consumption habits. Globally, people are buying more and more without giving a thought to where all these products end up when their usefulness runs out. Landfills don't have unlimited capacity, and our resources are not infinite. For this reason, instead of chasing after the latest fashions and gadgets every season, we should focus on buying goods of quality that will stand the test of time. In this way, each and every one of us can do our bit to ensure a more sustainable future.

PURCHASING: FAR FROM LUXURY

We may be buying goods with increasing frequency, but for many, rather than a luxury, this can often be due to necessity. The 'Boots' theory, imagined in a Terry Pratchett book, explains how people with lower incomes can't afford quality products that last longer, and so are trapped in a cycle of having to opt for lower quality equivalents, which need replacing more frequently. This costs them more money in the long run. We just need to look at the abundance of throwaway fashion and cheap gadgets that are constantly being snapped up to understand how frequently this happens today.

Model answer

The high rate of consumerism is a modern problem that has no immediate solution. Where goods are readily available at a cheap price, there will always be people willing to pay for them. However, the reasons behind these high levels of consumption are arguably far from clear cut.

Opening statement to engage the interest of the reader

Hedging to make the opinion more reasonable and less subjective

The first text appears to put the blame for overconsumption firmly on the shoulders of the consumer, indicating that people should think more carefully about their spending and its associated environmental effects. The writer implies that buyers whimsically follow trends with no concern for the wider world. However, their suggestion that the solution lies in buying quality items is perhaps a little unrealistic: modern items are simply not built to last. One idea could be involving customers in a more sustainable product life cycle, where the majority of components are reused or recycled.

Use of a specific reporting verb to show the writer understands what the text explicitly states, and what is suggested.

The second text states that the consumption habits of many people stem from necessity, describing a vicious circle in which low-income earners cannot afford up-front investment in quality items, and therefore are left with little choice but to buy cheaper and more often. This argument holds a lot of weight, as the price difference between low-cost and premium items can be incomparable. Nonetheless, it also oversimplifies the issue, disregarding the fact that shopping and trend following are also social activities. To really mitigate overconsumption, we must stop and ask ourselves more often, 'do I actually need this?'

Summary of text 2

Writer's opinion on text 2

In conclusion, while the current cycle of consumption may be set to stay, shoppers should consider how to dispose of their items more responsibly, as well as consider whether their purchases are in fact necessary in the first place.

Task

Read the two texts below.

Write an essay summarising and evaluating the key points from both texts. Use your own words throughout as far as possible, and include your own ideas in your answer.

IS HISTORY WORTH TEACHING?

In most history classes, students spend countless hours memorising dates and names that they will promptly forget as soon as they have taken their exams. I do not think it unfair to say that history is a burden for young minds. Would it not be more productive to stop pondering over what has been done in the past and start thinking about what has to be done now to address pressing issues like the climate crisis? Today's students should focus on subjects like science and technology, languages and economics, where they acquire the knowledge and develop the skills they will need to face life's many challenges.

IN DEFENCE OF HISTORY

History teaches humility. Time and again, humankind has thought they had everything figured out, only to find their world view overturned by new ideas. It is for good reason therefore that debates about the value of studying history invariably lead to the oft-quoted words of philosopher George Santayana, 'Those who cannot remember the past are condemned to repeat it.' It is self-evident that studying historical events and trends, especially over the last century, helps us reach a deeper understanding and appreciation of current events. When we know the origins of the problems we face, we are one step closer to solving them.

Write your Essay in **240–280** words.

Useful language for essays

Referring to the source texts

Both texts address the issue of ...

In the (first / second) text, the writer asserts ...*

... is stated in the first / second text*

One assertion made in the first / second text is that ...

The second text, on the other hand, takes an opposing view ...

* alternative reporting verbs: *argue, contend, contest, dispute, maintain, outline, propose, suggest, state*

Integrating others' views with yours

This is an argument that holds a lot of weight ...

This is a notable / noteworthy point ...

This point shouldn't be taken for granted ...

(However) One (fundamental) flaw in this view is ...

(Nevertheless) This argument doesn't take into account ...

Expressing your own viewpoint

It is probably accurate to claim / say / suppose that ...

There is little doubt that ...

It could be debated that ...

The idea is debatable whether ... because / due to ...

Expressing contrast

However ... | *On the contrary, ...*

In contrast, ... | *Nevertheless, ...*

Nonetheless ... | *Even so, ...*

On the other hand, ... | *At the same time, ...*

Despite / In spite of (the fact that), ...

Writing Part 2 Article

A youth arts magazine is running a series on the personal benefits of live entertainment. The magazine has invited readers to send in articles briefly describing a memorable experience of an in-person event involving music, arts or culture. The article should explain the advantages of attending or participating in live events and consider how this can foster better understanding of oneself and others.

Write your **article.**

Model answer

catch title to grab the reader's attention →

What's your vibe?

Little can beat the thrill of standing amongst a thronging crowd all jumping in time to the beat of their favourite group. Live cultural and arts events, be it music, theatre or whatever takes your fancy, can leave us all with a feeling of rich contentment and belonging that is hard to find elsewhere.

← Descriptive introduction to draw the reader in to the writer's imagination

writer's own anecdote to engage reader →

Personally, this came in the form of seeing my favourite musician, The Wkend, at a recent concert in Madrid. Even before entering the wide expanse of the stadium, seeing the hordes of people queuing to enter, all with the same passion, was a complete blast – I felt like part of an unspoken group, tribe even. Once inside, this unspoken and immense sense of bonding just increased with every song we heard as we all moved in unison, as if in a trance from the music.

← Highlights show vivid, descriptive language. Often used when describing personal experience

Use analogy and comparison to enliven your writing →

Just think back to the last event where you could revel in your fandom. Didn't it feel good to be amongst crowds who really got the point of it all too? For me, and I suspect many, it's this sense of bonding, albeit fleeting, that makes these events so magical. Whether a play, some opera, or a concert, the private love you've had for a certain style of music or production suddenly becomes public as you meet like-minded people that share these long-fostered emotions. These events can give you the validation and encouragement to seek out other similar kinds of entertainment, knowing that you'll always find some peers out there with whom to share it.

← Appeal to the reader to draw them into the opinion

On a wider scale, these kinds of events can bring people together as they trade views or music recommendations, in this way forging a sense of kinship. It gives you a homogenous pack with which to identify, perhaps helping you to refine your own styles and interests as well as giving you an outlet for your existing ones.

Task

A health and wellness magazine is running a series on the impact that spending time in nature can have on an individual's health. The magazine has invited readers to send in articles describing their experiences and pursuits in the natural world. The article should describe how you experienced nature, the impact it had on your health and how society as a whole can benefit from spending more time outdoors.

Write your **article** in **280–320 words.**

Useful language for articles

Expressing opinion	**Drawing the reader in**
In my experience, …	*Just think back …*
I'd go so far as to say …	*What would you do if …*
There's no doubt that …	*Have you ever considered …*
It's undeniable that …	*Consider …*

Using descriptive techniques

Adjective/adverb use – it was a deliberately ominous suggestion …

Relative clauses – A view which could take your breath away …

Similes – …the crowd moved in unison, like a wave rippling across the ocean

Metaphor – The place was a zoo, mess everywhere and children climbing all over …

Writing Part 2 Letter

You have recently taken part in an evening course run by your local community college and the college director has requested some feedback. You decide to write a letter in which you briefly describe the course and the positive aspects of it. You should also suggest improvements that could be made.

Write your letter.

Model answer

Dear Mrs Potter,

I have recently attended your six-week evening beginner's art course, held on Tuesdays at 7 p.m., and, as requested, I would like to give you my feedback on the course. ← Context setting and reason for writing stated in the opening lines

Over the six weeks, we learned a wide range of skills and techniques. The course was clearly staged, looking initially at the elements of drawing and perspective, and then experimenting with a variety of mediums such as oil, watercolour and pastel. Having had no prior basis in art, all of these classes were invaluable for me and for many of my fellow classmates. The instructor was clear and patient at all times, doing his best to divide his time between those of us who were slightly more advanced and those who took longer to get the hang of things. I also think the classes were very reasonably priced.

Writer addresses last part of the task {

If I could give any advice for improvements , it would be to suggest slightly smaller class sizes. There were sixteen students in our group, but the facilities were only sufficient for around twelve in my opinion, both in terms of art supplies and physical space. This also put the teacher in an unenviable position, having to stretch himself rather thinly amongst the students to advise and assist. In general, while the instructor was second to none, the general state of the college buildings could be improved. There are many signs of wear and tear. I know this is a budgetary issue, but it is worth pointing out that these poor conditions do not go unnoticed.

Having said that, I would not hesitate to enrol on another of your courses and am already looking at Step 1 Watercolours. If it is anything like the beginner's art course, then it will almost certainly be well worth my while. ← Positive closing remark and summary of overall opinion

With many thanks,

Ania Brozda

Task

You have recently read some letters in a newspaper discussing the question 'Is there still a sense of local community?' The newspaper has invited its readers to join the debate. You decide to write a letter in which you briefly describe an experience that made you feel part of your community. You should also analyse the reasons why, in general, it is important to belong to a community.

Write your **letter** in **280–320 words**.

Useful language for letters

Stating reasons for writing

I would like to give you my feedback ...

I thought I'd share my own thoughts ...

I'm writing in order to highlight ...

With respect to the article entitled ...

Writing about a large amount

There is an abundance of groups to ...

The tutor has a wealth of knowledge.

People couldn't be more friendly ...

There is no shortage of ...

Writing about a lack or small amount

There is a dearth of courses that ...

... This kind of help is few and far between ...

This feeling is almost certainly lacking in ...

The teacher was stretched rather thinly ...

Writing Part 2 Report

You work as a volunteer on the website for your children's secondary school. The principal has asked you to help produce social media guidance for students. Write a report for the school principal that evaluates the negative impact of social media and gives advice on how students can avoid these problems and use social media responsibly.

Write your **report.**

Model answer

Social media guidance report

Brief introduction outlining the purpose of the report → This report is to assist Heslington Common Secondary School in the development of a social media policy for new students, outlining the potential issues they may face and how they can avoid them.

Sub headings to clearly separate sections of the report → **The perils of social media**

In the modern world, children grow up immersed in social media and become proficient users of it at a young age. As such, it is a prime concern to monitor their use of social media more effectively. Teenagers are naturally curious and, as is commonly known, there are precious few limits to the types of content they can lay their hands on, some of which could possibly be violent or subversive. In addition to these worries, adolescents are at an age where they actively share information amongst their peer groups on social media, such as jokes or photos of others, but have not always become fully rounded as individuals. They are therefore not always ready to take full responsibility for their behaviour and recognise the psychological impact it can have on others.

Use a variety of linking words and phrases to make the overall text cohesive.

Facing the dangers

To counter such concerns, the first thing is to educate all groups involved: teachers, parents and students. Starting with adults, we need to ensure teachers and parents are provided with information about how to control and monitor teenagers' browsing activities. This does not mean 24-hour surveillance, but rather raising awareness of tools available to block websites with malevolent content. As for the children, the school needs to focus on the development of empathy, helping students to understand the negative effects of insensitive and irresponsible use of social media. Studies show that activities involving case studies or role plays can be particularly effective.

Use of 'is to' to avoid subjects

Use referencing to avoid repetition but aid the reader.

Conclusion

Summarising sentence. → Overall, social networking is a key part of a teenager's life, and while we should never deprive them of it, we should make every effort to make sure it is used kindly and responsibly.

Task

You recently helped organise a charity event in your local community. The charity has asked you to write a report about the event. In your report, you should briefly describe the event, evaluate the extent to which it was effective and recommend what should be repeated and what should be done differently in future events.

Write your **report** in **280–320** words.

Useful language for reports

Introducing the report

The aim / purpose of this report is to ...
This report comprises / contains ...
It will also include / evaluate / advise on ...
The basis for this report lies in ...

Making recommendations

This could be done by ...
One solution is to ...
In light of this, I'd advise/recommend ...
It would be advantageous to ...
To counter this, the first thing to do is to ...
It is particularly important / absolutely essential to ...

Writing Part 2 Review

A style and culture magazine has invited readers to submit reviews of restaurants that are institutions in their local area. You decide to send in a review of a restaurant describing the dining experience there, as well as outlining the restaurant's importance for the area. You should also say why you believe restaurants can become so meaningful to diners or communities.

Write your **review.**

Highlights show vivid, descriptive language that reviews require

<u>Regans' – A hug on a plate</u>

When it comes to restaurants, many people tend to look for the next big thing, whether it be a much-hyped new kind of cuisine or an unusual dining experience. Certainly, whimsy like this has its place in eating out, but we as diners so often tend to overlook the cultural mainstays that have fed us all our lives through thick and thin. Perhaps we take it for granted that they will always be there, yet they most certainly deserve recognition. Regan's is such a place. ← Brief summary of what the review is about

Understated in its décor and totally devoid of any pomp, Regan's has been serving customers in the city's docklands for over a hundred years. Whether for a wedding, birthday or work promotion, you would be surprised to find a local anywhere in the neighbourhood who doesn't remember celebrating a special event at this institution. While you might not get a velouté or a macerated strawberry, what you will get is hearty portions of decent, honest food that will make you reminisce about what your mother cooked when you were still in short trousers. And perhaps that's what makes it the institution it is – local food, for local people, a place where you fit in and feel at home. After all, restaurants aren't just about the cuisine or the décor; they can also fulfil a social and emotional function, and Regan's does just that by creating a home from home.

} Description of the restaurant

Reasons why the restaurant is important for the community → (it the institution it is – local food, for local people ...)

General comment on the importance of restaurants in communities →

A restaurant is often a meeting place where we make memories, whether a proposal of marriage or a celebratory dinner. As such, they are places to keep close to our hearts and cherish, especially those that have been with us and the generations of our families. Would I recommend Regan's? I think the review speaks for itself. While it's nice to get out of your culinary comfort zone on occasions, it's well worth getting into that zone too!

} Final recommendation and snappy end

Model answer

Task

Your college magazine is asking for reviews of films that have had a great impact on people. You decide to write a review about a film you saw, outlining what the film was about, explaining why it had such a great impact on you, and assessing how films can be much more than just entertainment.

Write your **review** in **280–320** words.

Useful language for reviews

Praising

What I found particularly interesting / poignant / thought-provoking was ...
It provides a fascinating / captivating / terrifying look / insight / into ...
What makes it so excellent / dramatic / thought-provoking is ...
That's what makes it the smash hit / cult classic / blockbuster / mainstay that it is.

Evaluating critically

One element which let it down was ...
Perhaps it's weak link was ...
The (only) downside to the ... was ...
One element that left it wanting was ...

Encouraging

I wouldn't hesitate to recommend ...
Would I recommend it? It's a no-brainer.
Don't think twice about going/seeing/ reading ...

Discouraging

Give this a miss!
Avoid it like the plague.
It's not for everyone ...
It's not worth (the entrance fee/ the paper it was written on).

ADDITIONAL MATERIALS

UNIT 2

Writing Part 1 Essay

Write an essay summarising and evaluating the key points from each text. Use your own words throughout as far as possible, and include your own ideas in your answer. Write your answer in **240–280** words.

PASSENGERS ALONE TOGETHER

To be a passenger is to be alone in a crowd. An elderly man reading a book on the commuter train, a businesswoman typing furiously on her laptop on a short-haul flight, a toddler watching cartoons on the Tube – these are all individual bubbles, worlds barely intersecting. But this is how we like it. Imagine if every passenger began shouting into their mobile phone or blasting their music on wireless speakers. The result would be cacophony. So we carefully police the boundaries of our bubbles to peacefully coexist during the remainder of our journey.

PASSENGERS AND PASSIVITY

The role of a passenger is no doubt a comfortable one to inhabit, but there is also something undeniably passive about it. After all, to become a passenger you must cede the right to ride, drive, steer, navigate, conduct or guide. You can't usually influence the trip in any meaningful way; you're just along for the ride. This, of course, suits most of us just fine – that is, until we become bored or hungry or tired. Then it becomes clear that we have paid a price for our passivity, and we must resist the urge to say, 'Are we there yet?' in the tone of an irritable child.

Go back to page 25.

UNIT 6

Pronunciation Assimilation

SPEAK Student A

1 Read the sentences as quickly as possible. Use assimilation as much as possible. Student B has 20 seconds to write what they hear.

A good cook should put ten grammes of coconut butter in it.
The brown bear had gone through the side gate to take a short cut.
He might be a good painter if he bought proper paints and white paper.

2 Change roles.

3 Check each other's sentences and give one point for each underlined word which is spelt correctly.

Go back to page 83.

UNIT 7

Writing Part 2 Review

While there are more descriptions of nouns in this review, key examples are underlined.

Mystery is an umbrella term for many different microgenres, ranging from detective stories to fantasy adventures, and one of these genres which is increasingly popular is the psychological thriller. Perhaps one of the best examples of this is *The Girl on the Train*, <u>the compelling **debut** novel by Paula Hawkins.</u>

<u>This split-narrative **story** of a woman trying to unpick the details of a crime she witnessed</u> was a best-selling blockbuster that also went on to be a hit Hollywood film. The story centres around three women with tragically interlinking narratives. Megan is everything Rachel could want to be. Anna has everything that Rachel could have had. When one of the trio mysteriously disappears one evening, it falls to another to unpick the dark truth of that fateful night.

What sets it apart from many books of the same genre is the <u>cleverly woven **narrative**, which moves back and forth in time and perspectives</u>. This means that the reader is trying to solve the puzzle of the disappearance in the same way that some of the characters are. With each new piece of information, another clue is given to the reader. This <u>clever **technique** of drip-feeding information</u> keeps the reader hanging on, trying to find the answers. Another element, which is essential in all storytelling is, to have characters you believe and care about, and this book has characterisation that is second to none. The main characters aren't one-dimensional, but rather they come with history and are fallible people with perhaps circumstances that have led them to where they are. This gives us a <u>crucial element of **investment** which is indispensable in all, but especially mystery, novels.</u>

Mystery is about needing and wanting an answer, and in this way, there is no denying that Hawkins' debut delivers more than enough, making it a great example of the genre.

Go back to page 109.

UNIT 8

Idioms Noticing similarities and differences

make someone's blood run cold: if a sound, sight, or thought makes your blood run cold, it really frightens you.

make someone's blood boil: to make someone feel extremely angry.

rock the boat: to do or say something that will cause problems or upset people.

make waves: to be busy or act in a way that causes other people to notice you, especially if causing problems or trouble.

be between a rock and a hard place: to be in a difficult situation and be stuck with choosing between undesirable alternatives.

be in a tight spot: to be in a difficult situation, often without being able to see a solution.

be out of line: to behave in way that is considered unacceptable.

be/get out of hand: to become unmanageable or uncontrollable.

UNIT 10

Speaking Part 3 Discussion

Discuss the following questions.

1 In what ways do you think reading enriches people's lives?
2 How important is it to engage with the literary works of other cultures?
3 Should the study of literature be a compulsory subject on the school curriculum?
4 Why do some people reject fiction altogether in favour of non-fiction?

Go back to page 149.

UNIT 11

Speaking Part 3 Long turn

Student A: Talk for about two minutes about the question below.

Student B: When Student A has finished, say how you think most people will do their shopping in the future.

How has shopping changed in urban areas?
- shopping centres
- online shopping
- family-run businesses

Student B: Talk for about two minutes about the question below.

Student A: When Student B has finished, say whether you think cities are becoming more or less liveable.

What is the most important factor in making a city liveable for all its residents?
- affordable housing
- public services
- community outreach

Go back to page 161.

UNIT 12

Speaking Part 3 Discussion

Discuss the following questions on the topic of health and wellbeing.

1 It is said that society places too much emphasis on how people look nowadays. How much truth is there in this?
2 What would you consider the most important personality traits for maintaining health and happiness? Why?
3 Do you think people will be healthier or less healthy in the future? In what ways?
4 To what extent does a person's lifestyle contribute to their wellbeing? What changes to lifestyle can people make to improve their wellbeing?
5 Do you think employers have responsibility for the work–life balance of their employees? Why / Why not?
6 Should young people be taught stress management techniques like meditation in schools? Why / Why not?

Go back to page 178.

UNIT 12

Writing Part 2 Letter

Dear Sir / Madam,

I hope this letter finds you well. I noticed your request for stories about health improvements in the recent edition of *Best Life* and, as such, I am writing to share my own recent lifestyle changes with you in the hope of inspiring your readers.

Recently, I noticed that I'd become rather lethargic in my day-to-day life, which was undeniably due to a lack of exercise. As someone with a full-time office job, it can be near impossible to find the time to work out or eat healthily, and I'm afraid I let these kinds of activities slip. So, I decided to start making incremental steps to transform my lifestyle.

Initially, I made small changes, like getting off the bus a stop earlier on my daily commute and buying a pedometer to gauge my step count. This worked fantastically and I became quite competitive with myself. Soon I was going for brisk walks during my lunch hour rather than spending it immobile in front of the screen. Next, I decided to introduce some dietary changes. I'm not a fan of calorie counting, so I just made a commitment to cut back on takeaways to just one a week. With just these initial steps, I'm feeling so much better than I did before.

To anybody wanting to make lifestyle changes, my advice would be to make sure you set realistic goals that you can build around your existing routine. Start with an initial set of small changes and when they become second nature, slowly build upon them. This is a much better approach than making sweeping changes on day 1, as these kinds of promises to yourself are always very hard to stick to. Lastly, don't give up! People can do anything, if they only set their minds to it.

With best wishes

Samina Kendrick

Go back to page 180.

UNIT 6

Pronunciation Assimilation

Student B

1 **Read the sentences as quickly as possible. Use assimilation as much as possible. Student A has 20 seconds to write what they hear.**

We could prepare that cake for our garden party on Monday.

That money might be a good present for my second cousin.

You should put that pot plant by the front gate then people will see it.

2 **Check each other's sentences and give one point for each underlined word which is spelt correctly.**

Go back to page 83.

UNIT 1

Vocabulary Adjectives and nouns with *self*

SPEAK Work in pairs. Say to what extent you agree or disagree with each statement. Justify your answers.

- My parents' generation was more **selfless** and **self-sacrificing** than my own.
- Some societies prize **self-reliance** too highly. It's perfectly fine to turn to others for help, support and guidance.
- Too many people in this world equate **self-worth** with the accumulation of wealth.
- The problem with influencers on social media is that they pedal the notion that being **self-indulgent** and materialistic can somehow buy you happiness.

Go back to page 5.

UNIT 11

Writing Part 2 Report

SPEAK Read the model answer and discuss the questions.

Report on Transport in Anderford

Introduction

Last week there was a meeting in the town hall where citizens were called on to share their concerns with regard to transport issues in Anderford. Over 50 people came to the meeting and a general consensus was reached on what the overriding issues are.

The key issue: reliability

Over 90% of those in attendance called for an improvement in the reliability of public transport. For many, buses are the only practical way of getting around town, due to limited parking and high car park charges in the centre. Although a schedule is provided at stops, it was felt that buses do not run to this, and, on some occasions, do not appear at all, despite several people reporting having waited for over an hour. The knock-on effect of this has been felt, with some passengers subsequently being late for medical appointments, their jobs, trains, etc...

Pinpointing the problem

While this problem may be solved by providing a more frequent service, it was acknowledged that such an addition may incur extra charges. A far more viable and more cost-effective option was considered to be investigating the root causes of the issue and finding effective solutions, such as altering routes to avoid traffic heavy zones. Another initiative that may ease the inconvenience to travellers is to post regular live updates online, so that passengers can stay abreast of any incidents or delays.

Summary

It is my belief that, with such heavy reliance on one form of transport, the council must offer citizens an immediate solution to this unreliability. I strongly recommend developing an app with live status reports to better assist travellers with planning their journeys. Further investigation into factors impacting the schedule should be carried out, and diversions or additional routes put in place as necessary. Only once this has been undertaken will trust be restored in the system.

1. How have they organised their report? Are there clear, appropriate headings for each part?
2. Have they answered the question and included all the relevant information?
3. Is the tone of the report correct? Underline any examples of advanced language structures and vocabulary.

Go back to page 169.

UNIT 4

Word formation Nouns

1 **In 1–10 below, the suffix at the beginning of the line can be used to form nouns with all of the words in the line, except one. Underline the odd one out and write down the noun forms of all the words in your notebooks. You may need to make further changes to the word given.**

0	**-ty**	tranquil	humble	scarce	sustain	<u>adhere</u>
		tranquillity	*humility*	*scarcity*	*sustainability*	*adherence*
1	**-al**	memory	intellect	announce	portray	deny
2	**-sion**	justify	persuade	intrude	collide	include
3	**-ive**	initiate	tolerate	sedate	narrate	explode
4	**-ance**	resemble	resist	comply	emerge	ignore
5	**-tion**	recognise	aspire	assume	resolve	fuse
6	**-ence**	indifferent	depend	correspond	reside	dominate
7	**-ment**	resent	bright	engage	amend	attach
8	**-ness**	clumsy	good	gratifying	wild	righteous
9	**-ist**	resilient	extreme	physics	final	piano
10	**-ing**	crave	say	publish	serene	gather

2 **Complete the crossword with the missing nouns in sentences 1–8. Use the words given in capitals at the end of the line to form the missing nouns.**

1 Once I realised my mistake, I had no choice but to **beg** for ____________, hoping my boss would give me a second chance. FORGIVE

2 It's an NGO dedicated to **reversing** the ____________ of mangrove forest ecosystems worldwide. DEGRADE

3 A former sports correspondent, she later **rose** to national ____________ for her insightful, provocative commentary on the evening news. PROMINENT

4 When a ____________ is **made** on one side of the negotiation, the other party is expected to make one in return. CONCEDE

5 To recover years of unpaid taxes, the local government has **begun** legal ____________ to repossess the property. PROCEED

6 The neighbourhood has **enjoyed** a notable ____________ and is now home to a broad mix of artists, designers and tech professionals. REVIVE

7 After a lacklustre debate performance, she **announced** her ____________ from the presidential race. WITHDRAW

8 Our company recently **formed** a strategic ____________ with an Irish firm, allowing us to jointly identify and evaluate potential business opportunities. ALLY

Go back to page 54.

UNIT 7

Word formation Adjectives

1 Your goal is to reach the other side of the board, moving one space at a time and correctly completing the sentence by putting the word given in capitals into its correct form to fit the gap. Try to stop your partner reaching the other side of the board before you by winning the spaces in their path.

2 Use a coin or counter and place it on your start position.

3 **Student A:** Choose the space you want to move to and write down the missing word on a piece of paper. You must spell the word correctly to win the space. You can only move to adjacent spaces.

Student B: Check the answer and decide if it is the correct form and spelling of the missing word. If both are correct, **Student A** can move into that space.

4 **Student B:** Do the same. Then, take turns until you reach the other side.

The __________ theme of the novel is to do with identity. ARCH

Given the amount of forensic evidence, the guilty verdict was a __________ conclusion. GO

Despite an __________ search of the area, the police were unable to find any clues. EXHAUST

As these two terms are __________, you can switch them without any difference in meaning. CHANGE

It was an __________ and finite decision with grave consequences for future law enforcement. REVOKE

STUDENT A START

The ring might not have been of any __________ value, but in terms of sentimentality, it was priceless. MONEY

It was the country's __________ population that most worried the government. DWINDLE

Following these steps, if the programme remains __________, try restarting your computer. RESPONSE

I turned the job down: the hours were very long and the salary was __________. PITY

It had been a __________ mistake and she bitterly regretted saying it. THOUGHT

For some __________ reason, they decided to relocate the head office to the suburbs. FATHOM

The event was an __________ success and raised five times more money for the charity than expected. PRECENDENCE

Finding him to be of __________ moral standing, she decided not to take up his offer of a second date. QUESTION

To do the job well, you have to be very __________ RESOURCE

The route through the mountains was __________. PERIL

STUDENT B START

It's a __________ possibility that she could win the election, but highly unlikely at this point. THEORY

We need find the __________ causes of your pain and then we can discuss treatment. LIE

The impact of the tornado is __________ as it is not just the cost to businesses that we must consider. MEASURE

The bird wings were __________ and leaving it unable to fly. DEVELOP

Despite initial assessments, the manuscript was in fact found to be a forgery and completely __________. WORTH

With 1000 votes to 14, we can confirm Martha as the __________ winner of this year's competition. DOUBT

It was Byron we suspected of spreading the __________ gossip. MALICE

Thank you so much. Your help on this matter has been __________. DISPENSE

This is the third __________ government who has failed to make any significant changes to the situation. SUCCESS

Without so much as a __________ glance, she marched out the room. BACK

Go back to page 105.

UNIT 11

Pronunciation Stress timing

1 SPEAK **With your partner, do the city quiz. Match one of the cities (a–f) to each of the facts (1–5).**

CITY QUIZ

1 The world's first skyscraper was built in the city of ___________.
2 The world's oldest restaurant is located in ___________.
3 Pavements in ___________ are heated by a snowmelt system underground.
4 The cities of ___________ and ___________ are built on largely reclaimed land.
5 In ___________, there are more journeys made on bike than by car.

a Calcutta
b Chicago
c Helsinki
d Madrid
e Miami
f Songdo

2 SPEAK **Underline the stressed words in the quiz in Exercise 3. Take it in turns to practise saying the stressed key words and speeding up the unimportant words.**

Go back to page 168.

READY FOR READING AND USE OF ENGLISH PARTS 5–7

Reading and Use of English Part 5 Multiple choice

Complete the sentences with a noun from the box. Use the collocates in bold to help you.

allowances comparison fault importance lie light shift tribute

1 For some, a product's sustainability has become just as important as its quality or price, and this **reflects** a paradigm ___________ **in** consumer behaviour.
2 During his speech in Ankara, he **paid** ___________ **to** the memory of modern Turkey's founding father, Mustafa Kemal Atatürk.
3 Investors had been in the dark about whether the company would enter the VR headset market, but yesterday's presentation **shed** some ___________ **on** its plans.
4 The reviewer **made** no ___________ **for** the artist's youth and judged his work rather harshly.
5 Kowalski's column **finds** ___________ **with** the way New Zealand regulates GM foods, saying its policies limit innovation needed to fight climate change.
6 Throughout her directorial career, Berta has attached **great** ___________ **to** sets and lighting, which for her are inseparable from the story.
7 In her latest book, he **draws** a ___________ **between** disorders which are innate and those which are due to environmental factors.
8 These repeated breakdowns **give** the ___________ **to** widespread assurances that were given about the reliability of the new hydropower plant.

Go back to page 62.

READY FOR GRAMMAR

1 The present

A The present continuous vs the present simple

The present continuous is used:

- to emphasise that a situation is temporary or takes place for a period of time around the present.

  *Our dogs **are staying** with our neighbour while our house is being refurbished.*
- to emphasise change, development or progress.

  *As information is more readily available and accessible, we **remember** / **are remembering** less about the past.*
- to make requests or demands sound less direct and more polite.

  *I need to crowdsource a new project and **I hope** / **I'm hoping** you can lend a hand.*
- with indefinite adverbs of frequency, such as *always*, *constantly* to show that something happens so often that it is characteristic of that person, group or thing.

  *My cousin is so helpful. **She always offers** / **she's always offering** to check my homework.*
- to show the speaker is less confident about something.

  *Our horse always runs well on this track, so we **expect** / **are expecting** him to qualify for the final.*
- to add a tone of disapproval or annoyance, or to emphasise the surprising/undesirable nature of events.

  *My four-year-old son **always knocks** / **is always knocking** over cups during breakfast. (= it's annoying)*

  *We **are constantly finding** the kids' toys hidden in odd places around the house. (= it's surprising)*

B Narratives

The present tenses can be used for certain types of narratives. Generally, the present simple is used for quicker actions and events, while the present continuous describes longer actions and situations.

1 In live commentary (e.g. sporting events or ceremonies). Here, the present continuous captures actions that are unfolding at the time of speaking.

  *There**'s** 35 seconds to go, this **is** the one. It**'s coming** back for Johnny Wilkinson. He **drops** for World Cup glory. It**'s** up, it**'s** over, he's done it.*

2 When giving directions, instructions or demonstrations.

  *Okay, let's go over it again. You **wait** behind the hedge until Dad arrives. Then you **signal** to Francesca, who**'s crouching** behind the car.*

3 In storytelling – whether in jokes, anecdotes or works of literature. The present tenses are used to make a story sound more vivid, as if it were happening now.

  *Two goldfish **are** in a tank. One **looks** at the other and says, 'You **know** how to drive this thing?'*

  *So, one day **I'm heading** home from work and the traffic **slows** to a crawl. I**'m waiting** for it to get going when THUD! A deer **jumps** onto the bonnet.*

4 In summaries of films, books or TV series to give a sense of immediacy.

  *It**'s** easy to find gaps in existing laws, the author **argues**, as they **fail** to keep pace with technological change.*

C Other uses of the present tenses

1 In headlines, the use of the present tenses helps ensure the headlines are short, punchy and dramatic.

  *Man **bites** dog (= a man bit a dog)*

2 In rhetorical questions, both the present simple and continuous can be used. In speech, these are often used to call attention to negative situations:

  *What**'s** the world **coming** to? (I'm disillusioned.)*

  ***Do** you **know** what time it is? (You're late.)*

3 *have to have* + past participle is used to express a present obligation about experiencing a past action.

  *It's indescribable – **you have to have seen** it for yourself. (= the only way for you to understand is if you see it for yourself)*

D Stative verbs

Stative verbs are rarely used in continuous forms. These verbs include those which describe:

1 the experience of our senses: e.g. *feel*, *hear*, *notice*
2 appearance: e.g. *appear*, *be*, *look*, *resemble*, *seem*
3 possession: e.g. *belong to*, *have*, *own*, *possess*
4 mental states or processes: e.g. *agree*, *astonish*, *deny*, *doubt*, *gather* (= understand), *guess*, *imagine*, *impress*
5 attitudes and emotional states: e.g. *appreciate*, *desire*, *despise*, *envy*. **NB** two exceptions are *long for* and *enjoy*
6 other: e.g. *concern*, *consist*, *contain*, *depend*, *hold* (= contain), *owe*, *reach*, *require*, *signify*, *weigh*

*Novakivsky's style during his Cracow period **resembles** that of his contemporary Stanislawski.*

Some verbs can have different meanings in their stative and dynamic forms, e.g. *appear*, *attract*, *conclude*, *consider*, *depend*, *expect*, *feel*, *fit*, *have*, *imagine*, *look*, *measure*, *see*, *smell*, *taste*, *think*, *weigh*

*It's a chewy, perfect cookie that is loaded with chocolate and **tastes** faintly of toffee.*

*The cook **is tasting** the sauce to see if it has enough salt.*

NB the verb *be* can be used in a dynamic way to talk about behaviour and actions, but not feelings.

*He **is being** extremely nice. ~~He **is being** pleased.~~*

E Performative verbs

We use performative verbs to perform an action by saying them, e.g. *acknowledge*, *assure*, *authorise*, *congratulate*, *contend*, *declare*, *demand*, *deny*, *forgive*, *guarantee*, *order*, *pledge*, *predict*, *promise*, *quit*, *refuse*, *resign*, *second*, *swear*, *vow*, *warn*.

***I second** the idea of taking a novel approach to this article.*

***We acknowledge** the complex reality of the situation.*

Modals can be used with performative verbs to make a statement sound either more tentative or more polite.

***I must apologise** for being somewhat tardy in my reply.*

Introductory phrases with performative verbs can be used with a present perfect or past simple meaning, e.g. *I gather*, *I see*, *I understand*.

***I hear** you're getting married. (I've heard...)*

1 The present

1 Complete Text A with the correct present form of the verbs in the box. Then do the same for Text B.

A

allow finish measure need promise seem think

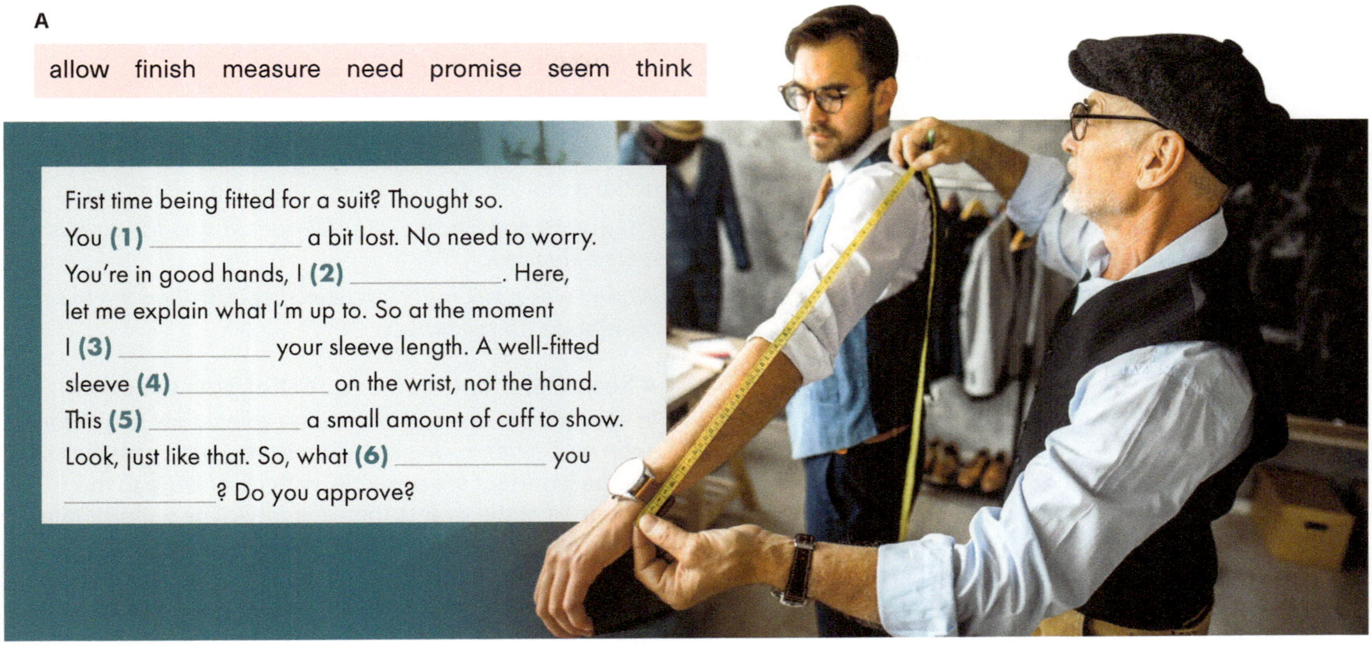

First time being fitted for a suit? Thought so.
You **(1)** ____________ a bit lost. No need to worry.
You're in good hands, I **(2)** ____________. Here,
let me explain what I'm up to. So at the moment
I **(3)** ____________ your sleeve length. A well-fitted
sleeve **(4)** ____________ on the wrist, not the hand.
This **(5)** ____________ a small amount of cuff to show.
Look, just like that. So, what **(6)** ____________ you
____________? Do you approve?

B

belong decide enjoy hear recognise taste weigh

Not your typical wedding reception, is it?
I **(1)** ____________ the DIY vibe that they've gone for.
I **(2)** ____________ some of these chairs from Samantha's
flat! And I **(3)** ____________ some of the serving dishes
(4) ____________ to her grandmother. Good DJ, too.
And the food! What a spread. I **(5)** ____________ what
to have for dessert right now, but I can't make up my
mind. I **(6)** ____________ my options. I recall somebody
saying how good the cupcakes **(7)** ____________,
so I'll probably start with one of those.

2 Tick the correct sentences. Correct the sentences with mistakes.

1 ☐ The photo is magnificent – it is always astonishing me how the right light can breathe such life to the bland contours of the city.

2 ☐ In a recent development, the demand for at-home care is increasing significantly as populations age.

3 ☐ It started as just a family business, but they look for additional partners to help scale up the operation.

4 ☐ Rather than lapses in concentration, mistakes are typically involving failure to correctly interpret available information.

5 ☐ This time I have no corporate backers footing the bill, so I'm depending on you to finance this venture.

6 ☐ This place is owing much of its beauty to the fact that it has remained largely agricultural, untouched by urban sprawl.

7 ☐ What are we to do about these students who are constantly dawdling in the corridors and arriving late?

Go back to page 8.

2 Past forms

1 Unfulfilled past actions

The following structures can be used with both the past simple and the past perfect for intended actions that did not take place:

- *be supposed to* is used to describe an action that had been intended but did not happen.

  The speaker ***was supposed to*** *give practical advice for young musicians, but she focused on something entirely different.*

- *be going to* and *be about to* are used for actions that were interrupted or were no longer necessary.

  He ***was going to / was about to*** *open the front door when the phone rang.*

  I had been ***going to / was about to*** *send her a message to check where she was, but then she arrived.*

- *be due to* or *be to* are used in formal English to describe scheduled or timetabled events that are no longer necessary.

  Before the hurricane hit, the President ***had been due to*** *meet her German counterpart.*

  The conference ***was to be held*** *in Tokyo but then it was called off.*

- the past perfect equivalent of *be to* uses the perfect infinitive of the main verb.

  The delegates ***were to have signed*** *the agreement before the end of the summit but one country would not agree.*

2 Forward-looking verbs in past tenses for unfulfilled past plans and polite or tentative suggestions

Verbs such as *aim, hope, expect, intend, mean, plan, think,* etc. can be used:

- to describe plans and actions that did not actually take place.

  What kind of feedback ***had your employees been expecting*** *to receive?*

  He ***had meant to leave*** *before it got dark.*

- To make a polite suggestion for a present or future situation, use a past tense.

  We ***thought*** *we could stop by later, if you're around.*

  We ***were hoping to meet up*** *this summer, if you're interested.*

- Verbs, such as *hope to, plan to* and *think of* can be used with the past continuous to talk about future possibilities. The use of the past tense instead of the present shows that the plan or prediction are more tentative.

  I was thinking of taking a sabbatical and travelling around Greece.

  I was planning to go to the shopping centre this weekend to get a outfit for the wedding.

3 Unexpected or annoying past actions

The past continuous, when it is used with adverbs or phrases like *constantly, always, continually, all the time, every day,* etc., can be used to describe repeated past actions that you did not expect or you found annoying.

They ***were continually cancelling*** *trains as the strikes were extended.*

When I was a kid, my mum ***was always telling*** *me to take my elbows off the table.*

4 Sequential and non-sequential past actions

In subordinate clauses with time expressions (e.g. *after, as soon as, before, by the time, once,* etc., both past simple and past perfect are possible, with no change to the sequence of the events they describe. The subordinate clause can come before or after the main clause, with no change to the sequence of events.

They ***started*** *playing as soon as it* ***stopped*** *raining.*

As soon as it ***(had) stopped*** *raining, they* ***started*** *playing.*

In such cases, the past perfect adds an element of 'because' (i.e. they started playing **after and because** it had stopped raining / They couldn't play earlier **because** it was still raining).

5 Past habitual actions or states

Both *would* + infinitive and *used to* + infinitive can be used to describe past habitual actions.

My aunt ***used to send*** *me to the shops to run errands for her. She* ***would*** *always* ***let*** *me keep any leftover change.*

However, to describe past states only *used to* + infinitive or the past simple are possible.

He ***used to have*** *a toy kitchen when he was a child.*

He ***had*** *a toy kitchen when he was a child.*

~~*He would have a toy kitchen when he was a child.*~~

It is possible to use the negative form *used not to* + infinitive, instead of *didn't use to* + infinitive. **NB** this is very formal and considered old-fashioned.

In days gone by, the idea that it is worse to do wrong than to suffer ***used not to be met*** *with blank incomprehension and incredulity.*

In a narrative, we can add background with *as* + subject + *used to* + infinitive, often to focus on something unusual.

He was promoted to Sub-Assistant Commissary-General, a post for which, ***as he used to say,*** *he was eminently unqualified.*

2 Past forms

1 Correct the sentences. You may need to write more than one word.

used to love / loved

0 She ~~would love~~ going there on holiday but now she hates it.
1 The gallery had opened the inaugural exhibition just as we arrived.
2 I thought you were to ring us before you left.
3 He would have an old friend he visited each and every time he was in Belgium.
4 When she was supposed to eat her way through all the local dishes, she went back to her old favourites.
5 As soon as he had been locating his seat on the plane, he started missing his family.
6 We used to leave for Italy that evening to attend a climate change summit, but it was abruptly cancelled.
7 According to the plan, they were meaning to check out of the hotel before breakfast, but they overslept.
8 Sorry to hear that you were to have to leave the arts and crafts festival early and come home. How long were you thinking of staying?
9 The boat had turned into the canal just as the sun came out, lighting up the Bridge of Sighs.

2 Complete the text with an appropriate form of the verb in brackets.

The first time I ever went to Spain was on a family holiday to Malaga when I was fifteen. I **(1)** ____________ (*never / see*) anywhere like it: the food, the weather, the people! When we got home, I **(2)** ____________ (*declare*) my intention of taking Spanish lessons and told my mum that I **(3)** ____________ (*contemplate*) the possibility of living in Spain permanently one day. My mum just laughed dismissively. She **(4)** ____________ (*always / do*) that and it **(5)** ____________ (*drive*) me to distraction. But her reaction only **(6)** ____________ (*strengthen*) my conviction. Before long, my Spanish was becoming quite fluent and I even had Spanish friends online, who I **(7)** ____________ (*chat*) with most days after school. When I turned sixteen, I **(8)** ____________ (*start*) working at a local supermarket and after two years, I **(9)** ____________ (*set*) aside more than enough money to get me to Spain. That was it! I was convinced that my Spanish dream **(10)** ____________ (*about / come*) to fruition. That's when I **(11)** ____________ (*meet*) my girlfriend (who would go on to become my future wife) and all my plans changed. It turned out that Mum **(12)** ____________ (*be*) right all along.

Go back to page 20.

2 Adverbs and adverbial phrases

A Position of adverbs

Adverbs are normally found in one of three positions within a clause: front, end or mid-position.

__Fortunately__, they had remembered their umbrellas.

The kids are playing __upstairs__.

I __wholeheartedly__ agree.

Adverbs in the mid-position go before main verbs, between auxiliaries and main verbs, and after the verb *be*.

The company has __completely__ remodelled the existing facilities.

Sport for sport's sake though is __undeniably__ fun.

Remember that adverbs do not usually come between a verb and its object.

It __completely__ slipped my mind.

~~*It slipped __completely__ my mind.*~~

The position of an adverb can depend on the type of adverb used, as well as what the speaker or writer wants to emphasise. While some adverbs can go in more than one position, the rules below can be used as a general guide.

1 Frequency

Adverbs of frequency usually go in the mid-position, but some (*frequently*, *normally*, *occasionally*, *often*, *sometimes, usually*) can be put in the end or front positions to add emphasis to the adverb:

He __occasionally__ attends classes.

He attends classes __occasionally__.

__Occasionally__, he attends class.

Longer adverbial phrases of frequency usually go in the end position. We can also put them in the front position if the adverb is not the focus of the sentence. **NB** These hardly ever go in the mid-position.

He goes to the cinema __every now and then__.

__Every now and then__ he goes to the cinema. (less emphasis on frequency)

2 Manner

Adverbs of manner usually go in the end position, but they may also go in the mid-position to put more emphasis on the adverb.

They accepted the offer __immediately__ and moved out.

They __immediately__ accepted the offer and moved out.

3 Time and place

Time and place adverbs (or adverbial phrases) usually go in the end position.

He learned to find solace __in the great outdoors__.

The ceiling paintings are best seen __in the afternoon__.

But, to add a literary tone, particularly in writing, they can go in the front position.

__Downstairs__, a vaulted cellar awaits visitors.

When combined, the order of adverbs is usually: manner / place / time.

We __chatted__ animatedly in the kitchen __after dinner__.

4 Degree

We normally put adverbs of degree right before the word they modify, whether they be verbs, adjectives or other adverbs. This type of adverb can change the meaning of sentence depending on its position:

You __really__ must look at Paula's beautiful drawing. (= modifying must)

You must __really__ look at Paula's beautiful drawing. (=modifying look at)

You must look at Paula's __really__ beautiful drawing. (= modifying beautiful)

5 Focusing: *even, only* and *just*

We can use *even* to suggest that something is unexpected or surprising and *only* to express some kind of restriction. Both these adverbs go in the front position when modifying the subject and in the mid-position when modifying the verb.

We were seated promptly and __even__ got a window seat.

__Only__ business domain email addresses are accepted.

Just can mean 'only' or 'exactly'. It goes directly before the word it modifies.

Although this was __just__ a joke, many people took it to heart.

This crowd-pleasing curry recipe is spiced __just__ right.

6 Comment and viewpoint adverbs

Adverbs like *clearly*, *obviously* and *theoretically* allow us to express a view about an action or comment on it. These adverbs can modify entire clauses when they go in the front or end position. In the mid-position, we use them to comment on, or even to distance ourselves from, what we are saying.

__Honestly__, the flat is not really our style.

The concert is completely sold out, __unfortunately__.

Franc's decision to move on was __apparently__ for personal rather than professional reasons.

B Adverbs with different forms

Some adverbs have the same base form but different meanings: *high / highly*, *deep / deeply*, *wide / widely*, *late / lately*, *hard / hardly*, *fine / finely*, *short / shortly*.

The race started 45 minutes __late__ due to heavy rain. (= after the expected, arranged or usual time)

The best book I've read __lately__ is, without a doubt, The Rings of Saturn *by W.G. Sebald. (= recently)*

C Adverbs to modify adjectives

Adverbs are often used to modify adjectives. Many of these combinations are strong collocations.

utterly useless

highly successful

painfully shy

strikingly different

2 Adverbs and adverbial phrases

1 Complete the sentences with a word or phrase from the box.

afterwards	around the bend	even	every now and then	just	only	sparsely	strategically	uphill	wholly

1 My wife and I aren't super outdoorsy, but we do like to go trekking ______________.
2 'Don't worry,' she said. '______________ if it does rain, I'm sure we'll have a great time.'
3 Thinking ______________, we packed our bags to bring the absolute minimum.
4 The area around the national park is ______________ populated. The nearest shop is miles away.
5 According to the map, a freshwater spring should be coming up just ______________.
6 The dried fruit we packed was so tasty that I ate too much and felt sick soon ______________.
7 After walking steadily ______________ for five kilometres through the mountain pass, we both needed a break.
8 ______________ immersed in the breath-taking landscape, I hardly noticed the passage of time.
9 We only ______________ made it back to the car before it started to pour.
10 I told her she could come into the house ______________ if she took off her muddy boots.

2 For sentences 1–7 choose the correct alternative.

1 The project got off to a flying start but ultimately it fell *short* / *shortly* of expectations.
2 That theory has been *wide* / *widely* discredited.
3 *Fine* / *Finely* chop the garlic and add it to the pan.
4 They dived off the boat and swam *deep* / *deeply* under the sea.
5 She hit the ball *hard* / *hardly* with her racket, sending it hurtling across the net.
6 Many people in the audience are said to have found the comedian's joke *high* / *highly* offensive.
7 There's been a surge of interest in the director's films *late* / *lately*.

3 One of the sentences in each pair below contains a mistake. For sentences 1–4, choose the better option, a or b.

1 a When the airline cancelled his flight, he immediately posted about it on social media.
  b When the airline cancelled his flight, he posted about immediately it on social media.
2 a The man next to me fidgeted for the entire duration of the flight.
  b The man next to me for the entire duration of the flight fidgeted.
3 a I didn't say we had to take the guided tour; merely I suggested it.
  b I didn't say that we had to take the guided tour; I merely suggested it.
4 a You should only take photos if you ensure the flash is turned off.
  b You only should take photos if you ensure the flash is turned off.

4 Match each of the adverbs in the box with the group of adjectives (1–4) which collocate with it.

bitterly	deeply	staggeringly	utterly

1 ______________ offended, ashamed, hurt

2 ______________ disgusting, disastrous, ridiculous

3 ______________ disappointed, cold, upset

4 ______________ beautiful, expensive, high

Go back to page 22.

3 Talking about the future

A Future forms

1 *Will*, the present continuous and *going to* are used to talk about future plans and intentions. Depending on the context, there might be slight differences in meaning or emphasis.

__Will you stay__ in Bairro Alto while you're in Lisbon?

(to ask if clear plans have been made)

__Are you staying__ in Bairro Alto while you're in Lisbon? (emphasis on fixed arrangements)

__Are you going to stay__ in Bairro Alto while you're in Lisbon? (emphasis on intentions)

2 The future continuous is used:

- to emphasise that a plan or activity is one of a repeated series of events or part of the normal course of events.

  __Will you be staying__ in Bairro Alto while you're in Lisbon? (as usual)

- to talk about something in the future we perceive as inevitable, or to convey that it is going to happen 'anyway.'

  We can ask the specialist to check the routers tomorrow because __she'll be fixing__ the server anyway.

- to make polite enquiries about future plans, emphasising that we don't wish to be nosy or influence the decisions of the listener. In contrast, *going to* sounds more direct.

  __Will you be going__ out this evening? (very polite – suggesting, I just want to know your plans.')

  __Are you going to go__ out this evening? (pressing for a decision)

3 The future perfect simple and continuous can be used:

- to imagine looking back at something from a point in the future. The future perfect simple shows that the action will be completed by a point in the future.

  __I'll have spent__ all the budget by the end of the week.

- the future perfect continuous emphasises that it will be in progress up to a point in the future.

  This summer __I'll have been mentoring__ young inventors for twenty-five years.

- to make assumptions in the present.

  The accident happened so long ago, most people __will have forgotten__ about it.

4 In future time clauses and conditional clauses, after conjunctions like *as soon as*, *if*, *in case*, *when*, *unless*, *until*, present tenses (including present perfect simple and continuous) are used, rather than *will* or *going to*.

The kids will regret leaving their umbrellas behind when it __pours / has poured / is pouring__ with rain!

B Other ways of talking about the future

1 Some verbs have future meanings in their present forms, e.g. *agree*, *aim*, *expect*, *hope*, *intend*, *look*, *plan*, *promise*, *resolve*. The present simple refers to a fact; the present continuous, to a process.

We'll need lots of hands to finish the prototype, but we __aim / are aiming__ to get it done this year.

2 Various expressions can be used to refer to the future:

- *be* + *about to* – to say something is close to happening

  The minister __is about to give__ a press conference.

- *be* + *on the point / verge / brink of* – an idiomatic way to say something is very close to happening

  Using wearable devices to pay in shops is __on the brink of__ mass adoption.

- *be* + *likely / unlikely to* – to talk about probability

  The company's next generation smartphones __are likely to be released__ this autumn.

- *be* + *due to* – to talk about something scheduled

  The next round of talks __is due to be held__ on Monday.

- *be* + *bound to* – to say emphatically that something is certain to happen

  This new user interface __is bound to receive__ mixed reviews from customers.

- *be* + *expected to* – to say something is based on an expectation

  The much talked-about gadget __is expected to be unveiled__ at this year's conference.

- *be* + *set to* – to make a strong assertion or to say someone is prepared for something to happen

  Poll numbers say she __is set to__ win re-election.

- *be* + *to* + infinitive – to talk about future arrangements in formal contexts

  The semi-final __is to be__ broadcast live on all major television networks.

- *be* + *to be* + past participle – passive form of *be* + *to* + infinitive

  The small data storage company announced it __is to be taken__ over by a large multinational.

C Future in the past

- Most of the structures in Sections A and B also have past forms (e.g. *was / were* + *going to / about to / due to / planning to,* etc. We can use these forms to talk about past plans, etc., especially those that didn't actually happen.

  I __was planning to__ go to Bella's get-together, but at the last minute I had a change of heart.

  I hadn't accepted the invitation because Rick and I __were set to fly off__ on our holiday that very weekend.

  NB *would* is rarely used as a future-in-the-past form. Its use is mainly restricted to reported speech and literary narratives.

  He decided to skip lunch. There __would__ be plenty of time to eat later.

3 Talking about the future

1 Decide which answer (A, B or C) best fits each gap.

1 **A:** I like my computer programming course, but right now I'm feeling a bit overwhelmed.
B: By the end of the course, I'm sure you ___________ all the ins and outs of it.
A are to understand **B** will have understood **C** will be understanding

2 **A:** I've spent all day trying to solve this engineering problem.
B: I'm sure if you keep racking your brain, you're ___________ find a solution eventually.
A bound to **B** due to **C** set to

3 **A:** I thought Conor had planned one of his pranks for the graduation ceremony.
B: He ___________ a Hawaiian shirt, but, in the end, he didn't go through with it.
A was wearing **B** was going to wear **C** would be wearing

4 **A:** I understand you've been with the company for a while.
B: This time next month, I ___________ here for three years.
A will be working **B** am going to be working **C** will have been working

5 **A:** Dad, we're going to be late to the birthday party!
B: Until we ___________ up the house, we're not going anywhere.
A tidy **B** will tidy **C** would tidy

2 Complete the second sentence so it has a similar meaning to the first sentence, using the word given. Use between three and eight words, including the word given.

1 He was close to resigning from his cabinet position to run for Prime Minister, but then he lost his nerve.
ABOUT
He ___________________________ from his cabinet position to run for Prime Minister, but then he lost his nerve.

2 Since we have so many chores to catch up on this Saturday, we can't make it to the game.
WILL
We can't make it to the game this Saturday because we ___________________________ on housework.

3 By graduation, Ji-ho and Shi-ah will have been dating for more than a year.
COUPLE
Ji-ho and Shi-ah ___________________________ for more than a year by the time they graduate.

4 The government was going to announce at any moment that it would remove trade restrictions.
VERGE
The government ___________________________ of trade restrictions.

5 Susan has no plans to stay in her current position for more than two years.
AIMING
Susan ___________________________ longer than two years in her current position.

6 The expiration date for your yearly subscription is the last day of this month.
DUE
Your yearly subscription ___________________________ the end of this month.

7 When this meeting has finally come to an end, is there a possibility of having a word with you?
SPEAK
When this meeting has finally come to an end, will it ___________________________ you in private?

8 I'm sure she will be unaware of what is happening around her most of the time.
IDEA
She is bound ___________________________ on around her most of the time.

Go back to page 36.

READY FOR GRAMMAR

3 will, shall and would

will

1 *Will / won't* is used to make predictions about the present or future, based on knowledge, experience or expectations.

*She's in Turkey. Hopefully she has warm clothes because at this time of year it **will be** a bit chilly.*

2 *Will have* + past participle is used to make predictions about the past.

*We can't go and see them now – they **will have gone** out.*

3 *Will* is often used to talk about willingness, unwillingness and refusal.

***Will** you get the door?*

4 *Will* can be used to make instructions or requests sound more polite and less direct.

***I'll have** to ask you to take a seat and wait to be seen.*

5 In spoken English, sentences with extra stress placed on *will* can be used to criticise the way people behave.

*Well, if you **will** keep saying that to his face ...*

Shall

1 *Shall* is used to make offers or suggestions.

***Shall** I fix you a sandwich?*

It is also used to express determination.

*I **shall** discuss the matter with him and see if we can get some kind of resolution.*

2 *Shall* can be used instead of *will* to talk about future intentions or make predictions, but this is less common.

*In the coming months, the firm **shall / will** continue to grow its online presence.*

3 In formal writing, such as in legal documents, *shall* is often used to refer to obligations or duties.

*The customer **shall** be responsible for the maintenance of the vehicle. (in a legal document)*

4 *Shall* is still used in a number of fixed expressions and idioms based on old speech patterns.

*Seek and ye **shall** find; never the twain **shall** meet; this too **shall** pass, etc.*

NB Shall is rarely used is American English.

Would

1 We can use *would not* (but not *would*) for a refusal on a single occasion in the past.

*The driver **wouldn't** let me on because it was packed.*

2 The informal expression *would you believe* (*it*) is used to show surprise and annoyance.

*And, **would you believe**, she didn't even say sorry!*

4 Modal verbs 1

1 Modals in rhetorical questions:

- *Can* is used to reflect on things in rhetorical questions.

  *How **can** the deal go ahead if both parties are still at loggerheads?*

- In formal discussions, the question form of *need* can be used rhetorically.

  ***Need** I say more?*

- Rhetorical questions with *ought* + subject + (*not*) *to* + verb are also possible.

  ***Ought** we **to** worry about microplastics in our seas?*

  ***Ought** we **not to** create a timetable for the meeting?*

2 Modals for criticism:

- *Can't* and *must* are used in questions for reproaches and criticisms.

  ***Must** you keep playing that terrible music?*

- *Could* and *might* are used to criticise. *Should* and *ought to* put an emphasis on an unfulfilled obligation.

  *You **could / might** have asked before borrowing my car.*

  *You **should / ought to** have told him Jakob was coming.*

3 Modals for judgement and advice:

- *Should* (but not *ought to*) can express personal judgements and reactions in a formal way, particularly for facts which have already been mentioned.

  *It's surprising she **should** say that to you.*

- *Shouldn't* and *oughtn't to* are used to give advice.

  *We **ought not / oughtn't** to buy this product as it is so harmful to the environment.*

4 Modals for obligation and lack of obligation:

- *Have to* + *-ed* is used to express obligation in the past.

  *In those days, you **had to have** graduated from a top university to get a job at the firm.*

- *Needn't have* + *-ed* is used to refer to past events the speaker considers unnecessary.

  *You **needn't** have waited for me.*

- *Shouldn't have* is used in spoken English to be polite and show appreciation when you receive a gift.

  *Oh sweetheart, you **shouldn't** have!*

5 Other uses of modals:

- *May* (but not *might*) is used to express wishes and hopes in a formal way.

  ***May** this year bring you all your heart desires.*

- *Might* is used in the phrase *try as* (she) *might* for emphasis.

  *Try as we **might**, we couldn't open the jar.*

- *Can / could* + *always* implies *if there is nothing better*.

  *What are we going to eat? Well, we **can / could** always just warm up that leftover soup.*

- *Should* and *ought to* are used to talk about logical probability.

  *I bought three loaves, which **should / ought to** be enough.*

3 *will*, *shall* and *would*

1 Match each sentence (1–5) with the appropriate response (A–H). There are three extra responses which you do not need to use.

1 It might be a bit early to ring up Tom and Derek.
2 What do you think your parents got up to this weekend?
3 I'm going down to the shops.
4 I thought you were going to quit.
5 Here's a list of what's on deck for the year ahead, but there are still some decisions to be made.

A And would you believe they want to charge me an extra £100.
B Will you pick me up some potting soil while you're out?
C They'll still be having breakfast at this time, so I'd wait a while.
D OK. Let's get down to business, shall we?
E How shall we respond to all this bad press, given the circumstances?
F Well, they will have cleaned the flat from top to bottom, for starters.
G Personally, I prefer people who will speak their minds, even if they're obnoxious about it sometimes.
H They wouldn't let me out of the contract until after I hard-coded the server URL.

2 Use *will*, *shall* or *would* plus the correct form of one of the verbs in the box to complete the gaps. Sometimes there is more than one possible answer.

be call calm do feel let make pass send

1 I'm so sorry to hear that the two of you have fallen out. You know what, though? Right now your friend **(1)** ____________ just as upset. Remember that you're a good and worthwhile person. This too **(2)** ____________, as they say, and tomorrow the world will be better. **(3)** ________ I ________ you a cup of tea? That **(4)** ________ your nerves.

2 **(5)** ________ you just ________ me explain, please? It says right here, 'Confirmation of shipment of the goods from the port **(6)** ____________ to the purchaser prior to payment.' It's right there in black and white, but I have yet to receive any confirmation. What **(7)** ________ I ________? Normally, I **(8)** ____________ them directly to complain, but, of course, it's a bank holiday today, so they **(9)** ____________ in the office.

Go back to page 43.

4 Modals

1 Complete the dialogues using a modal or semi-modal verb. You may need to use the negative. Sometimes more than one option is possible.

1 A As you can see, we've gone all out for your birthday lunch – three courses plus dessert.
B Oh, you ________ have gone to so much trouble!

2 A I can't find my glasses. What does this holiday card say?
B It says, '________ all your hopes and dreams come true in the New Year.'

3 A You've already tried on 10 pairs of glasses. Why ________ you be so picky?
B This is an important decision! I have to look at myself every day with these on.

4 A Do we need to buy any more potatoes for that dish we're making later?
B I don't think so. We've got two small bags at home. That ________ be more than enough.

5 A In light of the internal investigation, ________ we not to take more precautions to prevent such a colossal error from ever being made again?
B Yes, I second the need for more oversight in this sort of key financial decision.

2 Correct the mistake in each of the sentences and dialogues.

1 Customers don't read the fine print carefully enough. Must I mention the number of people who end up paying for a service that starts out as 'free'?
2 We racked our brains for days, but try as we may, we just couldn't find a solution to the problem.
3 You need to have said you weren't staying for lunch. We were waiting around for you!
4 You really don't ought to allow that student to speak to you in such an insolent, rude manner.
5 Back then, to be actively trading, you must purchase a membership to a stock exchange.
6 His apology was so evident in his gaze that he shouldn't have uttered a word to show her how he felt.

Go back to page 50.

4 Noun phrases and nominal clauses

A Types of nouns

1 Some nouns can have countable (C) and uncountable (U) forms which have similar meanings (e.g. *business*, *cinema*, *delight*, *injustice*). Others can have countable (C) and uncountable (U) forms with different meanings (*heat*, *jam*, *production*, *quality*, *strength*, *toast*, *trust*).

The children opted to put the family estate in a ***trust****. (C)*

Their business dealings remained informal, based on mutual ***trust*** *and respect. (U)*

NB some uncountable nouns in English refer to things that are countable in other languages, e.g. *advice*, *knowledge*, *luggage*, *machinery*, *news*, *research*.

2 Some nouns look plural but they are in fact uncountable, e.g. *aerobics*, *athletics*, *billiards*, *economics*, *measles*, *physics*.

Billiards is *renowned for its sportsmanship.*

3 Some nouns have the same form in both singular and plural, e.g. *aircraft*, *crossroads*, *corps*, *insignia*, *offspring*, *salmon*, *shellfish*, *species*, *trout*, *(TV) series*.

Some female bees remain with the nest after their ***offspring have*** *hatched.*

One of Berlin's famous furry ***babies has*** *found a new home in Eberswalde Zoo.*

4 Some nouns have no singular form and are always used in the plural, e.g. *binoculars*, *belongings*, *headphones*, *earnings*, *outskirts*, *premises*, *pyjamas*, *savings*, *scissors*, *surroundings*, *tights*, *tweezers*.

He isn't carrying much luggage because most of his ***belongings have*** *been sent ahead by sea.*

5 Some collective nouns can be either plural or singular, depending on whether the speaker or writer considers them to be a group of individuals or a single unit, e.g. *audience*, *committee*, *company*, *crew*, *enemy*, *government*, *public*, *team*.

The ***government is / are*** *hoping to implement a fiscal stimulus package.*

6 The possessive *'s* can be used to ellipt a noun.

He asked whose pen it was and I said it was ***Sara's****.*

B Subject–verb agreement

1 When determining the subject of a sentence, disregard information contained in relative clauses, brackets, or after phrases such as *together with*, *as well as*, *in addition to* and *along with*.

The first author as well as the last three authors ***has*** *signed off on the final proofs of the journal article.*

2 Two subjects connected by *and* generally take a plural verb – unless the writer is thinking of them as just one idea instead of two.

Getting my paper accepted in Nature and seeing it in black and white ***was/were*** *the* ***highlight/s*** *of my career.*

3 When two or more subjects are joined by *or* / *nor*, the verb agrees with the closest subject.

Either the students or the ***teacher has*** *to give in.*

Either the teacher or the ***students have*** *to give in.*

4 Subjects introduced by singular quantifiers, e.g. (*more than*) *one of*, *the number of*, *neither/either* take a singular verb form, even if the subject has a plural meaning.

There are two posts available, but neither (of them) ***interests*** *me.*

5 Fractions or percentages can take a singular or plural verb depending on the word that follows them.

Two-thirds of the students ***are*** *on a field trip.*

Two-thirds of the class ***was*** *wasted due to a fire alarm.*

6 Indefinite pronouns (*somebody*, *anybody*, *no one*, etc.) always take a singular verb,

Everybody ***has*** *finished eating dessert.*

C Nominalisation

Nominalisation, the process of turning verbs or adjectives into nouns, is a common feature of formal writing. It can make the text sound more objective and academic.

Although the equipment was ***unstable****, the research staff was still able to* ***complete*** *the trials.*

The ***instability*** *of the equipment did not preclude the* ***completion*** *of the trials.*

- Some multi-word verbs can be nominalised.

  Budget talks ***broke down*** *over the issue of using discretionary funds to repair roads.*

  Disagreement about using discretionary funds to repair roads led to a ***breakdown*** *in talks.*

- Adverbs change to adjectives when the verbs they modify are nominalised.

  I do remember a prominent columnist ***bitterly*** *complaining about this issue.*

  I do remember reading ***bitter*** *complaints about this issue by a prominent columnist.*

NB If overused, nominalisation can create unclear writing. Generally speaking, it is easier to understand ideas expressed in verbs.

D Adding information to noun phrases

- *Namely* and *that is* are used to add information to noun phrases.

  The interview showed off the star's best qualities, ***namely*** *her quick wit and perfect comedic timing.*

  She will become our community manager; ***that is****, she'll manage the company's presence on social media.*

- Appositive noun phrases provide information that further identifies, clarifies or defines another noun. Note that appositives are set off with commas if they are 'restrictive', meaning the sentence would still make sense without them.

  The tall clown, ***the one with the shiny purple shoes****, is my big brother.*

4 Noun phrases and nominal clauses

1 Complete the sentences with a verb from the box in the correct tense.

call contain consist damage express list plan

1 In the last hour, each of the three brothers ____________ a desire to sleep on the top bunk at the lakeside cabin.
2 In the last two decades, more than one of the university's ancient artefacts ____________ by vandals.
3 Today, the insignia of the armed forces ____________ of a single star worn on a golden epaulet.
4 Neither the paper in question nor the previously published papers ____________ into question the premise of this report.
5 The completely refurbished premises ____________ a yoga studio and meditation room.
6 Maria, in addition to her friend Silvia, ____________ to volunteer abroad before starting university this winter.
7 I'm looking at the website now, and none of the open positions ____________ an MA as a requirement, in a break with tradition.

2 Rewrite the underlined part of the report using noun phrases and nominal clauses. You may have to make other changes to the sentences.

This study explores the effects of parent-child relationships on the academic performance of university students. Using Social Cognitive Theory, the study proposes a method to validate the chain-mediating role played by psychological capital, that is, the internal resources that help us successfully manage difficult situations. The results show that academic performance and parent-child relationships strongly and positively correlate. Furthermore, this study also proposes mental health guidelines, which if the university adopted them, could help students to better handle their relationships with their parents. This could in turn could help students better accumulate psychological capital. The study concludes by arguing why there is no way to justify how little mental health is being emphasised in higher education.

Go back to page 54.

READY FOR GRAMMAR

5 Cohesion

1 Possessive pronouns (e.g. *hers / his / ours / theirs / yours*) can be used to refer back or forwards to stated people, things, events or ideas. This can help avoid any unnecessary repetition. They can be used:

- in the subject and object position of a clause or sentence.

  *Considering all the entries in the competition, **hers** ~~her effort~~ was not the best of efforts.*

  ***Theirs** ~~Their house~~ was not the cleanest of houses, but Hannah and Chloe worked so much they barely had time to pick up a duster.*

  *Do you have any spare tennis balls, please? The people we were playing with left and took **theirs** ~~their balls~~.*

- after the verb *be*, when used as the main verb, to complete the clause or sentence.

  *Although they desperately wanted the class to continue, the decision wasn't **theirs** ~~their decision~~.*

  *Daniel's name is written on the inside cover of this book, because it used to be **his** ~~book~~.*

  *She was my best friend, and I was **hers** ~~her best friend~~.*

- after prepositions to complete the clause or sentence.

  *With a face like **his** ~~face~~, Graeme could have been a model.*

  *Make sure all passengers in the minibus are wearing their seatbelts. It's for your safety, as well as **theirs** ~~safety~~.*

2 *The one that / The ones* followed by a relative clause can be used to focus on one thing in a particular group.

*I've looked into all the cruise ships that go around Greece and **the one that** I think is best for us is the Royal Celebration ship.*

*Can you see those trainers that man's got on? Those are **the ones that** I want for my birthday!*

3 *Each (+ noun / pronoun)... the other(s)* can be used to refer to two related things to say there is a reciprocal relationship.

*The survival weekend was a great way of team building, with **each of us** helping **the others**.*

*Although they all taught different subjects, there was no doubt that **each of the teachers** respected **the others'** knowledge.*

4 We can use ellipsis (the omission of words) to avoid repetition. In informal (often spoken English) the subject can be omitted in the structure with modal perfects (e.g. *must / should / could have + ed).*

*I can't find my house keys. **Must've left** them in the car. (I must've left them in the car)*

*Listen to all those sirens coming. **Could've been** an accident. (There could have been an accident)*

5 Demonstratives

Demonstratives can not only indicate a physical distance or closeness, but also a psychological one. They can be used to emphasise a particular thing and to create emotional distance from something / someone. They can also be used to avoid repetition.

- *this / these (that / those)* + noun / noun phrase can introduce new information and replace words such as *a / an* and *some*. They are used to give a sense of immediacy in the sense that it brings the listener and reader into the narrative and makes them feel involved (usually in informal narratives).

  *In my class there's **this** girl who says she knows you and your parents!*

  *There's **this** machine at the gym that I never use because it's rather intimidating. Well, yesterday, I plucked up the courage to use it!*

  *My cousin gave me **these** beads that she said would bring me good luck.*

- *that / those* + **noun / noun phrase** is used to convey distance and/or disapproval

  *I don't appreciate **that** type of attitude in my class, thank you!*

  *Almost every week there is a different study on the effectiveness of diet on illness. I think **those** so-called experts need to think again.*

- *those* is used in more formal contexts to mean *the one(s)*. This is usually followed by a defining relative clause. In sentences where no other context is given, *those* is generally used to mean 'the people'.

  *New cars are subject to emissions regulations, but **those** that were manufactured before 2000 are exempt.*

  ***Those** who travel by train will see an increase in their fares from January.*

  *A free wireless speaker will be sent to **those** who register before the end of the month.*

- *this / that / these / those* + noun + *of* + possessive is used to highlight a particular thing in the sentence, often to draw attention to a positive or negative aspect.

  ***This car of mine** has never let me down yet!*

  *Colin is such a delightful man, but **those kids of his** are an absolute nightmare.*

  *Have you read any work by Penny Carter? **This new book of hers** is brilliant – I can't put it down!*

5 Cohesion

1 Correct the mistake in each of these sentences.

1. Like humans, the animals worked together, with each pack member looking out for others.
2. He wasn't the most professional looking presentation, but his ideas were second to none.
3. They're such an amazing team! A partnership like them is very hard to find.
4. Everybody has a weak spot, and this, unfortunately, theirs.
5. Do you enjoy travelling, find stressful or have no strong feelings about it?
6. Please use safety goggles when working with the chemicals, especially the one that give off noxious fumes.

2 Rewrite the sentences using the form of cohesion in the brackets.

1. She had great talent. She could have been a singer. (hers)
   With ______________________, she could have been a singer.
2. The ad for the intern position had over 400 responses. There were more but I didn't read them all. (ones)
   The ad for the intern position had over 400 responses, and they were just ______________________.
3. With a twelve-hour workday, and then a family to cook and clean for, he didn't have an easy life. (his)
   ______________________ easy life, with a twelve-hour workday and then a family to cook and clean for.
4. "It was such bad weather last night. I'm sure that's what caused the accident." (been)
   "I'm sure of what caused the accident. ______________________."
5. They were a great double act, and you could see that they played off each other. (each)
   They were a great double act, with ______________________.

Go back to page 70.

5 Demonstratives

1 Rewrite the underlined parts of the sentences using demonstratives.

1. We should really say something to the neighbours. <u>Their dog</u> spends most of the night barking!
2. There will be a free room upgrade but it's <u>only for people</u> who book through our website.
3. The price of everything is skyrocketing at the moment. They should really give discounts to <u>the people</u> who can't afford to pay.
4. In our house there's <u>a door. It's</u> always been locked up. We've never known what's behind it.
5. Scholarships will only be offered to <u>the people</u> who got over 80 marks in their entrance exams.
6. I don't know how Chloe copes. <u>Her child</u> is always in trouble!

2 Complete the text with the correct demonstrative.

There's **(1)** ____________ new restaurant in town that I'm dying to go to if you fancy coming. **(2)** ____________ friend of mine, who's a total foodie, says it's already making a name for itself, and, despite the incredible menu, it's not one of **(3)** ____________ places that charge an arm and a leg either. We could go for the set lunch menu, which is only £12, or there's 10% off the a la carte menu for **(4)** ____________ who go on a Monday if you can make it then!

Go back to page 76.

6 Conditional clauses

A The following structures can be used in place of *if* in conditional clauses.

1 To express necessary conditions with past, present or future reference, we can use *so long as, provided that, on provision that, on (the) condition that* + clause.

We agree to the contract terms ***on condition that*** *we extend the project by one month should any unforeseen circumstances arise.*

2 To express that a situation is really possible, we use *in case of* + noun or noun phrase.

In case of a malfunction, please do not attempt to fix the photocopier; contact the engineer.

3 To express possible conditions with present or future reference, we can use *in the event that* + clause and *in the event of* + noun.

In the event that *the central electrical system fails, power will be restored through the use of generators.*

In the event of a failure *to the central electrical system, power will be restored through the use of generators.*

4 To express imaginary conditions with past, present or future reference we can use *suppose, supposing, provided (that), imagine, what if, in case + clause.*

What if *we provided additional resourcing, would that help meet the deadline?*

Here is a copy of the report ***in case*** *I forget to give you one later.*

5 To express unexpected or unlikely conditions, we can use *even if* + clause. The phrase *it's doubtful whether / that* can be used instead of a negative verb form for emphasis.

We wouldn't make it to the airport on time, ***even if*** *we took a taxi.*

It's doubtful whether *we would make it to the airport on time,* ***even if*** *we took a taxi.*

6 To express a lack of importance of an outcome, we can use *whether or not* + clause, *regardless of whether* + clause.

I'd accept that job, ***whether or not*** *my boss offered me a promotion.*

They'd definitely go to see that play, ***regardless of whether*** *the critics slam it.*

Whether or not can also be used to express the idea of choice. This is used in very formal contexts.

Whether or not *to take out a bank loan in the current climate is difficult to say.*

B The following conditional structures can be used to explain alternative outcomes, express regret, and make predictions or requests. We can use:

1 *If it wasn't / weren't / hadn't been + for + noun phrase.* to explain what particular thing or event prevents a situation from being different.

If it weren't for *the support of my line manager, I wouldn't have applied for the job.*

Rose would probably still be a footballer ***if it hadn't been*** *for the injury.*

This can also be expressed with *but for* + noun or noun phrase.

The performance would have been a resounding success ***but for*** *the power cut during the final act.*

2 *If* + subject + *were* + *to* + infinitive to make formal predictions.

If it were to take off*, the design could be one of our most profitable.*

3 *If + clause + shall* + clause to refer to the future.

We ***shall*** *soon feel the effects of the energy crisis if the government does not provide subsidies.*

4 A variety of phrases introduced by *if* clauses, e.g. *If it isn't / wouldn't be too much trouble, If you wouldn't mind, If you will / would be so kind* + clause to make polite requests in formal contexts.

If it isn't too much trouble, *could we rearrange our upcoming appointment for later in the month?*

5 To express regret, we can use the structure *If only* + past perfect.

If only I hadn't spent *that money, we'd be able to go away this summer.*

C Mixed conditionals

1 The most common types of mixed conditionals are used:

- to speculate about how a different situation in the past could have affected the present.

  If I had gone *to the party last night, I* ***would be*** *completely exhausted now.*

- to speculate about how changes to a present situation might have influenced the past.

  If I weren't working *in the office today, we* ***could have met*** *for lunch.*

We can also use mixed conditionals:

- to speculate about how a different present / past situation might affect the future.

  If he was *one of the directors at the company, he* ***would be travelling*** *to Japan this weekend.*

  If he had taken *the director role, he* ***would be travelling*** *to Japan this weekend.*

- to speculate about how a different situation in the future might affect the past/present.

  If I was playing *in the match next week, I* ***would be*** *at training right now.*

  If I was playing *in the match next week,* ***I would have gone*** *to training last night.*

D Ellipted conditional structures

Conditional structures can ellipted in certain circumstances:

1 To refuse a request in a more polite way, we can use the phrase *I would if I could. The reason for the refusal can be* omitted.

I was wondering if you'd be able to cast an eye over my report for the sales manager.

I would if I could *(but I've got other work to do)*

2 To give advice when replying to a question we can use the phrase *I would / wouldn't if I were you.*

A: Do you think it's a good idea to push for a promotion when I have my appraisal?

B: ***I would if I were you.***

3 Sometimes the subject + *be* can be omitted in an *if* clause.

If in doubt, *leave early than you normally would in case there's congestion in the city centre.*

4 In some conditional sentences about possibility, likes and preferences, ellipsis can be used to avoid repetition. The ellipsis form can be at the beginning or end of the sentence.

If you can, *pick up some fresh herbs for dinner on your way home.*

We could go over your presentation once more later, ***if you want.***

If you have time, *I'd really appreciate some help with installing some software updates on my laptop.*

6 Conditional clauses

1 Choose the correct phrase a, b or c to complete the sentences.

1 ________ the increase in sales over the last quarter, we would have been forced to scale down the business.
 a It's doubtful whether b Provided that c If it weren't for

2 I'll book the restaurant ________ enough people commit to coming by the end of the week.
 a provided that b but for c in case of

3 ________ your laptop had crashed, the presentation would have been a complete disaster!
 a Imagine b Shall c In case

4 The report has to be sent tomorrow ________ the marketing team receive more survey responses.
 a in the event of b were it for c whether or not

5 The website is ready to launch ________ some final checks, which won't take long.
 a but for b so long as c what if

6 ________ you didn't need to work ever again; how would you spend your days?
 a In case b Suppose c Whether or not

7 The government is likely to raise taxes ________ the economy appears to be doing well.
 a but for b in case c even if

8 ________ we win the contract, we'll be working much longer hours than now.
 a In case of b In the event that c What if

2 For sentences 1–8 complete the second sentence so it has a similar meaning as the first sentence.

1 In order for the new pay form to be useful for all departments, it would need to be online.
 If it is ________________.

2 One idea that could help us save money quickly is to go out for dinner less often.
 What if ________________.

3 I handed in my report late because someone had broken the printer.
 But ________________.

4 Olivia's quick thinking was what enabled us to make the sale.
 If it ________________.

5 I regret accepting the promotion because I'm so stressed now.
 If only ________________.

6 I don't think the team will win the World Cup, even if they win the next two matches.
 Whether or not ________________.

7 The only reason why I stayed working at that company for so long was my manager.
 If it hadn't ________________.

8 Unless the whole community takes part in the project, I don't think it will likely have any effect.
 It is doubtful ________________.

Go back to page 84.

7 Modal verbs 2

1 *May / might / could* can be used:

- to express possibility, draw conclusions and deduce information in the present, past and future.

  *You **may find** it easier to book via the website, rather than by telephone.*

  *It **might have been** the same burglar who committed both those crimes.*

  *Unemployment **could rise** in the coming months.*

- to summarise points, often in formal contexts, using *It* + *may / might be* + past participle.

  ***It may be assumed** that consumer spending habits will follow this trend for the next few years.*

  ***It might be summarised** as the worst economic policy ever introduced in this country.*

- before *well* to express a stronger possibility.

  *Look at how overcast it is over there. It **may well** rain.*

  *It **might well** have been delivered to your house by mistake. Would you check when you get home?*

NB Don't confuse may well with may as well.

*He **may well** decide to give up acting after that last terrible review = expressing a possibility.*

*He **may as well** give up acting after that last terrible review = stating something should be done because there is no better alternative.*

2 *Can't / couldn't* can be used:

- to express lack of possibility.

  For present deductions about the past, we use *can't*; for past deductions about the earlier past, we use *couldn't*.

  *What is this? It **can't be** a squash, it's the wrong texture.*

  *The teacher **can't have been talking** about the subjunctive when he said this. It doesn't make sense.*

  *They sent a search party out for the missing explorer in the hope that he **couldn't have got** far on foot.*

NB *couldn't have* + past participle can also be used for sarcasm: *You couldn't have taken a worse route to get out of town.* = You picked a really bad route to get out of town.

3 *Must / mustn't* and *have got to:*

- to make deductions and express a lack of possibility. For deductions about the past we can use *must (not) have been* (especially with *easy*). This is not as common as *can't / couldn't have* + past participle.

  *It was an amazing speech, although it **must not have been easy** to stand up in front of all those people.*

- In informal contexts *have got to* can be used to speculate about the past. In this context it is usually followed by a form of be.

  *It's got to **have been really emotional** for them, seeing her get such a warm reception at the awards ceremony.*

  *It's got to **be difficult** to work full-time and study as well.*

7 Adjectives and fixed expressions

We can use adjectives and fixed expressions to add clarity, focus, descriptive details and complexity to our sentences.

1 Adding detail

By using a string of adjectives, we can add descriptive detail to sentences, joining the final two adjectives in the string with *and*. The order of these words will usually be from shorter to longer, simpler to more complex, less vivid to more vivid, less important to more important in order to build to a climax. This is called climactic order.

*Her behaviour was **unkind, impolite** and **outrageous**.*

*Only a **vain, shallow and self-absorbed** individual would care so little for others around them.*

We can also add focus to descriptive terms, using adjectives in a verbless clause (i.e. where the subject and *be* have been ellipted) before and after a noun for focus. This is particularly useful in written narratives.

***Cold, sparsely furnished and uninviting**, it was located on the other side of the campus.*

*The building, **imposing, soulless and utilitarian,** stood out as a blot on the landscape.*

2 Adding intensity

To add intensity to a description, use a degree adjective before a noun. *Very* can be used to emphasise exactness or preciseness. *Major* can be used to emphasise importance or seriousness, e.g. *very nature, very place / spot, very existence, very idea, major role, major issue, major reason, major influence.*

*It was in this **very** spot that I first met my husband.*

*The discovery of penicillin had a **major** impact on global health.*

3 Using fixed expressions

To add focus, use fixed expressions in a front position, e.g. *All of a sudden, All in all, As a matter of fact, As it stands, As it turns out, At any rate, At best, At the same time, By all means, By the same token, Come to think of it, For / To all intents and purposes, For the most part, For the time being, In actual fact, In much the same way, Out of nowhere, Sure enough, Taking everything into account, To a certain extent, Up to this point, What is more.*

***All in all**, it was considered by everyone to have been a resounding success.*

Two fixed expressions can be used together for added focus.

***In actual fact, all in all,** it was considered by everyone to have been a resounding success.*

***All of sudden, out of nowhere** the skies opened and it absolutely poured down on all the spectators.*

7 Modal verbs 2

1 Correct the mistakes in each sentence.

1 It mustn't had been very pleasant to have the operation without anaesthetic.
2 It got to be uncomfortable to have to meet the person you're going to replace.
3 Although they were trapped on the mountain, they mustn't have called anyone as they had no reception.
4 Don't worry that your results haven't arrived yet. They may as well come tomorrow.
5 It may revealed that the company had known about its impending downfall for months.

2 In 1–4, complete the second sentence so that it has the same meaning as the first.

1 It's possible that José didn't steal the ring after all.
José ______________________________ the ring after all.
2 There's a high chance that Tara was exaggerating when she relayed that story.
Tara ______________________________ when she relayed that story.
3 I can't see any point trying to get this finished. We'll never do it in time.
We ______________________________. We won't finish in time.
4 It's not possible that Juno is graduating this year. It was only last year that started her course!
Juno ______________________________. She only started her course last year!

Go back to page 101.

7 Adjectives and fixed expressions

1 For sentences 1–8, choose the correct alternative in italics.

1 I've always been a language enthusiast. *As a matter of fact / Sure enough*, I used to read the daily news in both French and Arabic!
2 I knew the politician would deny the allegations and blame everyone else. *As it turns out / Sure enough*, he's hitting out at the colleagues who leaked the story to the press.
3 This is the *very / major* house I was brought up in. I never thought I'd see it again.
4 They expected a turnout of a hundred at the AGM. *At best / To a certain extent*, they reckon that just thirty people attended the meeting.
5 The patient is stable, which is great news. *For the most part / For the time being*, we're going to keep her in this ward to monitor her progress and then we'll reassess in a few days.
6 The company has suffered a *major / very* shortfall in funding and staff are now facing redundancies.
7 *For the most part / By all means*, I enjoyed the film but it was a little slow in places.
8 We've now lost six matches in a row. *To a certain extent / As it stands*, we'll be in line for relegation at the end of the season.

2 Combine the following pairs of sentences. Use strings of adjectives, verbless clauses and climactic order.

1 The throngs of fans outside the stadium were chaotic, noisy. They were also out of control.
2 The professor, determined and brilliant. He was also passionate about his work and was the idol of many of his students.
3 The perks of the job are incredible, but let's get this straight, it's often lonely. It's a high-paced, and chaotic role.
4 The jumper was thread-bare and tatty. It was her favourite item in her wardrobe as it was filled with so many memories.

Go back to page 108.

8 Comparatives

1 Review of comparatives

- *now more* + *adjective* + *than ever* to express a greater amount/quantity of something now

  Action on climate change is ***now more critical than ever.***

- *the* + *comparative, the* + *comparative* to express a proportionate increase (or decrease)

  In terms of single-use plastics, ***the less we produce the better*** *in my opinion.*

- *like* + *noun / pronoun / gerund*

  Trying to convince my parents to recycle is ***like talking to a brick wall.***

- (*just / every bit*) *as* + *adjective* + *as* to say two things are equal, or *not* (*quite*) *as* + *adjective* + *as* to mean two things are unequal

  Limiting waste production is ***not quite as important as*** *dealing with climate change, in my view.*

2 Expressing similarity

We can use *as* + *adjective / adverb* + *as* to compare something, someone or a situation to another thing, person or situation.

Finding effective alternative energies is ***as complex to deal with as*** *food scarcity.*

When using a singular countable noun after the adjective, the indefinite article comes between the adjective and the noun.

Leonardo de Caprio is as vocal ***a*** *champion of environmental causes as you can find in Hollywood.*

We can use *as if* or *as though* to compare the situations described in the two clauses.

The fish were laying on the coast ***as if*** *they had jumped right out of the water.*

3 Comparative structures with so

We can use *so* + *adjective / adverb* + *that* to say something happened to such a degree that it caused a specific result. In formal contexts, we can use *so* + *adjective / adverb* + *as* + *to infinitive* in the same way.

Companies should never be ***so bold as to*** *ignore their impact on the environment.*

4 Limiting a comparison

We can use *no / not any* + *comparative adjective* to limit a comparison (say it is no more than another thing).

The animals in this zoo are ***no worse off*** *than they would be in the wild.*

We can use *not that much* + *comparative adjective* (+*than*) to indicate a small amount more.

In my view, organic vegetables ***are not that much tastier than*** *other vegetables.*

5 Phrases of comparison

We can use *the faintest / the slightest* before certain nouns to express the least amount possible, usually after a negative verb form. This can also be expressed by putting *in the slightest* at the end of the clause.

I didn't have the ***faintest*** *idea what was happening.*

The restrictions didn't make a difference ***in the slightest****.*

We can use *tantamount to* as an adjective to compare two negative things and express their similarity.

The destruction of forests for their resources is ***tantamount to*** *criminal behaviour, in my view.*

We can grade comparisons with adjective + noun collocations: a *marked improvement*, a *vast difference*

We've noticed ***a marked improvement*** *in the town's care of the local environment following the talks.*

8 Expressing contrast

1 *while* and *whereas* to contrast people, places and situations in the same sentence.

While *some governments are making real progress, others seem more reluctant to engage with the issue.*

2 *not nearly as / so* + *adj* + *as* and *nothing like as* + *adj* to emphasise something that is not the case.

Even as little as twenty years ago, cities were ***nothing like as*** *crowded as they are today.*

3 *more* + *adjective than* + *adjective* for related qualities.

The lack of sales is ***more worrying than*** *frustrating.*

4 *slightly, comparatively, far, a great deal, considerably, significantly* + *adj* to indicate a degree of difference.

The mayor's office has been ***comparatively successful*** *at reducing air pollution.*

5 *Although/though* + participle clause or verbless clause.

Though *officially retired, Amy did some freelance work.*

6 *adjective* + *though* and *superlative* + *by far / by a long way* to add emphasis.

Interesting though *the film sounded, Laura couldn't persuade anyone to watch it with her.*

7 *And yet* to introduce an unexpected contrast.

I was convinced I had done badly in the exam, ***and yet*** *a month later my certificate arrived.*

8 *Nonetheless* at the beginning or end of a sentence, or between a subject or auxiliary verb and the main verb.

There were very few flights available. I have ***nonetheless*** *managed to find one.*

9 *Even so / All the same* come at the beginning of a sentence or join two clauses with a conjunction.

Addressing pollution in the city is difficult, but ***all the same****, the council should up their game.*

10 *Albeit* introduces a comparison using a noun, adjective or adverb phrase. It cannot be followed by an independent clause.

The proposal to invest in the rewilding project was welcome, ***albeit*** *long overdue.*

8 Comparatives

1 Complete the comparative structures in the text. Use one word only.

Some people might think that gardens don't make the **(1)** __________ difference to the general health of a city, but they can actually have huge beneficial effects, and despite what many people think it's actually **(2)** __________ more difficult to create gardens in urban spaces than anywhere else. Vertical gardens are now popping up in cities around the world, and they are **(3)** __________ environmentally friendly that local governments are starting to promote them in some places. They help clear the air of pollutants, and they also can make residents feel **(4)** __________ if they live in a green haven – making a marked **(5)** __________ to health and quality of life! They are as good **(6)** __________ answer to improving our urban spaces as you can find. In fact, the more creative solutions we can find to improving and greening urban spaces, **(7)** __________ better for us all it will be!

2 Underline the mistakes and correct them.

1 Dealing with climate change is as difficult challenge as any government can have right now.

2 Taking the car is no that much quicker than going by bus.

3 The judge ruled that when the defendant posed as someone else to enter the building, it was tantamount of a break-in.

4 Buying electric cars won't make faintest difference to pollution in general.

5 Every person should act so though they have a personal responsibility to the global environment.

Go back to page 116.

8 Expressing contrast

1 Which ONE of the following options (a, b or c) CANNOT complete the sentences.

1 Critics were quite negative in the reviews of the book on going green at home. __________ it topped the best seller list for over a year.

a All the same b Though c And yet

2 The report was submitted on time, __________ after a stressful last week of writing for all concerned.

a although b even so c albeit

3 Modern waste disposal can be extremely costly. __________, it is essential for good public health.

a Nonetheless b Even so c Although

4 __________ eco-friendly in many ways, electric cars don't grab my attention like the old petrol classics.

a Though b And yet c Although

2 Choose the correct words to complete the text.

Controversial **(1)** *though / than / albeit* nuclear power is, like renewables, it is another way of producing energy that does not use fossil fuels, **(2)** *all the same / albeit / and yet* an expensive one.

Advocates cite its safety and efficiency as key benefits, **(3)** *all the same / more / and yet* many governments are wary of it as it alienates some voters. For nuclear scientists, this lack of interest in nuclear is **(4)** *more / although / all the same* frustrating than surprising, as it contributes to lower levels of investment and therefore impacts their work.

(5) *And yet / All the same / Although* rejected by politicians, it is often embraced by climate scientists since it has an almost non-existent carbon footprint. **(6)** *Though / All the same / Albeit*, trying to convince less scientifically literate politicians and members of the public of its safety can be a daunting task.

Go back to page 121.

READY FOR GRAMMAR

9 Expressing concession, contrast, purpose and reason

Concession

To express concession in subordinate clauses, we can use:

- *however* + adjective + *it* / *this* + *may be* / *seem*.

  The effect is caused by light waves, ***however surprising this may seem****.*

- *whatever, whoever* + *it* / *this* + *may be*.

  Find a mutually acceptable way to work together as a team, ***whatever it / this may be****.*

Contrast

To build on a previous, related negative clause, and to focus on an additional negative factor, we can use:

- *neither* / *nor* + inverted *be* + subject

  It isn't possible to guess what he's working on. ***Nor is it*** *worth trying as he'll never divulge the details.*

- *neither* / *nor* + inverted *do* + subject

  Cooking fine food does not have to be prohibitively expensive. ***Nor does it*** *have to be complex.*

Purpose

To introduce a purpose, we can use:

- *in order (not) to*

  In order to *establish a better procedure, all staff will be asked to complete a questionnaire.*

- *so as (not) to*

  We came by taxi ***so as not to*** *be late for the event.*

Reason

We can use:

- *as* / *since* in place of *because* to express reason.

  Since *there had been some storms in the vicinity, we sheltered in a café rather than continuing.*

- *as* / *while* to talk about time and reason together.

  While *we're in the neighbourhood, we should check out the restaurant options.*

  Why don't I review the rest of your presentation ***as*** *we've got some extra time.*

- *now that* / *as* / *since* to introduce a clause explaining a present situation.

  Now that *I understand his inspirations, we're making much better progress.*

  Since *we met, my life has expanded in so many different respects.*

- *in that* instead of *because* as a subordinating conjunction, to give greater in-depth explanation. This is more commonly used in formal contexts.

  The village is delightfully picturesque ***in that*** *it's tucked away in the hills and is full of period cottages.*

- *as for myself* as a discourse marker to introduce or focus on a personal viewpoint.

  As for myself*, working in a one of those intimidating office buildings would be a somewhat overwhelming.*

9 Passive and causative structures

The passive can add complexity to clauses as well as a degree of sophistication.

1 In subordinate clauses, we can use the *-ing* form of the perfect passive to give explanatory background information from the past to main clauses. These are more commonly used at the beginning of a sentence.

  Having been trained *at a top university, Nina managed to find a good job soon after graduating.*

  The kitchen ***having been cleaned*** *and the clothes* ***put away****, it was now time for everyone to relax.*

  They can be used as the complement of prepositions in subordinate clauses at the beginning or in the middle of a sentence.

  They went to the opening of the new library in spite ***of not having been invited*** *by the mayor's office.*

  In spite ***of not having been invited*** *by the mayor's office, they went to the opening of the new library.*

2 We can build more complex clauses by positioning two or more passive constructions consecutively. This describes a process where two or more actions follow each other in a specific order. Avoid repeating the auxiliary forms.

  The photos ***have been*** *framed and* ***hung*** *on the wall.*

3 Causative structures

  have + *object* + infinitive and *get* + object + infinitive with *to* can be used to show you arranged for someone else to do something.

  We should ***have the decorators paint*** *the ceilings.*

  Let's ***get the children to tidy*** *their rooms.*

  This structure can also be used to mean experience something, but in this case only *have* can be used.

  The driving school ***hasn't had anybody fail*** *their test.*

  get / *have* + object + past participle can be used to make promises. The person can either be promising they will do the action or that someone else will.

  I'll ***have your complaint reviewed*** *thoroughly and then we'll assess how to proceed.*

  The imperative form of *have* / *get* + object + past participle can be used to make commands. It can be the person being spoken to or someone else who will do the action.

  Have that report written *and on my desk by noon.*

  get + past participle for situations where someone has been affected by an experience that they did not do or cause. Common past participles used in this way are: *caught, involved, left, stuck, trapped.*

  We didn't get going early enough and ***got caught up*** *in the congestion through the town centre.*

9 Expressing concession, contrast, purpose and reason

1 Add the missing word or phrase to the correct place in the sentences.

1. Our sales techniques always get results, however unorthodox may seem.
2. As myself, I'm drawn to urban life with all its cosmopolitan sights and sounds.
3. I hadn't downloaded the app on my phone I couldn't access the details.
4. My strength is visibly improving that I've got a personal trainer.
5. The restaurant isn't appropriate for gluten intolerant people. Nor it that great for vegetarians.
6. We tiptoed softly around the house as not to wake the children.
7. Her sculpture invokes the true spirit of her homeland that she uses locally sourced stone.
8. We should fetch the heavy boxes from upstairs there's two of us here.

2 Cross out the words which cannot be used to complete the sentences.

1. We've decided to delay the refurbishment *while / since / as* the quotations we got were out of budget.
2. The images cannot be used for commercial purposes, *whatever they may be / whatever they may seem / whatever these may be*.
3. *Since / Now that / In order to* we've agreed on the colour scheme, we should choose some fabrics.
4. *While / As / In that* we're all together, why don't we go over the plans for the loft extension?
5. The construction workers are working round the clock *so as to / in that / in order to* complete the stadium on time.
6. I can't see them refunding the cost of their error. *Nor does it / Neither does it / Nor is it* look like you'll get an apology.
7. I enjoyed the intricate plot of the book *because / in that / now that* it kept me guessing until the very end.

Go back to page 131.

9 Passive and causative structures

1 Decide which answer (A, B, C or D) best fits each gap.

1. Leave it to us. We ____________ the catering organised for the event so you can get on with other things.
   A will get **B** have been getting **C** have got **D** be getting
2. The walls ____________ and the floors laid, the room was ready for the new furniture.
   A getting painted **B** having painted **C** got painted **D** having been painted
3. Have those pots ____________ by the time I get back.
   A cleaning **B** to clean **C** cleaned **D** been cleaned
4. The manager ____________ all new staff ____________ on a health and safety training course.
   A is having / go **B** have / to go **C** has / to go **D** is having / going
5. Georgia was proud of ____________ to exhibit her work at the gallery.
   A she had been asked **B** asking to have **C** having been asked **D** get asked
6. We searched for the cat for hours yesterday until we noticed she'd ____________ under the garden shed.
   A had trapped **B** got trapped **C** been trapping **D** got trap

2 Rewrite the sentences with passive or causative structures. Use the word in brackets.

1. They repaired and varnished the old door remaining faithful to the details of the period. (*was*)
2. A local artist was commissioned to do a series of murals in the town by the council. (*had*)
3. I contacted the company about my order because they hadn't sent an email with the delivery details. (*due to*)
4. I want somebody to order the flowers for the wedding today to avoid delays. (*have*)
5. I'll ensure that someone brings you the dessert menu in just a moment. (*get*)
6. The caterers prepared the food and then we waited for the guests to arrive. (*having*)

Go back to page 134.

10 Inversion

In more formal or literary contexts, we can use certain adverbial structures at the beginning of a clause to emphasise something or convey a sense of drama. Following the structures, the order of the subject and the verb is inverted. In sentences without an auxiliary verb, *do, does or did* is added.

1 Inversion for emphasis

- Inversion is used after the following phrases:

  at no time, barely, hardly, scarcely, rarely, hardly ever, never, in no way, little, on no account, never again, no sooner, not since, not until, not only, only later, only then, only when, under no circumstances.

  ***Hardly ever will** you find this type of deciduous tree growing at this altitude.*
- *Not until, Only when, Only after, Only once, Not since* are followed by a subordinate clause. The inversion of the subject and the verbs happens in in the main clause.

  ***Not since** we were children **have** we spent an evening playing board games.*

  Many of these phrases can also be followed by a noun and then the inverted verb form.

  ***Not since** last spring **has** a stranger been seen here.*
- We can use *not only... but also* and *never / nor + must +* subject to emphasise the importance of something.

  ***Never must they** uncover how we knew where to look for the files; **nor must they** ever access to the records.*
- We can use *never again + will + subject* for predictions.

  ***Never again** will our paths cross at such an auspicious point in the history of this universe.*
- We can use *may + subject* to introduce a clause describing a strong wish.

  ***May next year** bring all the joys you could hope for!*
- Clauses which start with *as, than* and *so* can be used with inversion, especially in literary contexts.

  ***So far had they** walked through the sweltering jungle that Kristina had lost all track of time.*

  *Authors of fiction tend to command higher advances **than do** nonfiction authors.*

2 Inversion in conditional clauses

Conditional structures can be inverted to give emphasis. This happens in the *if* clause when *if* is omitted.

- *Were it not for* + noun / noun phrase.

  ***Were it not for his persuasive manner**, we certainly wouldn't have attended the event.*
- Past perfect + inverted subject

  ***Had the hero known** what fate held in store, he surely would have told Ada he loved her.*
- If we think something is unlikely, we use *were* + subject + *to* + infinitive.

  ***Were they to take up** the fight, they'd clearly need many more resources.*
- We can use an inverted *should + subject* in more formal contexts.

  ***Should you** fail to complete the quest, there will be consequences. (If you fail to complete ...)*

  Notice the difference with negative clauses.

  ***Should you not** complete the quest, there will be consequences (If you don't complete....)*

3 Inversion with adverbs of time, place and movement

- We can use adverbs of place or time + *be* or verb of place or movement. The subject comes after the whole verb form (i.e. not just the auxiliary). Do not add *do, does, did.*

  ***Inside the chest should have been** the golden amulet.*

  ***First was** a sumptuous soufflé, **then came** the prawns.*

  Here and *there* when they are used as adverbs of place. These types of exclamations are sometimes used in everyday speech.

  ***Here comes** the rain, we'd better head indoors.*

  ***There stood** my parents with huge smiles on their faces.*

  However, remember that if the subject is a pronoun, you cannot use an inversion structure.

  ***There goes the bottle**, washing out to sea.*

  ***There it goes**, washing out to sea.*

10 Creating emphasis and cleft sentences

To add emphasis to a person, thing or a clause we can use:

1 Question words

What, Who, How, Why or Where + clause as the subject of a sentence to emphasise certain information.

***How** the agency will respond to these requests is unclear.*

2 Using nouns with premodifiers

the (+ premodifier) + *thing / fact / point / problem / reason / issue + be (that).*

***The underlying problem has always been** the council's reluctance to spend money on public transport.*

3 Emphasising a person / thing

it + be + noun phrase + relative clause.

*In the play, **it's May who notices that the necklace has been stolen**, whereas in the film version it's her maid.*

4 Negative Not

Not a + noun for focus (often with a passive structure). This is usually a literary device.

***Not a day** goes by that I don't think of what could have happened differently.*

10 Inversion

1 Correct the errors in the sentences.

1. Hardly had Scott crossed over the rope bridge as it collapsed behind him.
2. There the bus is going – it looks like we've missed it.
3. Only when you've handed in the final manuscript you will feel satisfied.
4. Freya was having a tantrum about not getting her own way, than do all children of that age.
5. Only later it became apparent that Simona had deceived us all with her cunning disguise.
6. Were we have given them the news now, I think they'd react worse than if we waited.
7. Not only you must hide this book safely, but also you shouldn't mention that you've seen it.
8. Was behind the old cottage a rambling garden which no one had tended for generations.

2 Choose the correct alternative. In some cases both options may be possible.

The detective surveyed the scene in her usual attentive manner. On the side of the road were a jacket, a pair of boots and a hat. They'd been put there deliberately, suggesting that someone was coming back for them. She needed a closer look, but **(1)** *rarely / hardly* had she bent down to examine the clothes **(2)** *then / when* her deputy ran over. **(3)** *Here it comes / Here comes* trouble she thought to herself as she stood up.

(4) *Were it not / Had it not been* for his anxious expression, she might have had him wait till she was done, but something about the scene was nagging at her anyway so she motioned to Fraser to talk. He informed her that he had just received a call from the station – the inspector wanted an update.

Iris was well aware that **(5)** *if the fugitive should not be found / should the fugitive not be found*, her job would be on the line, so reluctantly she pulled her mobile out of her pocket. She cleared her throat and focused her mind. The inspector shouldn't sense she was uneasy, **(6)** *nor must / must nor* he suspect the investigation was stalling. The call was mercifully short. She hung up and tried to remember what she'd been thinking before the call. She gazed across at the scene and **(7)** *only then / only when* did she realise what had been on her mind. Sticking out of a bush on the other side of the road **(8)** *was something that looked like a scarf / something that looked like a scarf was.*

Go back to page 147.

10 Creating emphasis and cleft sentences

1 Complete the sentences with words from the box.

how	it is	it was	not	was that	why

1. At the end of the story, ____________ Jackson who lives to fight another day.
2. ____________ you managed to complete the project on time, I'll never know.
3. ____________ my daughter who first alerted me to the broken garage window.
4. ____________ a cloud was in the sky as we approached the mountain's summit.
5. ____________ the application was not received in good time is still to be ascertained.
6. At that time, the primary issue ____________ nobody took responsibility for the mistakes.

2 Rewrite the underlined sections of the text to add emphasis.

(1) <u>Lewis, a friend of mine from work,</u> asked me to join him on a trip to the Hay literary festival. I didn't really know what to expect because, although an avid reader, I wouldn't have labelled myself as a literary festival goer. **(2)** <u>I didn't have a clue</u> about these kinds of events, but I thought I might as well tag along and vowed to keep an open mind. A couple of days before he emailed me the programme and I was astounded by the sheer number of talks. **(3)** <u>I didn't know how I'd be able</u> to see everything I wanted to! Anyway, I did a bit more investigation and **(4)** <u>conveniently</u> the festival had an app to help people plan their visit. It turned out to be invaluable as vastly improved my experience of the whole event.

Go back to page 152.

READY FOR GRAMMAR

11 Reporting structures 1

Verb patterns with *that*

1 Verb + *that* + clause (*that* can be left out of many informal structures of this type)

e.g. *add, agree, announce, argue, boast, concede, consider, doubt, echo, estimate, feel, forewarn, go on to say, imply, insist, mention, mumble, mutter, predict, reckon, remark, report, snap, suppose, warn*

*The Chair **went on to say (that)** the meetings would be cancelled should attendance remain so poor.*

*After a series of poor performances, **they doubted** their team would be promoted.*

*The article in the College News **implied (that)** there had been problems on campus.*

2 Verb + object + *that* + clause (*that* can be left out of many informal structures of this type)

e.g. assure, forewarn, inform, persuade, reassure, remind, warn

*The council **didn't inform us (that)** this road would be closed today.*

*The air steward **warned the passengers that** any further disruption would have them thrown off the flight.*

3 Verb + (*that*) + (modal verb) + present subjunctive

Following certain verbs, e.g. *advise, demand, insist, propose, recommend, request, suggest, urge,* we can use the present subjunctive form of the verb, i.e. there is no *-s* form in the third person. The same form is used in both the present and the past.

*The host **insisted that we (should) leave** our passports at the front desk.*

*The town planner **recommended that the developers resituate** the development further outside of the city.*

In negative subjunctives, the verb *do* is omitted.

*The town planner recommended that the developers **not situate** the development so close to the centre.*

Verb patterns with *to*

1 Verb + infinitive with *to*

e.g. *agree, beg, claim, forewarn, guarantee, offer, predict, refuse, swear, threaten, vow*

*The newspaper article **claimed to know** the reasons behind the sudden increase in crime.*

To show that the action in the main clause is in the past, we use the perfect infinitive.

*At least three people **claim to have seen** the incident, but no report has been filed yet.*

*At least three people **claimed to have seen** the incident.*

2 Verb + infinitive with *to* + object

e.g. *beg, claim, offer, mean, refuse, threaten, volunteer, vow*

*As Carla hadn't been there before, **Maria offered to show her** around the town.*

*Residents **volunteered to clean the building** rather than pay the extra charge.*

3 Verb + object + to infinitive

e.g. *authorise, beg, bribe, call on, convince, encourage, nag, plead (with), urge, warn*

*The local council have **encouraged all inner-city residents to use** public transport with a new reimbursement scheme.*

*The police **warned them not to park** there, so they're bound to get a ticket for doing so.*

NB The structure in the passive becomes passive structure + reporting verb + *to*

*They **were warned not to park** there...*

Other verb patterns

1 Verb + preposition + gerund / noun phrase

e.g. *boast, complain, exaggerate, hypothesise, quibble, wonder* ***about***

advise, protest, warn ***against***

attack, blame, criticise, defend, excuse, praise, tell off, **(+ object)** ***for***

discourage, forbid, **(+ object)** ***from***

accuse, speak **(+ object)** ***of***

congratulate **(+ object)**, *insist* ***on***

confess, consent, object, own up ***to***

*The local council **confessed to ignoring** warnings about traffic congestion during the sporting event.*

*The onlookers **hypothesised about** the causes of the crash.*

2 Verb + gerund

e.g. *advise, debate, deny, mention, recommend, regret, suggest*

*The guide **recommended going** to see the castle, but **suggested taking** a taxi, as it was quite a steep climb.*

*The residents **denied having seen** anything on the night of the fire.*

3 Some reporting verbs can be used with the impersonal passive structure when we want to distance ourselves from what is being said. This is more common in written reports or formal spoken reporting.

e.g. *accept, acknowledge, anticipate, assume, claim, conclude, consider, estimate, expect, know, maintain, observed, prove, say, suppose, recognised, report, rumour, think*

***It is anticipated that** council members will meet again last week with local businessmen to discuss the proposals.*

*The redevelopment of this area **is estimated to have cost** over $3 million.*

11 Reporting structures 1

1 Match each sentence beginning (1–8) with an appropriate ending (a–h).

1 The forecast **warns against**
2 We had only pulled over for a moment, but the warden still **threatened**
3 The singer thanked her fans and **went on**
4 When questioned by police, the suspects **denied**
5 The whole class had to stay behind until someone **owned up**
6 The minister is widely **rumoured**
7 James didn't think it would but I **assured**
8 It's Helen's own fault. We all **warned her**

a **to have accepted** bribes from the construction firm.
b **to share** how proud she was to accept the award.
c **not to take** that job, but she wouldn't listen.
d **him that** my car would make it all the way to Madrid.
e **taking** any unnecessary risks such as venturing outdoors during the blizzard.
f **being** anywhere near the scene.
g **to having defaced** the textbooks.
h **to give us** a ticket.

2 Rewrite each sentence using the reporting verb in brackets.

1 Anna: 'I'm not sure you should take the exam so soon, Jim.' (DISCOURAGE)

2 Politician: 'If you vote for us again, I promise that we will continue to improve the economy of this country.' (SWEAR)

3 Dad: 'If you don't make more of an effort with your schoolwork, Adam, you'll regret it.' (WARN)

4 Daniel: 'I'm sorry. It was me. I broke the window!' (CONFESS)

5 'Some people say that the actor has been sacked from the movie franchise after publicly criticising the director.' (RUMOUR)

Go back to page 165.

11 Reporting structures 2

1 In informal conversations, it is common for people to use *went* or *be* + *like* instead of *said*. This is very colloquial. *e.g.*

*The traffic warden was pretty rude and without even looking up she **went** 'you can't park here' and gave me a ticket, and I **was like** 'I can park here, can't you see my resident's permit?'*

2 In informal speech, certain reporting verbs can be used to express speaker opinion, e.g.

drone on about	*(talk in a boring way for a long time)*
blather on about	*(talk in a silly / annoying way for a long time).*
bang on about	*(continue to talk about something repeatedly/for a long time).*
sound off at	*(express opinions in a loud/ forceful way)*
keep on at	*(complain, moan or nag).*
go on and on	*(talk, for what the speaker thinks is too long, or nag).*
go off at	(speak angrily).

*My father's always **droning on about** the vegetables he's growing in the garden, but I couldn't care less!*

*It takes us hours to go out. My partner is always **blathering on about** this top or that, and these shoes or those.*

*If people don't like the state of the roads, there's no point **banging on about** it to friends – they need to petition the council.*

*My dad always **keeps on at** me about cleaning my room, but I just don't want to do it.*

*There's no point **sounding off at** the waiters if you don't like the food. Just ask to change what you've ordered.*

*I wish my boss wouldn't **go on and on** about how important the presentation is. It makes me nervous!*

*Dan's child nearly ran into the road and he completely **went off at** him.*

3 Reporting using adjectives

Adjectives can be used to report feelings or opinions, indicating the style of which the information was delivered previously.

e.g. adamant, grateful, insistent **+ that**

doubtful, unsure, uncertain, skeptical ***that/whether***

complimentary/insulting **about**

critical/scornful ***of***

abusive/sympathetic ***towards***

*The council were **adamant that** the road works were essential.*

12 Participle clauses

A Types of Participle clause

1 Present participle clauses, e.g.

***Hoping** to learn more about eating healthily, I signed up to a vegetarian cooking course.*

NB Stative verbs can be used in present participle clauses.

2 Perfect participle clauses, e.g.

***Having researched** all the options, she settled on the yoga retreat in Corsica as it had the best reviews.*

3 Passive participle clauses, e.g.

***Having been given** a stark warning by his doctor, Jim realised he had to make serious lifestyle changes.*

4 Verbless clauses, e.g.

***Alone and afraid**, she wrapped herself in a blanket.*

B Use of Participle clause

1 to refer to simultaneous events (i.e. to replace a *while* clause).

***Running down** the street for the bus, I tripped over.*

2 to refer to earlier events (i.e. to replace an *after* clause).

***Having spoken** to the fitness instructor, I have a clearer idea of what his classes with involve.*

3 to refer to a reason (i.e. to replace a *because* clause).

***Not wanting** to wake anyone else up, I snuck out of the room and quietly closed the door.*

4 to refer to a condition (i.e. to replace an *if* clause).

***Given** a choice, I'd rather dance than go to the gym.*

5 to provide information about a noun phrase (i.e. to replace a defining or non-defining relative clause).

*The message **posted** today was about meditation techniques*

NB unlike relative clauses, these can often come before the noun phrase.

***Built in 1066**, the castle is a major tourist attraction.*

C Adding a subject to a participle clause

The subject of a participle clause is usually same as that of the main clause. However, we can introduce a different subject:

1 if the actions are happening at the same time as events in the main clause, or are used to give extra information.

*Her eyes **filling** with tears, Yasmin was clearly overwhelmed at her gold medal win.*

2 when *with* is used to introduce a different subject.

***With** exercise classes **running** throughout the day, the centre is perfect for everyone's schedule.*

3 To add a subject without without *with*

***There** being no further matters to discuss, we closed the meeting early.*

11 Reporting structures 2

1 Choose the correct option to complete the sentences.

1 At the press conference, the mayor was absolutely ________ that he hadn't taken any bribes during his time in office.
a sceptical b adamant c critical

2 The members of The Beatles are generally ________ to be Liverpool's most famous export.
a acknowledged b admitted c refused

3 Did you see the way that man went ________ at the shopkeeper just then? I've never seen someone so angry!
a on b off c out

4 After such a serious tackle, it's ________ whether Thomas will be able to play for the rest of the season.
a doubtful b critical c insistent

5 He keeps ________ on about the price of petrol being so dear, but I don't see him walking any more than usual!
a sounding b complaining c banging

6 When I told her what she'd done wrong she ________ on and on about it not being her fault.
a was b went c did

7 All the neighbours are being so ________ about my front garden. I'm so happy they like it.
a scornful b grateful c complimentary

8 If you don't like the subject you're studying, why don't you ________ to change classes.
a declare b request c admit

Go back to page 167.

12 Participle clauses

1 Correct the mistakes in the sentences.

1 With the marathon come up in just a few months, Jessie knew she had to start training.
2 Finished her course of antibiotics, Sara felt much better.
3 Vegetarianism becoming ever more popular, lots of restaurants serve meat-free options.
4 Watched the instructor giving an example, I realised I'd picked a class way above my level.
5 The spectators watched the referee march around the pitch, book players for minor infractions.
6 The race was so hard that Ciarán was the only person in the over 60s category finishing.

2 For sentences 1–8, choose the correct alternative in italics.

1 *Posting up / Having posted up* flyers all around town for her new nutritional therapist business, she was disappointed not to receive even a single call from them.

2 She had really hoped to be able to make a go of it, *to see / having seen* a number of her friends from college all manage to jump straight into jobs, but there weren't the same opportunities in her town.

3 *Using / Used* for short evening classes as well as full-time courses, the local college always had rooms available, and, even more importantly, there were a couple of classrooms for catering studies, fully equipped with kitchens.

4 *Having been taught / With being teaching* in the very same college, she was sure that she might be able to get some special rate for classroom hire too.

5 As a teacher, the participants would listen to her *talking / talked* about foods and their nutritional values.

6 *Plans making / Plans made*, she decided she'd go into the college first thing in the morning.

Go back to page 176.

12 Verb patterns

A Gerunds

Gerunds are used:

- as the subject, object or complement of a verb.

  __Working__ from home has multiple benefits.

- after prepositions as well as after certain phrases (e.g. *have difficulty / problems, there's no / little point, it's no good / use, it's not worth*)

  There's __little point starting__ a diet if we're going travelling next month.

- after certain verbs (e.g. *anticipate, contemplate, handle, imagine, miss, prevent, propose, risk, tolerate*)

  Why would you __risk damaging__ your health in that way?

  NB Some of the verbs above can follow the structure verb + object + *ing*

  I can't __imagine him making it to__ the top division.

- after an object with certain verbs, especially when describing repeated actions or those in progress. (e.g. *catch, discover, find, hear, leave, notice, see, spot, watch*)

  The teacher left __the students doing__ their homework.

- to explain that something is not permitted or not a possibility, we use no + *ing*

  __There's no taking photos__ during the match.

- to create a noun phrase in the structure *the* + *ing* + *of* + object

  __The eating of unhealthy food__ at schools contributes to the country's obesity epidemic.

  __The burning of calories__ happens naturally throughout the day, but we can aid it with movement and exercise.

- in formal English, we can use a possessive pronoun + gerund to replace object pronouns + gerund when the subject of the main verb and the gerund differ.

  Do you mind __my taking__ this seat? = more formal

  Do you mind __me taking__ this seat? = more informal

- to indicate who is doing an action after a possessive 's. This structure is not usually used with verbs of the senses, e.g. *hear, see, feel,* etc.

  __Rachel's lashing out__ at me over the smallest things is really starting to wear me down.

  The entire sports club turned out to celebrate __Kyle's winning__ the marathon.

  In informal English, the possessive *'s* is often dropped.

  The entire sports club turned out to celebrate __Kyle winning__ the marathon.

B Infinitives with *to*

Infinitives with *to* can be used:

- after certain verbs (e.g. *appeal, arrange, deserve, dread, hesitate, manage, offer, prepare, pretend, succumb, struggle, vow*)

  I __dread to think__ what would have happened if you hadn't been there.

- as the subject, although this is less common.

  __To stay calm__ while all around you is panic is one of the hardest skills to master.

- after *for* + subject. However, this is more common when preceded by *it is*.

  For them __to lose__ now is a disaster.

  It is a disaster for them __to lose__ now.

- after certain adjectives (e.g. *eager, elated, formidable, reluctant, stunned, traumatic, thrilled*)

  The public were __stunned to find__ out that the winner had cheated.

- in a perfect form to refer to things that may or may not have happened in the past.

  He pretended __to have been__ on the diet for months so he could get compensation.

  In a non-finite clause, the perfect infinitive can refer to events which happened (or could have but didn't).

  __To have gone__ to an Elvis Presley concert must have been incredible.

- after certain nouns (e.g. *ability, capacity, chance, decision, determination, mistake, proposal, tendency way, willingness*).

  It was a __mistake to open__ the community centre in the evenings.

- to express purpose and result.

  He takes those pills __to help__ his arthritis.

  When the subject of the infinitive is different from the subject of the sentence we use *for*.

  We went to the class to show Matt what it was like / We went to the class __for__ Matt __to see__ what it was like.

- after *only* to indicate a surprising or frustrating subsequent event.

  They battled through the rain to get to the match __only to discover__ it had been cancelled.

- when certain verbs of liking are used after *would*.

  I don't go to the park often, but __I'd hate not to have it__ nearby.

- in informal English we can split the infinitive. This should generally be avoided in formal English.

  Adam started __to gradually cut out sugar__ from his diet.

  The doctor decided __to immediately address__ the issue with the patient.

C The bare infinitive (without *to*)

The bare infinitive (without *to*) can be used after certain verbs (e.g. *had better, would rather / sooner, let, dare*)

***We'd better shape up** if we want to enter the race.*

D Difference in meaning

Some verbs can be followed by both the gerund and the infinitive, but there is a difference in meaning *(e.g. forget, mean, regret, remember, stop, try)*

*We'll never **forget travelling** through Italy by bike. / Don't **forget to take** your ticket when you travel.*

*I **regret signing up** for that boot camp class. / I **regret to tell you** that the class is closing.*

12 Verb patterns

1 Rewrite the sentences 1–10 using gerunds and infinitives.

0 The doctor advised me to give up fast food, but I can't bear the idea.
I'd hate ______*to have to give up*______ fast food, like the doctor advised.

1 I know I came last in the sailing race I entered, but I don't regret it.
I'll never regret ____________________ the race, even if I did come last.

2 The teacher wasn't too happy that I had to leave the class early.
I don't think the teacher was too happy with ____________________ class early.

3 The only reason I got fit was because my friend wouldn't stop nagging me about it.
Without ____________________ I would never have got fit.

4 Nobody realised how unhealthy he was until it was too late.
They failed ____________________ how unhealthy he was until it was too late.

5 Her preference was to go camping but everybody else insisted on staying in a hotel.
She would ____________________ but everybody else insisted on staying in a hotel.

6 It is the local council who run the gym on a day-to-day basis.
The daily ____________________ is undertaken by the local council.

7 Nobody likes that Daniel talked all through the yoga class.
I don't think anyone was impressed with ____________________ all through the yoga class.

8 They were cheating on their test and the examiner spotted it.
The examiner ____________________ their test.

9 It's brilliant that the women's team are getting paid as much as the men!
For ____________________ as much as the men is brilliant!

10 You can't eat or drink inside the auditorium.
There's no ____________________ inside the auditorium.

Go back to page 179.

AUDIOSCRIPTS

1.1

W = Woman M = Man

Extract 1

W: It's true that clothing is a basic need, like food or water. But I think we can all agree it's become so much more than that. In today's world, the clothing we wear is a mirror that reflects who we think we are and who we want to be.

M: But is that really new?

W: Well, yes and no. Of course, clothing has always been meaningful. Traditionally, the clothes people wore symbolised cultural affiliations and values, age and ethnicity. But these days our wardrobe choices encompass all that plus a sense of fashion and personal style. Not to stray too much into jargon, but this is why we behaviour theorists call clothing an 'artefact of extended self'.

M: And that's where brands come in, which I know is a particular focus of yours.

W: Exactly. Thanks to globalisation and the internet, most of us, in our own way, are becoming brand conscious consumers. We splurge on certain clothing brands because of their association with celebrities, subcultures or leisure activities – or, more often than not, as much as we are loath to admit it, to project a sense of having arrived, mixed with a certain vibe of aspiration.

Extract 2

W: Are you saying your job defines you?

M: I'm not sure I'd go that far, but I would say that jobs in general tend to reinforce certain traits. For example, as a news editor, I'm being trained every day to prioritise what's happening right now. At this moment. And it's not hard to see how that mindset spills over into the rest of my life. If only I were a bit better at compartmentalising things.

W: Yeah, same here. Being a dentist, I'm so much less trusting than I used to be. Day after day, people who are decent and upstanding in their everyday lives, well, they cancel their appointments, saying something just came up. Sure it did. And when they do show up, they sit down and start lying to me straight away about how much they've flossed. And the next time I see them, what do you know? They've continued to neglect their teeth, despite their promises. Being in this particular psychological environment for years, well, it's definitely affected me. Instilled particular habits of mind.

Extract 3

M: Let me just read you a quotation from an oral history interview. It's from a man who as a child worked in the circus during the 19th century:

'Most children, their parents are proud when their kids grow. Not mine. One day my dad's measuring me for a new costume and discovers I've sprouted up. Oh my, does he curse. You see he's hoping I stay small, so it's easy to throw and catch me.'

Memorable, isn't it? You see, it's one thing to read facts and figures about the lives of working-class children a century ago; it's quite another to hear about it from someone first-hand. In their own voice. In their own words.

You see, at the end of the day, history consists of stories, and what stories get told and who gets to tell them is important. Traditional history courses usually only touch on major events – on the whos, whens and whats. Oral history brings depth to our understanding of the past, giving apparently peripheral characters a starring role. Through the exploration of their identities, we are drawn closer to their reality. And this tends to complicate the story a bit. It helps avoid the sort of sweeping generalisations that reinforce prejudice, stereotype people and overlook key variables in the historical context.

2.1

What made me want to write about travelling in the desert? I guess the short answer is that, after years of travel writing, I'd walked along so many tropical beaches and looked out at so many mountain views, and I was getting a bit tired of it all. Deserts sort of felt like the last frontier, you know? Over the past few years, I've been visiting and writing about deserts and today I'll share a bit about what I've learned.

Deserts are such special places. Where else can you see land so dry that it cracks? Or rock formations, formed by centuries of weathering and erosion, that are every bit, if not more, beautiful than the sculptures you find in art museums? For me, photos never do justice to a desert. You need to experience it for yourself. In the desert, even the sound of your own footsteps is different.

There are actually four main types of desert. Subtropical deserts are very hot and dry all year-round. Coastal deserts, on the other hand, have cool winters and warm summers. While in cold winter deserts, summers are long and dry and winters are extremely cold, in polar deserts, it's below freezing all year-round.

I must admit, before I started my research, I didn't know that the Arctic and Antarctica were deserts, but I now know that any place that receives less than 25 centimetres of precipitation a year counts as one – no matter how cold it is!

My most recent trip was to the Sahara – the most legendary and expansive of the subtropical deserts. After flying to Marrakech, I took a scenic 10-hour car ride into the desert. I had fallen asleep during the last leg of the journey and woke up just outside the town of Merzouga to views of the towering and majestic Erg Chebbi dunes. Soon I found myself on the back of a camel, walking slowly into the sands of the Sahara. That night I slept out in the open, under a sky full of stars.

Before going into the Sahara, I was warned to prepare carefully. Sunglasses, sun cream, extra water – any sensible person will bring these. But you'll also need specialised gear like wide-brimmed hats and hooded shirts that breathe well and provide UV protection. Long trousers are a must. They protect you from abrasion caused by camel fur, which is quite rough, but above all from local shrub brush that can easily pierce the skin.

When it comes to travelling in the desert, there's a lot to be said for layers. Bring like 20, I'd say. You begin piling them on in the evening, when temperatures drop quickly, and then start stripping them off at dawn. Oh, and don't forget a waterproof – night-time can get quite damp from the heavy dew.

One thing I didn't see much of in the Sahara was wildlife – apart from camels, of course. This is because most desert animals like beetles, hedgehogs and owls are nocturnal. On the last day of my trip, though, I did see a scorpion. I almost stepped on it – and it scared the life out of me!

There is one kind of desert animal that I love – a rare antelope called the addax. Their heads are marked with black patches, forming an 'X' over their noses, and they have scraggly beards and prominent red nostrils. Their spiral horns are strikingly beautiful. I'd love to see an addax on the trip I'm currently planning to the southern Sahara, but I may not get the chance. It is estimated that the current population living in the wild could be in the low hundreds, or possibly even less. Time will tell whether or not they can be saved.

Unfortunately, it's not just desert animals that are in danger these days but desert landscapes themselves. Recently I've been looking into 'desert greening,' where great swathes of land are irrigated intensely with the goal of growing crops, supposedly in the name of saving mankind from the climate crisis. This I don't like one bit. If there is one thing I've learned in my travels, it's that deserts are not barren wastelands, but rather places worth saving in their own right.

3.1

Speaker 1

Good training relies on objectivity. That's why baseball coaches like me were such early adopters of video analysis way back in the days of reel to reel. They came to depend on it in a big way. Review footage allowed them to praise or correct without bias. These days though it's a whole new ball game. You can create a database that accurately shows the progress your players have made – great for morale – and that's what got me into video analysis initially. The tech has a long way to go, though. There's still way too much fiddling about, endlessly moving things between different programmes and apps. And the ability to easily capture motion in 3D – now that would really be something.

Speaker 2

I bet most of you out there in the audience have never worked without email, but I have. Back then we welcomed email as a way to open up channels with business partners in faraway places. And how many trees we ended up saving when we reduced paper-based office correspondence, I can only imagine. But for most of us, the shine has thoroughly worn off. In the modern office, we take it for granted that a good chunk of our working day will be dedicated to emptying our inboxes, like people bailing out a leaky lifeboat. Our very sanity is under attack, and every day the deluge continues with no solution in sight. People today talk about 'techno-stress.' I'd say, in all likelihood, email is one of the main culprits.

Speaker 3

I don't know what I'd do without the software and that worries me a bit. And I do see the ethical issues people have with police like me using facial recognition tools to identify suspects. But, at the end of the day, it's just another tool. It might be less time consuming to track people down, but the technology is susceptible to error and doesn't replace traditional police work. It's not as if computers are solving crimes in seconds all by themselves. People who think that have watched too much TV. I will say, however, that police themselves have not been immune to this sort of wishful thinking, which is one of the reasons why we demanded access to the software and quickly embraced it.

Speaker 4

This year we took the plunge and installed crop sensors around the farm. The goal is to decrease leaching and runoff into groundwater, but the technology should create other knock-on effects. The sensors can communicate information about the level of moisture present at certain depths in the soil, which means I can save time and money by making adjustments to my irrigation systems on the spot from a phone or computer instead of driving to each field. In theory, anyway. To be honest, the whole system is still a bit temperamental, and the farm is seriously lacking when it comes to connectivity infrastructure, but I'm sure these are just bumps in the road.

Speaker 5

Like most of my patients, I was wary of virtual visits at the outset. I saw it as yet another decision aimed at improving the hospital's bottom line that would come at the expense of patient care, which it undoubtedly was, but with time – what do you know? – I've come to embrace it. Talking to people on a computer has obvious limitations, but if your ailment is minor, say a fever, cough or cold, I can offer decent care from a distance. And virtual visits are so much more convenient for underprivileged patients, who sometimes don't have access to transport or are unable to leave their homes. Plus, I like how quickly I can check in with my patients, just to see how they're getting on.

3.3

I = Interviewer P = Professor
W = Woman M = Man

Extract 1

I: Professor Yavuz, what first attracted you to blended learning?

P: Well, going back nearly 20 years, I was working as an associate lecturer, teaching on a module designed to inspire creative entrepreneurship, and I had an unusual group – or at least that's what I thought at the time. Attendance at lectures was dreadful but the students would turn in brilliant work and respond instantly to any email I sent. This was a real 'aha moment' for me. These days, emerging talent has different expectations, but we're still trying to lure students into traditionally structured courses because it's more effective for our institutions. This experience made me think outside the box and consider what parts of the course might work better online.

I: Is it hard to get the balance right?

P: The principles of blended learning are largely in place now: a large part of the material is still learned synchronously, through what we call 'contact moments,' i.e. in class, while much of the preparation and processing happens asynchronously, essentially freeing up space for higher-quality interaction during those contact moments. The exact ratio is dynamic, however. There are didactic factors to consider but also practical ones like available technology, the intensity of the course, predetermined student competencies and needs, and so on.

Extract 2

W: It's not hard to see why the electronic spreadsheet has been such a hit. Imagine writing down individual numbers by hand in rows and columns across the double spread of an A2 ledger. The electronic spreadsheet has made it infinitely easier to manipulate data, in the process wiping out millions of jobs for desk clerks and giving birth to the world of modern finance. The problem is, though, that we have become so enchanted with spreadsheets, they've become a curse.

For example, back at my first data analyst gig, I was tasked with creating a tool to track and analyse the performance of my company's suppliers. A spreadsheet was the natural choice, but once the team started using the file in their daily workflow it quickly became bloated and burdensome to use. Sound familiar? But that's not all: as the operations got more complex, with formulas referencing other formulas – sometimes incorrectly – it got harder to trace back how some calculations were being performed. I've since learned that there are programming languages that allow for a more systematic manner of performing analytics, making it much easier to troubleshoot, and that data can be stored more sustainably through SQL databases, where it can be queried in a centralised location.

Extract 3

M: Lobsters have developed a remarkable way of seeing the world. Their eyes are mounted on long stalks and each eyeball is made up of thousands of tapered square tubes. Unlike a human eye, which relies on 'refraction' or the bending of light, a lobster's eye reflects tiny amounts of light from a wide viewing area and then focuses them into a single image. Outside of their natural habitat, lobsters are effectively blind, but in the dark murky water at the bottom of the sea they can spot predators without so much as moving their heads.

What does all this have to do with space, you might be wondering? Well, scientists have copied the design of the crustacean's eye to create a new type of telescope that can monitor a wider section of the sky. With this brilliantly innovative technology, still in the works, scientists aim to detect X-rays emitted by marvellously rare events in the cosmos – the sort of fleeting, hard-to-capture energy unleashed when neutron stars or black holes collide. These are hard to find because we don't know their location in advance. But a lobster's eye telescope, whose 'eye' is curved and dotted with tiny tubes, could be able to pick up X-rays coming from a wide variety of angles. Who would have ever thought a lobster would help us see into space?

4.1

I = Interviewer H = Hanya
J = Jeffery

I: Welcome to the programme. Today our guests are the sociologists Hanya Richardson and Jeffery Walsh, who study friendship. Hanya, friendships too easily fall by the wayside in adulthood, don't they?

H: They do indeed. In the research for our book, we found that people make the most friends between the ages of fifteen and twenty-five, and then, try as we might to keep up with people, our friendship circles shrink as we move into adulthood. We become engrossed in our careers. We get married, have kids. We might even end up relocating for one reason or another. In our daily lives, we're still surrounded by people, of course, but they are in the same position as ourselves – busy, short on energy and free time.

J: We have fewer friends as adults, but not usually by choice. One study found that the average adult won't have made a new friend in the last five years, even though about half would have liked to.

H: And so the question is, how can we fill this friendship gap? It's a bit of an uphill battle, as we all know. It can take between forty and sixty hours to develop a casual friendship. But of course it's also possible to spend hundreds and hundreds of hours with someone and think of them as just a workmate or an acquaintance.

I: So, what else can be done to turn these everyday encounters into real friendships?

J: Most of us, we assume friends will just sort of fall into our lives, and it's not entirely unreasonable that we should make this assumption, because it fits with the way many of the friendships developed when we were younger. Back then, we were stuck in the same building with lots of potential friends, and it was as simple as going through shared experiences. As adults, we have to put ourselves out there a bit more.

H: And it can't be a one-off thing. It's not enough to go to just the one networking meeting. Better to look for a professional development group. Don't go to a book lecture; look for a book club.

I: What about those of us who find it hard to relax and be ourselves around people who we don't know?

J: That's very common, and it's often due to a cognitive bias known as the 'liking gap.' This describes people's tendency to underestimate the degree to which they are liked by strangers they interact with.

H: Like it or not, to make new friends, we simply have to get used to those small bouts of anxiety that come from engaging with new people. All too often we resort to overt or covert avoidance strategies, like looking at our phone or playing with the host's pet. We ought not to let ourselves fall into this common trap. By trying to protect ourselves from rejection, by limiting our eagerness or enthusiasm, we only make the chances of rejection more likely. Other people, after all, are just as afraid of getting the brush off as we are.

I: So let's say you meet someone you really click with. What then?

H: Here also a bit of courage can pay dividends. We sometimes get too caught up in our own heads about who chose to invite whom to do what when, and whose turn it is now. But the truth is there are a lot of people out there who really appreciate being asked but are really terrible at asking. It's normal to worry about being clingy, but we probably underestimate that nice-to-be-wanted feeling that people get when you pick them to spend time with.

J: And, to fast forward a bit, once a friendship is established, if or when things don't live up to our expectations, we shouldn't get too hung up about it. Because they won't. People need the space to be imperfect. With friends, it's best to avoid resentment and reserve judgement when life gets in the way.

I: Speaking of tough times, these days there is a school of thought that says we should ditch one-sided friendships and take better care of ourselves. Hanya, what's your take on that?

H: So, I wouldn't advise anyone to be friends with a person who actively does things to hurt them. But this kind of self-focused attitude, you know, avoiding toxic people and all that – it muscles out the reality that we're all imperfect. Friends need us most when they're acting poorly and not thinking about the consequences. True, it can be tough when a friend is doing all the talking and you're doing all the listening. But they still deserve your respect and attention. And you know what? In the long run, it's actually very good for us to stick through other people's struggles. It's how we become better people.

4.4

Hello. My name is Samira Joshi and I've been asked to come here and talk to you about my job as a professional mediator. Workplace mediation, in a nutshell, is an informal way of resolving employment-related disputes. It involves a mediator, like me, acting as an impartial third party, who facilitates a meeting between two or more people in conflict.

When considering mediation, there is no need for a company to take seniority into account, but voluntary agreement from both parties, on the other hand, is essential. Without this commitment to proceed, the mediation process is not really worth pursuing.

Workplace mediation is by no means a panacea, but it can be an effective way of dealing with many common workplace issues, including relationship breakdown, personality clashes, miscommunication and so on. In my experience, though, it's workplace incivility that company representatives most often mention when they contract my services. This could involve any kind of behaviour with an intent to harm, with social undermining on the low end of the spectrum and bullying on the more serious end.

Generally speaking, mediation is a chance to resolve disputes without resorting to legal processes or disciplinary action or, ultimately, dismissal. Ideally, it's better to mediate a conflict at the beginning – that can avoid escalation – but even if a conflict is well entrenched and employees have, say, resorted to sick leave to escape anxiety generated in the workplace, mediation can still be an effective way to get them back at their desks.

So what does the mediation process look like in practice? Well, in the first stage, I meet with each individual in separate rooms. Everything said here is completely confidential; note-taking is usually fine, but recording devices are generally prohibited. My job here is to actively listen while each party walks me through their experience of the dispute. This helps me wrap my head around the key issues. Here flip charts are a mediator's best friend. They're a great place to brainstorm ideas.

In the second stage, called the facilitated joint meeting, both sides come together and try to settle their differences. I act as facilitator, first letting each side say their piece – with no interruptions – and then I lead a discussion of the key aspects of the dispute. Here mediators need to keep a close eye on pace, because the goal is to reach a mutually acceptable solution on the day. At the same time, though, we need to be led by the parties in terms of what they are ready to discuss. It's a delicate balance.

Particularly during this second stage, emotional intelligence is crucial, I think. To excel in this profession, you really have to be able to understand not just what people are saying but also what they aren't saying – listening between the lines, so to speak. Good problem-solving skills also come in handy, not to mention lots of patience. You might think of these competencies as innate, but in my experience it's possible to develop and greatly improve them over time.

On a personal note, I've long thought the key to successful mediation is to get people to move away from the past – that is, their grievances and obsessed-over life experiences – and focus on the future. This sort of subtle alteration in mindset can be hard to achieve but is ultimately very powerful.

All right, so, if the first two steps of the process have gone well, we then move into the final stage, where I prepare a written agreement for both parties to sign up to. Everyone involved has to not only agree to the statement, but also to share responsibility for its enactment. It's important to note that this agreement is morally, but not legally binding.

Talking of legal questions, I should mention that whether or not the mediation process succeeds or fails – and every so often it does fail – the entire process is what lawyers would call 'without prejudice,' meaning that if an employee wants to go on and pursue an employment tribunal, for example, they can take their case straight on and don't have to worry about any information from the mediation process being disclosed.

So, before I move on, I thought this would be a good time to open the floor to any questions you might have ... [fade]

5.3

Speaker 1

Still to this day, I can't believe it happened. I wanted to visit my uncle in Australia, and *there was this flight* I saw online that was a bargain. To be fair, I was in a rush and the kids were playing up, so I suppose I only had one eye on what I was doing. We didn't even realise the error until we were on the plane... to Sydney Nova Scotia, Canada! It took both me and my wife a while to find the funny side – but we made the best of it, and spent three weeks there, seeing the area. Obviously, our luggage was completely unsuitable. We'd packed for 30 degrees and ended up in around 0 degrees! But it was a trip to remember!

Speaker 2

I still feel like an idiot when I think back to this. I'd generally consider myself quite bright, which is why when I read this story about someone falling out of a plane and surviving, due to a *type of cloud*, I was amazed! Apparently, it was particularly dense, and I'm no scientist, so I took it as read. Anyway, I was telling this to people for years – always ending with an exclamation like 'Isn't it incredible?' or something like that. It turns out it is incredible, because it's simply not true. I checked it years later only to realise that the lucky survivor had a parachute. I must've misread the article all those years ago. Mortifying! I still wonder how many people are telling *that ridiculous 'fact' of mine*... simply because of my stupidity!

Speaker 3

In my job, communication is key and I'm often flying around the world. Well one day, I was in Japan interpreting for an important US dignitary who for some unknown reason decided to go off-script and make a joke in a bid to get everybody on side. It's so hard to plan for *those sorts of deviations*, and the joke just couldn't work in Japanese at all, so I had to think on my feet. I told the audience 'Mr Shephard told a funny story. Everybody please laugh now.' And thankfully they did! Although I did get some looks from the dignitary himself who asked me what I'd said as it was far shorter than his joke. I had to come clean about it and thankfully he saw the funny side!

Speaker 4

I used to work as a runner on a news show... this basically means running around helping out and being a general dogsbody. I was straight out of college and was completely out of my depth to be honest. One day, we had someone who was going to be interviewed for a slot about industrial waste. I ran into reception and saw a guy sitting there. 'Are you here for the interview?' He nodded his head, so I had him miked up and ready within 10 minutes. But the interview was really strange. It was like he didn't know the first thing about industrial waste. It was only after that I found out here was in the building for a job interview, not to talk about environmental problems on the TV! Needless to say, I didn't last long there.

Speaker 5

Back in the day, I volunteered at a local community organisation. They would put on talks and events, mainly to keep retired people busy. Anyway, it was when one of these events was being organised... on local history as I remember, and the organiser mentioned that 'Enis and Margaret were doing the slide show'. Well, I was dumbfounded! *Princess Margaret* doing the slide show?! What a coup! I diligently spread the word, totally unaware that I had got the wrong end of the stick. *Well, that error of mine* caused the biggest turnout they'd ever had! And probably the most disappointed audience too. To be honest, I did think it was a little out of the ordinary, I mean, why would a member of the royal family turn up in our village to talk about local history!?

5.4

M = Man W = Woman

Conversation 1

M: Did you hear what happened to Katie?

W: No, what's that? Spill the beans!

M: Well, I'm not really sure I should really.

W: Come on! Don't beat around the bush! Tell me!

M: Well... she's been fired from her job!

W: Katie?! No way...but she's normally so responsible. What did she do?

M: I'm not totally sure. It was news to me! And probably to her too!

Conversation 2

W: When you send the agenda out, can you let me know please?

M: I've already done it – I thought it was ready.

W: Oh no! I had to make some tweaks to it. Well, don't worry, I think we probably got our wires crossed. I wanted you to just double check it.

M: Oh, I'm sorry.

W: Don't worry. Can you make sure the catering is all organised? I think it's going to be a long meeting if you catch my drift...

M: Yes, there are some quite difficult items on the agenda.

W: Still, it will be nice to catch up with all the other department heads...

6.1

W = Woman J = Jacob Z = Zandra
I = Interviewer N = Nick

Extract one

W: Provided that you don't want to earn a fortune, the job is great. I mean the hours are not for everyone, you're on duty from the crack of dawn until whenever the clients want, but if they're good people, and you get the right captain, being First Officer is not a bad job at all. You're responsible for supporting the captain and offering those extra touches that really make the difference and guarantee the onboard experience is second to none, which I find really fulfilling. Not to mention the fact that you get to sail these amazing vessels in some spectacular locations.

The downside is that the number of good crewing jobs has plummeted in recent years, largely due to the soaring costs of fuel. The knock-on effect has been that a lot of people have realised that they're paying through the nose for their hobby and that it's no longer financially viable. People generally think that yacht owners are rolling in it, but you'd be surprised. Most people are drawn to them for the same reason as me – they love sailing, not the flashy lifestyle that people associate with them. And of course, the range of crafts is vast so anyone can own one if they want, even if their budget isn't enormous.

Extract two

Z: I really wish I had a job that allowed me to travel more. Sitting in that office all day, with a view of the car park is so depressing, it's like life is passing me by.

J: We're all in the same boat here though. It doesn't look like any of us is going to quit and have a massive career change any time soon, does it?!

Z: Hey! thanks for the vote of confidence. I guess no one knows what's around the corner.

J: True. Supposing your job was remote, like a digital nomad, so all you need is a laptop and your passport and you're good to go. Where would you go?

Z: Um, well, so long as money were no object and I could afford to come back and see my family as and when I wanted, I think I'd opt for a village in the mountains. I wouldn't want to be too isolated, but I've always wondered what it would be like to just pack up and move on whenever you fancied a change.

J: Mmm, I can see this working for you, but I suspect I'm in my comfort zone workwise. I can't see me moving on anytime soon.

Extract three

I: So, Nick Morgan personal finance advisor at Life & Futures always gives us some real food for thought on making our money go further on everyday expenses, but there's something that he's keen to talk about in more detail today. Over to you Nick.

N: Thanks, Jess. Okay, well, I've been getting some emails from listeners asking for advice about what to do in the event that an unexpected expense arose. These happen far more frequently than you might imagine, and even if you don't earn plenty of money, it's not that hard to future-proof your finances in order to give you some peace of mind. Or at the very least feel like you're somewhat prepared. Just putting aside a small amount per week would mean you'd build up a large enough nest egg soon enough in case of any nasty surprises. Then there won't be any stress or panic if, for instance, a household appliance breaks down without warning.

I: Yes, I see what you mean. Squirrelling money away little and often could help make sure life ticks along a lot more smoothly.

N: Indeed. When it comes to money, we want our resources to gradually swell over time as opposed to everything being a rollercoaster. And this really just comes down to being sensible. Unfortunately, there's no magic bullet here.

6.3

When it comes to work, we humans have always been tempted to shun hard graft in favour of earning a quick buck for no real effort. Some of these get-rich-quick schemes are nefarious scams selling products of dubious quality. Some could even be described as downright criminal, such as asking people to invest in non-existent companies. But in recent years a more wholesome variety has emerged. Enter the side hustle. Essentially this is just a second job, but it has morphed into an attitude towards life for many, or perhaps even an extension of their identity.

The phrase was coined in the 1950s but it wasn't until the early 21st century that it really took off with the rise of the internet and the gig economy. They presented opportunities for entrepreneurship that many people hadn't previously considered and enabled those with a pioneering spirit to capitalise on their untapped creative skills and talents.

Many of these side hustles combine the internet and creativity: online stores selling thousands of items of jewellery or hand-crafted kitchenware, millennials posting hours of videos on cosmetic techniques, the list is endless. To be honest, much of the creative output is mediocre at best which then begs the question of why people are willing to spend countless hours trying to grow a side hustle, yet they seem incapable of devoting the same energy levels to their career in marketing or retail. After all, one brings clear and obvious paths to increased wealth over time whereas the prospect of an actual, sustainable income from the other is far lower.

But the tantalising promise of being master of your own destiny seems to have much more appeal for some. There's that famous quote that gets attributed to various philosophers which claims that if you choose a job you love, you'll never work a day in your life, the implication being that doing something you love will bring more meaning to your life or to your career. This is in contrast to jobs that feel more burdensome because they don't spark a sense of feeling joy even if they come with a hefty pay check.

Added to that is the sheer number of online videos about 'how I made millions from such and such a hobby'. It is quite astonishing to see how content of this type has soared as well as the number of hits that some of these videos get. This relentless promotion of working for yourself from these self-styled business experts that claim to have foolproof ways for all of us to make millions out of our hobbies is real clickbait.

What I want to know though is whether or not side hustles are too good to be true? When you think about the number of hours people are putting into these side hustles, one wonders whether they would be better off channelling their energy elsewhere in their lives.

It turns out that there are three main categories of side hustle. One is freelancing, that is selling your professional skills to companies for a fee determined by yourself. This is nothing new, but with the rise of online working, these people are able to be digital nomads. The key to earning power is in the words 'professional skills'. Contrast that with the gig workers delivering food or using the family vehicle as a taxi. These people sit at the bottom of the side hustle ladder when it comes to income and do not get a snappy job title. Their existence serves as a reminder of how the idea of a side hustle being something desirable rather than necessary has been co-opted by tech start-ups and large corporations. Finally there is the entrepreneur who creates a scalable business from scratch and represents the ideal of this whole concept – while the risks may be high, the carrot of greater rewards is forever present and achievable for a few.

7.1

I = Interviewer H = Helena
A = Anthony

I: Today, we're talking to acclaimed film director, Antony Murphy, and Helena Fitzpatrick, an expert on psychology of film and lecturer at Central University. Both masters of mystery in their own way today, we hope to unlock the secret of why people love a mystery so much and what tricks are used to keep viewers hooked. So, Antony, some people call you the master of this genre, tell us how you keep the audience on the edge of their seats...

A: Well, in my films, there's one thing I want to give the audience, and that's suspense... that anticipation you have right before something happens. To get that as film-makers we've always got to keep something back and make the audience keep guessing what happens. We don't need to draw this out, it can be done in short sharp shocks. Think of a door opening – it's not the end result that excites us, it's the potential threat lingering behind that door.

I: And what makes us enjoy that so much Helena? It's not exactly pleasant, is it?

H: Well, science shows that this kind of suspense gives humans a physical pay-off too. When we watch a suspenseful film, we're actually micro-dosing ourselves with neurological signals that would be activated in a real-life emergency. This gives us a rush, but in controlled conditions, because thankfully we're highly unlikely to have to cope with the conditions we see on screen, and in the cold light of day, we know that too.

A: Yes, and these rushes should happen at set moments throughout a film too... and in the overall story arc. In films, you can't just rely on the story to create this effect. Music, lighting, timing all ramp up the tension. Film-makers are an old hand at using these effects these days, but sometimes they fall flat by over-maximising these tense moments, which can stop the audience caring. You've got to keep the stakes high ... know that the character might well end up in grave peril and hope they don't. The excitement can be tangible. Thrillers are THE genre that makes suspense such an incredible experience, and we as film-makers have got to be careful not to waste it. It's a whole other ball game from other genres like mystery books, and their film adaptations. And I imagine the psychology is quite different too.

H: Mmm, it is. Although there is one common strand for both experiencing mystery AND suspense. Both offer a way to be absorbed by something that is far away from our own worries and this is what people enjoy in general, but whereas the audience are generally all squirming through a suspenseful film, with something like a detective novel, there is far less of that and much more mulling over all the possibilities. People tend to be attuned to information related to survival, and in a way trying to solve a mystery is a subconscious effort to hone this skill. Along with this is our inherent desire to know all the facts. That's also what keeps us hanging on with a mystery novel.

A: It's got to be quite tricky to write that kind of story, because the main event has usually happened before the start, and the whole story is the unravelling of the truth. It's a completely different approach to how we as film directors work in general.

I: And do you think that mystery and suspense ever has a negative side psychologically?

H: Well, yes, and one that's relatively novel. It's the rise of on-demand, series, or seasons as we now nearly ubiquitously call them. Watching a series like that can be quite a stressful activity. In the days of terrestrial shows, it was easy enough to avoid a spoiler, because each episode was aired at a certain time. Now, you can binge everything in one night, and spoil it for others around you sometimes unwittingly. Even if someone is just ahead of you, the speculation of who could or couldn't have been the culprit, suddenly becomes terrifying. I've inadvertently done it to other people and it drives me up the wall when someone does it to me... It's not generally a conscious activity. People sometimes try to avoid this kind of frustration by trying to steer clear of social media, and the overpicking of ideas, and even sometimes their friends, just in case they stumble across what's going to happen. As a psychologist, I would say that's not a particularly healthy recourse of action, but I think it's a very common one.

8.1

Speaker 1

Understandably, my job involves paperwork. It's vital that before any new requests for solar panels to be put on public buildings or offices are given the go ahead, the application has no legal loopholes. If companies get things right at this stage, it's far more likely that the permissions will be granted quickly further down the line. It stops the painfully slow progress of applications that we used to see. Before, after several months people would get requests for more documents and still be no further along in the process. Over the last couple of years there's been a marked increase in those that we've authorised. I get a real kick out of being able to tell companies that their project has been given the green light straight away.

Speaker 2

Rewilding projects are becoming more popular these days. But I'm constantly amazed at how many people are bitterly opposed to them around here. I'm forever getting emails from people in the local community who don't like the idea of leaving nature alone – which is what rewilding is all about after all. Unfortunately, all they see is a blot on the landscape, and trying to explain the environmental benefits to them doesn't make the slightest difference. Nonetheless, I'm firmly committed to the cause. I've noticed that in the last few talks I've given at the town hall, more people seem to be coming around to the idea, so at least that's a start.

Speaker 3

The national park suffers from a lot of forest fires, and prevention is our main focus of attention. Managing the ecosystem here is a delicate balance of a variety of strategies for all the team and I am involved in considering where the budget goes. It's a lot of analysis but it's never wasted as the insights I get help us decide how to use what we've got and where, so we get the most out of it. The only issue is that climatic conditions are so changeable these days that we have to review everything year on year. Often there are a couple of overriding concerns though and that helps with the decision making.

Speaker 4

Here at the Nature Society, we carry out a series of surveys every year to determine how well the local bird and mammal populations are managing in woodland habitats. Once I've laid out the objectives, the team gets to work. The scientific side of things is far beyond me I'm afraid, but my team are as competent a group as you'd find in any university research department. During the course of the surveys, the team works in conjunction with a local wildlife group. That's a real advantage because it gives us more eyes on the ground so to speak. They are genuinely concerned about the local wildlife and their data has been invaluable in informing a lot of what we do over the years.

Speaker 5

I don't know whether many people would find my job particularly stimulating, but I enjoy working on complex problems. And to be honest, figuring out how to reduce air pollution is tantamount to figuring out the size of the universe! I'm often in touch with the council. They provide me with all sorts of statistics and reports on air quality, as does the environment agency. In return, they get our insights on the most effective measures for the community as a whole. We ruled out pedestrianising the city centre last year in favour of congestion charging. Although highly controversial at the time, it has proved itself to be the better decision by a long way.

8.2

So, today I want to focus on the issue of household waste and when I say that, I mean the appliances and gadgets which we can no longer live without and the utterly disastrous effects that this throwaway culture we live in is having on the environment.

The problem of electronic or 'e-waste' is one that has been building up significantly and now we desperately need to get to grips with it as part of the ongoing fight against climate change. I would go as far as to say that we are currently living in what is tantamount to the era of waste rather than the era of technology since the world economy is, to a large extent, dependent upon it. The cycle of production, use and waste is constant and is repeated across almost all industries.

Even so, I want to stress that humans are not wasteful by nature. In fact, until very recently, (relatively speaking) the way in which humans were able to forage for food and materials from their surroundings, the way they would fashion rocks, wood, metal and what have you into reusable tools that could improve their lives, can best be described as extraordinarily resourceful. Part of this was due to having to use what was available locally, whereas today, innovations in transportation, which have dramatically sped up international trade, allow us to access materials easily and as a result, create and consume more.

It wasn't until the birth of the modern consumer lifestyle in the mid-20th century that we became passive over-consumers instead of active makers and menders. And yet here we are a few decades later in a world where most of the world's gold reserves can be found not underground as had always been the case, but in the vast number of electronic devices already in existence.

Now, let's talk about how modern products are made. Part of the problem these days comes down to a concept known as planned obsolescence, a modern term which refers to the idea of forcing customers to buy replacements by making products which are bound to fall to pieces after a short time, and which are difficult to repair. The rise of large factories and the rapid growth of corporations competing for a share of the market drove companies to sell things at cheaper rates too, thereby making it far less important for people to maintain their possessions as they could easily afford to go out and get a new one. This trend became especially prevalent in small consumer electronics and led us to the state we are in with e-waste.

Planned obsolescence is not a new phenomenon, but over the last couple of decades it has become more widespread, so much so that in France there is now a law which states that manufacturers must provide clear information on how to repair products. This is mostly due to the success of a company that started publishing free online instructions for repairing household products such as laptops and washing machines and who put pressure on governments to amend laws to remove planned obsolescence.

The future of electronic waste may well be based on a wholesale change in materials and processes. Using completely different materials is as attractive as upping the amount we recycle. For instance, rather than investing in ways of dealing with hazardous byproducts from devices, scientists and engineers are exploring ways to make some components from natural materials so that they either biodegrade or can be dismantled easily via a method known as e-processing. This means that materials could be artificially grown and that destruction of natural habitats in order to extract metals could become a thing of the past. Currently the list of viable options for more sustainable manufacturing includes plants such as hemp, bamboo and seaweed all of which have a range of advantages over mined materials. Researchers are really excited about the future – they are convinced that the materials science and engineering are the key to improving the e-waste situation and bringing in a new era.

9.1

Architecture has an aim that diverges from art at some level because it involves pushing the boundaries of what it is physically possible to make when something has to be functional as well as aesthetically pleasing on such a vast scale. As such it presents far greater opportunities to shock and surprise, at times being a real eye opener into the creativity of the human mind. A quick glance around the world's most renowned buildings – be they ancient or modern – will confirm that the architects of these kinds of landmark buildings are extremely single-minded people, dead set on leaving behind some kind of legacy project or grand statement that might earn them a reputation for all eternity.

If I were to ask you to illustrate this point, no doubt you'd come up with some classics – the Colosseum in Rome, the Guggenheim in Bilbao, the Sydney Opera House, the list goes on. But these buildings all have one common function in that they're designed for pleasure and entertainment and, as a genre, have been reimagined and reworked over and over. However, what we're going to home in on today, is the lowly office building, where many of us spend our days. As we will see, this is an area where architects have really blazed a new trail. The eye-watering costs of these buildings are clearly beyond all but the most ambitious or wealthy organisations and therefore it is no surprise that many are located in financial districts in capital cities.

It is worth noting that these have been met with mixed reviews.

Take Lloyd's of London – considered by some to be the first step into innovative workplace architecture. Opened in 1986, its pioneering high-tech architecture can be seen in the fact that the building's services – including lifts, water pipes and staircases, are actually located on the building's exterior, opening up the interior and creating a space of breath-taking proportions. It reimagined what an office space could look like. However, with the plans having been drawn up with attention to function rather than form, it is perhaps unsurprising that the initial reception could be described as lukewarm at best. It was variously nicknamed an oil rig and a motorbike engine with some even going so far as to call it an eyesore. However, over the years the building has been embraced, being seen as iconic and a game changer of its time. In fact, it was granted Grade I building protection, affording it the same elite status as other key buildings and monuments in England, such as Buckingham Palace, the Royal Albert Hall and Nelson's Column.

Another fascinating example for us to look at is the F&F building, in Panama City, completed in 2011. And look, it is in the shape of a corkscrew. What is particularly intriguing to note, is that the spiral design actually started out as merely a theoretical project by the architect company, but despite not having been intended as an actual building, it caught the eye of one the company's clients and the decision was taken to go ahead with this design. The building is covered in glass and so appears to shimmer in the sunlight and is really eye-catching. It is also remarkable insofar as its budget was relatively low for a building of this magnitude – $50 million. Again, opinions are divided on its appeal, although this could be down to the fact that a considerable amount of the space has not been able to be rented out, so for some, it might be deemed a waste of money.

These buildings seem to have been more controversial than their cultural counterparts that I mentioned earlier like the Guggenheim, and these could also be described as not fitting everyone's ideas of great design, although it's not altogether clear why this should be. Anyway, both these buildings are definitely imposing, intended to communicate the expertise of their designers in addition to the success and dominance of the companies that are located in them.

Let's now compare those with this one which I'd say is much more whimsical – the office of the National Fisheries Board of India in the city of Hyderabad, which was based on Frank Gehry's Golden Fish in Barcelona, although it possesses none of his trademark flowing design and is instead an altogether more simple representation of a fish. Motives for a design like this? Well, I suppose it offers employees who would otherwise be stuck working in some bland, nondescript government building an element of fun, or perhaps a topic for the watercooler, but I wonder what you think of this. Do you think its novelty value will wear off in the future? Is it liable to date quickly and require a revamp or replacement?

9.2

1. At some level architecture has an aim that diverges from art.
2. so, instead of showcasing a building that might earn its designers both money and a good reputation, it could be deemed a waste of money.

9.4

O = Olga E = Edward

O: So, the working life of a reproduction artist must be quite rewarding? I mean, having a studio chock full of masterpieces from throughout the ages – is it like being immersed in the sum of all western art day in day out?

E: At times you could say so, and while I know it does sound fantastically creative and a bit risqué, it's driven by the tastes of my clients who mostly tend to commission typically populist things, which essentially can be quite dull. You know, those paintings which despite having been lauded by critics over the years are actually not that difficult to do – between you and me I can knock out a Klimt or a Monet in no time, but I'd far rather be presented with something that I could get my teeth into a bit more, something very technically demanding that needs some real thought put into it.

O: Yes, I can totally see where you're coming from. Essentially, it's like when people ask me to stick a vase back together that's just some old family heirloom with only sentimental value. It's hardly a ringing endorsement of my finely honed technical skills. What I really want is to have someone bring me something which entails getting out my microscope and chemical testing kit, not a tube of super glue.

E: For me, the bottom line is people just want to look at a painted version of their favourite painting, because of the kudos of having an actual piece of art in the house, even if there were no way it could be an original. The whole technical prowess part of my job doesn't interest the average buyer either. Then it all becomes more of a chore than a pleasure since, like you, I don't feel like I'm being stretched – it's more like a paint by numbers gig and now and again I feel like telling them to get a print offline.

O: I can imagine! My situation is slightly different in that I'm more embedded within large organisations. They can be pedantic in their requirements, but a technical challenge is almost always there. Especially when working with pigments that have a complex, historical and lengthy production process or certain types of canvas.

E: And how do you go about the research for something like that? How much leeway are you given in terms of time allocated and where do you even start?

O: Well, often I'm part of a team working on a collection and at the outset there'll be at least one art historian and a chemist or forensic art expert tasked with working this out. Sometimes we work to deadlines, but more often than not it's contingent on the problems we uncover as we go along. Working out how to cope with something we hadn't foreseen can mean the deadline goes out the window. For large museums and country houses or palaces, getting it right is paramount so actually they're usually quite generous. The objects restored have to be historically accurate before they are allowed to go on display to the public.

E: Mmm. I see. I'm not sure I'd be any good at heading up that kind of project, I wouldn't like to be constantly juggling so many bits and pieces, but the team aspect sounds nice. As it stands my job can be a bit solitary – you know, isolated up in the studio for hours on end, not that I'm complaining. I'm not sure I want someone around all the time, but I'd often quite like to be able to get someone to cast an eye over what I'm doing when I'm painting something like a Rembrandt. You have to painstakingly layer on the colours and gradually build it up – it's quite time-consuming and tiring and you can lose focus if you're not careful. Obviously, you have the option of going back and correcting what you've done but I find that disrupts my flow.

O: Yes, I see what you mean. With what I do, there's quite a lot of stop start since we're working on small parts of a painting rather than the whole thing at once. It's vital to regularly step away from the microscope to check what we're doing fits in with the work, and we haven't accidentally made a section look out of place. Anyway, going back to the time issue, what about your clients – do they have reasonable expectations as to what is achievable in their timeframe? How do you go about managing this?

E: I have a fairly reliable approach actually, which always works, which is to meet with the customer and talk through timescales and prices, but I have an ace up my sleeve! I show them three examples of the same painting – one which took a couple of days to complete and the others which took a couple of weeks and a month respectively. They soon get the picture so to speak.

10.1

Speaker 1

The recording should have been straightforward since we'd contracted an experienced freelancer, so we only had the studio for two days. The author, some up-and-coming novelist who was on the radar of the literary magazines, decided she wanted to come to the recording, which I thought would be a nice touch. Well, it was an utter disaster; she kept interrupting the voice artist to explain how she wanted certain lines delivered. This obviously didn't go down well, and they went back and forth bickering about it for hours. At the end of day one, we'd barely even finished the first chapter. I had no one to blame except myself though and next time I won't get carried away with any notions of bringing people together to collaborate on an audiobook and will just get it done.

Speaker 2

I had reservations at the outset to be honest. The network had gotten itself all worked up about a movie version of Gina Lee's latest novel and asked me to write the screenplay. I suppose I was flattered even though it was a daunting task to say the least. Anyway, one day, all of a sudden, production halted, and we were all sent home. Only later did I discover that they'd gone way over budget on the CGI and the investors had pulled out so, the whole thing was shelved. But at least I now know that, were I to ever get asked to be involved in something similar, I should just walk away – it's not worth the stress regardless of any promises of potential box office fortunes.

Speaker 3

Had I known how it would end up, I would have definitely approached things differently. It turns out that subtitling is actually really technical, but we wanted to avoid having to hire a load of dubbing actors. With all the characters in the film, it would have taken forever and been incompatible with our schedules. And the production team was pretty bilingual, so we went with subtitling instead, thinking it would be way less effort. But it soon became apparent that there's much more to it than meets the eye. Subtitling is all about where you split the sentences to fit logical sections on to the screen so that people can follow what's going on, but with these never-ending monologues from some of the characters it was a nightmare and we had to get some actual closed caption specialists in to review everything at the last minute, which was unimaginably stressful.

Speaker 4

Never have I been involved in such a disastrous film adaptation of a book. As the lead scriptwriter I should have been more outspoken and dismissed their suggestions out of hand. I know that there's a place for artistic licence, but I should have stood my ground. I tried to warn the production team not to cast an actor with blond hair if they didn't want to alienate the legions of fans loyal to the book. For them the protagonist's flaming red hair is fundamental to his character. Then, inexplicably, they decided to omit the part where he abandons his homeland, the very part that drives most of the narrative. Instead, they gave the film a romantic slant for reasons best known to themselves. It's not surprising it bombed spectacularly at the box office.

Speaker 5

We wanted to stimulate good discussions amongst professionals in order to get the most accurate translation, so we had our translators work in mini groups of three for each language. We expected them to self-manage and were pretty hands off at the beginning. What we did not predict however, was such vastly different team dynamics and so our schedule went out the window as some teams got on with it while others went round in circles. Anyway, we acted fast and got two of our in-house project managers to step in and impose some kind of order. No sooner had they started coordinating the discussions than the production schedule got back on track, and we managed to publish the translations simultaneously in China, Brazil, Germany and Turkey.

10.3

1 Only later did I discover that they'd gone way over budget on the CGI.
2 Had I known how it would end up, I would have definitely approached things differently.
3 Never have I been involved in such a disastrous film adaptation of a book.
4 No sooner had they started coordinating the discussions than the production schedule got back on track.

10.4

S = Stefan C = Carla

S: As I see it, reading is the most valuable skill we can give our children. It's fundamental to getting on in life and I'm a firm believer in parents taking every opportunity they can to read with their kids.

C: Well, I'm not sure that forcing children to read more than they want to is particularly beneficial.

S: Um, sorry. What I meant to say was parents should read with their children often, but in a way that generates a love for it.

C: Ah, okay I see what you mean. You know it doesn't always follow that children who read a lot continue to do so as adults. Reading can become more or less attractive at different times in our lives.

S: Hmm. Now you mention it, maybe it depends on the child and their circumstances. As you say, we all change our interests even as young children and adolescents.

11.2

C = Councillor W = Woman
M = Man I = Interviewer M = Matt

Extract one

C: We want our city to be the envy of the country, somewhere that people can look up to as a place ahead of its time. As such, we're inviting all residents to consult on our plans to raise the quality of life here for all residents via new technologies. Plans that past councils have woefully neglected to implement. The proposal we have encompasses a range of green, smart initiatives from monitoring pollution levels to wildlife counts, as well as creating 'green buildings' – spaces at one with nature and accessible to all. We're also proposing enhancements in cycling provisions around the city, like bike lanes and information on rentable bike availability which, we hope, will be an incremental step in making commuting not just easy, but carbon zero. We believe it is an exciting time for our city, but we want to narrow down your priorities as residents in terms of smart cities and that's where we need you. We'll be holding public consultations over the coming months, and everybody is welcome to air their views. There is a full proposal document which can be downloaded from the council website, so please do take a look and get to know our propositions in more depth.

Extract two

W: Look I've really had about enough of this centre, and I want you to do something about it for a change.

M: I'm so sorry to hear that. We've got a complaints form if you'd like to...

W: When I spoke to you before, you advised me to fill out a complaint form, which I did and I've heard zero back. I want some action here! Look at the place... it's littered with rubbish and it's all from your groups here. I don't mind you putting things on for the most vulnerable, but they shouldn't be lurking around outside at all hours. One of them even went off at an old man last week, I saw it for myself. No, it's not on at all.

M: Ah yes, I remember your form now. I've taken it to the manager, and she should be in touch with you about it. I'm sorry I can't help more.

W: Well, I should hope so too. And I'm not the only one... I'm sticking up for the whole community here. Everyone has had it up to here.

Extract three

I: Matt Reid, thank you for joining us today. So, for any budding transport planners out there, can you give us what you consider the most important factors when planning routes?

M: Good question. The paramount factor has to be safety, and planners like me have to anticipate any potential hazards – these could be blind spots, bottlenecks et cetera.. But after that, I suppose it's thinking about all the road users – not just car drivers... because people aren't very sympathetic towards a new route when it's more inconvenient. And no detail is too small when it comes to factoring in problems. Take for example the bridge that was added near the town hall. Lorry drivers were, understandably, up in arms about it because, well, while height was considered, the tunnel underneath couldn't fit wide loads.

I: That must be rather tricky!

M: Not really, nowadays we can model these kinds of things, which really takes the headache out of working out any unintended problems before they happen. The real uphill battle can be working with multiple stakeholders who all tend to have their own agenda... and these don't always meet in the middle. Fortunately, this has never resorted to full-blown arguments, but it hasn't always been pleasant!

12.1

I = Interviewer A = Alex
N = Nadiya

I: Today we're discussing access to hiking trails in our outdoor spaces and specifically national parks. With me are Alex Rogers from local community action group, Access All Areas, who advocate for improved access for people with disabilities, and Nadiya Thompson from the National Parks Service. Alex, let's start with you. Could you give us an outline of what the key issues are for disabled people in this particular context.

A: Sure. Our countryside is criss-crossed by a network of fantastic walking and hiking trails, many of which can be found in national parks, and yet the vast majority of them are completely inaccessible to those people living with disabilities. This is in contrast to many urban settings where provision is quickly becoming more widespread. I mean just think about public transport, municipal buildings, hospitality and tourism. These sectors have been making great strides in accessibility either due to legal obligations or for commercial reasons. It sends a positive message about inclusivity that is absent in our national parks.

I: Nadiya, how would you respond to that?

N: The National Parks Service is fully committed to improving accessibility and is working hard to implement positive changes in this area as soon as possible. We understand full well that disabled people have as much right as everyone else and are just as keen to get out and about in our beautiful natural spaces. In recent years complaints have been mounting up from groups such as yours, Alex, and after a lot of consultation with charities, local government and health experts, I believe we've now got a solid and workable proposal finalised which will improve access for wheelchair users, as well as for people with other health conditions or impairments.

A: It's good to finally get this plan agreed, but it is a shame that it takes so much effort to move things in the right direction. Community action groups like mine have to constantly pile on the pressure and keep at it in order for change, however frustrating the process can be.

N: I appreciate your frustration Alex, but we are making progress. We've come a long way in the last decade, and I agree that we mustn't let up now. One of the largest obstacles that I think the National Parks Service faces is a lack of funding both government and private. What we're trying to do with our latest funding applications is highlight the benefits of spending time in nature and make it clear that the National Parks Service has a responsibility to provide access for all citizens. That's why we're now consulting people like Alex to help us present our case.

I: And do you think that this is a good approach Alex?

A: We have been trying to get more involved for some years now, so yes. However, there is not much that we can do when it comes to attracting investment. We can definitely continue to make the case for the health benefits though.

I: Is this a fair assessment of the situation in your view Nadiya?

N: In my view, yes, it is. We see the role of community action groups as more connected with campaigning and raising awareness among the disabled community. Their data gathering is also a valuable support.

A: We focus on encouraging participation; you know, taking groups of wheelchair users on a hike to give them the confidence they need to open their eyes to the possibilities. We want to urge them on to be more adventurous and challenge themselves through outdoor activities like hiking. More than just inspirational, their lived experiences can be very powerful at persuading people of the need to upgrade paths and trails so that they are wheelchair-friendly and cater for people with other disabilities, such as prosthetic limbs. We have started running workshops for the national parks service employees so they can learn about the achievements of disabled hikers in places with proper access. It's about getting everyone on board to change the mindset of wider society.

I: Yes, I see how they could be really meaningful to a lot of people. How have the parks service employees reacted to these workshops?

N: Very enthusiastically in all the parks we've tried them in. Working with Alex on this has not only been really enlightening but also given us a fresh perspective on why it's needed. Actually, among the national parks and other organisations that manage outdoor spaces, there are plenty of initiatives being thought up, but the key thing is that we have to actually go through with them and not just pay them lip service. Unfortunately, some of these plans can lay idle on someone's desk, gathering dust while other things take priority.

I: Ah, right. And do you have any way of addressing this?

N: We're trying to make Alex and groups like hers more of an integral part of what we do.

A: And we are delighted to bring a raft of experience to the table.

0.1

N = Newsreader W = Woman
M = Man I = Interviewer
Mi = Minister

Extract 1

N: The city centre is seeing its fifth day of gridlocked traffic thanks to the closure of the south side of the inner ring road. The road is closed to allow repairs to the tarmac to take place. However, residents only learned about this closure through social media posts of photos as the cones were put in place to block off entrance and exit points to the road. The council had said that the roadworks were due to take place towards the beginning of last month, and duly notified to city residents, but due to issues with materials, this had to be delayed. No further updates were issued however. Local residents, hauliers and taxi drivers are only some of the groups to have severely criticised what they consider to be the council's ineptitude, inundating their offices with calls of complaint. In a statement to us this afternoon, the council, while explaining the necessity of the works, remains defiant in the face of the complaints of citizens. A response which will almost certainly leave citizens wanting further answers.

Extract 2

W: Did you see the news last night? They had scenes from all over the US – it appears that the cold snap has really hit them hard.

M: It's incredible really, how the infrastructure there just isn't prepared for extreme weather. Especially as blistering cold weather isn't really anything new for them.

W: Well actually, I read that apparently these acute cold weather events are getting fewer and further between, so maybe that's why it's caused so much havoc. I mean, why plan for the unexpected? It's really the animals I feel sorry for rather than us humans...

M: Really? I hadn't even considered that. I suppose they must really be feeling it…

W: No doubt… Most animals are accustomed to being in the elements, which is the last place to be at the moment, so a lot of them are in a bad way, even those that are built to deal with the cold. I think most animals tend to retreat as winter approaches, but they simply aren't equipped for what can come out of the blue. Poor things. Lots of volunteers have been out there lending a hand, but, needless to say, they can't get to them all.

Extract 3

I: So, today, you're announcing a new housing scheme. Tell us about it, and why you think this is adequate to address the real long-term housing problems we're facing in this country?

Mi: We think this scheme is an ideal way to deal with the issues we have with housing at the moment. Basically, our towns have been laid to waste in recent decades following the influx of people to the core cities, and we want to regenerate these areas. Anyone with empty housing in these places can apply for a grant to restore their property, improve its energy efficiency and basically give it a new lease of life. Making these places more attractive would eliminate the need to keep building on our green spaces, and now in the days of remote working, towns, not just cities, are a much more viable offering.

I: But why not tackle the real problem head on by investing in our cities and the lack of affordable and decent accommodation?

Mi: We mustn't be too city centric in our thinking. Policies also exist for our cities, they have been fruitful, especially recently.

I: And do you really think that people will flock from cities into these, might I call them, deserted towns? Being a pioneer in a place with limited services hoping for better days doesn't sound ideal to me.

0.2

Thank you for inviting me here today to talk about new and inventive ways people are harnessing energy, which I hope some of you might adopt. In modern life, energy has become somewhat of a predicament for both individuals and countries, as costs of energy prices soar, and the environmental costs of energy production become increasingly obvious. But this does not necessarily need to be the case, and research into non-traditional energy production is coming on <u>leaps and bounds</u> with solutions showing great inventiveness, both in small- and large-scales which are either ready, or almost ready, to deploy.

Let's start with a case study. You might not think of the force of gravity as a viable energy source, but surprisingly, it is used in the production of energy in some forms and has much higher <u>reliability</u> than solar or wind energy, as it is a <u>constant</u>. It has been put to use in some localised projects to make a huge difference to certain groups of people. Take for example, the GravityLight in Kenya, a device which is bringing light to homes which are normally off-grid, and doing it, safely and cost-effectively. Where they once used <u>kerosene</u> to power their lighting, they are now doing it with rocks linked to a dynamo with a pulley system. It may be a small amount of power that is generated, but it's making a real difference to communities in far flung areas, especially as <u>running costs</u> are virtually non-existent. And there is no reason why this couldn't be scaled up. In fact, there are some companies that are considering gravity, in terms of energy storage this time, on a much larger scale, so it seems as if this is just the tip of the iceberg for its potential.

The next step for small-scale energy production might lie in exploiting the kinetic energy we generate all around us. In the UK, there are smart panels in some <u>pavements</u> to capture the energy of the pedestrians, channelling it into the streetlights. In Japan, some nightclubs are using similar techniques but on their dancefloors. This kind of energy could change our daily lives as we know it, perhaps for example to the point where we are using our fingers as a <u>charging device</u> every time we send a text message or scroll on our mobiles. That could also mean that we never run out of battery again!

Now these are great inexpensive energy sources, but, while having potential for expansion, at present they are localised projects. However, there is one rather unusual resource which involves the adaption of an existing energy source – solar energy – and this could be a <u>game-changer</u>. While solar energy is considered, and quite rightly, as one of the green energies, it's not as perfect as it at first seems. The actual <u>construction</u> of the panels is where the problem lies, because of the need for silicon as a <u>conductor</u> in the panels, which is neither cheap nor particularly environmentally friendly due to its <u>energy-intensive</u> production process. The replacement scientists are working on for this actually comes from a creature of the deep – the jellyfish. A specific protein is being developed that is derived from the green fluorescent protein, or GFP, contained in jellyfish that gives them their distinctive <u>glow</u>. This protein reacts to UV light which in turn activates electrons… mirroring the kind of process that happens in solar panel energy. Scientists have the ability now to artificially create this protein, so there is little reason why this couldn't be <u>commercially sold</u> in the form of solar panels, and also deployed as bio cells floating in the ocean, collecting power whenever the sun shines.

These are just some of the ways that our traditional sources of energy can be complemented, or even replaced over time, both on a local and global scale. As I mentioned at the start, it's an exciting time for energy, as talented young scientists are shooing away <u>finite</u> generators of power to look to things that are abundant and limitless in our natural world. And this is essential if we are to counter the challenges that climate change, limited resources, and population growth, present to us.

0.3

I = Interviewer K = Kevin J = Julia

I: Today I'm joined by town councillor Kevin Eastwell and conservationist Julia Wright to talk about a much-loved household pet that's causing some controversy here in New Zealand at the moment… the cat. So, Julia let's start with you. Enlighten us on the problem. Surely everyone loves a cat.

J: Thank you, Dan. And yes, cats are close to our hearts, that can't be denied, but we shouldn't be blind to a much more significant issue they bring about – the elimination of a variety of species, particularly birds, here in the country. All countries have to protect their native species, but for New Zealanders the need is so much stronger, because whereas other countries may be able to repopulate depleted species by bringing the same species in from other countries, they just don't have that luxury as many of their species are completely unique to their country. Cats are great pets, sure, but they're also predators, and they've killed off more than eleven bird species in New Zealand.

K: But let's make it clear that we're talking about feral cats, not the common domestic cat we find within homes, and while I do accept there is a sensitive problem to deal with here, we need to be careful not to demonise those with cats. I'd say nine out of ten of them already take their responsibilities as owners seriously.

I: But let's backtrack a moment…how has this occurred? I mean, it's common knowledge that cats kill birds… but are they actually responsible for killing off whole species of birds?

J: What you need to take into consideration here is how unique this country is. Never historically being home to mammals, unlike other countries, the bird population flourished. However, with very few threats to counter, they didn't cultivate the necessary survival skills for living amongst the varieties of life that have now been introduced. So, for example, a cat finds a bird and in other places that bird just flies away, hopefully, but some of their birds can't even fly!

K: This isn't a modern problem though as far as I'm concerned. It's been taking place over centuries since humans first populated the islands. Take for example the Lyall's wren, a bird which thrived in New Zealand, well, up until the first human settlement in the 13th century. Then fast forward to the start of the 19th century and this bird population was all but wiped out on the main islands. Numbers had dwindled to just a colony on St Stephens Island.

J: But, much later, when that became home to a lighthouse, with a cat that produced more feral cats, that was another nail in the coffin for the Lyall's wren, so to speak.

I: So, what can we do about this?

K: Well, I imagine Julia has much more drastic ideas than I do on what needs to be done. For me, it's fundamental to respect and protect the rights of our citizens, and as a nation where almost half of us are cat owners, we shouldn't bombard them with restrictions and make cat owning a headache. What we DO need to do, I believe, is to agree on a working system for the reduction of feral cats, which are the main problem, but this should be nationwide, not a localised initiative, as I'd argue the major damage is done in rural areas.

J: I'm sorry, but for me that's just burying your head in the sand and ignoring the simple fact that cats travel. Certainly, we shouldn't outlaw pet ownership, but we've got to cut this problem off at the source. The issue with household cats is twofold – of course they are predators themselves, but the fact that feral cats are born from household cats is the real nettle we need to grasp. Only around 90% of cats are spayed or neutered and that is 10% too low, especially when there's more than one cat within the home – and for me this is what needs to change, or at the very least cats that are within that 10% need to stay indoors.

I: Is that a policy you see working?

K: Not for the residents in my town, I'm afraid, and I agree with them. We mustn't restrict freedom of choice and most importantly, we shouldn't scapegoat the household cat when the issue is far more complex. There are plenty of other predators affecting our wildlife that I think we should prioritise over this issue.

I: So, what is being done about the predator threat in general?

J: Well, there's a programme called Predator Free 2050, aimed at eradicating rats, stoats and possums, considered by some to be their most dangerous predators, which has received widespread backing from numerous areas. It is undeniably a noble cause, but one that would do well to stretch its ambitions by including feral cats. Nobody knows the feral cat population in the country, but it is estimated at around 2.5 million, and this is 2.5 million too many.

0.4

Speaker 1:

Ultramarathons are so much more than an endurance sport for me. There's no doubt to everyone around me that I'm a competitor that basically eats, sleeps and breathes the challenge. I think that's because people underestimate what ultramarathons are about and just train physically, but you've really got to be meticulous in your mental preparation. For example, nutrition is of the utmost importance when training for these events as being in peak condition not only externally, but internally too is an absolute must. To run a normal marathon, it's enough to be in shape, but an ultramarathon takes discipline, for months beforehand as well as during the race. This is something that catches people unawares but without a doubt it's the key to the finish line.

Speaker 2:

Occasionally I moonlight as an ultramarathon training guide where I train women like me to prepare for the experience. I became instantly hooked on ultramarathons after my first one, which took place in the Himalayas and was such a mind-blowing experience. My colleagues mostly think it's a ludicrous hobby, but I just love having a crack at things that are a little out of my league. In my talks, I make sure people know what they've let themselves in for, and, I know this might sound contradictory, but prepare yourself for a few curve balls. Carefully planned packing is essential as the most minute detail can make such a difference, but despite everything that you do you can't tell until you're out there, which is half the excitement.

Speaker 3:

One of the most common beginner training errors is focusing on just distance, but focusing on speed, particularly running slowly, is necessary too, constantly monitoring your heart rate so it's not elevated. What I'd have given for someone to have mentioned that before my first ultramarathon, and unfortunately also my first 'did not finish'. Now, I understand that only a fine-tuned approach will get results, but that's also the joy of them... the constant progression. Now, I look to not only my physical program, but the course layout, poring over it meticulously for any red flags as this is crucial if you don't want to be in agony. And next time, to avoid the dreaded problem of getting sand in my running shoes, I'll definitely be tying plastic bags around my feet!

Speaker 4:

Having just finished my first ultramarathon last year, I'd say the experience was rather bittersweet, and to be honest, I feel like it could be my last. The preparation was tough enough, but I really had no idea what I was in for. I tested myself to the limits, at points on my hands and knees and in tears, but no matter what, I kept going to the very end and I'll always look back on it with a unique sense of accomplishment, without forgetting how tough it was. To anyone thinking of doing an ultramarathon, well, I'd say you've got to be a particular type of human being, one that can reckon with themselves in the darkest moments. While some competitors can do this, I, and many others, just aren't equipped for it.

Speaker 5:

I don't know where I'd be without ultramarathons as I completely relish the challenge that each one has presented whatever they throw in my path. Having struggled on a jungle night course after breaking a toe, very little can faze me now, neither at work or at home, and I'm hoping that will only continue. What people often don't tell you about ultramarathons is the likelihood of hallucinations, which has happened to me a few times. It's hard to counter this, but maintaining a high level of fluids is important, then try not to get sleep deprived, and rely on the other runners if you do have an episode because the teamwork can be incredible, and they'll always help you get through.

0.5

I = Interlocutor S = Sofia
M = Mario

I: Good afternoon. My name is Helen Walker and this is my colleague Scott Harrison. And your names are?

S: My name is Sofia.

M: I'm Mario.

I: Could I have your mark sheets please? Thank you. First of all, we'd like to know something about you. Where are you from, Mario?

M: I'm originally from Rome, the capital of Italy, but a few years ago I moved with my family to a town on the coast.

I: And you, Sofia?

S: I come from Jerez, in the south of Spain. It's a beautiful town and very popular with tourists.

I: Are you working or studying at the moment?

S: I'm halfway through a degree in Engineering, and right now I'm on an internship at a construction firm. I'm really enjoying it so far.

I: And you?

M: I've just finished university and I'm going on a year abroad. I'm actually leaving in two weeks!

I: Sofia, what made you decide to study English?

S: Most people study English in Spain from the age of five upwards, but not many people continue for as long as I have. When I realised I wanted to be an engineer, I knew I wouldn't be able to do it without English, so I've continued. It's an essential skill for me, as lots of Engineering journals are in English, and Engineering is also a field which is quite international. English is nearly always the language of any international projects in this area.

I: And Mario, what do you enjoy about where you live?

M: Well, as I said, I moved a while ago. My parents moved because my mum got a new job, and now we're in a coast town... coastal town. It's much more relaxed than city life, and it's easier to travel around. I can walk everywhere, so I guess that's what I like most.

I: Thank you.

0.6

I = Interlocutor S = Sofia
M = Mario

I: Now, in this part of the test you're going to do something together. Here are some pictures of people in different situations. First, I'd like you to look at pictures one and two and talk together about how these people might feel. You have about a minute for this, so don't worry if I interrupt you.

M: Well, in picture one they look pretty happy, but they seem exhausted too, don't you think?

S: Yes, it looks to me as if they've just completed a marathon. I think marathon runners, or long-distance runners at least, get those kinds of blankets when they finish a race.

M: Yes, I think they do ... and they've got medals too!

S: They must be feeling an immense sense of achievement I imagine. Both of them.

M: Why do you think that? Because it's a difficult thing to do?

S: Yes, but also because they must have trained quite hard. It's something that takes a lot of time and effort to achieve. And also, you can tell, not just by the medals but also by their expressions, that they've done something they are very proud of and pleased about!

M: Hmm.... and image two reminds me of when I'm playing with my niece! They both look really happy. What kind of relation do you think the little girl is to the man?

S: It's hard to tell, but they definitely look like family to me. It seems to me that the man feels overjoyed to be around the child, and they clearly have a close relationship. Perhaps it's a family member like an uncle who hasn't seen his niece for a long time and they're both delighted to be in each other's company. What do you think?

M: Yes, it could be.

S: It could even be a father and daughter, and this is just an everyday occurrence – where they play and really enjoy just being together. I say that because I could totally imagine that being me and my father when I was little.

I: Thank you.

0.7

I = Interlocutor S = Sofia
M = Mario

I: Now, I'd like you to imagine that a lifestyle magazine is planning an article on the theme of personal achievement. They want a picture to accompany the article. Talk together about the ways in which these activities contribute to personal achievement, as shown in these pictures. Then, decide on which image you think would be best to use. You have about three minutes to talk about this.

M: It's an interesting subject, isn't it? For me, it's very obvious in picture four that it is about personal achievement. She's a young woman, and the picture indicates that she's just bought a house.

S: Yes, she looks very pleased. It's not surprising.

M: I think those are the keys of the house... the house keys. That's something to be proud of, don't you think?

S: Yes, especially being so young. That makes it quite a significant achievement. She looks over the moon to me.

M: Yes, she does. Let's look at image three maybe.

S: I don't think I'd use picture three as I can't really see how it's related to achievement. What's your opinion?

M: Yes, I'm not sure either. It looks like they are rehearsing for a play.

S: Maybe it's about writing a play or being an actor.

M: Well, being a famous actor would probably be quite a good achievement.

S: On second thoughts, it could be about getting outside of your comfort zone. After all, not everyone likes being up on stage. But maybe we should rule that picture out anyway.

M: Yes.

S: I mean, the link between the picture and the topic of the article isn't immediately obvious. I'm not very keen on two either.

M: Really? Why not?

S: I don't know. I suppose it's just a bit vague. I mean, can you "achieve" having a family?!

M: Hmmm.... I see what you mean.

S: Also, even if it's just a relative playing with a child, I'm not sure that's really about achievement. In my mind, that would be more about contentment in your life. You don't really achieve being an uncle, do you? It's not something you do.

M: No, I suppose not. For me, it's between one and four.

S: Yes, I'm torn between the same two. They are just more obviously linked to what the article's about.

M: If I had to make a decision, then perhaps I'd go for picture one. The one thing that stands out for me is that they've done something... challenging... and their sense of happiness. Also, sometimes people do these kinds of things for charity. I think that's an even bigger achievement!

S: Yes?

M: Yeah, because they are doing something hard, but for other people.

S: Well, let's go with that then. I agree with you. Picture one is probably the best for the article. I think it's got the most global appeal, rather than the others that just focus on certain sections of society. People can buy houses because they've got rich parents, or win some money. It's not always like an achievement, it can be down to luck essentially, whereas running a marathon is different.

M: Yeah, anyone can do it, and it's something that requires dedication and determination. One hundred per cent.

I: Thank you. Can I have the pictures please?

0.8

I = Interlocutor S = Sofia
M = Mario

I: Now, in this part of the test you're each going to talk on your own for about two minutes. You need to listen while your partner is speaking because you'll be asked to comment afterwards. So, Sofia I am going to give you a card with a question written on it and I'd like you to tell us what you think. There are also some ideas on the card for you to use if you like. All right? Here's your card. Please let Mario see the card. Remember Sofia, you have about two minutes to talk before we join in. Would you like to begin now?

S: I think competition can be a double-edged sword. There are lots of advantages and disadvantages to competition in all walks of life. In my opinion, in terms of sports, the sense of competition is the main reason that people like to take part and train so hard too. It spurs them on to be the best in their field. I mean, would we ever have had so many records broken if people didn't want to win against others? I'd probably say no. Also, it would make for pretty boring TV too, if sports had no sense of competition. Could you imagine a football match without scoring goals?! Who would watch that?

Competition at work, well, I think that's a bit different. People are usually competitive in jobs because they want to get promoted or get noticed and by that I mean getting noticed for the right reasons, instead of getting noticed for doing something wrong. But, I'm not sure it's the best attitude to have in the workplace. In many jobs, being a team player is an important skill and I think more competitive people aren't always great team players. On top of that, at work, being very competitive can be quite selfish, I believe. People can do all sorts of things to get one up on their colleagues... it's not a very nice trait. No, I'm not really sure I see the benefits of workplace competition. I know I'd like to just be happy at work, not trying to be better than the rest and vying against my workmates all the time.

I also see no reason why anyone would want to compete with their friends for anything at all. I'm not a competitive person and my friends aren't either. In fact, we support each other as much as we can. I'm always borrowing things from them and giving and asking for advice. Overall, I think it's a much better way to be.

I: Thank you. Mario, are you a competitive person?

M: Yes, I suppose a little. I do a lot of swimming, and although I do it for me personally... because I enjoy it, I also find the competition side very exciting. I was quite competitive at school too with my exam results... always comparing them against my friends. But I always wanted my friends to do well too. I think just a small dose of competition is probably a good thing. It makes us try harder.

I: How about you?

S: No, not really. I suppose in some areas I am maybe a little bit competitive. I've entered a few competitions online to try to win things, like concert tickets, but I never have. I'm not a very sporty person so those kinds of competitions aren't really my cup of tea.

I: Thank you. Now, Mario, it's your turn to be given a question. Here's your card. Please let Sofia see your card. Remember, Mario you have about two minutes to speak and there are some ideas on the card to use if you like. All right?

M: Ohh! I find this question interesting. As someone who does sports myself, I'm quite a big fan of large events like the Olympics or the World Cup. In terms of benefits, well, I think there are...is... an overwhelming amount of benefits to these kinds of sporting events. To start off with, they provide amazing entertainment for people all around the world. You just need to look at a World Cup for example, and see the happiness in the faces of the fans on the screen. I truly believe people at home feel the same way. I know I do.

I think these events also encourage people to have a more international outlook. Viewers often become interested about the host nation and want to know more about them. I remember when the Olympic games were held in Rio in Brazil, and my uncle and his friends went to it and came back telling incredible stories of what Rio was like. I think we could call him a... Brazilophile after that experience. But you don't need to go there in the flesh to see that kind of thing.

Normally the coverage on TV shows, not just sporting things, but cultural elements too, and we can all learn something from that.

I would say that there aren't many drawbacks to these kinds of competitions. Some people might think that it causes some anti-social behaviours like when football hooligans get violent but I think this is isolated. In my view, international sporting events bring everybody together, not pull them apart. I also imagine that it brings in a lot of money to the host country, and the people in the country too. Also, governments can turn a whole area around when a sporting event is coming to their country. Look at Barcelona. When the Olympics were there, the local government transformed some parts of the city and they've stayed this way.

I: Thank you. Sofia, do you think competition in sports in general is a positive thing?

S: To be honest, I'm not really sure. Some people have more sporting ability than

others, and I'd imagine this would make them more competitive. I'd definitely say that people are competitive only when they've got a chance of winning.
If someone is not evenly matched against another person, well this can be quite demotivating and depressing. So, it's not always positive.

I: What do you think, Mario?

M: Yes, I agree one hundred per cent. You can see this kind of thing in professional sports, when a team just gives up... not actually, but in their spirit because they're outmatched. But also in everyday life too... people who aren't sporty, aren't generally competitive and don't like it.

I: Thank you.

0.9

I = Interlocutor S = Sofia
M = Mario

I: Now, to finish the test we're going to talk about competition in general. Do you think more competitive people tend to be more successful than people who aren't very competitive?

S: Shall I begin?

M: Okay, sure.

S: Unfortunately, yes, I think that's quite often the case. The problem with very competitive people is that they will stop at nothing to get what they want, whereas less competitive people won't do certain things. I believe this means that competitive people often win over others.

M: That's quite a depressing thought but I see what you mean. I think that's why sometimes politicians do well. The ones who are more competitive tend to succeed.

S: Yes. The problem with competition is when it affects the person's morals. There's a big difference to just, for example, wanting to win a quiz, compared to desperately wanting to be more successful than the people around you, and doing this for example by... well... I think the series *Succession* is a good example of that. Have you watched the show?

M: No, but I've heard of it.

S: Well, it's about the children of a media mogul and how they do some really underhand things to ensure their own success in the business, often at the cost of one another. This is naked ambition, but I think that's just another form of being competitive.

I: Do we learn to be competitive or are we born competitive?

M: I think we learn it... thinking back to what we talked about in terms of sport. I think competitiveness is always there a little, but it's something that grows inside us if we think we've got a chance of winning. I wonder how much difference it makes whether you win or lose a lot in your early childhood. Perhaps the feeling you get if you lose often when you're young makes you less competitive in your adult years, just because it doesn't make you feel very good. What's your opinion, Sofia?

S: I would say that how competition develops in children often depends on their influences. So, for example, if their parents are competitive people and show them this mentality, then they are more likely to be like that themselves. Whereas some other people grow out of that early childhood sense of competition and start to focus on other things that perhaps they think are more important... like understanding others, sharing or kindness.

M: That's an interesting point. I definitely think your parents can affect how competitive you are too, but so can everybody. I don't know if it was the same for you, but we used to have sports days and quizzes at school where there would be winners and losers. Competition is everywhere, not just at home.

S: Yes, I do agree that there is competition in many areas, but I think whether your parents encourage it is still pretty important.

I: Do you think it's ever a good thing to compare yourself against other people?

S: Hmmm... yes maybe sometimes it is useful. Perhaps it depends on the ways in which you compare yourself. If you have a role model, and you compare yourself to this, then I think that can be a good thing.

M: Yes, but.... Well, perhaps it depends on the role model.

S: That's true. While it might be a good thing to compare yourself to, for example, Malala Yousafzai, the girl who stood up for her human rights. But comparing yourself to someone who just poses for photos on social media all the time might not be so great. It seems to me to be about the underlying factors that you are looking to compare yourself to. Looking to others in terms of a sense of morals or achievement, well, I think that's worthy. But constantly comparing your looks or clothes to someone... for me I find that a bit shallow.

M: Yes, and also it's something that most people can never live up to. You look at these people in magazines or on social media, but you can never have a body like them.

S: Absolutely. What we don't see is the amount of time in the gym, or all the work they have done on their bodies and faces!

M: We must be realistic.

S: Yes, we can't be copies of other people. For me, the most important thing to remember is that we are all unique, and we must be ourselves.

I: Thank you. That is the end of the test.

M: Thank you

S: Thank you.

IDIOMS WORDLISTS

Idioms in alphabetical order

a blank canvas	something that can be developed or changed in many different ways	The flat is **a blank canvas.** We could do exactly what we want to make it our own.
a breath of fresh air	someone or something that is new, interesting, and exciting	After all the criticism, his positivity came as a **breath of fresh air**.
a likely story	used for telling someone that you do not believe what they have just said	What, she just found the watch on a park bench? **A likely story**.
a long shot	an attempt or guess that is not likely to be successful but that is worth trying	It's **a long shot**, but you could try calling her at work.
a sight for sore eyes	someone or something that you are very pleased to see	Hey Pippa, you're **a sight for sore eyes**!
a slow burner	a thing that slowly develops into something interesting or powerful	Be patient because the series is **a slow burner**. It gets far better in the second episode.
Achilles heel	a weak feature of someone or something that is otherwise strong, which makes them open to attack or failure	Spelling and punctuation has always been my **Achilles heel**.
agree to differ	to accept that someone else does not have the same opinion as you and agree not to argue about it any more	There are some issues on which my colleague and I have **agreed to differ**.
as dead as a doornail	completely dead or not working	I dropped my mobile phone in the bath and now it's **as dead as a doornail**.
as far as anyone can tell	used for saying what you think is true when you think that there may be facts that you or others do not know	There's been no damage to the property **as far as anyone can tell**.
at the leading edge	at the most modern and advanced point in the development of something	These scientists are **at the leading edge** of medical research.
be barking up the wrong tree	to be doing something that will not get the result that you want	If you think Hamish is going to help you, then I'm afraid you**'re barking up the wrong tree**.
be caught red-handed	to be caught doing something wrong	They **were caught red-handed** trying to break into the van.
be full of yourself	to be always talking about yourself or your achievements in a way that annoys other people	I'd rather not ask Ivan to do the speech – he's a bit too **full of himself**.
be made of money	to have a lot of money	I can't give you as much as that – I'm not **made of money**, you know.
be on a roll	to be having a lot of success or good luck	We'd be crazy to stop when things are going so well – **we're on a roll**.
be out of the loop	to not belong to a group that has information and makes decisions about something	There's no point in asking Kanami about it – she**'s out of the loop**.
be rolling in it	to have a lot of money	They sold their house in London and made a massive profit, so they**'re rolling in it**.
be stuck between a rock and a hard place	to be in a position in which you have to choose between two things that are not good	Either Pablo is disappointed or we upset Anna. We**'re stuck between a rock and a hard place** on this one.
be your bread and butter	to be something that provides your main income	Right now this kind of work is my **bread and butter**.
bear no resemblance to (someone / something)	to look completely different to someone or something	This is supposed to be a replacement but it **bears no resemblance to** the original.
beat around the bush	to spend a long time getting to the main point of what you are saying, often because it is embarrassing	I wish they'd stop **beating around the bush** and tell us what we need to know.

between you and me	used when you are telling someone something that you do not want anyone else to know about	**Between you and me**, I'm not sure that's the only problem.
bowl (someone) over	to surprise someone by being very beautiful, impressive, unexpected, etc	We **were bowled over** by the sheer beauty of the landscape.
break the mould	to change a situation completely, or to do something in a completely new way	A lot of those reality shows are very similar, but this one definitely **breaks the mould**.
by the book	correctly, following all the rules or systems for doing something in a strict way	I can't believe this is Sanjit's mistake, he always does everything **by the book**.
catch (someone's) drift	to understand the basic meaning that someone is trying to express	I couldn't hear everything Alex was saying but I think I **caught her drift**.
catch (someone's) eye	if something catches your eye, you suddenly notice it	As she flicked through the pages, an attractive design **caught her eye**.
Catch 22 situation	a set of problems that is impossible to escape from because each problem must be solved first before you can solve any of the others	You can't get a job without an address and you can't rent a flat without a job – it's a **Catch 22 situation**.
clear the air	to discuss a problem or difficult situation with someone in order to make it better	Karina and I have had a little chat and I'm hoping this has now **cleared the air**.
cliff-hanger	an exciting end to part of a book or television programme that makes you want to read or watch the next part	There's a real **cliff-hanger** in the last chapter of this novel, so I'm guessing there's going to be a sequel.
collector's item	a rare or valuable object that collectors want to own	We never use that old teapot because we've been told it's a **collector's item**.
come out of your shell	to stop being shy and begin to confidently show your real character and feelings	Once Laurence **came out of his shell**, he was pretty talkative.
creature of habit	someone who likes to do the same thing at the same time every day	I drink coffee in the morning and water after lunch. I'm definitely a **creature of habit**.
dead end	a situation in which no further progress is possible	Unfortunately, it looks as though this line of inquiry has come to a **dead end**.
don't get me wrong	used when you want to make sure that someone understands your comments correctly, especially when you are criticizing something	**Don't get me wrong**, we love going to the theatre, but this just wasn't worth the money.
down the rabbit hole	used for referring to a situation in which you become so interested in something that you cannot stop trying to find out about it or doing it	Whenever I really enjoy a play I often end up **down the rabbit hole**, researching the cast.
draw the line at (something)	to say that you will definitely not allow or accept something	You can invite some of your friends, but I **draw the line at** more than ten.
feel the pinch	to have less money than you need	**Are** you **feeling the pinch** because of massive energy bills?
find common ground	to find something that people can agree about, especially when they disagree about other things	We don't agree on some things, but we**'ve** also **found** plenty of **common ground**.
for a split second	for an extremely small amount of time	Apologies, **for a split second** I'd forgotten your surname.
freelance	freelance work is done by a person who is not permanently employed by a particular company but who sells their services to more than one company	They commissioned a **freelance** artist to produce the drawings.
from scratch	from the beginning again, not using all the work that you have done before	Milo has rebuilt the entire car engine **from scratch**.

get (something) down to a fine art	to become very good at doing something, especially something difficult	After a whole year, I've got my commute to work **down to a fine art**.
get (something) off your chest	to talk to someone about something that has been worrying you, so that you feel better about it	You're looking worried. Is there anything you want to **get off your chest**, Ria?
get off on the wrong foot	to immediately establish a bad relationship with someone when you first meet them or first start working with them	I'm not sure why, but somehow Mike and I **got off on the wrong foot when I joined the company**.
get the wrong end of the stick	to understand something completely incorrectly	That's not what she means at all. You**'ve got the wrong end of the stick**.
get your wires crossed	if two people get their wires crossed, they become confused because they each think that the other one is talking about something else	Sorry, I thought we were going to Paola's house first. We must **have got our wires crossed**.
give (someone) the creeps	to make someone feel nervous or frightened	Having to walk through the forest at night **gave** me **the creeps**.
give (someone) the upper hand	to give someone control or an advantage over a person or situation	The break for rain seems to have **given** the Australian team **the upper hand in the match**.
go back to the drawing board	to try to think of a completely new idea because the one that you tried before was not successful	OK, we'll just have to **go back to the drawing board** and think of something else.
go down a storm	to be very popular	We've changed the recipe and the new version **is going down a storm** with customers.
go round in circles	to do something for a long time without achieving any results because you always return to the same problem that you cannot solve	There's no point in continuing this debate, we**'re** just **going round in circles**.
go-getter	someone who is determined to succeed and who works hard to achieve this	They only want to recruit **go-getters** who will make sacrifices in order to succeed.
grey area	a situation in which the rules are not clear, or in which you are not sure what is right or wrong	I'm afraid I can't give a definite answer to that question as it's still something of **a grey area**.
hands down	without any doubt	It's **hands down** the best restaurant in town.
hard up	not having much money	I'm not sure Lance can afford to come – he's pretty **hard up** at the moment.
have a chip on your shoulder	to be likely to become angry or offended very easily, especially about something that other people think should not upset you	Wim is really jealous about it, but then he's always **had a chip on his shoulder**.
have a head start	to have an advantage over other people in the same situation as you, especially in a competition	Students who do the course will **have a head start** when applying for jobs.
in a tight spot	in a difficult situation	I'm **in** a bit of **a tight spot** – can I borrow some money for a couple of weeks?
in the clear	no longer believed to be guilty of something bad or illegal	It's been confirmed now that you weren't there at the time – you're **in the clear**.
in the pipeline	being planned or prepared in order to happen or be available soon	The band has a new album **in the pipeline**.
in the same ballpark	not calculated exactly, but within a similar general range	Tom's on a good salary and although I don't know what Sam earns, I'd guess it's **in the same ballpark**.
it's news to me	used for saying that you didn't know about something, especially when you are annoyed about this	'So Natalia is having a party when you're away.' 'Really? **It's news to me**!'

jump the gun	to do or say something too soon, before you know that it is suitable or correct	We'll ask them when the time is right; we mustn't **jump the gun**, or we'll regret it.
keep (something) under wraps	to keep something secret	Next year's design is being **kept under wraps**.
keep your head above water	to manage to live or keep a business running even though you are not earning much money	He's had some unexpected bills, but is still managing to **keep his head above water**.
learn the ropes	to learn how to do something, especially a job	It didn't take her new assistant long to **learn the ropes**.
leave your mark	to have a very strong and noticeable effect on someone or something, usually a bad one that lasts for a long time	Yulia's difficult childhood **left its mark** on her throughout her life.
let the cat out of the bag	to tell someone something that was intended to be secret	It was supposed to be a surprise, but Frederico **let the cat out of the bag**.
like talking to a brick wall	used for saying that someone does not listen or react to you when you talk to them	Don't bother explaining it to my mum, it's **like talking to a brick wall**.
live and breathe (something)	to be very enthusiastic about a particular activity and spend all the time you can doing it or talking about it	The whole family just **lives and breathes** music.
love is blind	used for saying that when you love someone, it is difficult to see their faults	She's so selfish I can't really understand why they're together, but then **love is blind**.
make (someone's) blood run cold	to make someone feel suddenly very frightened or worried	A loud knock on the door **made** my **blood run cold**.
make waves	to cause problems by making suggestions or criticisms	I think your idea is great, but it's probably best to avoid **making waves** right now.
make your blood boil	to make you feel very angry	This should have been done weeks ago – it **makes my blood boil**.
meet (someone) halfway	to agree to do something that someone wants, if they do something that you want	If you're prepared to agree to these conditions then they'll **meet you halfway** on the price.
money for old rope	money that you earn very easily without much work or effort	We finished the job in half a day. It was **money for old rope**.
move the goalposts	to change the rules and make it difficult for people to achieve something or to know what to do	This issue is never going to be resolved if management keep **shifting the goalposts**.
nail down the finer points	to definitely decide the details of something	A plan of action is almost agreed, we just need to **nail down the finer points**.
nasty piece of work	someone who is unkind or unpleasant	Erik is being horrible to everyone again – he's such a **nasty piece of work**.
no holds barred	without any limit on what you are allowed to do	Some viewers complained the show was offensive and there were certainly **no holds barred**.
not be out of the woods yet	used for saying that a situation is still difficult, although it has improved	Things are definitely getting better, but I'm afraid we're **not out of the woods yet**.
not for love nor money	used for emphasizing that something is not available or possible, or that you will not do it	We want to do some alterations to the house but I ca**n't** find a builder **for love nor money**.
not say boo to a goose	to be very quiet and shy	Don't rely on Ciara to defend you – she **wouldn't say boo to a goose**.
on target	likely to get the result that you are trying to achieve	Are they **on target** to finish the work when we agreed?
on the right track	doing or thinking the right things	Thanks. This essay is looking great; you're definitely **on the right track**.

out of hand	not well controlled	You'd better say something before things get **out of hand**.
out of line	behaving in a way that other people do not approve of	Deb should apologise because what she said was way **out of line**.
people person	someone who enjoys being with other people and makes friends easily	The job mainly involves talking to customers so you definitely need to be a **people person**.
put your finger on (something)	to discover or understand exactly why a situation is the way it is, especially when something is wrong	Can you **put your finger on** where the problem is?
put your money where your mouth is	used for saying that someone should do something, especially spend money, to show that they mean what they say instead of just talking about it	He says he's prepared to invest some of his savings, but he needs to **put his money where his mouth is**.
red herring	something that is not relevant that makes you confused or takes your attention away from what you should be concentrating on	At first it looked as if the doctor was involved, but that turned out to be a **red herring**.
reinvent the wheel	to waste time and effort trying to do something that someone else has already done well	We've already got a good solution for that, so don't waste time **reinventing the wheel**.
ring a bell	something that rings a bell sounds familiar to you, although you cannot remember the exact details	OK, yes, that **rings a bell**. I think I might have been there a few years ago.
rock the boat	to cause problems by changing a situation that is considered satisfactory	Everyone is happy with the arrangements now, so please don't **rock the boat**.
scare the wits out of (someone)	to make someone feel extremely frightened	Don't scream like that, you **scared the wits** out of me!
skeleton in the/your cupboard	an embarrassing secret about your past that you do not want anyone to know	If you want to succeed in politics then you can't have too many **skeletons in the cupboard**.
small talk	informal conversation about things that are not important	I didn't know anyone at my table and had to spend the entire meal making **small talk**.
smell a rat	to believe that something dishonest, illegal, or wrong has happened	When she was working late every evening he began to **smell a rat**.
spill the beans	to tell someone something, often something that should be kept secret	I think Jeff knows what's going on, but he wouldn't **spill the beans** when I asked him.
sticking point	something that people cannot agree on and that stops them from continuing with a discussion	Deciding who should deal with this is now one of the main **sticking points**.
stroke of luck	something that happens by chance and that helps you to achieve something	By a **stroke of luck**, Finn had an identical jacket that I could borrow for the wedding.
stumbling block	a difficulty that causes mistakes or prevents progress	This is a major **stumbling block** to negotiations that will be hard to overcome.
take (something) on the chin	to accept something unpleasant in a brave way without complaining	Pelagia **took** it all **on the chin** but the rest of the team were furious about the comments.
talk (someone's) ear off	to talk to someone for a long time, often in a loud or boring way	We stood there for nearly an hour while he **talked** my **ear off**.
talk shop	to talk about your work, especially in a way that is boring for other people	Can we change the subject and stop **talking shop**?
talk the talk	to talk confidently about something in a way that makes people think you are good at it, know a lot about it, etc	Ed might not always get things right, but he can really **talk the talk**, can't he?
talk to the hand	used for saying in a slightly angry way that you do not want to listen to what someone is saying	'That's never going to work, Sian.' '**Talk to the hand**. I don't need advice from you.'

teething problems	minor problems that a new company, project, product, etc may have in the beginning	This model has had one or two **teething problems**, but we've managed to sort them out.
tell (someone) a thing or two	to tell someone some useful or interesting information about someone or something	I'm sure Felix could **tell** us **a thing or two** about electric cars. Shall we ask him?
tell (someone) where to get off	to tell someone very rudely that you are not interested in them or in what they are saying	Achim can never be trusted – she should **tell** him **where to get off**.
tell it like it is	to give the real facts about something, even if they are unpleasant	OK, I'm ready to hear the worst, just **tell it like it is**.
tell me about it	used for saying that you already know about something unpleasant that someone has just described because you have experienced it yourself	'We've spent hours on the phone to the insurance company.' '**Tell me about it**!'
tell me something I don't know	used for saying in a slightly angry way that you already know about something that a person is talking to you about, often because it is obvious	'But Jack hasn't finished this.' '**Tell me something I don't know**, I've been trying to sort his mess out all morning!'
the bottom line	the most basic fact or issue in a situation	This won't get better if you don't change your lifestyle. That's **the bottom line**.
the pot calling the kettle black	used for saying that someone is criticizing another person for a fault that they also have	He said she was stubborn? Well, that's **the pot calling the kettle black**. He can never admit he's wrong.
the world is (someone's) oyster	used for emphasizing that you can go anywhere or do anything that you want to	With those skills she'll find work wherever she wants. **The world is her oyster**.
there's a lot to be said for (something)	used for saying that there are many advantages in doing something	**There's a lot to be said for** living with your parents and saving on rent.
there's more to (someone / something) than meets the eye	used for saying that someone or something is more interesting, impressive, complicated, etc than they seem to be	Joshua might seem quiet and a little boring, but **there's more to** him **than meets the eye**.
think outside the box	to find new ways of doing things, especially of solving problems	We're looking for the ability to **think outside the box** and come up with innovative solutions.
throw in the towel	to stop trying to do something because you lack determination or because you think you cannot win	There are only three candidates now because two of them decided to **throw in the towel**.
time will tell	used for saying that you will know in the future whether something is true or right	It feels like it was the right thing to do, but **time will tell**.
to put it mildly	used for saying that the words you have chosen are not as extreme as they could have been	It was a rather awkward conversation, **to put it mildly**.
touch base with (someone)	to communicate with someone that you have not seen for some time in order to find out how they are, what is happening, etc	I'm planning to **touch base with** Becks when I'm in Manchester.
wet blanket	someone who spoils other people's fun by being negative and complaining	Don't be a **wet blanket** – it'll be fun!
wild goose chase	an attempt to find something that does not exist or that you are very unlikely to discover	There's no one with that name living there – I suspect you've been sent on a **wild goose chase**.

ANSWER KEY

1 THIS IS US

Vocabulary Feelings and emotions

1

1B despondent **2B** ballistic
3B elated **4B** besotted **5B** grossed
6B flabbergasted **7B** engrossed

Speaking Part 3 Long turn

Useful language

Introducing your first main point	Transitioning to another main point
First and foremost... To start off with...	Moving on... Now, turning to...
First of all... I'd like to start by...	My second/third point is... Now let's look at...
Introducing an example	**Summarising**
For instance... A case in point is...	In summary, ... To recap, ...
For example... I'll give you an example of what I mean.	To sum things up... In a nutshell...

Listening Part 1 Multiple choice

1

1 A **2** C **3** C **4** A **5** C **6** B

Pronunciation Consonant clusters with /s/

1

1 stray **2** splurge **3** consists

2

1 streak **2** stroll **3** risks **4** scrapped
5 boasts **6** springboard

Vocabulary Adjectives and nouns with *self*

2

1 satisfied **2** deprecating **3** sacrificing
4 respecting **5** possessed **6** made; indulgent

3

1 self-pity **2** self-worth
3 self-deception

About English

Goblin mode: behaviour that is unapologetically self-indulgent, lazy or greedy

Vax: related to a vaccine, e.g. fully vaxxed, vax sites

Climate emergency: a situation in which urgent action is required to reduce or halt climate change and avoid potentially irreversible environmental damage resulting from it

Toxic: poisonous, unpleasant, e.g. toxic friendship, toxic loans

Post-truth: relating to or denoting circumstances in which objective facts are less influential in shaping public opinion than appeals to emotion and personal belief

Reading and Use of English Part 6 Gapped text

1

1 D **2** A **3** F **4** H **5** B **6** G **7** E

Language Focus The present

1

1 is always looking **2** hope
3 is only getting **4** is spending

2

1A *appear* (stative): to give the impression of being or doing something

B *appear* (dynamic) to be in a film, play, television programme, etc.

2A *attract* (stative): to interest someone in a romantic way

B *attract* (dynamic): to create interest in something which makes people come somewhere or take part in something

3A *conclude* (stative): either to decide or believe something based on what you have heard or seen

B *conclude* (dynamic): to settle an agreement, treaty, negotiation, etc. with someone

4A *consider* (stative): to have a particular opinion about something

B *consider* (dynamic): to think about something carefully before making a decision or forming an opinion.

3

Ready for Grammar

1

A 1 seem **2** promise **3** 'm / am measuring **4** finishes **5** allows **6** do, think

B 1 am / 'm enjoying **2** recognise
3 hear **4** belong **5** am / 'm deciding
6 am / 'm weighing **7** taste

2

1 it always astonishes me

2 correct

3 they're / they are looking

4 mistakes typically involve

5 correct

6 This place owes

7 correct

4

1 absolutely adores **2** 're hanging
3 just wants **4** put **5** hits **6** jumps

6

Yes, the speaker followed all the tips.

Reading and Use of English Part 2 Open cloze

2

1 such **2** case **3** to **4** up **5** face
6 blow **7** Should **8** purpose

4

1 with **2** against **3** from **4** to **5** of
6 at **7** from **8** by/with

Writing Part 2 Article

2

1 A description of one or two ways your personal interests or views have been shaped by global trends.

2 An evaluation of how global trends influence our lives positively or negatively.

3

1 Yes. They discuss how a global trend, manga, has shaped their interests. They also evaluate to what extent global trends like manga are negative or positive.

2 First paragraph: to engage the reader's attention and introduce the topic.

Second paragraph: to explain how our online activities contribute to the development of our personal identities.

Third paragraph: to argue against the idea that global trends and local traditions are in conflict.

Fourth paragraph: to refer back to the opening paragraph – using the organisational pattern of 'topping and tailing' – and to reinforce a main point: that our personal identities can include a harmonious mixture of global and local elements.

3 Yes, the writer holds the reader's attention from start to finish, expressing a mixture of straightforward and complex ideas, using supporting examples and reasons to good effect.

4 *got sucked into the Japanese subculture; globalisation as a juggernaut, squashing local traditions; dulled my enthusiasm for our local festivities; my identity is rooted in the very soil of my home town; sipping a cappuccino at the local café; sporting my favourite Akira T-shirt*, etc.

4

1 "For me it's manga; for you, it might be.."

2 "...globalisation as a juggernaut, squashing local traditions..."

3 "Some see global trends as... Some see globalisation as..."

4 The two sentences in the last paragraph.

5 The reference to *Akira* in the final paragraph, which links back to the opening paragraph.

Useful language

1 The non-profit gave up on hosting the second fundraiser because the results of the first one were unsatisfactory and there was a general lack of enthusiasm among donors. OR The non-profit gave up on hosting the second fundraiser because of the unsatisfactory results of the first one and a general lack of enthusiasm among donors.

Sample answer

Article: The global tide

In our ever-shrinking world, personal identities are not merely shaped by local influences but also by global trends that ripple across borders and cultures. This phenomenon reflects the intricate interplay between our individuality and the larger currents of the world around us. Let's delve into two distinct ways through which personal opinions and interests are moulded by these global trends.

Firstly, the surge of digital connectivity has revolutionised how we perceive and interact with the world. Social media platforms, for instance, expose us to a plethora of ideas and lifestyles from various corners of the globe. A teenager in Tokyo can develop a fondness for Argentine tango, and an artist in New York can find inspiration in the intricate designs of Moroccan architecture. This cultural exchange has broadened our horizons, allowing us to engage with perspectives we might have otherwise missed. However, there's a flip side; the relentless pursuit of likes and shares can also breed a sense of insecurity and the pressure to conform to an idealised global norm.

Secondly, the growing concern for environmental issues has ignited a global passion for sustainable living. The recognition of climate change as a shared threat has prompted individuals from diverse backgrounds to embrace eco-friendly practices. From adopting plant-based diets to advocating for renewable energy, this trend highlights our collective responsibility towards the planet. Yet, it's crucial to acknowledge that the impact of such trends can vary across societies. For some, these lifestyle shifts might be empowering, while others view them as an imposition on cultural practices deeply tied to their identity.

The influence of global trends on personal identities is a double-edged sword, as they expose us to enriching experiences and foster a sense of unity, but they can also blur the line between authenticity and imitation. Therefore, we must recognise that the positive or negative impact of these trends is inherently complex.

Examiner's comments

Content: All content is relevant to the task. The target reader is fully informed about the two issues the writer raises about personal identities shaped by global trends. For each point, the writer weighs the pros and cons that global trends have on individuals in a convincing manner.

Communicative achievement: The writer follows standard article writing conventions by using appropriate combination of direct and indirect speech and a consistent, natural tone. They also communicate their views on the topic in a convincing manner, backing them up with examples.

Organisation: The text is well organised and coherent, and the organisation of the text is logical and easy to follow. The writer uses a variety of cohesive devices and organisational patterns effectively: *Let's delve into two distinct ways through which personal opinions and interests are moulded by these global trends. Firstly; However; Secondly; Yet; Therefore.*

Language: There is a wide range of vocabulary, with some natural turns of phrase and appropriate use of collocation, used effectively and with an appropriate style: *ripple across borders; delve into; a plethora of ideas; there's a flip side; deeply tied to their identity; a double-edged sword.* The wide range of structures is used naturally and all are well suited to the register and topic of the text.

Mark: very good pass

1 Review

Reading and Use of English Part 1 Multiple-choice cloze

1

Despite its potential drawbacks, the trend might be a way to make fashion more sustainable.

2

1 C **2** B **3** B **4** A **5** D **6** C **7** B **8** D

Vocabulary Feelings and emotions

1 by **2** over **3** in **4** with **5** to **6** out **7** in **8** to **9** out

Language Focus The present

1 both possible **2** guess
3 am minding **4** concerns
5 both possible **6** wish
7 both possible **8** holds

Idioms Personality

1

Sentence B is more concise.

A good reason to use idioms is because they convey a lot of information in relatively few words.

2

1 c **2** e **3** d **4** a **5** h **6** f **7** i **8** g **9** b

3

Suggested answers

Positive: come out of her shell, people person, go-getter

Negative: a nasty piece of work, full of himself, have got a chip on your shoulder, wet blanket

Positive or Negative depending on context: creature of habit, live and breathe something, by the book

Discussing idioms

A wet blanket and *a party pooper* are very similar in meaning. They both describe people who disapprove of a particular activity and/or refuse to participate. Generally, *a party pooper* is a childish term and is used more humorously or light-heartedly by adults.

A people person refers to someone who enjoys getting to know others and is particularly good at interacting with different people.

A people pleaser refers to someone who always goes out of their way to do things to please others and to get other people's approval.

A go-getter is someone who is energetic and eager to succeed whereas *a high flyer* is someone who is successful in their career.

2 WANDERLUST

Speaking Part 2 Collaborative task

Useful language

1 about **2** by **3** about **4** what

Vocabulary Travel

1

1 occupied **2** beaten **3** faraway
4 over-run **5** torrential **6** unrestricted

3

1 overseas travel **2** leisurely stroll
3 iconic landmark **4** bustling crowds
5 shoddy service **6** culture shock
7 backwater villages

Reading and Use of English Part 5 Multiple choice

2

1 D **2** C **3** A **4** B **5** C **6** A

Language focus Past forms

1

A 5 and 8 **B** 4 and 7 **C** 1 and 10
D 2 and 9 **E** 3 and 6

2

1 had been (non-sequential past actions)
2 was about to request/had been about to request (intended past actions)
3 was (always) questioning (annoying past actions), would always question
4 expected/had expected/was expecting (stative verbs) **5** ordered (sequential past actions) **6** began / were beginning (sequential past actions) **7** used to/would sit (used to/would for dynamic verb)

Ready for Grammar

1

1 opened, was opening **2** were going to **3** used to have **4** had eaten **5** had located / located **6** were supposed to / were about to / were going to / were to / were due to leave **7** meant **8** had to leave **9** turned into

2

1 had never seen **2** declared **3** was contemplating **4** was always doing **5** would drive / used to drive / drove **6** strengthened **7** would chat / used to chat / chatted **8** started **9** had set **10** was about to come **11** met **12** had been

Listening Part 2 Sentence completion

2

1 last frontier 2 (beautiful) sculptures 3 coastal deserts 4 towering (and) majestic 5 (local) shrub brush 6 layers 7 scorpion 8 (spiral) horns 9 desert greening

Language Focus Adverbs and adverbial phrases

1

1 c 2 a 3 b

2

1 'Even' in sentence A modifies the action 'got support,' expressing surprise about this support. In sentence B, 'even' modifies 'its most longest standing members,' expressing surprise about these members giving their support.

2 In sentence B, there is less emphasis on the adverbial phrase, and therefore the frequency of the action, than in sentence A.

3 In sentence A, the adverb 'reportedly' modifies the whole sentence, giving the speaker's view on the whole situation. In the second sentence, the adverb only modifies the verb 'travelling'. Here the speaker is commenting on that specific action.

4 In sentence A, 'really' modifies 'should', so the emphasis is on the fact that it's a good idea to look at the instructions. In sentence B, however, the adverb modifies the verb "read", so the speaker is emphasising that the person should not just look at the manual, but *really* read it carefully.

5 The meaning of the two sentences is the same, but sentence B has a more sophisticated, literary tone, more likely found in writing than in speech.

Ready for Grammar

1

1 every now and then 2 Even 3 strategically 4 sparsely 5 around the bend 6 afterwards 7 uphill 8 Wholly 9 just 10 only

2

1 short 2 widely 3 Finely 4 deep 5 hard 6 highly 7 lately

3

1 a 2 a 3 b 4 a

4

1 deeply 2 utterly 3 bitterly 4 staggeringly

Word formation Adverbs

1

1 knowingly, purposely 2 admirably, considerably 3 spatially, confidently 4 whereby, thereafter

3

1 clockwise 2 methodically 3 hurriedly 4 regardless 5 homeward

4

1 lengthwise, otherwise, likewise

2 admittedly, supposedly, reputedly

3 doubtless, nevertheless, nonetheless

4 strategically, analytically, thematically

5 onward, backward, seaward

5

1 indefinitely 2 momentarily 3 predominantly, predominately 4 periodically 5 wholeheartedly, heartily 6 relentlessly 7 allegedly

Writing Part 1 Essay

2

1 The parts of the text containing key points tend to use more general, abstract language, while the parts of the text containing supporting examples or reasons tend to be written in more specific and concrete language.

2 **Suggested answers:** for example / instance, like, to illustrate, case in point, e.g., examples include

3 *What's more, also*

4

'It can help you become more independent and self-confident.'

'... you don't have to negotiate your plans with other people, ...'

'Not only is it more fun to travel with other people, ...'

'... it is also more convenient.'

5

The rhetorical question introduces an issue that is central to the piece of writing. The following sentence, which answers the rhetorical question, is the thesis statement. This can be an effective way of organising an introduction to an essay.

6

Suggested answer:

But what about the disadvantages?

7

Sample answer

Journeying alone: Empowerment within or the allure of shared experiences?

There is a lot of public discourse surrounding solo travel these days, where enthusiasts tout its virtues as a path to self-discovery and self-assurance. Undeniably, voyaging alone can be empowering, engendering a sense of self-confidence that resonates deeply. The lone traveller emerges from their journey not just with an array of passport stamps but with a deeper understanding of themself. This newfound self-reliance isn't confined to distant shores; it infiltrates everyday life, making individuals comfortable in their moments of solitude. Beyond this psychological growth, solo travel offers a practical boon. It liberates explorers to indulge in whatever floats their boat, whether that involves unearthing eccentric museums or perusing local antique troves, freed from the constraints of group dynamics.

However, the romanticised allure of solo travel might not withstand scrutiny when faced with the inherent human need for connection. Life's vibrancy often emanates from shared experiences, a truth substantiated by the sentiment that an unshared joy is a joy diminished. This newfound self-reliance isn't confined to distant shores; it infiltrates everyday life, rendering them at ease in their solitude. Furthermore, the convenience of companionship cannot be disregarded. Solo travel lacks the accountability that a fellow traveller provides, leaving one vulnerable to misjudgements and ill-fated choices.

While advocates of solo travel extol its potential for personal growth, critics argue for the irreplaceable enrichment that shared moments provide. The dichotomy between individual empowerment and the inherent human need for shared experiences remains a point of contention. Ultimately, the choice between venturing alone and seeking camaraderie is subjective, hinging on the balance one strikes between self-discovery and shared joy.

Examiner comments

Content: All content is relevant to the task. The target reader is fully informed about the main ideas in the two texts. The writer presents a counterargument about the pros and cons of travelling solo: However, the romanticised allure of solo travel might not withstand scrutiny when up against the inherent human need for connection. The writer's own views are evident throughout the essay.

Communication achievement: Essay writing conventions are used naturally and with flexibility. The evaluation of the key points from the input texts is combined with the writer's opinions, and complex ideas are communicated convincingly. The writer has adopted a semi-formal tone, which is used consistently to engage and hold the reader's interest.

Organisation: The essay is well-organised and coherent. The shift between the different points in the input texts develops naturally. The writer also presents a counterargument, which enables the writer to express a range of opinions on the topic effectively: *While advocates of solo travel extol its potential for perrsonal growth, critics argue for the irreplaceable enrichment that shared moments provide.* Cohesive devices and organisational patterns are used flexibly: *This newfound self-reliance; it infiltrates; Beyond this psychological growth; However, the romanticised allure; Furthermore.*

Language: A range of less common lexis is used with sophistication and precision: *enthusiasts tout its virtues; engendering; array; infiltrates; boon; allure; emanates,* etc. The use of grammar is natural and sophisticated.

Mark: very good pass

About English

WFH = Work from home

BRB = Be right back

JSYK = Just so you know

IRL = in real life

AKA = also known as

2 Review

Vocabulary Travel

1

1 flight **2** arduous **3** far-flung
4 stroll **5** shoddy **6** travel

Reading and Use of English Part 3 Word formation

1 unprecedented **2** circumvents
3 faraway **4** picturesque **5** invariably
6 compile **7** periodically **8** scenarios

Reading and Use of English Part 4 Key word transformation

1 instant / moment / second / minute they set foot in

2 made no reference to / did not / didn't make (any / a) reference to the influence

3 improvement in the performance of the stock market / the way the stock market performed / how the stock market performed

4 was a lack of diplomacy in

5 was held up by / due to / because of / owing to / on account of / as a result of unforeseen

6 take exception to the rudeness of

Idioms Making stories interesting

2

1 life **2** tell **3** wrong **4** luck
5 second **6** mildly **7** me **8** hands
9 said **10** story

3

1 To scare somebody very much.

2 You will only know a result or outcome in the future.

3 Don't take what I'm saying as negative criticism.

4 Something very fortunate that happens unexpectedly.

5 Less than a second, an instant.

6 What I'm talking about is even more extreme than my words suggest.

7 Keep what I'm saying a secret.

8 Easily, without question.

9 Something has advantages.

10 You don't believe what somebody said.

4

1 // I did see a <u>scorpion</u> // I almost stepped on it // and it scared the <u>life</u> out of me //

2 // Time will <u>tell</u> // whether or not // they can be <u>saved</u>.

6

Discussing idioms

A split second is used, often in narratives, to describe a very brief amount of time. *For a split second, I thought I was going to fall down the escalator.*

A New York minute also means a very short amount of time, but it is more informal and can convey a sense of urgency. *I need that document in a New York minute.*

Don't get me wrong is used to clarify meaning. It is often used to make sure that the person you are speaking to doesn't misunderstand your message, especially if trying to avoid them taking it as negative criticism: *Work is just so stressful at the moment. Don't get me wrong, I love my job and being busy, but this is too much.*

Don't take this the wrong way is often used before you go on to say something a bit critical of the person you are talking to: *Don't take this the wrong way, but I don't think you've put much effort into this essay.*

A stroke of luck is used to indicate that something lucky happened by chance. *I found my dream wedding dress in the sale, so it was 50% off! It was a complete stroke of luck.*

A lucky break is when you have good things happen to you, especially with regard to your career. *Harrison Ford got his lucky break while working as a carpenter. He was asked to read the lines for Hans Solo and George Lucas was so impressed he gave him the role.*

Ready for Reading and Use of English Parts 1–4

Reading and Use of English Part 1 Multiple-choice cloze

2

1 B **2** A **3** D **4** B **5** B **6** C **7** D
8 A

3

0 c **1** c **2** c **3** c **4** d **5** c **6** a
7 d **8** c

Reading and Use of English Part 2 Open cloze

2

1 little **2** their **3** were **4** about **5** of
6 have **7** Not **8** provided

3

A

Reading and Use of English Part 3 Word formation

2

1 consistently **2** perfectionist
3 exemplify **4** miscalculation(s)
5 composition **6** irresistible
7 exceptional **8** practitioners

3

1 *consistently* is an adverb.

2 *perfectionist* is a noun.

3 *exemplify* is a verb.

4 *calculation(s)* is a noun. The answer could be both singuar or plural. The prefix *mis-* makes it negative.

5 *composition* is a noun.

6 *resistible* is an adjective. The prefix *ir-* makes it negative.

7 *exceptional* is an adjective.

8 *practitioners* is a plural noun.

Reading and Use of English Part 4 Key word transformations

1 would be given a hard time by journalists

It will be in the passive.

to give someone a hard time

2 couldn't / could not / could never / was unable to / was not able to / was never able to hold down a

to hold down

It should be in the past. It should be negative.

3 doesn't / does not stand a chance of

of often precedes the *-ing* form

stand a chance

4 was (feeling) / felt / had been (feeling) under the weather

It should be either in the past or past perfect

be / feel under the weather

5 it bore no / little resemblance to the pictures

Not at all.

bear no / little resemblance to

6 had been / were on the verge of walking out / leaving / resigning

The past simple or the past perfect; *on the verge of*

3 AHEAD OF THE CURVE

Reading and Use of English Part 7 Multiple matching

1

1 B **2** E **3** C **4** B **5** F **6** C **7** D
8 A **9** E **10** D

Language focus Talking about the future

1

If you say something *is likely to* happen, you are saying there is a good probability of it happening.

If you say something *is bound to* happen, you are saying emphatically that it is certain to happen.

If you say something *is due to* happen, you are saying it's scheduled to happen at a certain time in the future.

2

1 a **2** b **3** e **4** d **5** c

4

1 will come **2** will live **3** has been aiming **4** were seen to be

Ready for Grammar

1

1 B **2** A **3** B **4** C **5** A

2

1 was (just) about to resign

2 will be catching up

3 will have been (together as) a couple

4 was on the verge of announcing the removal

5 is not / isn't aiming to stay (for) (any)

6 is due to expire / run out at

7 be possible (for me) to speak to / with

8 to have no idea (of) what is going

Vocabulary Phrasal verbs and noun collocations

1

1 run **2** plough **3** hold

2

1 c **2** f **3** a **4** h **5** j **6** b **7** d
8 i **9** e **10** g

4

2 throw out **3** come round
4 meet with **5** come up with
6 stumble across **7** draw on
8 put forward **9** hold out
10 flick through

5

1 draw on **2** bring down **3** meet with
4 throw out **5** put forward, come up with

Writing Part 2 Review

2

Yes. In the second and third paragraphs, the writer mixes description with evaluation. This is common in reviews.

3

1 particularly **2** automatically
3 exceptionally **4** fiendishly
5 inadvertently

4

"I was smitten"

"This is particularly handy for ... "

" ... you can easily ... "

" ... is exceptionally / extremely good at ..."

"... got on my nerves"

"... is fiendishly difficult to find..."

" ... makes it far too easy to..."

"But the big problem is ..."

" ... does a poor job of ..."

" ... is also problematic"

"... is an atrocious place to..."

"Were it less aggravating ..."

5

distinguish itself **from**

similar **to** messaging apps

Just tap **on** a single email

Flow soon got **on** my nerves.

does a poor job **of** handling

my email **on** my computer

true **of** many apps

consider **for** a moment

6 Sample answer

In today's fast-paced world, where multitasking and constant distractions are the norm, staying productive has become a paramount challenge. Enter Habitica – a revolutionary habit tracker app that not only helps users build and track productive habits but also adds a gamified twist to the process. In a society where productivity is key, Habitica manages to stand out as a vital tool for individuals intent on making the most of their time.

Habitica is not just another habit tracker; it is a platform that transforms mundane tasks and habits into an engaging role-playing game-like experience. Users create their avatars and embark on a journey to conquer real-life tasks and goals. With each completed task, the avatars level up and unlock rewards, enhancing the sense of accomplishment and motivation. This ingenious blend of habit tracking and gamification has added an element of fun and excitement to otherwise mundane activities.

In contemporary society, where digital devices dominate every aspect of life, apps like Habitica play a pivotal role. They bridge the gap between our increasingly digital lifestyles and our desire for self-improvement. The app harnesses the addictive nature of technology for a positive cause, effectively turning procrastination into motivation. Habitica's approach aligns well with the modern mindset, providing a tangible sense of progress and achievement through virtual means.

Furthermore, Habitica addresses the need for holistic productivity. It tracks work-related tasks and encourages me to focus on my personal development, health, and well-being. This comprehensive approach to productivity reflects the changing dynamics of contemporary society, where work-life balance and mental well-being are of utmost importance.

In conclusion, Habitica is a shining example of the growing significance of apps in today's society. It not only aids individuals in enhancing their productivity but also demonstrates the power of technology to transform routine activities into exciting and rewarding experiences. As we navigate the challenges of the digital age, Habitica's blend of habit tracking and gamification offers a practical solution to the productivity puzzle, making it an essential tool for those striving to succeed in the modern world.

Examiner's comments

Content: All content is relevant to the task. The target reader is fully informed about the app, which the writer uses and endorses. The app is briefly described, giving some information about how it helps to positively reinforce productivity by gamifying tasks. The writer evaluates the importance apps have on contemporary society.

Communicative achievement: The conventions of writing a review, such as the use of an informative tone and a positive viewpoint, are used to communicate complex ideas in an effective and convincing way. The app and the impact it has had on the writer is described clearly and with enthusiasm. The target reader's attention is held with ease and all the communicative purposes of the task are fulfilled.

Organisation: The text is well-organised and coherent, and the paragraphs are well structured. A good range of cohesive devices and organisation patterns are used to link ideas across sentences and paragraphs in a natural way: *Habitica is not just another habit tracker; This ingenious blend of habit tracking; Furthermore; In conclusion.*

Language: A variety of topic-specific vocabulary, including less common lexis is used effectively and precisely to communicate specific ideas: *a paramount challenge; adds a gamified twist; a vital tool*, etc. A wide range of simple and complex grammatical forms are used with full control, flexibility, and sophistication: ... *not only aids individuals in enhancing their productivity but also demonstarates the power of technology; As we navigate the challenges of the digital age*, etc.

Mark: very good pass

Reading and Use of English Part 3 Word formation

1

1 inconceivable **2** windfall **3** enrolled
4 effectively **5** momentous **6** decoded
7 curiosities **8** definitive / definite

Listening Part 4 Multiple matching

1

1 B **2** E **3** H **4** A **5** C **6** B **7** A
8 E **9** F **10** C

Vocabulary Prepositional phrases

1

1 You say that something exists in *a big way* to emphasise its great extent or importance.

2 You are *under attack* if you experience aggressive or violent acts.

3 You say something will happen *in all likelihood* if you are almost certain it will.

4 You say something happens *on the spot* if it happens at that moment or place.

5 You say one thing happens *at the expense of* another if the first thing harms the second thing.

2

1 under **2** on **3** in **4** at

3

1 the forefront of **2** threat **3** jeopardy
4 odds with **5** a par with

Pronunciation Vowel length before voiced and unvoiced consonants

1

Sentence 1, the vowel in *man* is longer.

2

Words with a longer vowel sound (i.e. before voiced consonants): big, come, good, have, leave, reel, tool

Listening Part 1 Multiple choice

1

1 B **2** A **3** B **4** C **5** B **6** A

Language focus *will*, *shall* and *would*

1

1 B **2** A **3** B **4** A **5** A **6** A **7** A

Ready for Grammar

1

1 C **2** F **3** B **4** H **5** D

2

1 will be feeling **2** shall pass **3** Shall, make **4** 'll / will / would calm **5** Will / Would, let **6** shall / will be sent **7** shall do **8** would call **9** will not / won't be

3 Review

Reading and Use of English Part 2 Open cloze

2

1 Each **2** in **3** more **4** to **5** use **6** give **7** say **8** ways

Language focus

1 won't have bought **2** will be completing **3** bound to open **4** Would we have **5** would

Reading and Use of English Part 4 Key word transformations

1 as I love espresso, there is / I have no doubt / question

2 in for (some) unjust criticism

3 no circumstances is this laptop (ever) to be

4 full implementation of the policy

5 was told in no uncertain terms

6 from being irritated by the children's

Idioms Innovation

1

1 If you start *from scratch*, you do something from the very beginning, without using any work done earlier.

2 In races, runners used to scratch a long line in the ground, so that everyone would start from the same place.

2

1 c **2** h **3** e **4** b **5** f **6** d **7** a **8** g **9** i

3

Suggested answers

in the pipeline: in the process of being planned or developed

teething problems: when a new project or product has small problems at the beginning

stumbling block: something that causes problems and stops you from reaching your goal

on the right track: thinking or behaving in a way that will lead to success

dead end: a situation in which no progress is possible

long shot: something that has little chance of succeeding

at the leading edge: to be in the most advanced position in an area of activity, such as technology

think outside the box: to approach a problem in a new or innovative way that shows imagination

go round in circles: to work hard at something or discuss it at length without making any progress

4

1 on the right track **2** dead end **3** at the leading edge **4** think outside the box **5** in the pipeline **6** teething problems **7** go round in circles **8** long shot **9** stumbling block

These are examples of 'puns', a kind of joke that plays on two different meanings of the same word or phrase to humorous effect.

Discussing idioms

A stumbling block refers to an issue that impedes progress. *The chief negotiator has disclosed that there are still several stumbling blocks to overcome before peace can finally be restored to the region.*

A chip off the old block we say this about someone whose character or behaviour is very similar to their parent's. *Sam loves formula 1 like his dad. He's a real chip off the old block.*

Go round in circles to keep doing or discussing the same thing(s) without managing to achieve anything. *We're not making any progress! We're just going round in circles on this matter.*

Go round the bend an informal way to say you're going crazy, or beginning to behave in an unreasonable way. Also *drive around the bend. I'm going round the bend with all these forms. Why does it have to be so complicated?*

A long shot is something that is unlikely to succeed but worth trying. *When I applied for an internship at the company, I knew it was a long shot, but figured I'd do it anyway.*

A shot in the dark when you try to guess something but don't know anything about the subject, or have no knowledge about it. *My boss asked me about our team's finances. I said we had spent 20% of the budget. It was a total shot in the dark.*

4 MEETING IN THE MIDDLE

Listening Part 3 Multiple choice

2

1 B **2** C **3** A **4** A **5** C

Language focus Modal verbs

1

1 might **2** can **3** should **4** ought not to

3

1 Need I remind you that homework makes up 20 per cent of your overall mark?

2 The presence of the prime minister should be sufficient to bring about the necessary arrangement.

3 You needn't have picked me up at the airport.

4 You might have told me sooner that you were planning to drop the course!

5 You oughtn't to respond to an irritating email before you've had time to calm down.

6 What a wonderfully thoughtful gift! You shouldn't have!

Ready for Grammar

4 Modals

1

1 shouldn't / should not **2** May **3** must **4** should / ought to **5** ought

2

1 *Need* I mention the number of...?

2 ... but try as we *might*, we just couldn't find...

3 You *ought to / should / might / could* have said you weren't staying for lunch.

4 You really *oughtn't / ought not* to allow that student to speak...

5 ... to be actively trading, you *had to have purchased* a membership...

6 ... he *needn't have uttered / didn't need to utter* a word to show her how he felt.

Pronunciation Stressed modal auxiliaries

1

In the first sentence, we don't know the result. In the second, the speaker knows they didn't pass and they are implying they could have passed it if, perhaps, they had had better luck or studied harder.

2

1 B, A **2** A, B **3** A, B **4** B, A **5** A, B

Vocabulary Partitive expressions with uncountable nouns

1

D

2

1 e **2** j **3** g **4** h **5** c **6** i **7** b **8** f **9** a **10** d

Reading and Use of English Part 6 Gapped text

1

Suggested answers: Hostage negotiator / business people. Negotiation techniques include listening, asking open ended questions, gaining rapport and emotional intelligence / identification.

2

1 E 2 H 3 F 4 A 5 D 6 G 7 B

Language focus Noun phrases and nominal clauses

1

Sentence B sounds more formal and academic because the writer uses nouns to communicate their message.

The adjective *organised* and verb *preceded* change to nouns (*organisation* and *predecessor*) in sentence B.

2

1 careful analysis / dramatic increase
2 logical deduction / conclusion
3 efficient allocation
4 high tolerance / first encounters
5 argument / baggage allowance
6 emotional intensity / refusal

3

1 were 2 are 3 is 4 is 5 is 6 has 7 operates 8 promotes

Ready for Grammar

1

1 has expressed 2 has been damaged 3 consists 4 have called 5 contain 6 plans / is planning 7 list

2

Possible answer: *This study is an* **exploration of** *the* **effects** *of parent–child relationships on the academic performance of university students. Using Social Cognitive Theory, the study proposes a method* **for the validation of** *the chain-mediating role played by psychological capital, that is, the internal resources that help us* **succeed in the management of** *difficult situations. The results show a* **significant and positive correlation** *between academic performance and parent-child relationships, owing in part to the chain-mediating role of psychological capital. Furthermore, this study also* **sets forward a proposal** *for mental health guidelines,* **the adoption of which** *could help students to better handle their relationships with their parents. This could in turn* **lead to greater accumulation of** *psychological capital. The study concludes* **with an argument for** *why there is no* **justification for** *the relatively little* **emphasis** *currently being placed on mental health in higher education.*

Additional materials Word formation Nouns

1 memorial, intellectual, announcement, portrayal, denial

2 justification, persuasion, intrusion, collision, inclusion

3 initiative, tolerance, sedative, narrative, explosive

4 resemblance, resistance, compliance, emergence, ignorance

5 recognition, aspiration, assumption, resolution, fusion

6 indifference, dependence, correspondence, residence, dominance

7 resentment, brightness, engagement, amendment, attachment

8 clumsiness, goodness, gratification, wildness/wilderness, righteousness

9 resilience, extremist, physicist, finalist, pianist

10 craving, saying, publishing, serenity, gathering

2

1 forgiveness 2 degradation
3 prominence 4 concession
5 proceedings 6 revival 7 withdrawal
8 alliance

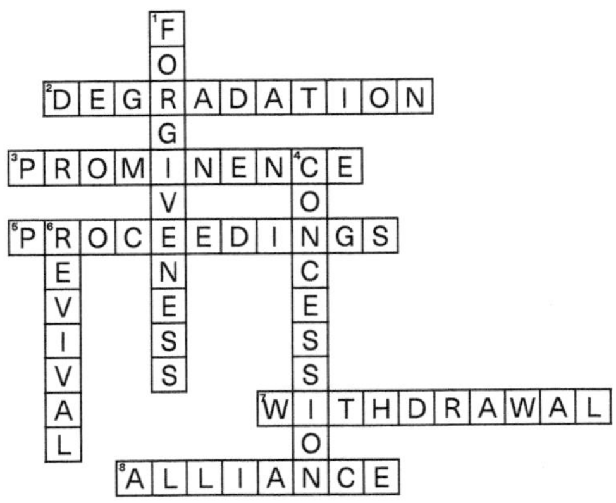

Vocabulary Closed compounds

1

1 scapegoat 2 wavelength
3 watershed 4 backlash 5 stalemate

2

1 If you *become a scapegoat*, you are blamed for a failure or for something bad that somebody else has done.

2 If you are *on the same wavelength*, you have the same way of thinking or the same ideas as somebody else.

3 If an event marks an important change in life or in society, it can be called a *watershed moment.*

4 If you *spark a backlash*, you experience a strong negative reaction from a large number of people.

5 If you break a *stalemate*, you overcome a disagreement or a situation where neither side can win or make any progress.

3

1 keepsakes 2 turnover 3 willpower
4 shortcomings 5 proofread

Listening Part 2 Sentence completion

1

1 seniority 2 (workplace) incivility
3 sick leave 4 flip charts 5 pace
6 emotional intelligence 7 mindset
8 enactment 9 without prejudice

Writing Part 2 Letter

1

The purpose of the letter is to share your own views and experiences with the readers of the magazine related to a feature called 'Have our relationships moved online?'

There are three points to include:
1) describe a personal or business relationship that developed online; 2) evaluate the quality of online relationships; 3) say to what extent they can replace meeting people face-to-face.

2

Suggested answer:

Opening paragraph: Disagree with arguments made in feature: *there are also benefits*

First paragraph : Focus on story: how I met Maria online and developed a friendship

Second paragraph: Focus on benefits:

1) breaking the ice 2) meeting people with mutual interest

Closing paragraph:

–'call to action': *this topic is worth further exploration*

3

Suggested answers:

1 **needs improvement (1)**: The writer tells the story of a relationship that developed online. However, she only indirectly evaluates the quality of online relationships and does not clearly state to what extent they could replace meeting people face-to-face.

2 **excellent (3)**: The writer appropriately begins (*To the editor*) and ends (*Best regards*) her letter.

3 **satisfactory (2)**: The writer uses a formal tone throughout, even when describing personal experiences (*It was with great interest...; ... she kindly agreed to ...*), but the use of contractions (*it's, she's, I'd*) is less appropriate in this context.

4 **excellent (3)**: The main ideas are divided into well-developed paragraphs. There is a clear progression from start to finish.

5 **excellent (3)**: The writer provides personal examples to support the two points made in the third paragraph (she is shy but finds it easy to interact online; the connections she has made are with people who share her interests).

6 **excellent (3)**: There are various examples of C2 Proficiency level vocabulary (*belittle, trigger memories, reclaimed wood, nook, blossom, join a flock of like-minded people, stepping stone*) and grammar (subordination, noun clauses, verb patterns, tense contrasts, relative and participle clauses).

7 Sample answer

Dear Editor,

I am writing to share my experience of a remarkable online business relationship that has not only defied physical barriers but has also transformed how I perceive virtual interactions today.

Several months ago, I stumbled upon an online platform dedicated to connecting professionals in my field. Intrigued, I decided to create a profile and engage with the community. It wasn't long before I crossed paths with Valentina, a like-minded entrepreneur who shared my passion for sustainable technology solutions. What started as a few comments on each other's posts soon evolved into extensive conversations about our respective ventures.

Our online collaboration led to joint projects, where we worked together regardless of being miles apart. The ease of communication through messages, emails, and video calls streamlined our decision-making process. For instance, we exchanged ideas, reviewed lengthy documents, and even presented proposals to potential clients, all without having met in person.

The quality of this online business relationship has been truly phenomenal. Despite the absence of physical proximity, our connection feels genuine and strong. The exchange of ideas has been as vibrant as any in-person meeting, and the convenience of scheduling virtual calls has allowed us to maintain a steady pace of progress.

However, while my experience has been overwhelmingly positive, I recognise that online relationships might not be universally seamless. Non-verbal cues, personal interactions, and the camaraderie forged during face-to-face meetings are irreplaceable. In certain complex negotiations, the subtleties of body language can make all the difference. Moreover, conducting business solely online can sometimes hinder building deep emotional connections, which are crucial for trust in certain business partnerships.

In closing, my journey with Valentina has underscored the incredible potential of online relationships in the business world, which can transcend geographical constraints and foster productive collaborations. Yet, it's important to acknowledge that while digital interactions offer convenience, they cannot fully replicate the richness of in-person encounters. Striking a balance between virtual and physical interactions remains key to nurturing well-rounded and enduring business relationships.

Sincerely,

Jules Diaz

Examiner's comments

Content: All content is relevant to the task and the target reader is fully informed. The writer has described their personal observations, illustrating their experience of conducting business online. The writer evaluates the pros and cons of forming business relationships online.

Communicative achievement: The conventions of formal letter writing, such as appropriate opening and closing salutations and a neutral tone, are used flexibly.

Organisation: The text is well-organised and coherent as a whole. A variety of cohesive devices and organisational patterns are used flexibly, and punctuation is used to good effect: *it wasn't long before...; Despite the absence; However, while my experience has been overwhelmingly positive; In closing; Yet, it's important to acknowledge.* Complex ideas are communicated in an effective and convincing manner, holding the target reader's attention with ease, and fulfilling the communicative purposes of the task.

Language: A range of vocabulary, including less common lexis, is used effectively and precisely: defied physical barriers; stumbled upon; crossed paths; respective ventures; truly phenomenal, etc... A wide range of simple and complex grammatical forms is used with control, flexibility and sophistication: *Having stumbled upon an online platform; as vibrant as any in-person meeting; The ease of communication through messages, etc...*

Mark: very good pass

4 Review

Vocabulary

1 willpower, round **2** stroke, comeback
3 scapegoat, scrap **4** breath, proofread
5 pang, keepsakes

Reading and Use of English Part 1 Multiple-choice cloze

1 A **2** B **3** B **4** D **5** A **6** B **7** D **8** C

Language focus

1 is / was going to **2** employs **3** trusts
4 doesn't **5** contains **6** Sophie's

Idioms Negotiation

1

emphasise a particular point

2

1 common ground **2** bottom line
3 sticking point **4** grey area **5** the air
6 finer points **7** to disagree **8** wrong foot **9** meet us

3

Suggested answers:

bottom line – the most important factor to consider in a situation

clear the air – to improve a situation of tension by discussing worries or doubts

nail down the finer points – to reach an agreement or decision about specific and/or complicated aspects of something

common ground – interests, beliefs or opinions shared by people who disagree about other things

grey area – an unclear situation that is difficult to define or deal with

sticking point – something that people can't reach an agreement on during a discussion or negotiation

agree to disagree – to accept you have different views and stop trying to change another person's mind

get off on the wrong foot – to begin badly by doing something in completely the wrong way

meet halfway – to reach a compromise in which you give the other person part of what they want

Discussing idioms

agree to disagree – also *agree to differ.* To accept that you have different opinions on a matter and decide to stop arguing about it or trying to persuade the other to change their mind.

see eye to eye – completely agree about something. *My parents never argue. They actually seem to see eye to eye on almost everything.*

clear the air – diffuse an angry or tense situation and get rid of bad feelings between people. *Raúl and I had a frank discussion, and finally opened up what had been irritating us. It really helped to clear the air and now things are so much better.*

break the ice – say something to relieve tension or get a conversation started between strangers. *At the dinner party, it was a bit awkward at first but once we had broken the ice, we had some really interesting conversations.*

find common ground – discover what shared interests or opinions you have with someone. *Although you may not like your neighbours, the key to getting along is to find some common ground.*

stand one's ground – not to retreat or lose advantage in face of opposition. *In spite of all the opposition's attempts to undermine her and intimidate her, Parvati stood her ground and won the lawsuit.*

Ready for Reading and Use of English Parts 5–7

Reading and Use of English Part 5 Multiple choice

2

1 B **2** C **3** A **4** D **5** A **6** C

Additional materials Reading and Use of English Part 5 Multiple choice

1 shift **2** tribute **3** light
4 allowances **5** fault **6** importance
7 comparison **8** lie

Reading and Use of English Part 6 Gapped text

3

1 D **2** E **3** H **4** A **5** F **6** G **7** B

Reading and Use of English Part 7 Multiple matching

3

1 C 2 E 3 B 4 D 5 C 6 A 7 E 8 A 9 C 10 B

5 NEWS TRAVELS FAST

Reading and Use of English Part 6 Gapped text

2

1 F 2 H 3 B 4 A 5 D 6 C 7 G

Language focus Cohesion

1

1 in publishing salacious and sensationalist stories

2 the hoax moon story in the *New York Sun*

3 stories

4 'yellow journalism'

5 omitting past participle 'used', i.e. the techniques are still being used

6 news sites

7 whip up excitement

8 other kinds of posts

Ready for Grammar

1

1 Like humans, the animals worked together, with each pack member looking out for the others.

2 ~~He~~ His wasn't the most professional looking presentation, but his ideas were second to none.

3 ... A partnership like theirs...

4 Everybody has a weak spot, and this, unfortunately, is theirs.

5 Do you enjoy travelling, find it stressful or have no strong feelings about it?

6 Please use safety goggles when working with the chemicals, especially the ones / those that give off noxious fumes.

2

Sample answer:

1 a talent like / such as hers 2 the ones (that) I read 3 His wasn't an 4 Must've been the bad weather. 5 each playing off the other

3

1 substitution 2 reference 3 substitution 4 reference 5 ellipsis 6 reference 7 substitution 8 ellipsis

4

1 Hers 2 ones 3 each 4 other 5 so 6 such 7 hers 8 one

Vocabulary Neutral and sensationalist language

1

1 *scrap* and *oust*. Newspapers use them because they are more sensational and tempt the reader more than *remove*.

2

1 quash 2 condemn, slam 3 pledge, vow 4 provoke, spark 5 laud, tout 6 clash, dispute 7 divulge, leak

3

1 both possible 2 touted 3 clash 4 axed 5 pledged 6 both possible 7 divulge

4

1 leaked 2 to quash 3 have vowed 4 are lauding / have lauded 5 clash 6 disputed 7 divulge

Reading and Use of English Part 1 Multiple-choice cloze

1

1 D 2 B 3 A 4 A 5 C 6 B 7 C 8 D

Vocabulary Binomials

1

cut and dried means completely decided

2

1 foremost 2 outs 3 forth 4 large 5 go 6 error 7 tested 8 starts 9 cheese 10 take 11 white

3

1 First and foremost 2 fits and starts 3 back and forth 4 ins and outs 5 tried and tested 6 By and large 7 cut and dried 8 trial and error

Pronunciation Binomials

1

1 *change* has the longer vowel sound

2 *chop* is the word that is stressed more

3 *chop* is connected to *and* – this is a general pattern that the first word is stressed, and the last word often (but not always) has a long vowel sound.

3

ins and outs, back and forth, by and large, touch and go, fits and starts, chalk and cheese, give and take, black and white (others tend to have a stress on the first word but longer vowel sounds at the beginning).

About English

here, there and everywhere; hook, line and sinker; beg, borrow or steal; blood, sweat and tears

4

They don't tend to follow the same pattern.

Listening Part 4 Multiple matching

1 D 2 G 3 A 4 C 5 F 6 G 7 H 8 B 9 F 10 D

Language focus Demonstratives

1

1 this 2 that 3 those 4 that

Ready for Grammar

1

1 That dog of theirs 2 For those 3 those 4 this door that has always been 5 those 6 That child of hers

2

1 this 2 This 3 those 4 those

3

Sentence one is neither positive or negative. Sentences two and three have a negative connotation. Sentence four, while looking like it may be negative is, within the context, positive due to the result.

4

1 this 2 those 3 this 4 those 5 that 6 this

Writing Part 2 Article

1

You have to describe someone who demonstrates the ability to communicate effectively in a second language, as well as explain what personal qualities make people effective communicators in international contexts.

2

Introduction B is more appropriate to an article because it grabs the reader's attention and makes them want to keep reading. The first introduction would be more appropriate for an essay.

3

Tip 1: Roger Federer is famous, so many readers will be interested in reading an article about him.

Tip 2: This advice is followed throughout the article, but it is particularly evident in the paragraph about where Federer grew up.

Tip 3: The writer does this in a variety of ways. They use phrases such as 'Let me explain.' But they also write sentences that create a bit of suspense, e.g. 'But Federer demonstrates a better approach.' The reader wants to keep reading in order to find out what this approach is.

Tip 5: The writer is clearly a fan of Federer and knows a lot about his life, but they don't go into too much detail, limiting themselves to details that support to the points they want to make.

5 Sample answer

Navigating the Labyrinth of Second Language Communication

In a world as interconnected as ours, the art of communication knows no boundaries. We find ourselves conversing with individuals from diverse linguistic backgrounds in languages other than our mother tongue. The beauty of effective communication, I believe, lies in its universality and ability to transcend linguistic borders.

Effective communication, irrespective of the language in question, hinges on some fundamental principles. First and foremost, one must be able to articulate ideas with precision, leaving no room for ambiguity. Secondly, actively listening to understand the nuances of another language. Lastly, it requires patience and a willingness to adapt, as languages constantly evolve and adapt to the cultural contexts in which they thrive.

However, when we step into the realm of second language communication, a unique set of challenges presents itself, as we grapple with unfamiliar grammar rules, idiomatic expressions, and cultural nuances. The fear of miscommunication can be paralysing, leading to self-doubt. This raises a valid concern: Is the pursuit of truly mastering a second language always worth the effort?

Indeed, there are critics who argue that mastering a second language is unnecessary in this day and age. In our increasingly globalised world, English often serves as a lingua franca, making it possible for individuals to merely get by in this universal language.

In my view, the key to becoming proficient in English lies in immersing myself in the culture and its people while embracing my mistakes as stepping stones to improvement. While this approach may require significant effort, the rewards of bridging cultural divides and truly connecting with people from different backgrounds are undeniable.

In conclusion, second language communication presents challenges, and valid arguments against it exist. However, it's essential to recognise its many benefits including how it can enrich our understanding of different cultures and perspectives, which ultimately contributes to a more interconnected and empathetic world. Embrace the labyrinth of linguistic diversity; it's a journey leading to deeper human connections and a more interconnected world.

Examiner's Comments

Content: All content is relevant to the task. The target reader is fully informed about the writer's point of view, and they present a counterargument to weigh the pros and cons of mastering a second language.

Communicative achievement: The writer follows appropriate article-writing conventions. They achieve this by using an engaging tone to hold the target reader's attention to communicate straightforward and more complex ideas. The use of a rhetorical question in the third paragraph sets up the counterargument well: *Is the pursuit of truly mastering a second language always worth the effort?*

Organisation: The text is well organised and coherent, using a variety of cohesive devices and organisational patterns to generally good effect: *First and foremost; Secondly; Lastly; However; This raises a valid concern; In my view; While this approach... In conclusion*

Language: There is a wide range of vocabulary, with some very natural turns of phrase and appropriate use of collocation, used effectively and with style: *transcend linguistic borders; leaving no room for ambiguity; grapple with; stepping stones to improvement; bridging cultural divides; Embrace the labyrinth of linguistic diversity.*

Mark: very good pass

5 Review

Reading and Use of English Part 2 – Open Cloze

1 so **2** tip **3** fast **4** own **5** up
6 much **7** by **8** take

Vocabulary

1 axe **2** sparked **3** cut and dried
4 leaked **5** touch and go **6** Touted
7 black and white **8** tried and tested

Reading and Use of English Part 4

1 as I might to persuade

2 it hadn't been for the influence

3 be all and end

4 not visible / invisible to the naked

5 be at the expense of

6 nothing short of a miracle

Idioms Communication

1

1 The first conversation is informal. It is two people, perhaps friends, discussing another person. The second conversation is a business context where one person has not done something they needed to.

2 The second conversation is more polite. The language is more formal than in the first conversation.

2

1 beat around the bush **2** it was news to me **3** got our wires crossed
4 catch my drift

3

1 out of the loop **2** touch base
3 the wrong end of the stick **4** boo to a goose **5** something off your chest

4

Used to soften meaning: get something off your chest, get our wires crossed, get the wrong end of the stick

5

Sentences to change: **1** touch base
2 got the wrong end of the stick
4 I'm completely out of the loop
5 get it off your chest

Discussing idioms

be out of the loop – if someone is out of the loop on something they are not up-to-date on a certain matter – they haven't been included in the process or conversation. This is especially common when related to work matters.

be in the dark also means you do not know about something, but it has the additional meaning that you have absolutely no information about it at all. Perhaps you do not even know that the situation exists. *We need to tell the staff soon about the takeover. We can't keep them in the dark for much longer – word will start to get out.*

touch base – to briefly get in contact with someone. *I'm just writing to touch base. How are you getting on with the project? Will you be able to send it to me soon?*

cover all bases = also *have all your bases covered.* to deal with something thoroughly and prepare for all eventualities. *In preparation for the job interview, keep in mind a set of different examples that you can use and adapt for different questions. They might not ask you about all of them but it's good to have all your bases covered.*

get something off your chest – get a feeling of relief after finally saying something you've wanted to say for a while. *I felt so much better after talking to my dad and getting that secret off my chest.*

get a monkey off your back = to get rid of something that is a burden or a problem. *Next week I'll make the final payment on my loan and I'll finally get that monkey off my back!*

6 HIGHS AND LOWS

Listening Part 1 Multiple choice

2

1 B **2** A **3** A **4** C **5** A **6** C

Pronunciation Assimilation

2

Because the sounds are very similar, the mouth naturally moves to the position for the second sound to make it easier to connect the words together in fluent speech.

1 /m/ **2** /k/ **3** /ŋ/ **4** /b/ **5** /m/
6 /b/

Vocabulary Expressions and phrases with *pay*

1

1 your own way **2** it forward **3** your respects **4** the price **5** dividends
6 through the nose **7** a compliment
8 lip service **9** tribute to

Language focus Conditional clauses

1

1 Provided that **2** even if **3** Supposing
4 in case of

2

1 on provision that / provided that **2** But for / What if **3** in the event that / supposing

3

1 second **2** first **3** zero **4** mixed
5 third

4

Sentence 4

5

1 a **2** c **3** b **4** d **5** e

Ready for Grammar

1

1 c **2** a **3** a **4** c **5** a **6** b **7** c
8 b

2

Suggested answers:

1 to be useful, the new pay form would have to be put online.

2 we didn't go out for dinner so often? We could save money more quickly.

3 for the broken printer, I would have handed my report in on time.

4 had not been for Olivia's quick thinking, we might have lost the sale.

5 I hadn't accepted the promotion, I wouldn't be so stressed now.

6 the team win the next two matches, I don't think they'll win the World Cup.

7 been for my manager, I would have left the company sooner.

8 the project will have any effect, unless the whole community takes part.

Vocabulary *Rise* and *fall*

2

1 spiralling / soaring, hike up
2 waned / dwindled, escalating / mounting **3** swelled **4** wane / dwindle
5 plummeted **6** spiralling / soaring / escalating, soar / mount

3

rise = escalate, hike, mount, soar, swell

fall = dwindle, plummet, wane

both = spiral

4

rise = accelerate, skyrocket, surge

fall = diminish, plunge, slump, recede

5

1 a & b = d **2** a & b = b **3** a & b = c
4 a & b = b

Reading and Use of English Part 7 Multiple matching

2

1 A **2** A **3** D **4** C **5** C **6** A **7** D
8 A **9** B **10** B

Writing Part 1 Essay

Useful language

Possible answers:

2 We have to consider the question of whether or not we should hike / to hike (our) prices to meet mounting costs and if that will pay off in the long run.

3 We could incorporate best practice into our new policies from a range of sources.

4 Our human resources department is likely to be more interested in techniques that pertain to relevant theories.

4

... the psychology of motivation in the workplace ...

... may reveal more areas for analysis ...

... a question to be discussed in more detail by a company's management ...

... those with a growing family ...

... expressing gratitude in a more personal way ...

5 Sample answer

The perennial question – the essence of the workplace conundrum – meaningful work versus the almighty dollar. It's a quandary that has confounded thinkers for generations, and today, we'll wade into these waters. On one side, there are the believers in the sanctity of meaningful work. They assert that it's not merely about financial gain; it's about the intricate connection between one's job and their identity. They'll argue that being recognized by the higher-ups for one's unique character traits and grappling with challenging tasks are the cornerstones of workplace satisfaction. Yet, they concede that those facets are profoundly subjective, akin to interpreting a complex riddle. On the flip side, there's the faction that champions financial compensation as the ultimate source of contentment. They proclaim that, for many individuals, especially these labouring beneath the weight of economic hardship, it's the money that truly matters. They assert that a modest salary increase can alleviate the pressing financial burdens faced by low-wage earners. However, both perspectives bring valid insights to the table. The proponents of meaningful work remind us of the importance of personal fulfilment and the idiosyncratic nature of individual interpretations. However, they may downplay the undeniable significance of financial stability, particulary for those dealing with the everyday challenges of survival. On the other hand, the champions of financial compensation make a compelling case for its pivotal role in employee satisfaction, especially among lower-income workers. They underscore the concrete impact a salary hike can have on financial well-being. In summary, the enduring debate surrounding the primacy of meaningful work versus financial compensation in fostering workplace satisfaction persists. While both facets are undoubtedly crucial, their relative importance varies among individuals. Striking a harmonious balance that respects the diversity of the workforce and tailors strategies to meet varying needs is the key to fostering lasting employee contentment. In essence, a holistic approach that combines meaningful work, equitable compensation, and individualised recognition is the recipe for success.

Examiner's Comments

Content: All content is relevant to the task and the reader is informed about the main ideas in the two texts. The target reader is informed of the writer's view on the content points and are appropriately developed.

Communicative achievement: The writer uses the conventions of the essay with sufficient flexibility to communicate complex ideas in an effective way. They manage to hold the target reader's attention with ease and fulfil all communicative purposes as set out in the task. However, the register is occasionally uneven. The evaluation of the key points from the input texts is combined with the writer's opinions.

Organisation: Text is a well-organised and coherent as a whole. The writer uses a wide variety of cohesive devices and organisational patterns with flexibility: *On the one side; Yet they concede that; On the flip side; On the other hand; In summary.* However, clear paragraphing would have enhanced coherence further.

Language: The writer uses a wide range of vocabulary, including less common lexis, with fluency, precision, sophistication and style: *perennial question; workplace conundrum; proponents; idiosyncratic nature*, etc... The writer's use of grammar is sophisticated, fully controlled and natural. Any inaccuracies occur only as slips (*those, these*).

Mark: good pass

Listening Part 2 Sentence completion

2

1 identity **2** pioneering spirit
3 mediocre **4** sustainable income
5 meaning **6** (relentless) promotion
7 (their) energy **8** earning power
9 scalable

6 Review

Reading and Use of English Part 3 Word formation

1 satisfactorily **2** standardised / standardized **3** fraudulent
4 systematically **5** unidentifiable
6 confidentiality **7** indisputable
8 worthwhile

Vocabulary Phrases with pay

1 respects **2** tribute **3** lip service
4 dividends **5** way **6** price
7 compliment **8** forward **9** nose

Reading and Use of English Part 4 Key word transformations

1 (from) getting out of hand

2 (they are) left / you leave them to their own devices

3 burning the midnight oil

4 gets / comes / jumps / goes straight to the point

5 to / for all intents and purposes,

6 brings out the best in

Idioms Money and wealth

1

1 pinch **2** water **3** butter **4** up
5 rolling

2

a is their bread and butter **b** feeling the pinch, being hard up **c** keep their heads above water **d** to be rolling in it

3

1 a **2** b **3** b **4** b **5** a

4

1 The phrase *let's hope it continues* suggests something positive, so it feels like option a is more likely.

2 *her lavish lifestyle* suggests she spends a lot of money therefore option b is more likely.

3 Two things – *love nor money* – are mentioned, so option b seems more likely.

4 The word *promise* suggests that no action has happened yet, so option b is more likely.

5 The word *astounded* makes it sound like the task is easy, so option a would be more likely.

Discussing idioms

be on a roll – be experiencing a period of good luck. *David was on a roll last night at the quiz. He guessed all the answers correctly!*

be in the groove – find a 'rhythm' and be doing something well. *At first it took her a long time to do each one, but soon she was in the groove, and managed to churn them out quickly.*

money for old rope – used to highlight that you earned money for doing something very easy. *Cat Sitting for my neighbour is money for old rope. Squiggles keeps himself to himself so all I have to do is feed him, really.*

money for nothing = has a similar meaning, but goes even further, emphasising that the thing you did was "nothing" rather than being easy to do. *It's not fair. Some people get money for nothing, while others work their fingers to the bone and earn peanuts.*

READY FOR LISTENING

Listening Part 1 Multiple choice

1

1 C 2 A 3 B 4 C 5 B 6 A

Listening Part 2 Sentence completion

1

1 leaps and bounds 2 reliability 3 running costs 4 fingers 5 (a) game-changer 6 conductor 7 (distinctive) glow 8 (commercially) sold 9 finite

Listening Part 3 Multiple choice

3

1 B 2 D 3 B 4 C 5 A

Listening Part 4 Multiple matching

2

1 E 2 G 3 A 4 D 5 B 6 H 7 C 8 B 9 F 10 D

7 WORKING IT OUT

Listening Part 3 Multiple choice

2

1 C 2 D 3 C 4 C 5 A

Language focus Modal verbs 2

1

1 might well 2 got to 3 couldn't have

3

1 c 2 b 3 a

Ready for Grammar

1

1 It mustn't have been 2 It's got to be 3 they couldn't have called 4 They may well 5 It may well be

2

1 might not / mightn't / may not have stolen 2 might / may well have been exaggerating 3 may as well give up / stop / not bother trying to get this finished 4 can't be graduating (this year).

5

1 couldn't have been made

2 has got to be / must be

3 must be / must have been / 's got to be / has got to be / 's got to have been / has got to have been

4 may / might be deduced

5 could have been

6 might / may (well) start

6

The ice cubes had been poisoned. Maria drank her lemonade so quickly that the ice cubes didn't have time to melt, unlike Eliza.

Vocabulary Phrasal verbs of deduction and investigation

1

1 stumble across something 2 keep something back 3 mull something over

3

1 D 2 B 3 H 4 G 5 F 6 E 7 C 8 A

4

1 root out / rooting out 2 staking out 3 mull over 4 keeping something back 5 caught up with 6 hit upon 7 tracked down 8 nosing around

5

1 troublemakers, a problem 2 a solution 3 a person, the competition 4 territory (to claim the land), a claim (to explain and defend a position)

Reading and Use of English Part 2 Open cloze

1

1 being 2 around 3 with 4 loss 5 called 6 on 7 wall 8 side

Pronunciation Chunking and asides

2

'Of course! / The brain is an extremely complex organ. / When I did my psychology course, / which I had to drop out of, / we learnt a great deal about the mysteries of the brain / and the limits to our scientific knowledge.'

3

1 One thing I've always been curious about is the deep sea. I've actually read that we, <u>incredibly</u>, know less about it than we do our own solar system.

2 I think it's an exciting time for scientific research and I, <u>for one</u>, can't wait to see what the next few years will bring. Immune responses has been one of the areas that has been so hard to fathom, but science is getting there slowly but surely.

3 / One thing that truly makes me wonder is my dogs! I'd love to know what's going on in their minds and be able to speak to them. Although maybe what I love so much about them is that they don't answer back, <u>unlike my kids</u>.

4 What has always puzzled me in regard to the human body is why we have a dominant hand. What makes it so hard for me to write with my left hand, <u>it literally looks like a 5-year-old's writing</u>, and not my right?

5 Space has to be the ultimate mystery! The vastness of it all is unthinkable, and I'm positive there must be life, <u>of some form</u>, on other planets.

4

There is no pause. The intonation doesn't change. Any humour, personal perspectives on the subject, added interest, etc. is lost.

Speaking Part 2

Useful language

think about contemplate, ponder, wonder

puzzled baffled, mystified, stumped

discovery breakthrough, finding, revelation

Word formation Adjectives

1

1 hesitant, vacant, compliant, repentant odd one: fraud (fraudulent)

2 abhorrent, reminiscent, apparent, prevalent odd one: decipher (decipherable)

3 mischievous, infectious, poisonous, miraculous odd one: convince (convincing)

4 tolerable, redeemable, regrettable, laudable odd one: repel (repellent)

5 reversible, perceptible, accessible, discernible odd one: mercy (merciless)

6 harmless, thoughtless, relentless, blameless odd one: awe (awesome)

7 troublesome, fearsome, wholesome, irksome odd one: rebel (rebellious)

2

1 imperceptible 2 unrepentant 3 unapparent 4 indecipherable 5 irredeemable / unredeemable 6 intolerable 7 irreversible

Additional materials Word formation Adjectives

1 overarching 2 monetary 3 unfathomable 4 theoretical 5 undoubted 6 foregone 7 dwindling 8 unprecedented 9 underlying

10 malicious **11** exhaustive
12 unresponsive **13** questionable
14 immeasurable **15** indispensable
16 interchangeable **17** pitiful
18 resourceful **19** underdeveloped
20 successive **21** irrevocable
22 thoughtless **23** perilous
24 worthless **25** backward

Reading and Use of English Part 6 Gapped text

2

1 E **2** D **3** A **4** F **5** C **6** G **7** H

3

eavesdropper – someone who listens to private conversations without them knowing

fruitless – unsuccessful or not productive, especially despite a lot of work

gibberish – nonsense

princely – (of an amount of money) large and generous

squiggles – a line with a lot of curves in it

unfathomable – impossible to explain or understand

Language focus Adjectives and fixed expressions

1

1 retrospect **2** cold, dark and dangerous **3** very

2

a 2 **b** 3 **c** 1

Ready for Grammar

1

1 As a matter of fact **2** Sure enough **3** very **4** At best **5** For the time being **6** major **7** For the most part **8** As it stands

2

1 The throngs of fans outside the stadium were chaotic, noisy and out of control.

2 Determined, brilliant and passionate about his work, the professor was the idol of many of his students.

3 The perks of the job are incredible, but let's get this straight – it's a lonely, high-paced and chaotic role.

4 Thread-bare, tatty and filled with so many memories, the jumper was her favourite item in her wardrobe.

4

1 all in all **2** In actual fact **3** All of a sudden **4** Up to this point **5** Sure enough

6

1 There is a three letter shift in the alphabet and the note says 'NOW IS THE TIME. LET'S GO.'

2 The note is unlikely to be for Mr Allman. His wife has been communicating in code with somebody. It's likely she has run away. We don't know who with or why.

Vocabulary Verbs of confusion and deceit

1

1 duped **2** deluding **3** bluff **4** double-crossed **5** swindling **6** confound **7** conned

2

1 *dupe* has the connotation of tricking someone, while *perplex* simply means to confuse.

2 *delude* is to make someone believe something is true when it is not (even to yourself), while *hoodwink* means to trick someone (usually by telling a story).

3 *bluff* is to try and make someone believe you will or have the ability to do something that you can't or don't really intend to do, while *hustle* means to forcefully encourage someone to buy something.

4 *double-cross* means to betray someone who you were cooperating with (usually in crime), while *blackmail* is to ask for something (usually money) to keep quiet about information.

5 *swindle* means to trick people out of money or possessions, while *stump* means to confuse someone.

6 *confound* means to confuse, while *scam* means to actively trick someone.

7 *con* means to trick someone or persuade someone to do something by lying to them, while *baffle* means to confuse

Writing Part 2 Review

2

... the compelling **debut** novel by Paula Hawkins.

This split-narrative **story** of a woman trying to unpick the details of a crime she witnessed ...

... cleverly woven **narrative**, which moves back and forth in time and perspectives.

clever **technique** of drip-feeding information ...

... crucial element of **investment** which is indispensable in all, but especially mystery, novels.

3 Sample answer

A Masterpiece of mystery: My Annihilation by Fuminori Nakamura

My Annihilation by Fuminori Nakamura is a mesmerising dive into the dark abyss of psychological thrillers, solidifying Nakamura's reputation as a master of the genre. This novel is an outstanding example of its kind, and here's why.

Nakamura excels in creating an atmosphere of relentless tension that pervades every page of the book. From the very first chapter, the reader is pulled into a labyrinth of uncertainty, mirroring the protagonist's disorienting journey. The palpable sense to unease never wavers, keeping you on the edge of your seat until the final page. The author's ability to sustain this level of suspense is nothing short of brilliant.

The characters in *My Annihilation* are deeply flawed and enigmatic, leaving you guessing their true intentions and loyalties throughout. The main character, who finds himself ensnared in a web of intrigue, is both relatable and perplexing. Nakamura's skilful use of unreliable narration adds layers of complexity, blurring the line between reality and delusion. The reader finds themself questioning everything, just as the protagonist does.

One of Nakamura's greatest strengths lies in his ability to explore the darkest corners of the human psyche. *My Annihilation* delves into themes of identity, obsession, and the blurred boundaries between wrong and right. Nakamura adeptly peels back the layers of his characters, revealing their innermost fears and desires, all while maintaining an air of mystery that keeps you guessing until the very end.

Nakamura's pacing is impeccable, gradually ratcheting up the tension while providing just enough breadcrumbs to keep you engaged and guessing. The revelations that unfold are shocking and thought-provoking, ensuring that *My Annihilation* stays with you long after you've turned the last page.

In *My Annihilation*, Nakamura has crafted a superbly executed mystery that showcases his mastery of the genre. With its relentless suspense, enigmatic characters, and exploration of the human psyche, this novel is an outstanding example of what a mystery should be. Nakamura's ability to keep readers enthralled and guessing makes *My Annihilation* an absolute must-read for any fan of the genre.

Examiner's Comments

Content: All content is relevant to the task. The target reader is fully informed about the mystery novel which the writer has read. The writer explains why *The Annihilation* is such an excellent example of this genre. However, the plot isn't briefly summarised to provide the reader with a clear idea of the overall premise of the story.

Communicative achievement: The conventions of writing a review, such as the use of an informative tone and a positive viewpoint, are used to communicate complex ideas in an effective and convincing manner and the writer shares their views on why the book is an excellent example of the genre.

Organisation: The text is a well-organised and coherent throughout the review. The paragraphs are well structured and a variety of cohesive devices and organisational patterns, such as substitution, are used with flexibility to link ideas across sentences and paragraphs in a very natural way. Phrases such as *here's why; From the very first chapter; The characters in My Annihilation; One of Nakamura's greatest strengths;* help guide the reader through different aspects of the novel and the author's abilities. Although there is a lack of more overt cohesive devices the use of parallel structure in phrases like *relentless suspense, enigmatic characters, and exploration of the human psyche* to list the novel's key features, make the text more organised and coherent.

Language: A range of topic-specific vocabulary, including less common lexis, is used effectively and precisely to communicate specific emotions and ideas: *palpable; adeptly; revelations; impeccable; delves into' enthralled.* A wide range of simple and complex grammatical forms is used with full control, flexibility and sophistication: *The main character, who finds himself ensnared in a web of intrigue, is both relatable and perplexing, and Nakamura's skilful use of unreliable narration adds layers of complexity, blurring the line between reality and delusion.* There are occasional errors, but these do not impede communication: *wrong and right, The palpable sense to unease, etc.*

Mark: good pass

7 Review

Language focus Modal verbs 2

1 may **2** must **3** has got **4** couldn't **5** both **6** might **7** both **8** could

Reading and Use of English Part 4 Key word transformations

1 place in classrooms for the time

2 set on being / becoming

3 to the contrary the head teacher did not

4 on no account should / must

5 is not / isn't likely to get

6 couldn't / could not have written that

Vocabulary

1 C **2** A **3** B **4** A **5** C **6** B **7** B

Idioms Mystery

1

1 c **2** b **3** e **4** a **5** f **6** d

2

caught red-handed (whereas *red herring* can be anything that fools us, and *smell a rat* can refer to anything we think is not as it seems)

3

1 b **2** a **3** a **4** b

Discussing idioms

ring a bell – used to say that something sounds familiar. *I don't remember her but her name definitely rings a bell.*

strike a chord – generate an emotional response and make a strong impression. *The story has struck a chord with football fans and women's groups alike and is the number one item currently trending on social media.*

keep something under wraps – to keep something a secret. *They're keeping her pregnancy under wraps for the time being. They'll let people know a little further down the line.*

keep something under your hat = ask someone to keep something secret. *If I tell you something, will you keep it under your hat?*

be barking up the wrong tree – is used to describe a situation where you think someone has chosen the wrong course of action or line of inquiry because they are mistaken in their belief or theory about something. *Tara thinks that selling the house will fix the problem but I told her I think she's barking up the wrong tree.*

get the wrong end of the stick – also indicates someone is mistaken, but indicates someone has misunderstood a situation. *My brother heard part of our conversation last night and got completely the wrong end of the stick. He thought we were talking about him!*

8 HUMAN IMPACT

Speaking Part 3 Long turn

Useful language

may, highly, bound, be having, have learnt

Listening Part 4 Multiple matching

1

1 E **2** G **3** C **4** A **5** D **6** B **7** E **8** A **9** H **10** C

Language focus Comparatives

1

1 no **2** slightest **3** so, that **4** as, as **5** to

3

1 b **2** b **3** a **4** a **5** b

Ready for Grammar

1

1 slightest / faintest **2** no **3** so **4** as **5** improvement **6** an **7** the

2

1 difficult a challenge **2** not that much **3** be so ignorant as to **4** make the faintest difference **5** act as though

5

1 tantamount to **2** as if **3** so forward thinking as to **4** the slightest **5** is not / can't be that much

Vocabulary Environment collocations

1

1 catastrophe **2** erosion **3** tourism **4** wind farms **5** habitats **6** waste **7** disposal

2

1 catastrophe **2** erosion **3** waste **4** habitats

3

Adjective + noun = hazardous waste, marine habitats, ecological catastrophe, sustainable tourism, offshore wind farms, coastal erosion

Noun + noun = waste disposal

Reading and Use of English Part 5 Multiple choice

2

Possible answers: It has become richer, it has more greenhouses, the landscape has changed, it has more plastic waste.

3

1 C **2** A **3** D **4** B **5** A **6** A

Listening Part 2 Sentence completion

2

1 (world) economy **2** resourceful **3** underground **4** fall to pieces **5** maintain **6** widespread **7** pressure **8** hazardous **9** plants

Language focus Expressing contrast

1

so, yet

2

1 c **2** e **3** a **4** d **5** b

Ready for Grammar

1

1 b **2** b **3** c **4** b

2

1 though **2** albeit **3** and yet **4** more **5** Although **6** All the same

4

1 a Though unusual **2** b Even so **3** b Although well designed **4** a has nonetheless been difficult **5** a Albeit difficult

Writing Part 1 Essay

5

1 The first sentences of paragraphs 2 and 3

2 In the rest of paragraphs 2 and 3

6

reduce = alleviate, minimise

defeat = overcome

7

1 combat, overcome, rectify, remedy **2** compound, exacerbate **3** alleviate, minimise **4** address, deal with, face, tackle

8

1 minimise **2** combat **3** deal with **4** exacerbating **5** address

9 Sample answer

In these two texts, we tackle the urgent issue of environmental sustainability amid our expanding global population. While each text offers unique perspectives and solutions, they share an undeniable sense of urgency and the recognition that immediate action is crucial.

The first text emphasises the pivotal role of the private sector in driving environmental change. It champions innovative business models like the circular economy, which minimises waste through recycling and repurposing to reduce reliance on environmentally harmful processes like mining. Additionally, it urges high-income countries to lead in investing and implementing these ideas. While pragmatic and forward-looking, some may criticise it for not holding businesses accountable enough for their environmental impact and relying heavily on market-driven solutions.

Conversely, the second text underscores the government's crucial role in catalysing substantial environmental transformation. It argues that individual lifestyle changes alone won't suffice and calls for governments to incentivise its people to have smaller families. Moreover, it advocates for stringent environmental regulations, especially against deforestation, and stresses international cooperation to safeguard water supplies and promote sustainable food production. This perspective prioritises policy and collective action, recognising that without strong governmental leadership, change may not occur at the necessary pace.

Evaluating these texts, it's clear that both perspectives have merits. Tackling environmental challenges necessitates a multifaceted approach, combining private-sector innovation with robust government intervention. Collaboration among businesses, governments, and civil society is paramount. Moreover, the urgency of the issue is a common thread, under scoring the need for immediate action to safeguard our planet for future generations. Ultimately, it's not a question of whether business or government should take the lead but how we can harness the strengths of both sectors in a coordinated effort to confront the environmental crisis before it becomes irreversible.

Examiner's Comments

Content: All content is relevant to the task. The reader is on the whole informed. The writer has taken a clear stance on the topic and has discussed three of the main ideas in the texts. However, the idea of exploring new technologies has been omitted. The circular economy is addressed: *like the circular economy, which minimises waste through recycling and repurposing to reduce reliance on environmentally harmful processes like mining.* Reducing family size is discussed: *It argues that individual lifestyle changes alone won't suffice and calls for governments to incentivise its people to have smaller families.* The writer expands on the point about international cooperation: *Collaboration among businesses, governments, and civil society is paramount.*

Communicative achievement: The conventions of essay writing are used naturally and with flexibility. The evaluation of the key points is sometimes combined with the writer's opinions: *While pragmatic and forward-looking, some may criticise it for not holding businesses accountable enough for their environmental impact and relying heavily on market-driven solutions.; Ultimately, it's not a question of whether business or government should take the lead but how we can harness the strengths of both sectors in a coordinated effort to confront the environmental crisis before it becomes irreversible.* The writer maintains a formal tone, using structured language to maintain a level of objectivity suitable for academic writing.

Organisation: The text is well-organised and coherent. The shift between the different points covered in the input texts develops naturally to express the opinions on the central topic effectively: *The first text emphasises; Conversely, the second text underscores the government's crucial role; Evaluating these texts, it's clear that both perspectives have merits.* Throughout the text, there is a use of contrasting and comparative language to highlight differences and similarities between the two perspectives: *While, Additionally; Conversely; Moreover; Evaluating these texts; Ultimately.* The text maintains a consistent structure when presenting contrasting ideas making it easier for readers to follow the argument: *The first text emphasizes; Conversely, the second text underscores; Ultimately, it's not a question of whether.*

Language: Some less common lexis is used with sophistication and precision: *catalysing; robust; incentivise; repurposing; safeguard; multifaceted.* Errors are minimal and occur either as slips with spelling or are due to ambitious use of vocabulary: *under scores; under scoring.*

Mark: good pass

Student's own answers

8 Review

Reading and Use of English Part 3 Word formation

1 revitalise **2** disrepair **3** unrealistic **4** deprivation **5** insignificantly **6** untapped **7** extraordinarily **8** overlooked

Vocabulary

1 waste collection **2** habitat preservation **3** ecological catastrophe **4** sustainable development **5** household waste **6** marine habitat **7** coastal erosion

Reading and Use of English Part 4 Key word transformations

1 was surprised in the

2 to let the applause die down / to wait for the applause to die down

3 take up too much (of his) time

4 interesting though it

5 the film was more thought-provoking than

6 (running) low on petrol

Idioms Noticing similarities and differences

1

A Different: *ring hollow* = seem untruthful or insincere; *ring true* = seem to be true

B Similar: *in the clear* = no longer in danger or under suspicion; *out of the woods* = no longer in danger or difficulty

2

1 different **2** similar **3** similar **4** different

Discussing idioms

rock the boat – do or say something that will cause problems or upset people. *I didn't agree with the new policy but I didn't say anything because I didn't want to rock the boat.*

upset the apple cart – also means to cause problems but usually by spoiling someone's plans or disrupting a procedure. *I have to go to this family get-together. If I didn't, it'd thoroughly upset the apple cart.*

be in a tight spot – to be in a difficult situation. *The revelations about the ministers' expenses have put the Prime Minister in a tight spot, with many asking for him to resign if he cannot provide a better explanation for this widespread misuse of public funds.*

be a tight squeeze – refers to a situation where people or things are very crowded together. *Of course you can stay! There will be six of us in the cottage, so it'll be a tight squeeze but I'm sure we'll manage.*

make your blood boil – to make someone feel extremely angry. *It makes my blood boil to think of all that toxic waste being pumped into our rivers. Those responsible simply must pay.*

get your back up – this also means to make someone feel angry but is to a much lesser extent than *to make your blood boil. Ignore your brother when he teases you. He's just trying to get your back up.*

9 BY DESIGN

Reading and Use of English Part 7 Multiple matching

2

1 D **2** A **3** B **4** D **5** A **6** B **7** C **8** E **9** D **10** C

3

1 I'm even more convinced that there's no threat as a result of (having had) this first hand experience.

2 Our whole industry was turned upside down by new technology in the 80s; therefore, I know more than most about losing out to AI.

3 Even though it may seem counterintuitive, they might be surprised by what it's like working with AI.

Vocabulary Prepositional phrases with *by, in* and *out of*

1

1 by 2 in 3 out of; out of

2

1 D 2 G 3 A 4 F 5 B 6 E 7 H 8 C

3

1 by invitation only 2 in your mind's eye 3 out of the ordinary 4 out of place 5 by any means necessary

Language focus Expressing concession, contrast, purpose and reason

1

concession: however

contrast: whereas

purpose: so as to

reason: as, in that, now that, since

2

1 in that 2 Since my children have flown the nest, I'll ... 3 whereas 4 however far-fetched that may sound 5 as / since

Ready for Grammar

1

1 ... however unorthodox it may seem. 2 As for myself, ... 3 ... so I couldn't 4 ... improving now that I've got ... 5 Nor is it ... 6 ... the house so as not to 7 ... her homeland in that she uses ... 8 ... from upstairs since there's ...

2

1 while 2 whatever they may seem, whatever these may be 3 In order to 4 In that 5 in that 6 Nor is it 7 because, now that

Reading and Use of English Part 1 Multiple choice cloze

1

1 A 2 C 3 A 4 D 5 B 6 B 7 D 8 B

Vocabulary Describing art and architecture

1

1 renowned 2 vulgar 3 swanky

2

1 utilitarian 2 renowned 3 understated 4 ostentatious 5 minimalistic 6 swanky 7 flamboyant 8 whimsical 9 imposing 10 garish 11 vulgar 12 unassuming

3

1 garish, ostentatious, vulgar 2 whimsical 3 imposing 4 unassuming, understated 5 renowned 6 minimalistic, utilitarian 7 flamboyant, ostentatious

Listening Part 2 Sentence completion

1

Suggested answers

1 Visual impact is very important for some companies – to demonstrate success to clients and prospective employees, especially when trying to attract talent.

2 Wealth and success, and perhaps a sense of moving forward to the future. It can be important for an image of a city like New York or London.

3 Open plan offices can foster a sense of teamwork or alternatively be disruptive for people who need to concentrate. Plants and colour can increase wellness in the workplace. Furniture should ideally be well made and ergonomically designed for employee comfort.

2

1 legacy project 2 function 3 mixed 4 services 5 iconic 6 theoretical 7 remarkable 8 expertise 9 government

Pronunciation Juncture

2

1 an aim 2 might earn

3

1 A2, B1 2 A2, B1 3 A1, B2 4 A1, B2 5 A1, B2 6 A2, B1 7 A2, B1 8 A1, B2

Language focus Passive and causative structures

1

1 have been reimagined and have been reworked

2 the plans having been drawn up

3 not having been intended

2

1 B 2 D 3 A 4 C 5 E

3

1 Picasso 2 Taj Mahal 3 Eiffel Tower 4 Leonardo da Vinci 5 Vincent Van Gogh

Ready for Grammar

1

1 C 2 D 3 C 4 A 5 D 6 B

2

1 The door was varnished and repaired, remaining faithful to the details of the period.

2 The council had a local artist do a series of murals in the town.

3 I contacted the company about my order due to not having received an email with the delivery details.

4 I want to have the flowers ordered for the wedding day to avoid delays.

5 I will get someone to bring you the dessert menu in just a moment.

6 Having prepared the food and poured the drinks, we waited for the guests to arrive.

Listening Part 3 Multiple choice

2

1 C 2 A 3 B 4 D 5 B

Writing Part 2 Review

2

Paragraph 1 to provide an introduction to what exhibition you visited, to give background information about an artist, and indicate whether the exhibition was a success or not.

Paragraph 2 to give a brief description of the exhibition

Paragraph 3 to evaluate the exhibition's layout, installations and overall experience

Paragraph 4 to provide a summary of the exhibition and make a recommendation

3

A long-awaited new exhibition at The Tate Modern <u>opened</u> last week, billed as a great display of works from Yayoi Kusuma, one of the world's most celebrated artists and as expected it <u>was</u> nothing short of a (2) big success. Titled *Infinity Mirror Rooms*, the exhibition <u>explores</u> themes of infinite space and endless replication through two immersive mirror room installations, reflecting her long career in conceptual and minimalist artwork since she (3) <u>arrived</u> onto the New York art scene in the late 1950s.

The installations are accompanied by photographic works (4) carefully documenting the artist's early sculptural work as well as images of her working in her New York studio, giving the viewer context so as to interpret the artist's work more deeply and <u>see</u> her as the (5) strong artistic force that she <u>is</u>. Some images <u>explore</u> the (6) emotional experience of moving to New York where feelings of alienation hint at this having been a (7) difficult period in her life.

The curation of the exhibition has been (8) nicely done, with attention to detail in the layout and flow throughout the gallery. The main draw <u>is</u> without doubt the installations themselves in which tiny, suspended lights <u>give</u> the impression of (9) shining out in all directions. It <u>gives</u> a sense that the light <u>has filled</u> the (10) large Tate modern building beyond the confines of the installation rooms.

This exhibition would be well worth a visit for (11) fans of the artist herself, but additionally it could easily capture the hearts of any installation art lovers as a fascinating way to experience a talented and (12) famous artist.

The past tenses indicate actions in the past.

The present tenses are used to indicate that the exhibition is still current, and that the artist is still alive. When discussing the exhibition and the artworks, it is used to make them seem more engaging and timeless.

4

They are usually followed by more extreme information or opinions

Useful language

1 dazzling **2** triumph **3** exploded **4** meticulously **5** powerful **6** poignant **7** turbulent **8** exquisitely **9** radiating **10** mighty **11** enthusiasts **12** renowned

2 *turbulent* is negative

Suggested answers: dazzling = dull; enthusiasts = critics; explode onto = bombed / failed; exquisitely = crudely; meticulously = carelessly; mighty = tiny; poignant = cheerful / unmoving; powerful = insignificant; radiate = absorb, renowned = unremarkable; triumph = failure; turbulent = tranquil

6

Positive: flawless, formidable, profound

Negative: appalling, crude, disillusioned, dubious, mediocre

7

1 mediocre **2** dubious **3** crude **4** profound **5** disillusioned **6** flawless

8

1 the pieces were organised by artist / made the curation feel rather crude.

2 The promotional materials had suggested that the work on display would give insight into the people and culture of the region and visitors would leave with a more profound understanding of their contribution to our national heritage.

3 I left, disillusioned at the state of art in the region and suggest that art lovers head elsewhere

4 the latest exhibition of local artists

5 ... I would rate the works as mediocre at best. There were few pieces containing anything original, while the technical prowess on display was somewhat dubious, with glaring errors in perspective and clumsy brushwork.

9 Sample answer

<u>*Philip Beesley's Techno-Art Odyssey*</u>

Walking into Philip Beesley's exhibition *Grove* is like stepping into a lucid dream. The ethereal quality of his Venice Biennial installation takes you on a journey through a mesmerising realm that blurs the boundaries between art, architecture, and technology. Beesley's exhibit, housed in a dimly lit gallery, left me utterly captivated and inspired.

The layout of the exhibition was a masterpiece in itself. The immersive design invited visitors to meander through a labyrinth of delicate structures that seemed to float in mid-air. The way the installations were arranged created a sense of discovery and wonder around every corner. I found myself completely immersed in a surreal landscape where reality and imagination intertwined seamlessly.

The installations, constructed from a blend of intricate 3D-printed components, transluscent materials, and an intricate web of sensors, were nothing short of awe-inspiring. They reacted to the presence of visitors, creating an interactive dialogue between the art and its audience. It was as if the exhibition had a heartbeat, responding to the collective energy of those in attendance. The delicate, almost fragile appearance of the structures contrasted beautifully with their technological complexity.

What truly took Beesley's exhibition apart was the emotional impact it had on visitors. As I wondered through the softly lit space, I felt a profound sense of tranquillity and connectedness to the world around me. The fusion of art and technology here wasn't just an aesthetic choice; it was a powerful commentary on the harmonious coexistence of humanity and the natural world.

In conclusion, Philip Beesley's latest exhibition is a breathtaking triumph of artistry and innovation. The overall experience left me in a state of wonder and contemplation, a testament to Beesley's genius as an artist and a visionary. If you're seeking an otherworldly journey through the realms of art and technology, this exhibition is an absolute must-see. Be prepared to be transported to a place where the boundaries of reality are delightfully blurred, and your senses are awakened to the magic of creativity.

Examiner's Comments

Content: All content is relevant to the task. The target reader is fully informed about Philip Beesley's exhibition. The art installation is briefly described, and the impact it had on the writer, who uses some persuasive language aimed at convincing readers of the exhibitions value and appeal. For instance, the writer uses rhetorical devices like parallelism: *the boundaries of reality are delightfully blurred.*

Communicative achievement: The conventions of writing a review, such as the use of a semi-informal tone maintains a level of formality, making it suitable for a professional context, such as a magazine review. The writer uses descriptive and evocative language to convey the experience of the exhibition. However, they also incorporate elements of subjectivity and personal reflection, which are somewhat less formal than purely objective and informational writing.

Organisation: The text is well-organised and coherent with well-structured paragraphs which link ideas across sentences and paragraphs in a very natural way. The writer's use of lexical cohesive devices is effective in that they relate words and synonyms to maintain a thematic connection between sentences and paragraphs which relate to the exhibition experience: *immersive design; interactive dialogue; surreal landscape.* The use of general to specific organisational pattern, broadly introduces the exhibition and its key features before delving into specific details about the layout, installations, and emotional impact. This pattern allows the reader to build a broad understanding before focusing on specific aspects.

Language: A range of topic-specific vocabulary, including less common lexis, is used effectively and precisely to communicate specific emotions and ideas: *left me utterly captivated and inspired; profound sense of tranquillity and connectedness; awakened to the magic of creativity; lucid dream; awe-inspiring; harmonious coexistence; breathtaking triumph; otherworldly journey.* A wide range of simple and complex grammatical forms is used with full control, flexibility and sophistication: *If you're seeking an otherworldly journey through the realms of art and technology, this exhibition is an absolute must-see. The delicate, almost fragile appearance of the structures contrasted beautifully with their technological complexity. Be prepared to be transported to a place where the boundaries of reality are delightfully blurred.* There are occasional errors, but these do not impede communication: *transluscent; took Beesley's exhibition apart; As I wondered.*

Mark: good pass

9 Review

Language focus

1

1 may be **2** since **3** having been hindered **4** check **5** in that **6** for myself **7** Having been

Vocabulary

1 F **2** J **3** H **4** K **5** A **6** D **7** I **8** L **9** C **10** G **11** E **12** B

Reading and Use of English Part 2 Open cloze

1 stage **2** Having **3** whether **4** Contrary **5** ease **6** on **7** bear / keep **8** towards

Idioms Art and creativity

1

1 B **2** A **3** C

3

1 mark **2** canvas **3** eye **4** art **5** mould

4

1 c **2** d **3** a **4** b

5

1 go down a storm **2** bears no resemblance to **3** reinvent the wheel **4** is / has been a breath of fresh air

6

1 A: a slow burner, a blank canvas B: collector's item C: a breath of fresh air

2 A: break the mould, reinvent the wheel B: go down a storm

3 A: bear no resemblance to something, leave your mark on something B: have something down to a fine art C: catch someone's eye D: go back to the drawing board

Discussing idioms

A blank canvas – If something is *a blank canvas*, no decisions or plans have yet been made about it, so it is free for someone to do whatever they like with it. *All the walls in the new flat have been freshly painted, so I have a blank canvas and can design the place exactly how I want.*

A clean slate – refers to a new opportunity or a second chance at something, especially when what happened in the past is forgotten. *She knows she made mistakes in the past but is now looking for a clean slate so we can start again.*

go down a storm and *go down like a lead balloon* – mean the opposite. If something *goes down a storm* it is very successful and popular. If something *goes down like a lead balloon*, it is very unpopular. *My idea for the new product went down a storm with the marketing team. They absolutely loved it and want to present it to the shareholders.*

The launch of the company's new mobile phone went down like a lead balloon with consumers. People just didn't understand the offer and weren't willing to pay $4000 for it.

catch your eye – get your attention. *I really enjoyed the exhibition and there was one painting in particular that really caught my eye. I'd love to find out more about the artist.*

catch your breath – to pause an activity so that you can breathe normally again. *Just give me five minutes to catch my breath and then we can carry on jogging.*

READY FOR SPEAKING

Introduction

1 yourself **2** reaction
3 decision-making **4** written
5 interact **6** interruption **7** attention
8 Demonstrate / Manage **9** speculating
10 initiate / manage **11** contributions
12 willing **13** organise **14** opinions
15 appropriate

Speaking Part 1 Interview

3

1 Both students give relevant responses to the questions.

2 Sofia's answer is very well developed. She not only answers the questions asked, but goes on to expand by explaining the importance of English in engineering and gives examples of why it is so important (it is an international field and lots of journals are in English). She demonstrates her ability to speak confidently by doing so and shows she can use a range of language.

Mario's answer, while relevant, is shorter and he does not demonstrate as much confidence in manipulating the language as Sofia. Mario also makes a couple of minor mistakes, 'a internship' and 'coast town', although these do not impede understanding, and he also corrects himself when he says 'coast town'.

Speaking Part 2 Collaborative task

2

1 Both students interact well together. Mario invites Sofia to give opinions throughout this part of the task: *'don't you think?', 'why do you think that?', 'What kind of relation do you think they are?'*, etc. While Sofia gives longer responses, Mario shows that he is listening and reacts to what Sofia says, e.g. *'Yes, I think they do', 'Yes, it could be,'* etc.

2 Sofia successfully demonstrates that she can use language of speculation and comparison by using expressions such as *'it looks to me as if', 'They must be feeling', 'It seems to me that', 'It could even be'*, etc. Mario also shows that he can use some language of speculation, *'they look', 'they seem'*, etc. While Sofia uses more complex language, both candidates successfully achieve this part of the task.

4

1 Both students respond successfully to the task. They discuss all four pictures, eliminate those they do not think would be suitable, and finally come to an agreement on one picture to accompany the article.

2 Yes. Both students invite the other to respond to their opinions, e.g. *'don't you think?', 'What's your opinion?', 'Yes?'*, etc. They also respond to each other effectively and show they are listening to what they are saying, e.g. *'I see what you mean', 'No, I suppose not', 'Well, let's go with that then'*, etc. Both students also demonstrate the ability to keep the interaction moving, e.g. *'Let's look at image 3', 'I'm not very keen on 2 either'*, etc. The interaction is overall very well managed by both students.

3 Contributions from both Sofia and Mario are relevant and coherent. They discuss each of the pictures in turn, and try to relate what each picture says about the theme of personal achievement which helps them evaluate how suitable it would be for the lifestyle magazine. Each of their contributions moves the discussion along in a coherent and meaningful way, which means they successfully carry out the decision-making task.

Speaking Part 3 Long turn
Total time: 4 minutes

5

1 Sofia gives a well organised and cohesive response that successfully achieves the task. She takes each of the prompts on the card in turn, and discusses the question with respect to each of them. Her overall point of view is that competition can be both a good thing and a bad thing in terms of affecting other people (she says it is necessary in sport, not a particularly nice trait in the workplace, and not something she experiences with her friends). Both Mario and Sofia answer the follow-up question with relevant responses.

Mario's response is organised differently to Sofia's, but it is still largely coherent and well-organised. Mario first discusses the benefits of large sporting events (they are entertaining and give people an international outlook) before talking about the drawbacks (they aren't many, and any drawbacks are isolated). Mario's overall point of view is that large sporting events are beneficial, and his answer successfully expresses this opinion. Both Sofia and Mario respond appropriately to the follow-up question.

2 Sofia demonstrates that she can successfully manipulate the language to effectively discuss the topic. She uses a range of high-level vocabulary and phrases, e.g. *'all walks of life', 'It spurs them on', 'trait', 'vying against'*, etc. She also shows she can use complex language structures with fluency and ease, and makes effective use of rhetorical questions to engage with the interlocutor while discussing the topic. Furthermore, she uses markers to help structure her answer, e.g. *'In my opinion', 'I mean', 'On top of that', 'I also see', 'Overall'*.

Mario largely shows that he can use a decent range of vocabulary and language structures, but in general his response is not as complex as Sofia's. Mario also makes a few minor yet basic errors, e.g. *'interested about', 'anti-social behaviours'*, although these do not impede understanding.

Speaking Part 3 Discussion
Total time: 6 minutes

2

1 Both students develop their answers well throughout the discussion. They also help each other in regard to this, e.g. in the first question, Sofia talks about competitive people in general, then Mario brings it to politicians to exemplify what Sofia is talking about, and then Sofia refers to a TV series to further exemplify her opinion on competitive people and success.

2 The responses of both candidates are appropriately detailed. For each question, they give examples of what they are trying to express, e.g. in the second question, Mario speaks about competition in sport as an example of competitiveness that is naturally inside us and speculates as to whether this grows or fades depending on our childhood experiences at winning and losing. Sofia's contribution further details this by evaluating the impact of parents' influence on a competitive mentality in young people.

3 Both candidates express their opinions clearly and react appropriately to each other's opinions even where they may disagree. In the second question, Sofia quite clearly and politely emphasises that she believes parents' influence on a competitive nature in their children is probably the most important, while Mario, although acknowledging this, points out that everybody plays a role. In the third question, they both agree on the type of role model it is useful to compare yourself to. Overall, both students carry out the discussion task very well.

10 ADAPTATION

Listening Part 4 Multiple matching

2

1 C **2** G **3** B **4** F **5** D **6** A **7** H **8** E **9** G **10** C

Pronunciation Accents

1

1 C **2** A **3** E **4** B **5** D

Language focus Inversion

1

1 Only later did **2** Had I known **3** Never have I **4** No sooner had

3

1 No sooner had the musical *Hamilton* opened in 2015 than it became a roaring success, ...

2 Under no circumstances could Miranda have predicted *Hamilton*'s incredible worldwide appeal, ...

3 Not only did it win 11 Tony awards, but also 8 Drama Desk Awards, a Grammy, an Emmy and a Pulitzer Prize.

4 Only then did his remarkable talent for writing songs that can communicate huge amounts of emotion and depth in relatively few words become apparent.

5 Scarcely had the song *We don't talk about Bruno* been released on Disney+ than it had become an international hit ...

6 ... were it not for two influential people in his life, ...

Ready for Grammar

1

1 than it collapsed **2** There goes the bus **3** will you feel **4** as do all **5** did it become **6** Were we to have given **7** Not only must you hide **8** Behind the old cottage was

2

1 hardly **2** when **3** Here comes **4** both **5** should the fugitive not be found **6** nor must **7** only then **8** was something that looked like a scarf.

Vocabulary Describing books and films

1

1 tearjerker **2** heart-wrenching **3** page-turner **4** far-fetched **5** cult classic **6** box office hit **7** long-awaited **8** spine-tingling **9** hard-hitting **10** star-studded **11** critically acclaimed **12** spellbinding

2

1 box office hit **2** spellbinding **3** tearjerker **4** spine-tingling **5** long-awaited **6** heart-wrenching **7** star-studded **8** far-fetched **9** page-turner **10** hard-hitting **11** cult classic **12** critically acclaimed

Speaking Part 3 Long turn

2

1 see **2** believer **3** meant **4** mention

Useful language

1 **A** thoughts **B** words **C** perspective **D** reflection **E** way **F** mind **G** Come **H** put

2 & 3

Expressing your opinion

To my mind

From my perspective

As I see it

I'm a firm believer in

Rephrasing your opinion

On second thoughts

Let me put that another way

In other words

What I meant to say

Changing your mind

On second thoughts

On reflection

Come to think of it

Now you mention it

4

Come to think of it and *Now you mention it* are more informal

Reading and Use of English Part 5 Multiple choice

2

Western Australia

A literary critic, George

Yes

3

1 C **2** A **3** C **4** B **5** D **6** A

Language focus Creating emphasis and cleft sentences

1

1 a **2** d **3** b **4** c

2

1 George got the idea for his next book at a writers' festival.

2 There aren't any crime novels that deal / dealing with commonplace low level events.

3 Nowadays he thought / was thinking more about things that / what might be in the water beneath him.

4 Unfortunately, crime fiction is often formulaic and predictable.

Ready for Grammar

1

1 it is **2** How **3** It was **4** Not **5** Why **6** was that

2

1 It was Lewis, a friend of mine from work, who

2 Not a clue did I have

3 How I'd be able to see everything I wanted to I didn't know

4 The convenient thing was that

Vocabulary Similes

1

1 got on **2** watched **3** stuck out **4** fight **5** sleep

2

1 mad **2** dull **3** tough **4** clear **5** sly

Reading and Use of English Part 4 Key word transformations

1 for fear of dropping

2 it is in operation

3 to narrow down our next holiday destination

4 found (some) common ground

5 were out of line / order / place

6 to get the hang of skiing despite never / not

Writing Part 1 Essay

2

Censorship usually conjures up ideas of banning of books in medieval times, whereas in contemporary society it manifests itself in more subtle ways. <u>These days writers and journalists can have their work sidelined inconspicuously</u>; a series of damaging reviews, or a change of leadership at a publishing company can relegate important author voices to a less prominent position and <u>move the public perception in a different direction</u>, effectively acting as a form of censorship. Publishing tends to reflect the public interest and as such <u>whichever genre or subject has captured people's attention will be more heavily commissioned</u>.

Unfortunately, the modern world is more complex and nuanced than many care to admit, and <u>censorship is no longer as clear cut an issue as it once was</u>. <u>Self-publishing and blogging have given authors platforms to write about anything</u> without the oversight which would previously have come from an editor. The result is that we can inhabit many weird and wonderful worlds through literature. The downside is that <u>we can also be exposed to writing which may be unnecessarily upsetting</u>, damaging or misleading. What constitutes censorship for some is merely <u>a way of protecting the vulnerable for others</u>, and in some ways, this is a laudable aim.

3

Referring to the texts

rightly question whether

They come from very distinct standpoints

both make valuable points

Referring to ideas in general

There is no doubt that

that ignores the fact that

What is undeniable is that

4

Suggested answers

A: These days writers and journalists can have their work side-lined inconspicuously; a series of damaging reviews, or a change of leadership at a publishing company can relegate important author voices to a less prominent position and move the public perception in a different direction

B: What constitutes censorship for some is merely a way of protecting the vulnerable for others, and in some ways, this is a laudable aim.

5

B

8 Sample answer

In today's world, censorship has transformed from the archaic idea of book-burning and overt suppression into a subtler form. Contemporary censorship operates discreetly, no longer relying on heavy-handed bans but employing manipulative tactics. Writers and journalists now navigate treacherous waters, where their work can be obscured through methods like scathing reviews or strategic shifts in publishing leadership. This shift reflects the adaptable nature of public perception, driven by a publishing industry that prioritises genres capturing the zeitgeist.

In our digital age, censorship gains complexity. Self-publishing and blogging grant authors unprecedented freedom, but also expose readers to diverse yet bewildering content. This democratisation of expression offers a wealth of voices and ideas, but also raises concerns about unsettling, misleading, or harmful content. What some decry as censorship, others view as a noble effort to protect the vulnerable, highlighting the issue's evolving complexity.

I personally advocate for a nuanced balance. In this era of publishing democratisation, striking a harmony between freedom of expression and responsible content dissemination is paramount. The challenge is to preserve individual liberties while safeguarding society from harmful material. It's a delicate tightrope walk, demanding ongoing dialogue and careful consideration. The evolving face of censorship serves as a reminder of society's perpetual transformation, urging us to develop adaptive solutions that uphold free speech while prioritising individuals' well-being.

Examiner's Comments

Content: All content is relevant to the task. The target reader is fully informed about the main ideas in the two texts and the writer's views are evident. For instance, the writer expresses that in the digital age there is a need to strike a balance between *freedom of expression* and *responsible content dissemination.* They also advocate for the development of *adaptive solutions* to address the evolving nature of censorship and acknowledge that censorship has evolved from its historical forms into subtler and more nuanced manifestations.

Communicative achievement: The writer follows essay-writing conventions to communicate complex ideas in an effective and convincing way, holding the target reader's attention with ease. While the thesis is not explicitly stated, the text presents a clear central argument, which is the need to balance freedom of expression with responsible content dissemination in the face of evolving censorship. The formal use of language and style in the text reflects an academic approach to the topic of censorship. For instance, the writer uses objective language, focusing on presenting information and analysis rather than expressing personal emotions or opinions in an emotional or casual manner.

Organisation: The text is well-organised and coherently uses a wide range of cohesive devices and organisational patterns with flexibility. For instance, the writer repeats and rephrases the central idea of censorship and its evolution, such as *censorship has transformed; contemporary censorship; evolving face of censorship* to reinforce the main theme and maintain coherence. The following transitional phrases help guide the reader through different sections of the text: *In today's world; In our digital age; Personally, I*. The use of parallel sentence structure in sentences creates a cohesive relationship between the contrasting goals of preserving freedom and protecting society (e.g. *The challenge is to preserve individual liberties while safeguarding society from harmful material*).

Language: A range of less common lexis is used with sophistication and precision: *multifaceted; insidious; dichotomy; kaleidoscopically; tightrope walk; perpetual transformation*. The writer uses language throughout the essay that often helps to express ideas more succinctly and precisely.

Mark: very good pass

10 Review

Language focus

1 Never must / Under no circumstances should **2** Around the corner was sitting / There sat **3** Only when / Not until **4** So **5** But / Were if not / Had it not been **6** Barely / Scarcely **7** Had **8** Hardly ever / Rarely

Reading and Use of English Part 1 Multiple-choice cloze

1 D **2** B **3** B **4** C **5** A **6** B **7** D **8** C

Reading and Use of English Part 3 Word formation

1 irrespective **2** technological **3** discouraged **4** detached **5** assumption **6** Regrettably **7** readership **8** credibility

Idioms Literature

1

Lewis Carroll: *Alice in Wonderland*

Miguel de Cervantes: *Don Quixote*

Geoffrey Chaucer: *The Canterbury Tales*

Charles Dickens: *A Christmas Carol*, *David Copperfield*

Thomas Hardy: *A Pair of Blue Eyes*

Joseph Heller: *Catch-22*

Homer: *Iliad*

Walter Scott: *Ivanhoe*

William Shakespeare: *The Merry Wives of Windsor*, *Romeo and Juliet*

Jonathan Swift: *A Complete Collection of Genteel and Ingenious Conversation*

3

1 *the pot calling the kettle black*: someone criticises a person for something when they also share this trait or habit

2 *Catch-22*: a situation which is impossible to get out of because the solution is also the cause

3 *Achilles' heel*: someone's weakness or vulnerable point

4 *freelance*: being self-employed and work for different companies on fixed term contracts

5 *a sight for sore eyes*: something or someone that a person is very pleased to see

6 *go down the rabbit hole*: to spend a long time doing something, especially something that becomes increasingly complex / strange (e.g. when searching for information online)

7 *a wild goose chase*: when you waste a lot of time searching for something that you can't find or doesn't exist

8 *give you the creeps*: to make someone feel afraid, nervous or uncomfortable

9 *the world is your oyster*: you have many opportunities available

10 *as dead as a doornail*: something that doesn't work or is completely dead

11 *love is blind*: people don't see the faults of those who they love

12 *a cliff hanger*: a dramatic ending to a TV show to make the audience want to watch the next episode

4

1 *the pot calling the kettle black*: *Don Quixote*, Miguel de Cervantes

2 *Catch-22*: *Catch-22*, Joseph Heller

3 *Achille's heel*: *Iliad*, Homer

4 *freelance*: *Ivanhoe*, Walter Scott

5 *a sight for sore eyes*: *A Complete Collection of Genteel and Ingenious Conversation*, Jonathan Swift

6 *go down the rabbit hole*: *Alice in Wonderland*, Lewis Carol

7 *a wild goose chase*: *Romeo & Juliet*, William Shakespeare

8 *give you the creeps*: *David Copperfield*, Charles Dickens

9 *the world is my oyster*: *The Merry Wives of Windsor*, William Shakespeare

10 *as dead as a doornail*: *A Christmas Carol*, Charles Dickens

11 *love is blind*: *The Canterbury Tales*, Geoffrey Chaucer

12 *a cliffhanger*: *A Pair of Blue Eyes*, Thomas Hardy

6

A wild goose chase – means to waste time searching for something that is unlikely to ever be found, either because the thing doesn't exist or because you were duped and given incorrect information. *After two hours searching the building, they finally realised they had been sent on a wild goose chase.*

A lost cause – means a person or thing that has no chance of succeeding or changing for the better. Unlike *a wild goose chase*, *a lost cause* does not infer having been tricked or misled. *At first I tried to stop the dog from jumping on the sofa but then I realised it was a lost cause.*

An Achilles heel – refers to a person or system's weak spot or vulnerability which can lead to failure. *The supply chain is the company's Achilles heel as it is completely reliant on one sole provider.*

A chink in the armour – also refers to a vulnerability, but this is more limited to a fault in someone's personality or line of argument. *The prosecution were relentless in their pursuit of finding a chink in the armour of the defendant's alibi.*

Give you the creeps – to make you feel uncomfortable or fearful. *I hate going up to the attic. It really gives me the creeps.* Or *The way the taxi driver looked at me really gave me the creeps. I was so relieved when I was safely back home.*

Give you the chills – is similar to *give you the creeps* but refers to an intense feeling of either fear and dread or of pleasure. *When I heard the man's voice in the message, it gave me the chills.* Or *When I heard the chorister sing the song, it gave me the chills.*

11 TALK OF THE TOWN

Vocabulary City dwelling

2

1 derelict **2** affluent **3** tree-lined **4** tight-knit **5** commuter **6** affordable **7** rustic **8** concrete **9** congestion **10** low-emissions **11** antisocial **12** welfare

Speaking Part 3 Long turn

Useful language: Cause and Effect

1 effectively **2** refined **3** closely **4** trigger **5** circumstances

Reading and Use of English Part 7 Multiple matching

2

1 B **2** A **3** D **4** E **5** A **6** C **7** D **8** B **9** C **10** E

Vocabulary Phrasal verbs for problems and solutions

1

1 run **2** resort **3** ruled **4** narrowing

3

1 resign **2** flooded **3** called **4** ran **5** saddled **6** revert **7** talked

5

1 narrow down **2** saddle (somebody) with / be saddled with **3** call for **4** resign yourself to (something) **5** be flooded with **6** revert (back) to **7** rule out **8** run up against **9** resort to

Language focus Reporting structures 1

1

1 suggesting **2** warned **3** urged **4** accusing **5** persuade **6** reassure

2

1 C **2** D **3** A **4** E **5** B

Ready for Grammar

1

1 e **2** h **3** b **4** f **5** g **6** a **7** d **8** c

2

1 Anna discouraged Jim from taking the exam so soon.

2 The politician swore to improve the economy of the country if people voted for them again.

3 Adam's dad warned him that if he didn't make more of an effort with his schoolwork, he'd regret it. / Adam's dad warned him against making so little effort with his schoolwork as he would regret it. / Adam's dad warned him to make more of an effort otherwise he would regret it.

4 Daniel confessed to breaking the window.

5 It is rumoured that the actor has been sacked from the movie franchise. / It was rumoured that the actor had been sacked from the movie franchise. (depending on the time of reporting)

4

1 to urge / urging **2** have warned **3** to blame **4** spoke / have spoken **5** have remarked / remarked **5** have vowed / vowed **7** are encouraging **8** arguing

Listening Part 1

1

1 C **2** B **3** A **4** A **5** B **6** C

Language focus Reporting structures 2

1

1 **Extract 2** – local resident

2 **Extract 3** – Town planner

3 **Extract 1** –City councillor

2

1 went off at **2** aren't sympathetic towards **3** we're inviting

3

"went off at"

4

All the verbs are informal reporting verbs. *Bang on* and *drone on* both indicate that someone is talking in a boring way. *Blather* and *keep on* both indicate that the way a person is talking is annoying. *Go off at / on* indicates someone suddenly became very angry.

Ready for Grammar

1

1 b **2** a **3** b **4** a **5** c **6** b **7** c **8** b

6

1 admitted **2** sounded **3** adamant **4** unsure **5** keeps **6** was **7** refused **8** insisting

Pronunciation Stress timing

1

Planners like me have to anticipate any potential hazards ... these could be blind spots, bottle necks et cetera.

3

1 b **2** d **3** c **4** e, f **5** a

Additional materials Pronunciation Stress timing

The world's first skyscraper was built in the city of Chicago.

Pavements in Helsinki are heated by a snowmelt system underground.

The world's oldest restaurant is located in Madrid.

The cities of Miami and Songdo are built on largely reclaimed land.

In Calcutta, there are more journeys made on bike than by car

Reading and Use of English Part 2

1

1 soak **2** had **3** way **4** took **5** with **6** reduced **7** put **8** beyond

Writing Part 2 – Report

5 Sample answer

Transport Issues and proposed solutions

The recent town meeting brought to light several pressing transport problems that require immediate attention. After a thorough analysis of the discussions, I have identified two primary issues that demand immediate attention.

Traffic congestion

The town faces chronic traffic congestion due to the increasing population and insufficient road infrastructure. Daily gridlocks waste time and contribute to air pollution and stress among residents. To tackle this issue, we should prioritise investments in infrastructure enhancements, such as widening roads and implementing intelligent traffic management systems. Additionally, promoting alternative transport options like bike lanes and pedestrian-friendly pathways can reduce congestion and encourage eco-friendly commuting.

Inadequate public transport

The inadequacy of our public transport system is a recurring concern. Limited routes, irregular schedules, and unreliable service dissatisfy residents and lead to a higher reliance on personal vehicles, worsening traffic congestion. Therefore, enhancing our public transport system is essential. This could involve expanding bus routes, increasing frequency during peak hours, and improving overall service quality. Investing in electric or hybrid buses would also make the system more eco-friendly and attractive to residents.

In conclusion, addressing these transport issues is critical to every resident's well-being. By reducing traffic congestion and improving public transport, we can enhance residents' quality of life, mitigate environmental impacts, and promote sustainable urban development. It is recommended that these issues be given priority in future planning and budgeting to create a more efficient and accessible transport system for our town, ensuring the long-term prosperity of our community.

Examiner's Comments

Content: All content is relevant to the task. The target reader is fully informed. The target reader is on the whole informed. The writer has taken a clear stance on the topic and has discussed two main issues (*traffic congestion, inadequate public transport*) and provided solutions (we should prioritise investments in infrastructure *enhancements; This could involve expanding bus routes, increasing frequency during peak hours, and improving overall service quality. Investing in electric or hybrid buses...)*

Communicative achievement: A good command of the conventions of a report is demonstrated and complex ideas are communicated in an effective way, holding the reader's attention with ease and fulfilling all communicative purposes (e.g. *mitigate environmental impacts, eco-friendly commuting; infrastructure enhancements; sustainable urban development*). The writer uses formal language and structure, addresses important issues in a serious manner, and presents solutions in a professional and organised way. The tone is objective and professional, suitable for addressing transport issues and proposing solutions in a formal setting, such as a town meeting or official report.

Organisation: The text is a well-organised and coherent whole that uses a variety of cohesive devices and organisational patterns with flexibility. For instance, in the following sentence, the comparative phrase *also* links the idea of eco-friendliness to the previous idea of enhancing the public transportation system: *Investing in electric or hybrid buses would also make the system more eco-friendly and attractive to residents.*

Language: A range of vocabulary, including less common lexis, is used effectively and precisely. For instance: *pressing; chronic; inadequacy; long-term prosperity; thorough analysis; pedestrian-friendly pathways; sustainable urban development.* A range of grammatical forms is used, generally with control and flexibility.

Mark: good pass

11 Review

Language focus

1 banging **2** admit **3** adamant
4 suggest **5** rumoured **6** urge

Vocabulary

1 affluent **2** derelict **3** antisocial
4 called **5** revert **6** ran **7** with
8 narrow **9** affordable **10** tree-lined

Reading and Use of English Part 4 Key word transformations

1 someone owns up to defacing

2 to the best of their knowledge

3 only to realise they had been

4 by him through thick and

5 clung (on) to the hope (that) he'd / he would

6 would go through with leaving

Idioms with *Talk* and *Tell*

1

1 talk **2** tell **3** tell **4** Talk **5** told
6 talk, talk **7** talking **8** Tell

2

1 e **2** h **3** g **4** d **5** a **6** b **7** c **8** f

3

Positive: Really detailed. You can learn the new vocab as you look into these different aspects.

Negative: Time consuming. Would be hard to do this for all new vocab.

4

Possible answers:

(To) talk your ear off: Talk to someone excessively and for a long time.

Common use: common and informal

Example sentence: "John's a massive fan of train travel. He'll talk your ear off about it if you give him a chance."

Paraphrase: Some people who are very interested in their hobbies will talk for a long time about them to anyone who will listen!

(To) tell it like it is: Say the facts, even if they are unpleasant

Common use: common

Example sentence: The teacher told it like it is and said to Kate that if she doesn't study more, she's not going to pass the course.

Paraphrase: My mother is always brutally honest about my cooking, and it's not always nice to hear, even if it's true.

To tell sb/so a thing or two (about):

1 to tell someone about something you know more about

2 to tell someone why you are angry

Common use: common

Example sentence: 1. I could tell you a thing or two about the history of that family. 2. I'm going to speak to her and tell her a thing or two.

Paraphrase: 1. I could give you a lot of information about the history of that family. 2. I'm going to speak to her and give her a piece of my mind / tell her I'm angry with her.

Discussing idioms

Small talk – refers to the polite conversation at social events about unimportant or uncontroversial matters, especially with people you are not familiar with. *We sat in the classroom waiting for the teacher to arrive and made small talk.*

Idle talk – refers to foolish, irrelevant or trivial conversation. *She didn't talk to the neighbours. had no time for their idle talk and preferred to keep her own company.*

talk the talk – means to talk or act so confidently that it makes people believe you are an expert and know what you're talking about. *Mike can talk the talk in front of management but he doesn't actually have a clue what he's doing.*

put your money where your mouth is – means to be willing to show with your actions that you believe what you say and are not merely talking about it. *If that politician really believes what he's saying, he should put his money where his mouth is.*

tell me about it – in informal conversation, this is used to show that you agree with what the person has just said and have had the same experience. *"The wifi issues in the office keep causing my computer to crash. It's so frustrating!" "Tell me about it!"*

tell it like it is – to explain all the details of a situation without holding anything back or sugarcoating it. *We're in a very serious situation, so I'm just going to tell it like it is."*

12 ON THE RIGHT TRACK

Reading and Use of English Part 5 Multiple choice

2

An opinion piece

3

1 B **2** B **3** A **4** D **5** A **6** C

Language focus Participle clauses

1

1 c **2** b **3** e **4** a **5** d

2

1 Having enough money, they decided to book premium economy tickets.

2 Having so many films to choose from / With so many films to choose from, they knew they'd spend ages flicking through all the channels.

3 Everybody looked at the man causing a massive scene in the restaurant just because he found a hair in his food.

4 Having finished the book, she decided to write a review about it.

5 Tired after a long day, he headed straight to bed.

6 Having been built on a toxic waste site, the apartments were a nightmare to sell. (Order of the clauses may change)

Ready for Grammar

1

1 coming up **2** Having finished
3 With (at start of sentence)
4 Watching / Having watched
5 marching / booking **6** to finish

2

1 Having posted up **2** having seen
3 Used **4** Having been taught
5 talking **6** Plans made

4

Possible answers

1 Working such long hours, Josh needed a cleaner to help tidy his flat.

With such long hours spent at work, Josh needed a cleaner to keep his flat tidy.

2 Hoping to take part in the next Olympics, Fiona trained hard every day at the pool.

While hoping to take part in the next Olympics, Fiona trained hard every day at the pool.

Fiona, having trained so hard, hoped to take part in the Olympics.

3 Tried and tested many times, the simple breathing exercise can produce favourable results.

Having been tried and tested many times, the simple breathing exercise can produce favourable results.

Producing favourable results, this simple breathing exercise has been tried and tested many times.

Vocabulary Health and fitness

1

1 damaging **2** cognitive **3** burning
4 genetic **5** Fad **6** limiting
7 health **8** intelligent **9** conservative
10 superior **11** demographic
12 proficient

2

1 system **2** strength **3** diet
4 perspective **5** circulation
6 practices **7** pain **8** intervention

Speaking Part 3 Long turn

Useful language

1

1 F **2** D **3** G **4** A **5** E **6** G **7** B
8 C

2

A 3, 6 **B** 8 **C** 2, 4 **D** 1, 5 **E** 7

Language focus Verb patterns

1

1 bare infinitive **2** gerund **3** infinitive with to

2

1 my / me trying **2** preparing / me to prepare **3** to learn **4** to taste **5** to not be able / not to be able **6** not attending **7** to have to **8** to have come **9** to stop **10** to be **11** put / have to put

Ready for Grammar

1

1 entering / my having entered **2** my / me leaving early **3** my friend('s) (constant) nagging **4** to realise **5** to make / to have made **6** running of the gym **7** Daniel('s) talking **8** spotted them cheating **9** the women's team to be getting paid **10** eating or drinking

Writing Part 2 Informal letter

Useful language

1 altering habits **2** realistic goals
3 incremental steps **4** fierce determination
5 staying committed **6** losing heart

4 Sample answer:

Dear Editors,

I wanted to share my journey towards a healthier lifestyle, inspired by your magazine's call to action. Over the past year, I've made some significant changes that have not only improved my physical health but also boosted my overall well-being. Firstly, I decided to prioritise regular exercise. I used to be a couch potato, spending most of my free time playing video games, but I realised that a sedentary lifestyle was taking a toll on my health. So, I started incorporating daily workouts into my routine, which wasn't easy at first, but I found activities I genuinely enjoyed, like hiking and yoga. Now, I can't imagine my life without regular exercise. Another change I made was adopting a balanced diet. I used to overindulge in fast food and sugary snacks almost on a daily basis; however, I knew that these habits were negatively impacting my energy levels and overall health. I began cooking at home more, focusing on whole foods, fruits, and vegetables. This shift not only improved my physical health but also gave me a sense of accomplishment and control over my nutrition.

The driving force behind these changes was a desire for a better quality of life. I wanted to have more energy to pursue my passions, improve my mood, and reduce my risk of health issues down the road. I was tired of feeling sluggish and wanted to feel more confident in my own skin. My advice to others wanting to change their lifestyles is simple. Don't overwhelm yourself with drastic changes all at once. Begin with one aspect of your life, like exercise or diet, and gradually build from there. In short, making these changes has been transformative for me. I'm now healthier, happier, and more confident in my daily life. I encourage anyone looking to improve their lifestyle to take that first step towards a healthier, happier you.

Sincerely,

Jude Alvarez

Examiner's Comments

Content: All content is relevant to the task, and the target reader is fully informed about the changes the writer has made to their lifestyle (e.g. *Firstly, I decided to prioritise regular exercise; Another change I made was adopting a balanced diet; I started incorporating daily workouts into my routine. I began cooking at home more, focusing on whole foods, fruits, and vegetables*). The writer's own views are evident throughout the text, and they provide some advice (e.g. *Don't overwhelm yourself with drastic changes all at once. Begin with one aspect of your life, like exercise or diet, and gradually build from there.*).

Communicative achievement: The conventions of letter writing, such as appropriate opening and closing salutations and a semi-informal tone, are used flexibly (e.g. *I wanted to share my journey towards a healthier lifestyle; In short, making these changes has been transformative for me; I encourage anyone looking to improve their lifestyle to take that first step towards a healthier, happier you*). Complex ideas are communicated in an effective and convincing way, holding the target reader's attention with ease, and fulfilling the communicative purposes of the task (e.g. *I wanted to have more energy to pursue my passions, improve my mood, and reduce my risk of health issues down the road; I used to overindulge in fast food and sugary snacks almost on a daily basis, however, I knew that these habits were negatively impacting my energy levels and overall health.*).

Organisation: The letter is a well-organised and coherent as a whole, using a wide variety of cohesive devices and organisational patterns such as following a chronological order with flexibility. However, clear paragraphing would have enhanced coherence further. Transition words and phrases organise the text and signal shifts between different ideas and points (e.g. *Firstly; Another change I made was; In short*). The writer uses cause-and-effect relationships to explain why they made these changes. For example, they explain that a sedentary lifestyle was taking a toll on their health, leading to their decision to incorporate daily workouts.

Language: There is a wide range of vocabulary, with some very natural turns of phrase and appropriate use of collocation, used effectively and with an appropriate informal style to convey the writer's message effectively and enhance the overall tone of the letter (e.g. *boosted my overall well-being; couch potatoe; sedentary lifestyle; incorporating daily workouts; overindulge in fast food; the driving force behind these changes; reduce my risk of health issues down the road; transformative*).

Mark: pass

Listening Part 3

1

1 C **2** B **3** A **4** A **5** C

Pronunciation Reading between the lines

1

1 B **2** A **3** A **4** B

Vocabulary Multi-word verbs

1

1 c **2** a **3** b **4** d

2

a mount up **b** urge on **c** keep at it
d go through with it

3

1 caught up with him **2** cling onto
3 get to **4** goes without **5** caught on
6 get through **7** count him in

5

1 madness **2** fear **3** time **4** your job

Reading and Use of English Part 1

1

1 B **2** D **3** A **4** B **5** C **6** A **7** C **8** D

12 Review

Vocabulary

1 makeup **2** through **3** intervention
4 cling **5** catch **6** immune **7** mount
8 strength

Reading and Use of English Part 4 Key word transformations

1 to be / get saddled with

2 had anything good / a good word to say about

3 err on the side of caution / safe side / cautious side

4 was in / had any / had the slightest doubt whatsoever

5 was completely taken in by

6 Julio had the faintest idea (about / of) how to

Reading and Use of English Part 3 Word formation

1 predominantly **2** simplicity
3 uncompromising **4** technically
5 exclusivity **6** unattainable
7 insignificance **8** landscape

Idioms Sports

1

1 to learn the basic knowledge / skills in order to do something well

2 do something prematurely or before you're ready

3 to give up something

4 to change the rules / requirements of a process or procedure during its course

5 to be more likely to succeed than someone / something else

6 to have an advantage at the beginning

2

1 ballpark **2** target **3** barred
4 bowled **5** chin

3

1 baseball **2** darts / archery
3 wrestling **4** cricket **5** boxing

Discussing idioms

Jump the gun – means to start doing something before it is time or before you should. *You haven't signed the rental agreement for the flat yet, isn't it jumping the gun to get address labels printed?*

jump on the bandwagon – means to start doing something because everybody else is doing it and it is fashionable. *I don't think Ann actually believes in the issue – she's just jumped on the bandwagon.*

throw in the towel – means to admit defeat and stop trying to do something. *You've been trying to fix that lamp for two hours now. Isn't it time to throw in the towel?*

throw your hat in the ring – means to announce you are entering a race, competition or content. *Miguel Santos is the latest mayoral candidate to throw his hat in the ring.*

Collocation revision: Units 1–12

Adjective + noun

1 personality **2** destination **3** problem
4 undertaking **5** source **6** costs
7 evidence **8** waste **9** design **10** film
11 effects **12** strength

Verb + noun

1 make **2** take **3** come **4** break
5 know **6** pay **7** hit **8** pose
9 go **10** fight **11** call for
12 bottle up

READY FOR WRITING

Marking

1 D **2** A **3** B **4** C

Planning and checking

1 D **2** A **3** A **4** A **5** B **6** B **7** C
8 C

Task conventions

1 article, report **2** essay **3** article
4 essay **5** article, letter, review
6 review **7** letter **8** review, report

Macmillan Education Limited
4 Crinan Street
London N1 9XW

Companies and representatives throughout the world

Ready for C2 Proficiency Student's Book with Key ISBN 978-1-035-11707-9
Ready for C2 Proficiency Student's Book with Key with App & Digital Student's Book ISBN 978-1-035-12010-9

Written by Fiona Aish, Ethan Mansur, Jo Tomlinson with contributions by Roy Norris 2024

The authors have asserted their right to be identified as the authors of this work in accordance with the Copyright, Designs and Patents Act 1988.

First published 2024

Designed by EMC Design Ltd.
Cover design by The Restless
Cover photograph by Getty Images/DieterMeyrl, Getty Images/Vernonwiley
Picture research by Emily Taylor

Authors' acknowledgements
Fiona Aish would like to thank all the Aish clan, Mike Burrows, the team at Macmillan and Roy Norris for their constant and valuable support throughout this project.
Ethan Mansur would like to thank Christina Anastasiadis, Hilary Anne Thomson, Ian Sowers, M.A. and Roger Brown at International House Madrid for their help piloting materials. I am also very grateful to Javier Fruns at the Instituto Cervantes for his invaluable lessons in C2 item writing. I would like to express my deep gratitude to my wife, Antonia, and my two children, Lola and Dylan, for their continued support and inspiration. And I would also like to thank Roy Norris for all his invaluable feedback and moral support during the writing process, as well as everyone else at Macmillan who was involved in the project.
Jo Tomlinson would like to thank everyone who worked tirelessly on the project, including Roy and the team at Macmillan. Thanks also to Noe, Chloe and Isa for their help and support.

The publishers would like to thank Andrea Littlewood (International House Madrid, Madrid), Frank Carrizo Zirit (Madrid), Ian Sowers (International House), Jade Turner (Chester School of English, Madrid), Mario Fernández (The Cottage English School), Vilafranca del Penedès (Barcelona), Megan Yoder (The Warehouse Madrid, Madrid), Mercedes Vivero (Eng-Age, Pontevedra), Renata Whitewood, Siboney Rabenstein (International House, Madrid).

The authors and publishers would like to thank the following for permission to reproduce their photographs:
Alamy Stock Photo/AJ Pics p14(bl), Alamy Stock Photo/B.O'Kane p174, Alamy Stock Photo/Patrick Bombaert p26, Alamy Stock Photo/David Cabrera Navarro p205(bl), Alamy Stock Photo/Colin Palmer Photography p161(tl), Alamy Stock Photo/Cinematic Collection p100(tcl), Alamy Stock Photo/Ashley Cooper pics p73, Alamy Stock Photo/Donald Cooper p134(2), Alamy Stock Photo/Ian Dagnall p149, Alamy Stock Photo/FlixPix p100(bl), Alamy Stock Photo/Richard Gardner p136(tl), Alamy Stock Photo/Aleksei Gorodenkov p135(4), Alamy Stock Photo/Group North America LLC p168(br), Alamy Stock Photo/Hikupic p100(tl), Alamy Stock Photo/JJs p100(bcl), Alamy Stock Photo/Kolvenbach p186, Alamy Stock Photo/LANDMARK MEDIA p14(br), Alamy Stock Photo/Nathaniel Noir p170(bm), Alamy Stock Photo/Frank Nowikowski p163(Mexico), Alamy Stock Photo/Sean Pavone p207, Alamy Stock Photo/Science Photo Library p104(1), Alamy Stock Photo/Universal Images p168(br), Alamy Stock Photo/Marcelo Vinante p163(Bengaluru), Alamy Stock Photo/Tony Watson p136(br), Alamy Stock Photo/Richard Williams p124; **DoraBella Cipher** (created by Sir Edward Elgar, date unknown), PeterBrooks, Creative Commons Attribution 3.0 p106(bm); **Getty Images/**2014 Silver Screen Collection p156, Getty Images/500px p120(bm), Getty Images/10'000 Hours p55, Getty Images/AELTC p77, Getty Images/AFP/Cesar Manso p106(tr), Getty Images/AFP/Cristina Quicler p1, Getty Images/Dmytro Aksonov p144, Getty Images/Allkindza p67, Getty Images/Luis Alvarez pp40(tl), 132(br), 154(bm), Getty Images/Anadolu Agency p139(bl), Getty Images/Andreswd p123, Getty Images/Andia/Universal Images Group p119, Getty Images/Miguel Angel Partido Garcia p153, Getty Images/Array p71, Getty Images/ArtistGNDphotography p130, Getty Images/Art Media/Print Collector p128(bl), Getty Images/Giacomo Augugliaro p170(tr), Getty Images/AzmanJaka p135(3), Getty Images/Daryl Benson p17(3), Getty Images/Bettmann Archive p70, Getty Images/Blend Images p91(4), Getty Images/Blend Images/Tanya Constantine p183, Getty Images/Boris SV p132(bl), Getty Images/Marco Bottigelli p21(tl), Getty Images/Mark Bridger p115, Getty Images/Buena Vista Images p21(bm), Getty Images/Gary Burchell p28, Getty Images/Peter Cade p94, Getty Images/CasarsaGuru pp135(cr), 177(cl), Getty Images/Chapin31 vp66, Getty Images/Marcus Chung p76, Getty Images/George Clerk p184, Getty Images/Corbis p131, Getty Images/Peter Dazeley pp68, 133(tl), Getty Images/De Agostini p128(tr), Getty Images/Artur Debat p99, Getty Images/Martin Dimitrov p22, Getty Images/Dougal Waters Photography Ltd pp151, 178, Getty Images/Downunderphotos p63, Getty Images/Dr0ng p10, Getty Images/Eclipse_images p142(b), Getty Images/Sam Edwards p59, Getty Images/Marcos Elihu Castillo Ramirez p159, Getty Images/EMILI_VISION p181, Getty Images/Pieter Estersohn p132(tm), Getty Images/EyeEm/Kazuki Kimura p15, Getty Images/Grant Faint p233, Getty Images/Rana Faure/Corbis/VCG p142(a), Getty Images/FG Trade p2, Getty Images/FilippoBacci p48(2), Getty Images/Fine Art Images/Heritage Images p128(tl), Getty Images/Fotog p160(bl), Getty Images/Fortgens Photography pp86, 87, Getty Images/Future Publishing p34(bl), Getty Images/Gajus p69(tl), Getty Images/Vladimir Gappov p179(tr), Getty Images/The Good Brigade p177(br), Getty Images/Halfpoint Images pp75, 79, Getty Images/Halepak p101, Getty Images/Jon Hicks p133(tr), Getty Images/Hirurg p93, Getty Images/Hobo_018 p205(tr), Getty Images/Nisian Hughes p168(bl), Getty Images/Hulton Fine Art Collection p128(tmr), Getty Images/Image Source p8, Getty Images/INTI OCON p39, Getty Images/Image Source p103, Getty Images/iStockphoto pp16(1), 64, 88(br), 90, 104(2, 3), 107, 158, 147, Getty Images/iStockphoto/Annaspoka p12, Getty Images/istockphoto/Baranozdemir p120(tm), Getty Images/iStockphoto/fizkes pp56, 189, Getty Images/iStockphoto/Gorodenkoff p46, Getty Images/iStockphoto/Mikimad p24(tm), Getty Images/istockphoto/Squidmediaro p112, Getty Images/izusek p4, Getty Images/Izf p98, Getty Images/JackF p179(br), Getty Images/Kali Nine LLC p3, Getty Images/Kelvinjay p19(tr), Getty Images/Ray Keller p125, Getty Images/Koiguo p36, Getty Images/Kupicoo p25, Getty Images/Rich Legg p185, Getty Images/LeoPatrizi p38, Getty Images/Ron Levine p190(br), Getty Images/Alex Linch p196(br), Getty Images/Natalia Lisovskaya p31, Getty Images/LuckyBusiness p48(1), Getty Images/Mangiwau p163(Jakarta), Getty Images/Jose Martinez Calderon p140, Getty Images/Maskot p196(tl), Getty Images/Maxiphoto p122, Getty Images/Kevin Mayer p88(tr), Getty Images/MesquitaFMS p139(br), Getty Images/MesquitaFMS p60, Getty Images/Mfron p160(tr), Getty Images/Tara Moore p69(bl), Getty Images/Sasipa Muennuch p19(bm), Getty Images/Aleksandar Nakic p54, Getty Images/Peerayut Nantajeeworawat p80, Getty Images/NicoElNino p165, Getty Images/Olezzo p82, Getty Images/Onurdongel p34(br), Getty Images/Justin Paget p114, Getty Images/Vadym Pastukh p142(d), Getty Images/Jeroen Pels p127, Getty Images/PeopleImages.com p177(tr), Getty Images/Deb Perry p95, Getty Images/Plume Creative p47, Getty Images/Photochristine p113, Getty Images/Photo12/Universal Images Group pp128(tml), 129, Getty Images/Photo Josse/Leemage p128(cl), Getty Images/Piranka p136(bl), Getty Images/Witthaya Prasongsin pp44, 81, 166, Getty Images/Chris J Ratcliffe p169, Getty Images/Recep-bg p154(tr), Getty Images/Douglas Rissing p105, Getty Images/Oliver Rossi p50, Getty Images/Patchareeporn Sakoolchai p173, Getty Images/Johannes Simon p33, Getty Images/Skynesher p69(cl), Getty Images/SolStock pp48(3, 4), 49, 142(c), Getty Images/Sylvain Sonnet p135(tr), Getty Images/Sorbetto p9, Getty Images/South_agency pp134(1), 157, Getty Images/Alexander Spatari p133(tm), Getty Images/Srdjan Srdjanov p154(tl), Getty Images/Siri Stafford p203, Getty Images/Stock Montage p111, Getty Images/StockPlanets p24(bm), Getty Images/StockstudioX p16(2), Getty Images/Sunset Boulevard p145, Getty Images/Tetra images pp5, 108, Getty Images/Willie Thomas p91(1), Getty Images/Thomas M. Barwick INC pp17(4), 35, 58, 179(cl), 180, Getty Images/Willie B. Thomas p43, Getty Images/Universal Images Group pp37, 133(br), Getty Images/Urbazon pp91(3), 229, Getty Images/Santiago Urquijo p42, Getty Images/Klaus Vedfelt p100(br), Getty Images/Vgajic p40(bl), Getty Images/VioletaStoimenova p78, Getty Images/We Are p199, Getty Images/Westend61 pp14(tr), 45, 52, 84, 88(bl), 175, 190(tl), Getty Images/Pipat Wongsawang p61, Getty Images/Jonathan Woodcock p109, Getty Images/Peter Zelei Images pp162, 191; **Brittany Greeson**/New York Times/Redux/eyevine p65; **Guardian**/eyevine. All Rights Reserved p6; **The Image Bank** pp96, 117; **Robin Moore** p30; **Shutterstock**/Alhim p91(2), Shutterstock/Lauren Elisabeth p29, Shutterstock/Alex Segre p161(tr), Shutterstock/Mark Wolters p97.

The authors and publishers are grateful for permission to reprint the following copyright material:
Bronwyn Adcock, "'I'd keep it on the down low': the secret life of a super-recogniser", The Guardian, © Guardian News & Media Ltd. 2023, www.theguardian.com, p.6.
"Are we reaching the limits of innovation?" © The Economist Newspaper Limited, London, 2017, p.35.
"From No Place to Park" by Alexander McCall-Smith © Alexander McCall-Smith, 2007, first published by The Strand Magazine, reproduced by kind permission by David Higham Associates, p.150.

Additional sources
"Anger is more influential than joy: Sentiment correlation in Weibo" by Rui Fan, Jichang Zhao, Yan Chen, Ke Xu; State Key Laboratory of Software Development Environment, Beihang University, Beijing; 10 Sep 2013; https://arxiv.org/pdf/1309.2402v1.pdf, p.68 .

Ready for conforms to the objectives set by the Common European Framework of Reference and its recommendations for the evaluation of language competence.

Printed and bound in Brazil

2024
8